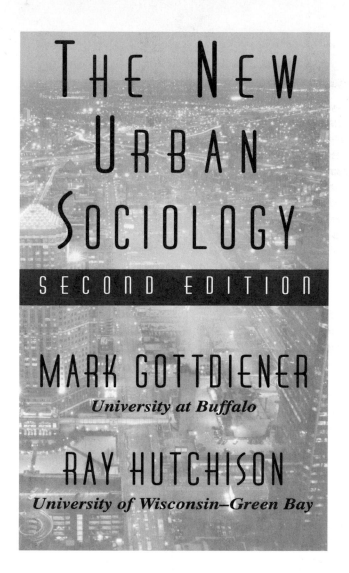

THE NEW URBAN SOCIOLOGY

SECOND EDITION

MARK GOTTDIENER

University at Buffalo

RAY HUTCHISON

University of Wisconsin–Green Bay

McGraw Hill

Boston   Burr Ridge, IL   Dubuque, IA   Madison, WI
New York   San Francisco   St. Louis
Bangkok   Bogotá   Caracas   Lisbon   London   Madrid   Mexico City
Milan   New Delhi   Seoul   Singapore   Sydney   Taipei   Toronto

McGraw-Hill Higher Education

A Division of The *McGraw-Hill* Companies

This book is printed on acid-free paper.

2 3 4 5 6 7 8 9 0 DOC/DOC   0 9 8 7 6 5 4 3 2 1 0

ISBN 0–07–289180–7

Editorial director: *Phillip A. Butcher*
Sponsoring editor: *Sally Constable*
Developmental editor: *Katherine Blake*
Marketing manager: *Leslie A. Kraham*
Project editor: *Susanne Riedell*
Production supervisor: *Kari Geltemeyer*
Art director: *Francis Owens*
Interior design: *Carol Barr*
Cover designer: *Carol Barr*
Cover image: © *PhotoDisc*
Photo research coordinator: *Sharon Miller*
Supplement coordinator: *Carol A. Bielski*
Compositor: *Shepherd Incorporated*
Typeface: *10/12 Times Roman*
Printer: *R. R. Donnelley & Sons Company*

Library of Congress Cataloging-in-Publication Data

Gottdiener, Mark.
  The new urban sociology / Mark Gottdiener, Ray Hutchison.—2nd ed.
    p. cm.
  Includes bibliographical references and index.
  ISBN 0–07–289180–7
  1. Metropolitan areas—United States. 2. Suburbs—United States. 3. Suburban life—United States. 4. Urbanization—United States—History. 5. Sociology, Urban—United States. I. Hutchison, Ray. II. Title.

HT334.U5 G657 2000
307.76'0973—dc21   99–045678

http://www.mhhe.com

ABOUT THE AUTHORS

Mark Gottdiener is professor and chair of sociology at the State University of New York–Buffalo. He received his PhD from the State University of New York–Stonybrook and taught at the University of California–Riverside before moving to Buffalo. Mark is the author of more than 10 books and edited volumes in urban sociology, urban semiotics, and urban theory, including *Las Vegas: An All American City, The Social Production of Urban Space, The Theming of America,* and *Postmodern Semiotics,* and serves as a managing editor for *Urban Studies.* He teaches courses in urban sociology, contemporary theory, and cultural studies. Mark is married and has two children.

Ray Hutchison is professor and chair of urban and regional studies at the University of Wisconsin–Green Bay. He received his PhD in sociology from the University of Chicago and taught at DePaul University and the University of California–San Diego before moving to Green Bay. Ray is series editor of *Research in Urban Sociology* and author of more than 20 articles and book chapters on urban sociology, immigration and refugee populations, and street gangs. He teaches courses in urban sociology, the city through time and space, and race and ethnic relations. Ray is married and has three children.

For Jennifer, Felix, and Zev
and
For Dulce, Leilani, Heather, and Jessica

CONTENTS

Chapter 6: The Rise of Urban Sociology   103

Chapter 7: Contemporary Urban Sociology: The Sociospatial Approach   127

Chapter 8: People and Lifestyles in the Metropolis   151

Chapter 9: Neighborhoods, the Public Environment, and Theories of Urban Life   183

Chapter 10: Metropolitan Problems: Poverty, Racism, Crime, Housing, and Fiscal Crisis

Chapter 11: Local Politics: City and Suburban Governments   239

Chapter 12: Urbanization in the Industrialized World: Western and Eastern Europe and Japan   261

Chapter 13: Third World Urbanization   281

Chapter 14: Environmental Issues and Metropolitan Planning   307

Chapter 15: Metropolitan Social Policy and the Future of Urban Sociology   335

PREFACE

The New Urban Sociology was the first textbook to present the sociospatial model and to apply this model to the study of urban sociology. In the five years since publication of the first edition, the theoretical discussion and applied study of "urban space" have emerged as the dominant paradigm not only in urban sociology but also in the various disciplines within urban studies, such as geography, architecture, and planning. New books by established scholars in the field, as well as special issues of scholarly journals and edited collections, offer insights into the social production and meaning of urban space. These developments reflect not simply a long-standing critique of earlier models of urban structure and process but a growing recognition that the emergence of global capitalism and the accompanying changes in the international division of labor have altered the social, political, economic, and cultural landscapes of metropolitan areas in the United States as well as in developing and industrialized nations around the world.

The second edition of *The New Urban Sociology* has evolved from our commitment to the study of urban sociology, a commitment forged over many years of experience in graduate school education and teaching in the classroom. We were introduced to urban sociology in graduate school by several well-known scholars and became passionately committed to the discipline. Mark studied with David Street and Gerald Suttles at SUNY–Stony Brook, and Ray studied with Morris Janowitz, Gerald Suttles, and William Julius Wilson at the University of Chicago. Urban sociology seemed to offer everything that was attractive about sociology. It required an interdisciplinary understanding of economics, politics, and culture. It was concerned with the reality of everyday life. It possessed great themes of immigrant adjustment, the making and unmaking of fortunes, active and exciting politics, the rise and decline of community ties, and even the dark side of human existence in the form of crime and vice. As graduate students, we were eager to learn about it all. From our experience, we came to an understanding that remains at the core of our work: Urban sociologists should be interested in actual reality. We should be inspired by daily life and be able to explain it in its full complexity. We agree with Robert Park that to understand urban life, one must move beyond the ivory tower of the university and "get the seat of your pants dirty" by actually doing research and becoming involved in urban communities.

While in graduate school, we learned about the theory of urban ecology, because that was the only explanatory paradigm taught at universities in the United States. Our dissertations were case studies of suburban development on Long Island (a suburban area adjacent to New York City) and of black suburbanization in Harvey, Illinois (an older suburb just south of Chicago). While revising these materials for publication, it became increasingly clear to both of us—even though we had not yet met each other—that the urban ecological paradigm could not adequately explain the changes occurring in the post–World War II period in metropolitan areas across the United States. Our dissatisfaction with mainstream urban sociology and our passionate interest in explaining the social, political, and economic changes that we observed in our field studies led us to reconceptualize the field.

Over the past decade and a half, we have devoted our work to introducing new ideas about the role of economics, politics, and culture in urban analysis. This effort culminated in a new kind of urban theory and a new paradigm for the discipline, as well as the first edited series devoted to urban sociology. Our work joined the efforts of others, such as Lefebvre, Castells, Harvey, and Pickvance, in what has come to be called the *new urban sociology*.

Over this same period, we have also devoted ourselves to the teaching of urban sociology. The limitations of the textbooks that presented urban ecology as a global paradigm made it difficult to instruct our students in understanding the complexities of urban life. Slowly we began to frame specific concepts and arguments that we felt improved the approach of urban sociology. The first edition of this book represented the culmination of Mark's efforts over several decades to develop a new theoretical model that was better suited to contemporary urban society and the systematic application of this theory to the topics studied by urban sociologists. This second edition represents our joint effort to expand the earlier material by including new topics (e.g., street gangs) and examples (e.g., the redevelopment of squatter settlements in the Philippines) that demonstrate the applications of sociospatial theory to the reality of urban life not just in the United States but around the world.

The central organizing concepts of this text were devised in response to the limitations of other textbooks in the field. Without exception, urban sociologists focus principally on the large central city as an object of analysis. Suburban considerations may be treated, but they are usually consigned to a separate chapter. This urban bias distorts reality. In the United States, the majority of people now live, work, and shop in the suburbs rather than in large central cities. Our text focuses on the entire metropolitan region, including cities, suburbs, industrial parks, shopping malls, recreational sites, and small towns. We believe this approach presents a more balanced account of contemporary urban life.

A second feature of this book also grew out of our response to the limitations of other texts, in which discussions about the nature of urban development are biased in favor of economic accounts. We believe that all environments function because they are meaningful spaces and that cultural considerations play a significant role in metropolitan life. In this text, we seek to show these relationships without bias toward a single factor. We strive to provide a balanced view of economic, political, and cultural considerations in the study of metropolitan development.

Too often, textbooks are written as a series of disconnected chapters reporting facts about one topic after another without providing a compelling vision. This book is an exception. The *sociospatial perspective* is an integrated paradigm of thinking about metropolitan life. Its basic premise is that spatial or environmental and locational considerations are always part and parcel of everyday social relationships. We cannot talk about one without also talking about the latter. The sociospatial perspective is not urban ecology, although it also stresses the role of location in social relations. Unlike urban ecology, it does not propose that explanation should follow biological principles, nor does it suggest that the drama of development can be reduced to the effects of technological change alone. In contrast, the sociospatial perspective is a synthesis of environmental considerations and the factors of class, race, gender, lifestyle, economics, culture, and politics to explore the development of metropolitan regions. Each chapter borrows from this thematic perspective to discuss specific topics ranging from crime to Third World development and, when possible, makes comparative distinctions.

The goal of this text is not just to be innovative but to be up to date. Its chapter topics are comparable to those found in other urban texts. The fruits of our discontent with the outdated mainstream perspective are realized in the execution of the material. When discussing the development of ancient cities, for example, cultural and political factors are considered to be as important as economic ones. In addition, the urban history of the United States is presented as high drama involving fortunes made through real estate speculation as much as through industry. Social problems are depicted as metropolitan and regional concerns rather than as the exclusive products of city living. The diversity of daily life is presented in terms of the full spectrum of race, class, and gender considerations. And finally, when we turn to metropolitan policy and the environment, we want to know *why* programs fail, *what* ideologies govern metropolitan growth, and *how* we can improve metropolitan life.

Some chapters, however, depart somewhat from the typical fare of other presentations. We consider the metropolitan changes occurring in the United States since 1960 to be so unique that we have devoted a separate chapter to their discussion. Furthermore, in the chapters on urban history and contemporary development, it is necessary to take a global perspective and provide comparative material. While a discussion of the development of Third World cities is now standard in urban texts, we have added a new discussion of metropolitan development in Europe and Japan to more fully incorporate a global perspective and provide comparative material. Finally, unlike most urban sociology texts, this book has a separate chapter on metropolitan politics and another chapter on metropolitan policy and the environment. Both are important for understanding how people manage and how they might improve the space of everyday life.

In the second edition, we have updated the material in the first edition and incorporated important new research. We have also sought to expand the approach presented in the first edition to include additional areas of research within the field of urban sociology. The reader will find not only a more complete discussion of earlier theoretical work but also an extension of the sociospatial model to incorporate both older and emerging areas of research.

Specific changes and additions to the second edition include the following:

- An expansion and elaboration of the basic sociospatial model (Chapter 1).
- New material on the origins of urban settlements and the origins of urban planning in Renaissance Rome (Chapter 2).
- Greatly expanded discussion of classical urban theory, including the work of Ferdinand Toennies, Roderick McKenzie's approach to human ecology, and social area analysis (Chapter 6).
- Thorough revision of the discussion of women, gender roles and urban space, and ethnic communities (Chapter 7).
- New material on street gangs and urban space (Chapter 10).
- New discussion of planned communities and the "new urbanism" (Chapter 14).

To make this edition more user friendly, we have enhanced the program of boxed inserts. In some cases, we have moved standard material in the text into boxes that highlight important work in the field. Some new boxes present important concepts discussed in the text (e.g., the sociospatial approach in Chapter 1; theories of urban problems in Chapter 10). Other boxes summarize classic studies in urban sociology (e.g., V. Gordon Childe's description of the urban revolution in Chapter 2; Ferdinand Toennies' discussion of community and society in Chapter 6; and Hunter's and Dahl's competing theories of urban political structures in Chapter 11). We have added boxes highlighting important recent scholarship in both urban sociology and urban studies (e.g., Massey and Denton's work on urban apartheid in Chapter 6; consideration of the impact of shopping malls in Chapter 9; William Julius Wilson's study *When Work Disappears* in Chapter 10; and a critical discussion of what has become known as the new urbanism in Chapter 14). We hope these boxes offer instructors additional opportunities to make the study of urban sociology come alive for their students.

The development of *The New Urban Sociology* through two editions has been an extended project stretching over many years. It could not have been accomplished without the crucial help provided by a number of people. We wish to thank friends in academia for their support: Bob Antonio, David Diaz, Joe Feagin, Harvey Kaye, Chigon Kim, Nestor Rodriguez, Eric Monkkonen, Peter Muller, Leonard Wallock, and Talmadge Wright in the United States; Phil Gunn, Lena Lavinas, Sandra Lincioni, and Sueli Schiffer in Brazil; Alexandros Lagopoulos and Nikos Komninos in Greece; Chris Pickvance in England; Dorel Abraham in Romania; and Jens Tonboe in Denmark. Randy Roethle and Tanya Krall (University of Wisconsin–Green Bay) provided editorial support for the second edition.

We have been most fortunate to have McGraw-Hill as a publisher because of the supportive relationship it nurtures with authors. The writing of the two editions of this text would not have been possible without the extensive help and support of editors Kathy Blake, Sylvia Shepard, Sally Constable, and Phil Butcher. For the second edition, we also wish to thank the editing/design/production team of Susanne Riedell, Francis Owens, and Kari Geltemeyer; Sharon Miller and Marty Levick for their management and research efforts on behalf of the photo program; and Leslie Kraham, our marketing manager.

We would like to thank our colleagues who served as reviewers for the second edition: Brian Barry, Rochester Institute of Technology; Scott Ford, Florida State University; Anthony Filipovitch, Minnesota State University at Mankato; Karl Flaming, University of Colorado–Denver; Judith Friedman, Rutgers University; Kevin Fox Gotham, Tulane University; Geoffrey Grant, South Dakota State University; Anthony Mendonca, Community College of Allegheny County; Charles Price Reavis, CUNY–John Jay College of Criminal Justice; and Thomas Shannon, Radford University.

We once again thank the reviewers of the first edition: Brian Aldrich, Winona State University; Craig Calhoun, then at the University of North Carolina, Chapel Hill, and now at New York University; Robert L. Carroll, University of Cincinnati; George Kephart, Pennsylvania State University; Jerry Lembcke, College of Holy Cross; Nestor

Rodriguez, University of Houston; Thomas Shannon, Radford University; Steven L. Vassar, Mankato State University; and J. Talmadge Wright, Loyola University.

Finally, as the writer of any textbook quickly learns, the long working hours and need for concentration can interfere with the everyday flow of family life. We are most fortunate to have two very understanding and supportive families. Mark's wife, Jennifer, and two boys, Felix and Zev, and Ray's wife, Dulce, and daughters, Leilani, Heather, and Jessica, were very patient as we prepared the second edition. It is they to whom we dedicate this book.

Mark Gottdiener

Ray Hutchison

CHAPTER 1

THE NEW URBAN SOCIOLOGY

It is morning across the United States, and people have brushed off sleep and prepared themselves for the day. Though most Americans live within metropolitan regions, they meet their circumstances in different ways. Using composite types constructed from case studies, newspaper or magazine stories, and personal observations, here are several examples of everyday life:

Larry Worthington lives in Costa Mesa, a section of Orange County, California, adjacent to Los Angeles. He is a lawyer and works for the county in another town, Santa Ana. Larry is married and has two children and a dog. Both he and his wife work. They own a house, two cars, and a small boat that they occasionally take sailing on weekends. The Worthingtons' combined income is over $100,000 a year, yet they are not affluent. Their housing costs alone amount to $30,000 a year, because housing in Orange County is very expensive. Car payments and maintenance add several thousand more in bills, but life would not be possible without an automobile in southern California. Because both of the Worthingtons work, they must pay for after-school day care for their children—another expense of several thousand a year. When all costs are added up, this family cannot meet every obligation, and so end each year in debt.

On this typical morning Larry is stuck in the inevitable lineup of cars on the freeway. His 20-mile commute to work takes him an average of 1½ hours each way. He has plenty of time to consider his looming debts as well as the daily needs of his job while waiting for the stop-and-go traffic to advance a few more inches. He tries to focus on music from the car stereo.

Every morning around five o'clock, Esther Hernandez wakes up with the first sounds of advancing traffic. She can't help it. She lives outdoors on a subway grate located on the corner of 40th Street and Lexington Avenue in Manhattan. Esther is homeless. When she first came to New York from the Dominican Republic, she found work in the garment center as a sewing machine operator. With the opportunity for piece-work (a kind of overtime), she was able to afford an apartment in the South Bronx.

Several years ago, she lost her job when the company she worked for declared bankruptcy. Due to the decline in garment manufacturing within New York City, she has been unable to find another job since that time. For a while she collected unemployment insurance, and when that ran out, she thought about going on welfare. Last March her building in the South Bronx burned down. She now lives on the street with all her possessions piled into a shopping cart. She has already been raped twice. As winter sets in, she thinks about going back to the Dominican Republic, but then she remembers that her family sent her to New York because there were no jobs at home. "Maybe things are better there now," she wonders.

Dave, Sean, Felix, and Hakim are playing free video games at the Nintendo booth in a mall located in Gwinnett County outside of Atlanta. School began a half-hour ago, but few people notice that the boys should be elsewhere. They've already spent well over one hour playing games at the video arcade. Few adults bother to look in there, since the arcade is tucked away on one of the more isolated arms of the giant mall. It's a perfect place to hang out while the school day is still on.

The four teens are good friends. Born and brought up in an affluent suburb of Atlanta, they are children of privilege. But they still have their complaints. Above all, they are terribly bored. They do not have enough exciting things to do. Every Friday evening, they pile into one of their cars and drive to Peachtree Plaza in downtown Atlanta. It's very much like their own mall at home, only bigger and constructed underground. There is more crime to worry about at Peachtree. But the girls who hang out there are cuter and more sophisticated, say the quartet. The boys don't always know what to expect, and that makes it exciting.

Wilhelmina Camacho and her family recently bought a ranch house in Daly City, just south of San Francisco. The last eight or nine years had been very rough on them, but now it seemed they would be alright. Wilhelmina came to the United States from the Philippines nearly a decade ago, leaving her husband and two young children behind. With a college degree from the University of the Philippines, she found employment quickly. For the first year, she lived with her sister's family in a crowded, two-bedroom house. Working long hours, she was soon able to afford an apartment by herself. Two years ago her husband and children were able to join her, and for a year they slept on mattresses on the floor, with no furniture except a few boxes for tables. Although her husband had a solid government job back home, he was only able to find work in a local fast-food restaurant. But after saving money for a couple of years, they had enough for a down payment. Last fall they moved into the house in Daly City, where their children would be able to attend a better high school and were safe from the gangs in the inner city. In Daly City they could attend church where mass was said in Tagalog, and shop at stores owned by Filipino merchants in the shopping malls. And in just a couple of months, they would become citizens of their new country.

Nancy and Irv Wright live in the Chicago suburbs. They've been married for less than a year. Nancy and Irv met in college at Northwestern University, dated for three years, and got married after graduation. Nancy has a job she likes at a branch of the public library.

She majored in library science and considers herself lucky to have found a permanent position so soon after graduating. Irv also likes what he does. He's a manager at a well-known department store in town. He majored in business administration and also considers himself fortunate to have a well-paying job. Irv and Nancy have more money than they can spend. In fact, they're saving up to buy a house. As part of their budget plan, they've decided not to buy a car, and they take public transportation to work every day.

Nancy grew up in a small town and is still fascinated by the sights and sounds of the city. Today she was a couple of minutes late getting to the train station, and she notices for the first time that the train coming out of the city is packed with people. As the train stops on the other side of the platform, she watches the passengers get off and hurry to the stairs to get the buses below; almost all of them are black or Hispanic. She looks around the platform and notices that almost everyone waiting to ride downtown is white and dressed for office work. Then she realizes that the people getting off the train from the city are going to work as well, but in the hotels, restaurants, and manufacturing plants around the airport. Chicago is a fascinating city, and she seems to learn more about it every day.

People speak about the city or the suburban town they live in, but rarely about the region. Yet the best way to understand urban growth is that it is regional in scale. Today we work, shop, attend schools, go to churches, synagogues, or mosques, and pursue recreation in an increasing variety of locations, all within an expanding metropolitan area. Urban texts in the past have addressed this issue, but they do not take it to heart as the central organizing principle of the discussion as this text does. In Eric Bogosian's brilliant film *Suburbia,* actress Parker Posey portrays an LA record promoter on tour who grew up in the affluent southern California suburbs. When asked by a group of small-town teenagers where she is from, she replies, "I come from an area." Bogosian insightfully understands that the words *city* and *suburb* fail to connect with the more contemporary reality of daily life.

The metropolitan regions of the United States contain an incredible array of people. Circumstances vary according to social class, race, gender, ethnicity, age, family status, and religion, among other factors. These important *social* variables, which are traditionally treated as the subject matter of sociology, in reality interact with locational, or spatial, factors such as the clustering of homes according to family income, the journey to work or school, shopping trips and the diverse ways people pursue a particular lifestyle, the particular patterning of our social networks, the regional search for cultural experiences, and the daily pattern of commuting. Consequently, this text captures the reality of contemporary life by studying daily phenomena as embedded within the urban and suburban settlement spaces that comprise the multicentered metropolitan region. These settlement spaces are given special cultural meanings and value by the people living within them. Discovering how these settlement spaces have come to be, the role that economic, political, and social institutions play in creating and destroying these spaces, and the processes by which these spaces are given meaning by local inhabitants is all part of the *sociospatial perspective* of the new urban sociology.

If we flew over our metropolitan regions, we would be struck most strongly by the immensity of scale. Urbanized development characteristically extends for 100 miles around our largest cities. The built-up region contains a mix of cities, suburbs, vacant space, intensely farmed agricultural land, malls, and recreational areas—all of which are interconnected and bridged by communication and commuter networks including highways, rail, telecommunications, and satellite- or cellular-based links. Figure 1.1 shows the regional extent of development across the United States.

The population of these areas characteristically ranks in the millions. Interestingly, most of the people residing in metropolitan regions live *outside* the large central cities and in the suburbs. They have lived that way in the United States since at least the 1970s, when census figures brought this change to our attention. At present, 86 percent of all Americans live in metropolitan regions. This pattern of urban growth was not characteristic of cities in the past.

Cities used to be highly compact spatial forms with a distinct center that dominated, in both an emotional and economic sense, the urbanized area surrounding it. Once inhabitants went outside the city, they would be traveling in the countryside. As the famous urban historian Lewis Mumford (1961) once observed, cities served as both huge magnets and containers that concentrated people and economic activities or wealth within well-defined, bounded spaces. Table 1.1 lists the 10 most populated cities in the United States. While some of the figures are impressive, such as a total of over 7 million or almost 3½ million for New York City and Los Angeles, respectively, they do not illustrate the massive regional growth of metropolitan areas and their population concentration in the United States. Compare this table with Table 1.2, which indicates the metropolitan regions associated with these large cities. The New York metro region, for example, contains 18 million people, while the area around Los Angeles is home to 15.3 million residents.

Today the city has exploded. There is no one focus or "downtown," as there was in the past. People live and work in widely separated realms. Most of the population is urban, so most live in or near some city. But progressively fewer people each year live within the large central cities that were the population foci of the past. Instead, we now call home the expanding regions of urbanization that are associated with a mix of cities, towns, suburbs, and exurban areas. This new form of settlement space is called the *multinucleated metropolitan region,* and it is the first really new way people have

TABLE 1.1
The 10 Most Populated U.S. Cities, 1980–1990, 1994

	Population			
City	1994	1990	1980	Percentage of Change, 1980–1990
New York City, NY	7,333,253	7,322,564	7,071,639	3.5
Los Angeles, CA	3,448,613	3,485,398	2,966,850	17.5
Chicago, IL	2,731,743	2,783,726	3,005,072	−7.4
Houston, TX	1,702,086	1,630,553	1,595,138	2.2
Philadelphia, PA	1,524,249	1,585,577	1,688,210	−6.1
San Diego, CA	1,151,977	1,110,549	875,538	26.8
Detroit, MI	992,038	1,027,974	1,203,339	−14.6
Dallas, TX	1,022,830	1,006,877	904,078	11.4
Phoenix, AZ	1,048,949	983,403	789,704	24.5
San Antonio, TX	998,905	935,933	785,880	19.1

Source: *Census of Population and Housing, 1990* (U.S. Department of Commerce, Bureau of the Census, Summary Tape), File 1C (CD-Rom); *Census of Population, Characteristics of the Population, Number of Inhabitants, U.S.* (U.S. Department of Commerce, Bureau of the Census, Summary), Table 27; 1997 Census.

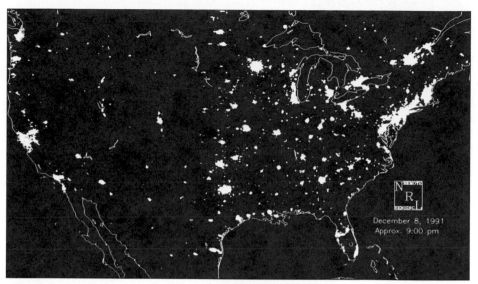

Figure 1.1   Satellite image of United States at night. Note the difference in settlement density between the West and the rest of the country.

The Los Angeles metropolitan area includes some 15 million persons and many different regional centers.

TABLE 1.2
The 20 Most Populated Metropolitan Areas

Area	Population				Percentage of Change		
	1995	1990	1980	1970	1990–1995	1980–1990	1970–1980
New York–No. New Jersey–Long Island, NY–So. Conn., NY–NJ–CT CMSA/NECMA	18,107,235	17,830,586	17,412,203	18,071,522	1.6	3.1	-3.6
Los Angeles–Anaheim–Riverside, CA CMSA	15,362,165	14,531,529	11,497,549	9,980,850	5.7	26.4	15.2
Chicago–Gary–Lake County, IL–IN–WI CMSA	8,589,913	8,239,820	7,973,290	7,778,948	4.2	1.6	2.0
San Francisco–Oakland–San Jose, CA CMSA	6,539,602	6,249,881	5,367,900	4,754,366	4.6	16.5	12.9
Philadelphia–Wilmington–Trenton, PA–NJ–DE–MD CMSA	5,967,323	5,893,019	5,680,509	5,749,093	1.3	3.9	-1.2
Detroit–Ann Arbor, MI CMSA	5,279,500	5,187,171	4,762,764	4,788,369	1.8	-1.8	-.7
Washington, DC–MD–VA MSA	4,509,932	4,222,830	3,250,921	3,040,307	6.8	20.7	6.9
Dallas–Fort Worth, TX CMSA	4,449,875	4,037,282	2,930,568	2,351,568	10.2	32.6	24.6
Boston–Lawrence–Salem–Lowell, Brockton, MA NECMA	5,768,968	5,685,763	3,662,888	3,709,642	1.5	3.3	-1.3
Houston–Galveston–Brazoria, TX NECMA	4,164,393	3,731,029	3,099,942	2,169,128	11.6	19.7	42.9
Miami–Ft. Lauderdale, FL CMSA	3,443,501	3,192,725	2,643,766	1,887,892	7.9	20.8	40.0
Atlanta, GA MSA	3,431,983	2,959,500	2,138,136	1,684,200	16	32.5	27.0
Cleveland–Akron–Lorain, OH CMSA	2,903,808	2,859,644	2,834,062	2,999,811	1.5	-2.6	-5.5
Seattle–Tacoma, WA CMSA	3,265,139	2,970,300	2,093,285	1,836,949	9.9	22.3	14.0
San Diego, CA MSA	2,644,132	2,498,016	1,861,846	1,357,854	5.8	34.2	37.4
Minneapolis–St. Paul, MN–WI MSA	2,723,137	2,538,776	2,137,133	1,981,951	7.3	15.3	7.8
St. Louis, MO–IL MSA	2,547,686	2,492,348	2,376,968	2,429,376	2.2	2.8	-2.2
Baltimore, MD MSA	2,469,985	2,382,172	2,199,497	2,089,438	3.7	8.3	5.3
Pittsburgh–Beaver Valley, PA CMSA	2,394,702	2,394,811	2,423,311	2,556,029	0	-8.0	-5.4
Phoenix, AZ MSA	2,563,582	2,238,498	1,509,175	971,228	14.5	40.6	55.4

Note: MSAs are metropolitan statistical areas; CMSAs are consolidated metropolitan statistical areas; NECMAs are New England consolidated metropolitan areas, which are based on townships and require a separate way of aggregating areas in the metropolitan region.
Source: State and Metropolitan Area Data Book 1991 (U.S. Department of Commerce, Economics and Statistics Administration, Bureau of the Census), Table 2; *State and Metropolitan Data Book 1986* (U.S. Department of Commerce, Economics and Statistics Administration, Bureau of the Census), Table A.

organized their living and working arrangements in 10,000 years. In contrast to the characteristics of the bounded city, the new form of space can be typified by two features: it extends over a large region and it contains many separate centers, each with its own abilities to draw workers, shoppers, and residents (see Table 1.2).

Some geographers have also begun to speak of multinucleated metropolitan regions. According to Peter Muller (1981), these areas can be understood best as composed of different *realms*. Realms are differentiated according to four factors: physical terrain, physical size, the level and kinds of physical activity within the realm (most particularly the kinds of minicenters), and the character of the regional transportation network. Commuting flows are particularly critical to multinucleation on a regional scale.

For example, Los Angeles contains six distinct realms within a region of approximately 50 square miles and a metro population in 1990 of 14,531,529. Development is sandwiched between several mountain ranges, especially the long escarpment created by the San Gabriel and San Bernardino mountains to the north that runs all the way east over 100 miles into the desert. On the West Coast is the Pacific Ocean, another barrier. The six realms are central Los Angeles (the old city center), the San Fernando Valley (the "valley"), the Pacific foothills (Santa Monica to Pasadena), the Pacific lowlands (beach cities—Hermosa, Redondo Beach), eastern Orange County (a separate metropolitan region that is exclusively suburban), and the San Gabriel and Pomona valleys (extending eastward and including Pomona, Ontario, and San Bernardino)—see Figure 1.2.

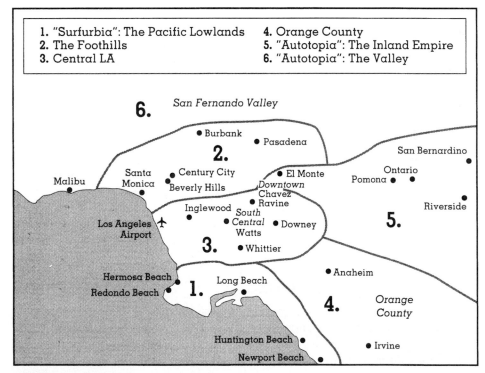

Figure 1.2   The realms of Los Angeles.

Defining the Metropolitan Region

As early as the 1940s, census takers attempted to capture regional and multicentered growth. They devised the term *Standard Metropolitan Area (SMA)*, which included a city of at least 50,000 and its surrounding suburbs within the county. This concept was changed again in 1959 to the current one, the *Standard Metropolitan Statistical Area (SMSA)*, when it was recognized that regional growth had spread across counties. By the 1980s, this concept was shortened to the term *Metropolitan Statistical Area (MSA)*. The MSA is composed of at least one large city of 50,000, along with its county and all surrounding counties that are linked economically with it. The latter link is determined by measuring the extent to which people in outlying counties travel to work to the designated MSA. If enough people commute to work from outside city boundaries, the county they reside in becomes part of the MSA. While the number of MSAs in the United States continues to grow (as of the 1990 census there were 254), two states, Wyoming and Vermont, still do not contain any (see Table 1.2 on page 6).

In the 1970s, it was recognized that regional growth and the sociospatial integration of cities was more extensive than the links captured by the MSA concept. A new term was devised, the *Standard Metropolitan Consolidated Area (SMCA)*. The SMCA was used for the first time in the 1980 census and does not do away with the MSA. It represents a higher order of integration for metropolitan areas that contain *several* MSAs, such as the Los Angeles/Orange County/Riverside/San Bernardino complex in southern California or the New York/New Jersey/Connecticut complex on the East Coast. Both of these regions contain more people than the entire country of Canada. At present there are 17 SMCAs in the United States (see Table 1.2). They are prime illustrations of the concept of *metropolitan region* that is so important to this text.

Table 1.2 reveals some interesting aspects of metropolitan growth. First, a significant number of areas have large populations rather than only one or two (see Chapter 12 on primate cities). Second, when comparing with Table 1.1, we can see that while some cities have large populations, their metropolitan regions are proportionately more populated. Philadelphia had a population in 1990 of over 1.5 million, but its metro region was more than three times that size, or 5.9 million; Phoenix's 1990 population was less than 1 million, but its metro region contained over 2 million people. Third, many regions of the Northeast or Midwest either grew slowly or lost population since the 1970s, while regions of the South and Southwest grew rapidly. This illustrates the Sunbelt shift discussed in Chapters 5 and 7. For example, the Detroit region declined by 1.8 percent and Cleveland by 2.6 percent, while the Los Angeles region grew by 26.4 percent and Phoenix by 40.6 percent between 1980 and 1990.

Megacities around the World

Not every country of the world is experiencing the new form of multicentered metropolitan growth, but all countries seem to be subject to a process of urban development that produces gigantic cities and regional urbanization. According to Dogan and Kasarda (1988), only 78 metropolises across the globe had populations of 1 million or more

Note similarity in skyscraper construction between New York City (above) and Hong Kong (below).

in 1950. By 1985 there were 258. Among these, 42 had more than 4 million population, 56 had between 2 and 4 million, 158 had between 1 and 2 million, and 300 had between .5 and 1 million. It is estimated that by the year 2010, there will be 511 metropolises across the globe with populations exceeding 1 million. By the year 2005, we will already experience a world urbanization of half the entire population. Growth of these regions is also expected to accelerate. By the year 2025, an estimated 135 giant urbanized regions will exist with populations of over 4 million. The United Nations estimates that by 2025, 61 percent of the globe's population will be living in cities. Table 1.3 indicates the 15 largest *megacities* in the world with their projected populations to the year 2015.

According to Table 1.3, it is expected that the megametropolises of the United States and Western Europe will lose population or grow slowly, while megaregions elsewhere will experience explosive growth. Thus, the population estimates for the year 2015 for Tokyo, New York, and Los Angeles, are expected to experience slow growth. In contrast, Jakarta, São Paulo, Seoul, Bombay, Shanghai, and Beijing, among others, are projected to grow substantially.

In the developed countries of the world, those located principally in Western Europe and the United States, the number of metropolises with a population over 1 million was 110 in 1985 and is expected to increase to 128 in the year 2000 and to 153 by the year 2025. In contrast, from 1950 to 2025, or 75 years' time, the number of metropolises with

TABLE 1.3
Population of the World's Largest Cities

Rank	City, Country	Population (thousands), 1994	Population (thousands, projected), 2015	Annual Growth Rate (percent), 1990–1995	Density (persons per square mile)
1	Tokyo, Japan	26,518	28,700	1.4	24,463
2	New York City, U.S.	16,271	17,600	0.3	11,473
3	São Paulo, Brazil	16,110	20,800	2.0	38,528
4	Mexico City, Mexico	15,525	18,800	0.7	37,314
5	Shanghai, China	14,709	23,400	2.3	87,659
6	Bombay (Mumbai), India	14,496	27,400	4.2	120,299
7	Los Angeles, U.S.	12,232	14,300	1.6	8,985
8	Beijing, China	12,030	19,400	2.6	37,816
9	Calcutta, India	11,485	17,600	1.7	54,607
10	Seoul, South Korea	11,451	13,100	1.9	45,953
11	Jakarta, Indonesia	11,017	21,200	4.4	122,033
12	Buenos Aires, Argentina	10,914	12,400	0.7	21,233
13	Osaka, Japan	10,585	10,600	0.2	27,833
14	Tianjin, China	10,376	17,000	2.9	47,291
15	Rio de Janeiro, Brazil	9,817	11,600	0.8	42,894

Note: The figures are United Nations estimates and projections, as revised in 1994, for "urban agglomerations" —that is, contiguous densely populated urban areas without regard to administrative boundaries.
Source: United Nations, Department for Economic and Social Information and Policy Analysis.

a population of over 4 million in the developing countries will increase from 31 to 486, or a multiple of 16 times. This explosive growth implies, as we will see in Chapter 12, an immense social crisis for the developing countries. But the growing multinucleated metropolitan regions in the advanced countries also represent serious challenges.

A New Approach to Urban Sociology

How did these changes come about? What is daily life like in the multinucleated metropolitan region? How does life there differ from that in the past? How has the city construction process, or *urbanization,* given way to the regional process of concentrated central city development, dispersed minicentered districts, and sprawling suburbanization? What is metropolitan culture like in the new regional spaces, and how does it differ from city life of the past? The answers to these and other questions are the subject of this book. Our discussion is about urban sociology, but it is not about the city alone. On the pages that follow we take an integrated perspective according to the regional focus of multinucleation. Both city and suburban life have to be considered. But there is much more.

The new urban sociology has three additional dimensions: the shift to a global perspective, attention to the political economy of pull factors in urban and suburban development, and appreciation for the role of culture in metropolitan life and in the construction of the built environment.

Global Capitalism and the Metropolis

Cities are the children of economic, political, and cultural forces. In recent years, urbanists have come to appreciate just how important the link is between cities or suburbs and changes in the economy. Prior to the 1970s, discussions about urban political economy assumed that the most critical influences emerged from the behavior of local businesspeople. A resident of a town might open up a store or factory. The owner would be known by others in the area. Jobs would be created, and local residents would apply for and fill them. Products of factories might be sold nationally, but locals would take pride in homegrown commodities and support the businesses of neighbors with their patronage, often because there was no place else to go.

This state of affairs no longer exists today. Since the 1970s, economic activity in metropolitan communities has become increasingly controlled by decisions made at the global level. Businesses are owned and managed by people from distant locations. The local TV repair shop, for example, may represent a manufacturer, such as Sony, whose headquarters are in another country, say Japan. The TV sets themselves may be assembled in yet another country, say Korea or Malaysia. Finally, foreign representatives of the manufacturer may live in this country and supervise the selling and repairing of their company's product. Reversing this example, many U.S. companies, such as Ford and General Motors, engage in such manufacturing, marketing, and administrative activities overseas. In short, economies today are linked across the globe, and the small, local factory with ties to the adjacent community has given way to the multinational corporation and to the global flow of investment as the dominant economic forces.

The global perspective has important implications for the study of metropolitan regions. Prior to the 1970s, urbanists saw changes in the city as emerging from the interaction of many local interests in a shared and common space. According to the sociologist Gerald Suttles (1972:8), this *ecological* approach, as it is called, meant that the organization of the city was not caused by "the planned or artificial contrivance of anyone." Rather, it emerged out of the "many independent personal decisions based on moral, political, ecological, and economic considerations." Today we possess a different understanding of urban organization as being caused by the actions of powerful interests, many of which have their home bases in places far removed from local areas. Their decisions, for example, to open a plant somewhere, close one down someplace else, buy up farms to build houses, or sell homes to put up minimalls or apartment buildings are all so important that they affect the well-being of the entire community.

The perspective adopted in this text, however, does not suggest that all important influences on metropolitan development derive from the global level. Important economic and political forces also arise from within community territory that can account for change. In the following chapters, therefore, we will consider the contribution to metropolitan development of all sociospatial levels: the global, the national, and the local. It is the interplay of the forces from the different levels within the local space that is the most interesting.

An additional change in perspective on urban sociology brought about by appreciating the global bases of economic activity involves a renewed emphasis on the study of capitalism as a socioeconomic system (Chase-Dunn, 1985). Our society is a capitalist one. In the recent past, our main ideological rival was the communist bloc in Eastern Europe and China, which advocated an alternative economic system. During the last decade, communism has been dismantled in most countries that practiced it, and a far greater number of countries than before now embrace capitalism. As a consequence, we can say with a great deal of confidence that the world today represents a global *capitalist* system.

The capitalist system is based on limited government regulation of business. Goods and services are bought and sold by private individuals or corporations in markets. People and corporations with money are free to invest it wherever they choose. Workers have limited job security and must sell their labor for a wage by bargaining with capitalist owners or their management representatives. The purpose of economic activity under capitalism is the pursuit of profit. Since the 1960s, capital investment has ranged the globe in an ever more fluid fashion, searching out the best combinations of costs and benefits for profit. Businesses compete with one another for the largest share of profit, and losers may go out of business or be bought up by winners. Job gains and job losses from mobile capital investment can occur in any country. Aspects of social needs (such as environmental quality or support for the community quality of life) that conflict with the profit motive are usually not considered unless the local citizens or their government requires it.

Since the 1970s, urban scholars have paid increasing attention to the relationship between capitalism and the metropolis (see Chapter 7). Competition among businesses that may not have a direct effect on space has been overshadowed by the competition among different places for their share of global investment (see Chapters 5, 12, and 13). Local populations and community well-being are also affected by changes in job needs, the level of economic activity, and growing lifestyle disparities between low-skilled or semiskilled workers and professionals living in the metropolis (see Chapter 10). All of these aspects constitute a new dimension to the study of urban sociology.

Pull Factors and the Political Economy of Real Estate

Prior to the 1970s, urban scholars looked at city and suburban growth as an expression of individual desires. For example, people moved from the city to the suburbs, it was believed, because they preferred the latter's lifestyle. In another case, investors picked a particular plot of land to develop because they liked its size and location. Individual actions based on individually held beliefs or needs might be termed the *demand-side* or push factor view of market activity, because they express the ways in which people and business act on their own desires. Urban sociology prior to the 1970s viewed growth almost exclusively in this manner.

At present, we are aware of several factors that operate to promote development in specific ways and thereby mold individual desires through incentives. These causes represent the *supply-side* or pull factor view of individual choice. Powerful social forces can create opportunities that persuade people to follow courses of action that they otherwise might not. Two supply-side sources of incentives in the development of metropolitan regions are government and the real estate industry.

The Role of Government in Development. The abstract model of capitalism represents this economic system as involving limited government intervention. This is not the case for modern economies. The United States, like other industrialized nations, has an economy that is influenced greatly not only by government regulations but also by the direct spending of government tax dollars on particular public projects. The combined action of laws or regulations and direct investment provides incentives for both businesses and individual consumers to behave in certain ways.

When city dwellers who are renters announce that they want to move to the suburbs, they are expressing their own personal preference. This decision may be occasioned by push (demand-side) factors such as problems with the public schools and high rents. Movers may also remark that the suburb they have chosen contains single-family homes that are affordable. Furthermore, due to government tax incentives on mortgage payments, it pays to own your home rather than rent. Government programs provide an enticement that pulls people in the direction of homeownership in the suburbs.

So the decision to move to the suburbs is a complex one that is prompted by both demand- and supply-side factors. For years urbanists neglected the latter dimension. Today we have a greater appreciation, in particular, for the way government at the local, state, and federal levels has operated to create opportunities and incentives that channel behavior in specific ways. In subsequent chapters we will see how this "political economy," the linked actions of business and government in the development of metropolitan regions, promotes growth.

The Role of Real Estate as a Special Factor in Growth. With some notable exceptions (Hoyt, 1933; Hughes, 1928; Form, 1954), early urban sociologists have neglected the critical role the real estate industry plays in metropolitan development. Recall from the discussion above that at one time, urban organization was viewed not as the product of any particular interest but as the interplay of many separate ones (the ecological approach). Presently, we understand that the opposite is often the case. Special interests such as global corporations can make or break a town depending on where they decide to invest new capital. But the single most important source of special interests in the development of the metropolis is the real estate industry.

The real estate sector includes all those corporations and banks, as well as land developers and construction companies, that invest in the development of land use and housing, including the land and the built environment themselves. The construction of new spaces proceeds through the actions of all those individuals, financial conduits, and corporations that make money from the change (turnover) in land use. Because a great deal of money often can be made through this type of activity, real estate interests are powerful special actors in the development of the metropolis, and their influence is greatly felt.

At any given time and on any piece of land, real estate forces can converge to turn over the existing use and engage in development that changes the utilization of local space. All of this is done in the pursuit of profit that comes as a consequence of development for different uses of land. Thus, in addition to understanding the political economy of production, it is important to understand the political economy of real estate. Consider an individual farm of 100 acres lying outside but adjacent to a developing city. Suppose its value as farmland is $400 an acre for a total of $40,000 as a working farm. Suppose too that an interstate highway is being built that will run from the large city parallel to this plot of land and on toward some other town. This highway, of course, is constructed with tax dollars by the government. Its purpose will be to open up the rural area to business and residential development.

Suppose now that a developer becomes interested in this tract of land. He or she could easily offer the farmer twice the value of what the farm is worth. Then, by dividing it up into streets and housing plots, he or she could develop a community. The 100 acres might, for example, contain 80 acres of housing plus a medium-size commercial shopping mall. Or perhaps 60 acres of single-family homes would be built along with 20 acres of condominium apartments, and the remainder of the land would be devoted to light manufacturing or minimalls. In any event, by some variation of land turnover into new uses, the developer typically could make several hundred percent in profit by building up and selling off developed land. In this way, not only has the environment changed, but turnover in this tract sets the stage for development of the land around it, thereby adding to the pressure to build up the entire region of what was once rural farmland around the city.

Perhaps one area of this same development is redeveloped for commercial use. Suddenly, structures in that section are also demolished to make room for a commercial building housing doctors' offices. The character of the community is altered again with the change in land use. And the process goes on as every few years new ways of utilizing land compel influential real estate investors to think up new ways to make money from the turnover in land use. In subsequent chapters, we will observe the important role real estate plays in the development of cities and the growth of metropolitan environments.

The Importance of Culture in Metropolitan Life

Many of the discussions of urban issues involve economic and political concerns. As we have seen, some of the more important aspects of the new urban sociology emphasize a greater attention to political economy. But this is not all there is to the new approach. People live in a symbolic world that is *meaningful* to them. They possess sentiments and ideas and attempt to communicate with others using common concepts.

Much of this interaction is organized through the direct use of spoken or written language. A significant part, however, employs expressive symbols that are objects used to convey meanings. One of the principal sources of symbolic life involves aspects of the built environment. For example, cities and suburbs are the sites of many subcultures— ethnic, religious, racial, gender specific, and age related. Neighborhoods within the metropolis composed of concentrations of these subcultures can readily be identified by objects that are signs of subcultural status. For example, ethnic areas of the city advertise themselves by the signs in front of restaurants, bakeries, specialty shops, and religious institutions (see Chapter 8). Urban subcultures may produce graffiti to show the boundaries of their neighborhood or to make claims over social space within the metropolis. People use such signs to orient themselves in the act of engaging in metropolitan life.

The study of culture and the role of objects as signs constitutes a significant part of the new urban sociology. Sociologists have studied metropolitan life as culturally meaningful for some time. What is new and different is the way such meanings are associated with objects in addition to words. For example, cities often try to develop an image that boosts attention to them in order to attract investment and tourists. A variety of images have been used, such as signs of industry ("motor city"), signs of regional growth ("the twin cities"), signs of vision ("the city of tomorrow"), and signs of life's good quality ("the city of leisure"). Slogans such as these are often linked to images or objects, such as a skyline or graphic logo of some kind. In this way, a particular symbolic identity is created for a place that gives the impression that it is special. The study of culture that links symbols to objects is called *semiotics,* and the special subfield that studies the built environment in this manner is called *spatial semiotics.*

Spatial semiotics studies the metropolis as a *meaningful* environment. Each individual building in the city, for example, performs a function for society. People often associate the appearance of the building with that function. In this way, the built object, the building, becomes a sign of its use. Thus, a large bank building represents what a bank does and what customers do there when they enter. Often banks are made of marble with brass fixtures and a kind of luxurious feel. We associate that atmosphere with banking. Government buildings, in contrast, represent political authority. Public buildings are usually constructed to convey the image of authority. Often they may incorporate a classic theme of Greek-style columns or convey political importance by the placement of auspicious statues at the entrance.

In the past, approaches to urban sociology have neglected the symbolic aspect of space, although some interesting early exceptions exist (see Wohl and Strauss, 1958). The perspective we will follow in this book integrates the symbolic nature of environments with more traditional factors that comprise social behavior, such as class, race, gender, age, and social status. Space, then, is another compositional factor in human behavior. We call this new perspective on metropolitan life the *sociospatial* approach.

Urban Semiotics. The famous Ginzu district in Tokyo lights up at night (top), while in Chicago graffiti announces the presence of a street gang (bottom). Both examples of urban signs make use of expressive symbols to convey meanings about power and urban space.

Summary: The Sociospatial Approach

In the past, urbanists have regarded space as only a container of social activities. But this view is limited. Space not only contains actions but also acts as a meaningful object to which we orient our actions. The factor of space constitutes a part of social relations and is intimately involved in our daily lives. It affects the way we feel about what we do. In turn, people alter space and construct new environments to better fit their needs. Hence, a *dual* relationship exists between people and space. On the one hand, human beings act according to social factors such as gender, class, race, age, and status within and in reaction to a given space. When a city converts a vacant lot into a basketball court, the type of activity and interaction of groups of persons within that space will change. On the other hand, people also create and alter spaces to express their own needs and desires.

The sociospatial perspective links the dual relationship between people and space with the social factors that are the bases of individual behavior. The most basic concept of this approach is *settlement space,* which refers to the built environment in which people live. Settlement space is both constructed and organized. It is built by people who have followed some meaningful plan for the purpose of containing economic, political, and cultural activities. Within it people organize their daily actions according to the meaningful aspects of the constructed space. In subsequent chapters we will discuss how sociospatial factors determine the construction and use of settlement space. Over time we will also see how change has occurred and how constructed environments are in turn molded by sociospatial factors.

In summation, the sociospatial perspective consists of attention to the following dimensions of daily life:

1. The urban and suburban settlement spaces that make up the built environment have developed within a larger metropolitan region. We adopt a regional perspective to study the older central cities, suburban communities, and new growth poles that make up the metropolitan region of the twenty-first century. We call this new form of social space the multicentered metropolitan region. We ask how and why multicentered metropolitan regions in the United States and across the globe came to be structured the way they are.
2. Settlement spaces are considered not only within their local and national contexts but as linked to the *global system of capitalism.* We pay special attention to the powerful forces of economics and politics, whose decisions influence the well-being of local areas. These economic and political decisions may derive from the metropolitan, the national, or even the international level.
3. Settlement spaces are affected by government policies and by the actions of developers, financiers, and other organizations and individuals that make up the *real estate industry.* These supply-side forces provide incentives and opportunities that pull and mold the behaviors, preferences, and choices of individual consumers and channel metropolitan development in certain specific ways. The real estate market does not simply respond to consumer demand; government policy (or the absence of such policy) at the local, state, and national levels has important consequences for metropolitan development.

BOX 1.1 THE SOCIOSPATIAL APPROACH

The basic propositions of the sociospatial perspective include the following:

1. The urban and suburban settlement spaces that make up the built environment have evolved within multicentered metropolitan regions.
2. Settlement spaces are linked to the global system of capitalism. Economic and political decisions at the metropolitan, national, and international levels influence the well-being of local areas.
3. Settlement spaces are affected by government policies and by the actions of developers, financiers, and others in the real estate industry. These supply-side forces channel metropolitan development in specific ways.
4. Settlement spaces are meaningful spaces. Everyday life is organized according to cultural symbols and material objects in the built environment.
5. There are meaningful differences among social class groups. These groups have more or less influence on decisions about how social space is allocated and structured.
6. The arrangement of settlement space influences human behavior and interaction; in turn, individuals and groups may alter existing spatial arrangements and construct new spaces to express their needs and desires.

4. The urban and suburban settlement spaces that make up the built environment are the products of human thought and action and are always meaningful places. Everyday life is organized according to cultural symbols and material objects that are part of the built environment; these symbols and objects are likely to have different meanings to different individuals or groups. We call the study of these symbols and objects *urban semiotics.*
5. Sociologists recognize that *social class groups* are an essential element of industrial and postindustrial societies. Social class groups differ from one another with respect to lifestyle, attitudes, beliefs, and access to political power and influence. As a consequence, these groups have more or less influence on decisions about how social space is allocated and structured within and across the metropolitan region.
6. The sociospatial perspective emphasizes the interaction between society and space. To class, gender, race, and other social characteristics that define difference among groups in contemporary society we add the element of *space* itself. The spatial arrangements found in urban and suburban settlement space have both manifest and latent consequences: They influence human behavior and interaction in predictable ways, but also in ways the original planner or developer may not have anticipated. But individuals, through their behaviors and interactions with others, constantly alter existing spatial arrangements and construct new spaces to express their needs and desires.

The Plan of the Book

In the following chapters, we explore the traditional topics of urban sociology in new ways. Chapter 2 addresses the origins of urbanization in the ancient world. Several explanations are proposed for the process of modernization that rely on the central role of cities. This chapter considers early cities around the globe and ends with a discussion of city growth in Western Europe. Chapters 3, 4, and 5 deal with the history of urbanization in the United States, covering, respectively, the colonial, metropolitan, and contemporary features of urban development.

Chapters 6 and 7 devote themselves to the field of urban sociology itself. The former considers classical urban theories, while the latter explores the *new urban sociology* and its relation to the *sociospatial perspective* of this text. The lessons of the first five chapters are also examined in light of the new perspective. Chapters 8 and 9 turn to the "lived" aspects of the city, or the people who make up urban life. Chapter 8 takes a detailed look at the people themselves and their ways of life, while Chapter 9 discusses theories of urban life and the methodologies sociologists have used to study people in cities and suburbs.

Chapter 10 deals with the important problems and issues facing urban communities at present. Aspects of contemporary sociospatial patterns or urbanization are highlighted. Chapter 11 considers local politics and covers both urban and suburban political activities. Chapters 12 and 13 turn to the globe and examine urban life in a variety of settings. Chapter 12 discusses the patterns of restructuring that are lately characteristic of the industrialized world and stresses common features with the U.S. case as discussed in Chapter 5. Chapter 13 focuses on urbanization in the Third World countries, stressing the features held in common as well as interesting differences.

The final two chapters look at ways of governing and administering urban and suburban areas. Chapter 14 considers the important issue of the environment, paying special attention to the sociospatial aspects of environmental costs. This chapter also considers the case of metropolitan planning in the United States and seeks to understand its limited success. Chapter 15 evaluates the changes that have occurred in the nature of government intervention within cities. Policy is seen to be closely related to ideological positions taken with regard to the limits of government intervention. This final chapter then looks at the prospects of metropolitan life and the relative well-being of urban sociology as a field of inquiry. It suggests that the uniquely "urban" emphasis of urban sociology be dropped in favor of the metropolitan perspective of the sociospatial approach.

CHAPTER

2

THE ORIGINS OF URBANIZATION AND THE CHARACTERISTICS OF CITIES

Historians estimate that urbanization, or the building of and living in compact, densely populated places, appeared as early as 10,000 years ago. Continuously used, densely populated settlements can be found in the Middle East that date back over 6,000 years and in the Indus Valley in India that date back over 4,000 years. Other centers of ancient urban life include the Minoan civilization of Crete (1800 B.C.) and the cities of China (circa 2000 B.C.).

The population of ancient cities tended to be small by our standards. Mohenjo-Daro in the Indus Valley had a population at its height of approximately 20,000 inhabitants. At its peak in the fifth century B.C., classical Athens, the birthplace of Western art, architecture, and philosophy, had no more than 150,000 inhabitants. Until the late Middle Ages, no city could compare with ancient Rome, which housed over 1 million people in the first century A.D.

Lewis Mumford, the great scholar of urban history and culture, has suggested that the first human settlements were cities of the dead—the Thanatopolis. The dead were the first to have a permanent dwelling (the caverns and mounds where paleolithic hunters buried their dead). Men and women would return to these ritual spaces to worship ancestors, and it is here that humankind first drew pictographs and paintings of not only animals for the hunt but also formalized figures of men and women. Mumford writes (1961:10), "The first germ of the city, then, is in the ceremonial meeting place that serves as the goal for pilgrimage: a site to which family or clan groups are drawn back, at seasonable intervals, because it concentrates, in addition to any natural advantages that it may have, certain 'spiritual' or supernatural powers, powers of higher potency and duration, of wider cosmic significance, than the ordinary processes of life."

Several ancient cities possessed remarkable structural features that made urban living not only possible but also quite comfortable. Mohenjo-Daro had a grid street system that made maximum use of space and an open sewer system that allowed for the elimination of waste and rainwater. Jericho, in ancient Israel, possessed a system of canals that aided the irrigation of fields outside the city. The palace at Knossos, on Crete, which is over 3,000 years old, was several stories high, and was designed to allow light to enter from the roof as well as the sides. However, it is easy to overemphasize these special cases. Most ancient cities, such as Athens, were plagued by unsanitary housing conditions and streets.

The citizens of the early towns lived an urban life that was fragile. Precariousness was, perhaps, an inevitable consequence of the growth of cities. According to Sjoberg (1960), cities were the sites of power. In order to be secure, it was necessary for early cities to exercise their strength and dominate the *hinterland,* the relatively less developed area outside the boundaries of the large city. Then, in order to prosper, it was necessary to expand the hinterland sphere of domination. As sites of wealth, ancient cities were protected by fortifications, and warfare between cities was quite common. Average town citizens lived under the constant threat of attack by roving bands of warriors or the armies of other towns. Often victors simply killed off or enslaved defeated city populations, and then the city itself was burned to the ground. In *Judges* we read, "And he took the city, and slew the people therein, and he beat down the city and served it with salt." The section of the Bible called *Lamentations* and the classic play *The Trojan Women,* by the Greek author Euripides, exemplify the ill fortune that all cities faced from the threat of war (see Box 2.1). In the former work, the ancient Hebrews lament the loss of their city, Jerusalem, from their exile in Babylonia. In the latter work, Euripedes wrote about the ancient city of Troy in Asia Minor after it was defeated by the Greeks. The men were killed or taken into slavery, and the women were parceled out to the victors.

Domination by successful rulers located in ancient cities led, in turn, to increased trade and commerce, but also to more war and the exercise of power over the countryside. Early urban existence constituted a drama involving such interwoven spheres of everyday life as agricultural production, regional and foreign trade, military conquest and rule, and the pursuit of arts and sciences based on the relative success of economic and political activities.

Most discussions of early cities focus on the apparent division of labor and economic activities around which the concentrated population was organized. In this way, city life is discussed as a progression from limited to complex specialization of work and functional organization. But not only were cities the locus of social functions; they were and remain *meaningful* space. Cities did not simply appear because certain fundamental social activities matured at a certain time. Cities had to be produced, or *constructed.* In ancient societies, every settlement was built by a group using a distinctive set of symbols and a model of space that was inherently meaningful to that group (Lagopoulos, 1986). For example, early cities, such as Ur in ancient Babylon, were

BOX 2.1   SOME CLASSICAL WRITINGS ABOUT CONQUERED CITIES

Lamentations (the Bible)

Oh how doth she sit solitary—the city that was full of people is become like a widow! She that was so great among the nations, the princess among the provinces, is become tributary!

She weepeth sorely in the night, and her tears are on her cheeks; she hath none to comfort her among all her lovers; all her friends have dealt treacherously toward her, they are become her enemies.

Exiled is Judah because of affliction, and because of the greatness of servitude; she dwelleth indeed among the nations, she findeth no rest; all her pursuers have overtaken her between the narrow passes.

. . . Jerusalem remembereth in the days of her affliction and of her miseries all her magnificent things which have been in the days of old: when her people fell in to the hand of the adversary, with none to help her, the adversaries looked at her, they laughed at the cessation of her glory.

(Chapter 1, verses 1–7)

The Trojan Women by Euripides

Scene: The action takes place shortly after the capture of Troy. All Trojan men have been killed or have fled; all women and children are captives. The scene is an open space before the city, which is invisible in the background, partly demolished and smoldering (Fitts, 1966: 151). [Hecuba is the former Queen of Troy whose husband, King Priam, has been killed.]

Hecuba: Such a state I keep
to sit by the tents of Agamemnon.
I am led captive
from my house, an old, unhappy woman,
my head struck pitiful.
Come then, sad wives of the Trojans
whose spears were bronze,
their daughters, brides of disaster,
let us mourn the smoke of Ilion.
And I, as among winged birds
the mother, lead out
the clashing cry, the song; not the song
wherein once long ago
when I held the sceptre of Priam
my feet were queens of the choice and led
the proud dance to the gods of Phrygia.

The ancient city of Babylon was built around a temple/palace complex along the Euphrates River. We know the temple as the Tower of Babel from the Old Testament.

often produced using cosmological codes that mandated geometrical relations between the city and the heavens, such as an east-west axis, and within the city through geometrical arrangements of the buildings.

Early religious codes distinguished between sacred and profane spaces, and also endowed structures with the protection of the gods. Around 500 B.C., the Etruscans, ancestors of the Romans, built cities first by plowing a "sacred furrow" as a large enclosure in a religious ceremony. The city could be built only within this space, signifying the sacred domain and separated from the profane space of the rest of the world. Only later, in fourteenth- and fifteenth-century Europe, did cities first appear without religious or cosmological codes guiding the construction of space. At this time, and continuing to the present day in Europe (and the United States), the meaning of a building (such as a bank) corresponded to the function it performed in the society with no necessary connection to some overarching symbol. In contrast, in the early settlements, there was a strong identification between what was meant by buildings and how individuals living within the city conceived of the meanings of buildings.

As the sociospatial perspective suggests, the ancient city was the combined product of political power, economic functions, and overarching symbolic meanings that expressed deeply held beliefs of the inhabitants.

Ancient Urbanization

Social scientists are interested in the origin of cities because the process of early urbanization holds insights into the origins of social structure. In particular, studies of early cities provide clues for an understanding of how complex social relations arose and how strong bonds were maintained among residents who were often unrelated. The best-known theory of the rise of cities was proposed by V. Gordon Childe (1950, 1954). According to Childe, ancient cities developed a social organization that differed from rural society in many respects and provided the social basis for modern life.

Childe viewed the development of society in terms of distinct stages and considered the emergence of urban life as a critical evolutionary phase in the rise of modern civilization. City building was part of an "urban revolution" that also brought a set of special social relations that are characteristic of modern life. The first step toward an urban society occurred when hunting and gathering societies shifted to food production in relatively stable and sedentary groups. According to Childe, once the urban revolution began, civilization progressed and evolved to more complex forms of social life sustained by an urban economy based on trade and craft production. It is principally from Childe that we have derived the idea that urbanization develops through specialization of work and the separation of different functions through increasing interdependence of societal tasks. These social relations were considered different from those found in rural society, and they provided the basis for modern civilization.

For Childe, the urban revolution possessed a number of distinct characteristics, including (1) a large population of several thousand inhabitants; (2) craftspeople, merchants, priests, and state functionaries who worked full time in these specialized occupations; (3) control of food production in the hinterland and the storage of the surplus; (4) a ruling class that possessed absolute control over the society; (5) numerical and alphabetical notational systems for information processing; (6) cultural forms of expression that were progressively refined, such as art and music; and (7) the existence of trade with other centers, some of which were at a considerable distance. In short, the large ancient city was the "cradle of civilization" (see Box 2.2).

Childe's theory of early urbanization was quite influential and may be accurate as a *descriptive* interpretation of ancient city life based on evidence from cities in Mesopotamia. Like other models of its day, it asserted an evolutionary view of development according to which civilization passes first through the stage of hunting and gathering, then to agriculture, and finally to urban-based economies, with an ever more complex and interdependent form of social organization leading up to a contemporary, "modern" stage. Other evidence suggests a discontinuous process of development.

Archeologists have known for some time that signs of civilization, such as the production of pottery in quantity or the use of writing, coexisted with the development of agriculture rather than appearing at the later stages of agriculturally based societies as evolutionary theories maintain. Jane Jacobs (1970) notes that some of the earliest human settlements, such as Catal Hyuk in northern-day Turkey, developed as commercial trade centers, not because of an agricultural surplus. For example, one of the oldest cities, Jericho, already possessed a complex urban culture based on trade and crafts over 4,000 years ago, *prior* to the domestication of grain in the surrounding region

BOX 2.2 V. GORDON CHILDE AND THE URBAN REVOLUTION

In his essay "The Urban Revolution," V. Gordon Childe described the features of early Sumerian cities that mark the beginning of urban settlement:

1. Increased population size and density: by 3000 B.C. Ninevah, Ur, Uruk, and other Sumerian cities each had as many as 20,000 persons, larger than other human settlements up to that time.
2. Concentration of agricultural surplus: farmers living within the region controlled by the city paid a tithe, or tax, to an "imaginary deity or a divine king" to support soldiers, priests, and other officials.
3. Public works and monuments: irrigation projects built by the state (through labor required of all citizens) allowed farmers to produce an agricultural surplus; the cities were dominated by temples (ziggurats) rising from a stepped brick platform.
4. Specialization of labor: the production of an agricultural surplus freed individuals to perform the specialized tasks required of artists, craftspeople, merchants, soldiers, and priests.
5. Invention of writing: systems of writing and numerical notation were developed to keep track of commercial accounts and tax payments.
6. Social stratification: priests, military leaders, and other officials formed a ruling class and were exempt from manual labor; workers and craftspeople were "relieved from intellectual tasks" but were guaranteed safety within the city.
7. Development of the decorative and fine arts: artists and craftspeople developed sophisticated styles and traditions in the depiction of persons and animals.
8. Development of sciences: sciences were developed to predict, measure, and standardize to assist in the production of agriculture and the keeping of tax records (arithmetic, geometry, and astronomy).
9. Membership in the urban community: participation in the community was based on residence and was no longer dependent on kinship.
10. Long-distance trade: raw materials not available in the local area were imported for craft production and religious ceremonies.

(Eisenstadt and Shachar, 1987:27). Because of the need to create a livelihood on marginal agricultural lands, early residents of towns innovated alternative economic activities including trade, full-time craft work, and even religion, whose products could then be exchanged for essentials, thereby providing the basis for an urban, city-based economy that could survive on trade.

While the social division of labor and its growing complexity certainly contributed to urban development, economic factors alone did not produce the first cities. The market by itself can never provide adequate control or guidance—that is, *regulation*—for social organization. In fact, the classical sociologists Emile Durkheim, Karl Marx, and Max Weber all argued that everyday actions in a market society generate problems and conflict that call for regulation by political and cultural means. "The most important of such problems were the construction of trust or solidarity (stressed by Durkheim), the regulation of power (Marx and Weber) and the provision of both meaning and legitimation for social activities so prized by Weber" (Eisenstadt and Shachar, 1987:50).

Classical Cities

Ancient Athens in Greece was constructed according to a cosmological code that was then overlaid by religious symbols linked to the pantheon of Greek gods, such as Zeus represented by a statue. The entire city itself was built to honor the goddess Athena. The figure used to design Athens was the circle, and all buildings followed geometrical design principles such as "the golden mean." In the center of the circle was the *agora,* which was not simply the marketplace but the public hearth or *hestia koine,* the center of the community. Over a period of 200 years, the agora at the base of the acropolis took form as public buildings—courts, libraries, temples, the gymnasium—gradually closed in the open area, creating an enclosed space where the public life of the city was focused. The public hearth was considered to be the *omphalos,* the center of the world.

Visitors would pass through the agora along the Pan-Athenaic Way and past the *stoa* (public marketplace), and then ascend the *propylaia,* the gateway to the sacred temples at the top of the acropolis, designed and built by the architect Mnesikles in 430–420 B.C. Robin Rhodes (1995:53) describes the ascent of the acropolis:

> Its architecture, in concert with the Panathenaic procession, progressed step by step from the west, from the realm of the secular, the human, the realm of stories, of human explanation, to the elemental religious experience of divine epiphany at the east side of the tenemos, at the front of the major temples to Athena.

The central organizing concept for Athenians became their political life, and the space of Athens became overlaid by a political code that supplanted the earlier cosmological/religious one. Thus, in ancient Athens the street network was a radial form emanating out from the center of the omphalos. This is to be distinguished from both the precocious grid planning of the Indus Valley cities and the haphazard growth of Mesopotamia.

The intent of radial development was dictated not by the economic concern of easy access to the market but by the political principle that all homes should be equidistant from the center because all Athenian citizens were equal. Within the center were placed the *citizen assembly hall,* the *city council hall,* and the *council chamber,* all structures linked to the institution of city politics.

In a second example, after 200 B.C., ancient Rome was constructed using a different model, one that emanated from a royal, or imperial, code that stressed grandeur, domination, and excess. Roman space was based not on the political equality of its citizens but on the military power of the state, even though it borrowed republican ideas

The Pan-Athenaic Way leads through the agora, the center of public life in ancient Athens.

from ancient Greece. In the case of Rome, as was also true of Athens, functional spaces serving principally an economic function were embedded in a larger, meaningful space governed by political and cultural symbols.

Initially the buildings of the Republican Forum at the center of Rome were built on a human scale and formed the focal point for activity within the city. As the empire expanded and the Republic was replaced first by a dictatorship and then by a monarchy, Rome was refashioned by the imperial code to a gargantuan style. The city of Rome became a physical representation of the empire itself. Monuments and public buildings were constructed to honor the personal accomplishments of each emperor. At its height in the third century, Imperial Rome contained a population of some 1 million people, many of them slaves (including secretaries, clerks, accountants, and foremen in addition to laborers). It encompassed a total area of eight square miles, much of which was given over to public space. The majority of the population lived in the 46,000 *insulae* (apartment buildings) within the city; these buildings usually were three stories tall, contained five flats, and housed five to six people. There were only 4,000 private homes within the city. Eight aqueducts brought the more than 200 million gallons of water needed to service 1,200 public fountains, 926 public baths, and the public latrines. The streets were narrow, twisting, and dark, averaging 6 to 15 feet wide; the largest street was just 20 feet wide. The city fire department consisted of some 7,000 men. The *circus maximus,* where chariot races took place, seated more than 100,000 people and was surrounded by taverns, shops, and eating places. The famous *Colosseum* rose more than 180 feet above the city and seated more than 80,000 people.

The Republican and Imperial Forums (located to the upper right of the Colosseum in this model) were the focus of civic life in ancient Rome.

Rome was very different from Athens and other Greek city-states in that it was the capital of the first urban civilization, with roads linking the city to administrative centers across Europe and the Middle East. These cities served as centers of political power, economic control, and cultural diffusion. By A.D. 200, more than 5 million people lived in Roman cities. As the empire prospered, the 1 million or more residents of Rome lived off the great wealth that poured into the city. Eventually the center became known for its decadence and idleness. At one time, a full 159 days out of the Roman year were declared public holidays! Of these, 93 days, or one-fourth of the entire year, were devoted to games at the emperor's expense. Alongside this parasitic existence emerged immense urban problems that we commonly associate with the modern city: the deterioration of housing, widespread poverty, public corruption, and a dangerous lack of proper sanitation facilities and other services for the residents.

Ancient Rome became a city of the rich and the poor, a society wedded to spectacle and consumption rather than commerce and trade. During the reign of Emperor Titus (A.D. 69–81), for example, some 5,000 animals were slain in the Colosseum in a single day as public entertainment. By the time the barbarians showed up at the city walls (after A.D. 400), the city had long since become mired in its own crises of excess and dependence.

Urbanization after A.D. 1000

When the Roman empire fell, urban space in Europe was reclaimed by the countryside and its feudal relations. Towns needed to defend themselves in the absence of a central authority. They became small, fortified settlements like the medieval castle. Consequently, in Europe during the Middle Ages, the level of urbanization was low. Few places exceeded 10,000 in population. In contrast, the cities of Asia, the Near East, and what is now Latin America housed thriving, populated communities during this same period.

Most historians contend that the cities that emerged around the globe after A.D. 1000 were the products of powerful national rulers and the success of regional trade rather than deriving from social relations that were uniquely urban in nature, as Childe's theory suggests. City life remained precarious and dependent on social relations that emanated from state power. It was not until the seventeenth century, with the rise of capitalism in Western Europe, that urban life appeared to be propelled by forces emerging from within cities themselves. In China, for example, towns were organized by the state under the infallible rule of the emperor and for the principal purpose of administration. These were secular kingdoms united under a political hierarchy to harness the economic wealth of the countryside. Under the imperial capital, the provincial capitals were dispersed throughout the kingdom, and under these were clustered the still smaller county capitals of the Chinese empire. In sum, commerce and trade combined with the power of the state to produce the towns of the Orient.

Much the same story characterized the Middle East, which also contained places with populations that eclipsed those in Europe after the year A.D. 1000. With the coming of Islamic hegemony, cities appeared that solidified the control of territory under the Muslim rulers or caliphs (see Chapter 12). Islam also took over older cities built by the Romans, such as Constantinople. To these it added two types of "new" towns across North Africa and the Near East: *Villes Crées* were fortress cities constructed by Islamic rulers as administration centers, and *Villes Spontanées* arose as trading centers constructed without preconceived plans but sanctioned by the caliph. Thus, Islamic society possessed a robust system of cities, but these were all products of state-directed territorial expansion and administration. As in the Chinese case, the rulers needed cities to control the territory and commerce of the hinterland.

The experience of India during this same period between the years 1000 and 1700 also replicates the combined role of royal administration on the one hand and the importance of local trade on the other in the sustenance of Oriental cities. As elsewhere in Asia and the Middle East, the size and well-being of Indian cities were a consequence of the power of central state authority rather than of social relations emanating from the urban community itself. Braudel (1973:413) provides an interesting illustration of the dependency of the city on the power of the state in his examination of India during the seventeenth century:

> The example of India shows how much these official towns were bound up with the prince—to the point of absurdity. Political difficulties, even the prince's whim, uprooted and transplanted the capitals several times. . . . As soon as its prince abandoned it the town was jeopardized, deteriorated and occasionally died.

While London (left) grew as a city in the Middle Ages, so did other, non-European places, such as Damascus (below).

Both cities contained a fortified wall for protection, religious buildings, and a palace or seat of government, as well as housing.

When a Mogul prince left Delhi

> on a journey to Kashmir in 1663, the whole town followed him because they could not live
> without his favors and liberality. An improbable crowd formed, estimated at several
> hundred thousand people by a French doctor who took part in the expedition. Can we
> imagine Paris following Louis XV during his journey to Metz in 1744?

Finally, in Latin America, the Aztec and Inca civilizations achieved impressive heights during this same period. As late as the 1600s, Spanish explorers marveled at the awesome scale of New World urbanization. Yet, as the example of Aztec civilization in Mexico shows, these places were closely connected to the agricultural relations of the hinterland and could not be considered modern cities. According to Murray Bookchin (1974:7–8),

> An illustration of the earliest cities can be drawn from descriptions of the Aztec "capital"
> of Tenochtitlán, encountered by Spanish *conquistadores* only three centuries ago. At first
> glance, the community is deceptively similar in appearance to a modern city. . . . The
> city's resemblance . . . rests on its lofty religious structures, its spacious plazas for
> ceremonies, its palaces and administrative buildings. Looking beyond these structures, the
> city in many respects was likely a grossly oversized pueblo community.

As Bookchin points out, in the case of Aztec cities, the horticulturally based activities of the family clans organized social relations within the city. These clan-based social orders reached into the very heart of city life. Integration around the agricultural economy was so complete that Aztec cities did not even develop money and retained a barter system. Just as in the Orient, commercial and craft activities carried on within Tenochtitlán could not explain either its immense physical space or the size of its population. The principal role of the city was to serve as the center for the Aztec rulers and their administrative functions.

It was not until the late Middle Ages in Europe that towns acquired political independence from the state. The classical sociologist Max Weber (1966) considered this autonomy as necessary for the establishment of an urban community. For Weber, the key to city life was the creation of an independent urban government that was elected by the citizens of the city itself. Classical Athens and early Rome were two examples. Weber believed that in the late Middle Ages, Europe also developed cities of this type. For Weber, an urban community consisted of a fusion of the fortress and the marketplace where trade and commercial relations predominated, a legal court of its own that had the authority to settle local disputes, and partial political autonomy that allowed residents to elect authorities who could administer daily affairs.

If the cities of the later European Middle Ages enjoyed autonomy, it was relatively short-lived. By the eighteenth century, nation-states had acquired control of territory, and the commercial-trading economy was global in scale, thereby making individual places dependent on one another. Weber's remarks about the city were meant to suggest that there may once have been uniquely *urban* social relations that characterized city life and helped to transform society from a rural, agriculturally based system of social organization to one that is considered "modern." For example, urban life was sustained by a mode of social organization that, when compared to rural areas, consisted of greater emphasis on specialized jobs, the decline of family authority and the rise of contractual and political relations, and a replacement of the strong ties binding people together based on kinship with those based on the interdependence of sharing the same fate as the city. In addition to Weber, other classical sociologists also developed ways of studying the contrast between premodern and modern societies. Ferdinand Tonnies, for example, called this the shift from *gemeinschaft* to *gesellschaft,* or the change from a society based on intimate contacts to one based on contract, while Emile Durkheim considered modernization as a change from a society based on mechanical solidarity, or a low degree of specialization, to one based on organic solidarity, or a high degree of specialization and interdependence.

In retrospect, it seems clear that the force that propelled the development of cities in Europe did not involve some uniquely "urban" cause but was a direct consequence of the rise of capitalism and industrialization. It is this change that defines the development from the relatively autonomous urban community in Europe of the seventeenth and eighteenth centuries to the large industrial and postindustrial cities that we know today.

The Medieval Order and the Birth of Planning

As we have seen, the spatial arrangement of the built environment is determined by the social structures of the larger society. Following the collapse of the Roman Empire, cities in the West declined in population and influence; we sometimes refer to this period as the Dark Ages, although Greek literature and philosophy were kept alive in the Moslem world and continuous development occurred in music and architecture in Europe. In Italy, where there was no centralized government and towns themselves often were beset by conflicts among wealthy families seeking economic and political control, fortified family towers dominated the skyline. This struggle for control of the Italian city-state is portrayed in William Shakespeare's play and Franco Zeffirelli's adaptation of *Romeo and Juliet,* filmed in Verona. The built environment of the Italian city-state reflects the underlying social order and social conflict of Italian society of this earlier period.

Just as classical cities developed around the *agora* and the *forum,* the medieval city developed around a central symbolic space. The buildings on each side of the central square represented the dominant social, economic, and political interests in medieval society: the cathedral, the town hall, and the merchants' hall and trade guilds. Medieval cities often competed with one another for economic and political dominance, and many were protected by city walls. Because the walls prevented the cities from expanding outward, the cities built upward, and by the late Middle Ages, four- and even five-story buildings overhanging crowded streets were not uncommon. As trade prospered, cities grew more crowded—and so did the problems of poverty, crime, poor sanitation, and ultimately disease. Daniel Defoe, in *A Journal of the Plague Year* (1722), describes the ravages of the great plague that devastated London in the seventeenth century, when houses containing persons suffering from the Black Death were boarded up by city authorities with the victims still inside!

By the mid-1500s, Rome had been restored to its position as the capital city of the Catholic world, and it grew in size and significance as trade and commerce in cities across Europe produced a new merchant class with the wealth and leisure time necessary to support pilgrimages to this most holy of sites. But continued growth and an aging infrastructure produced a medieval city of narrow streets, overcrowded housing, and massive traffic problems; in the last decades of the sixteenth century, nearly 450,000 pilgrims traveled to Rome each year. Pope Sixtus V (1585–1590) began an ambitious plan of urban redevelopment. Edmund Bacon (1970:117) described the plan for the redevelopment of Rome:

> Sixtus V, in his effort to recreate the city of Rome into a city worthy of the church, clearly saw the need to establish a basic over-all design structure in the form of a movement system as an idea, and at the same time the need to tie down its critical parts in positive physical forms which could not easily be removed. He hit upon the happy solution of using Egyptian obelisks, of which Rome had a substantial number, and erected these at important points within the structure of his design.

The seven holy pilgrimage sites within the city were linked by broad boulevards, providing for a new sense of movement and spatial ordering within the city. This plan for urban redevelopment was celebrated in engravings by the leading artists of the day. Implementing this plan would take more than 60 years and result in the destruction of neighborhoods of crowded medieval housing, but it produced a new city that would attract pilgrims from across Europe. New squares were built and monuments erected to symbolize the power of the church.

The redevelopment of Rome served as a model for urban planning during the Renaissance. New squares would be constructed with monuments to historical events and public figures; boulevards would connect these urban spaces with one another and direct traffic through the city. Older housing, now a crowded eyesore, would be demolished to make way for urban development. The design of the new metropolis would be replicated in Renaissance cities across Europe in the 1700s, and would serve as a model for urban planning in many other areas of the world, including Detroit and Washington, D.C. (Girouard, 1985).

Capitalism and the Rise of the Industrial City

Throughout the world, especially in North Africa, Asia, and the Near East, cities were the sites of vigorous trade and the economic activities associated with commerce. However, trade by itself did not sustain the rise of cities in Western Europe. Distinguishing the developing towns of the late Middle Ages from other such places was the emergence of capitalism based on a money economy.

The economy of the feudal manor, for example, was characterized by *simple commodity production;* that is, craft products were produced for exchange, but the owners remained the direct producers of the products themselves. Exchange itself could be facilitated using any object or service that was equivalent according to the cultural judgment of the society. This barter system prevailed for several hundred years in Europe after the fall of Rome and existed elsewhere in the Middle East and Asia.

In the later Middle Ages, beginning with the twelfth century, the general and accepted use of money and a fully developed commodity market within the city that was regulated by local government allowed the people with capital to hire both labor and resources to produce goods. The classical sociologist Karl Marx was the foremost student of the rise of capitalism. He called the type of economy made possible by capital and city regulation of markets *extended commodity production*. That is, unlike simple commodity production, which ended in the exchange of goods or services, extended production began with money, or capital, and, after production and exchange, ended with still more money, which was then invested in a new cycle of accumulation.

In this manner, commercial relations supported the accumulation of capital, and cities with such economies began to prosper beyond anything experienced until that time. In addition, social and cultural relations changed in the cities to sanction the pursuit of wealth through the accumulation of money. For example, the early Catholic Church prohibited the loaning of money, except within restricted guidelines, and limited the role of banks (see Vance, 1990). In the sixteenth century, the Protestant Reformation swept away these cultural and social restrictions on the free flow of investment, providing a cultural basis for capitalist development (Weber, 1958). Once that point was reached, the accumulation process spilled out into the surrounding area as the new, money-based capitalist economy penetrated relations in the countryside. The history of the Occidental city, as Braudel, Weber, and Marx all agreed, became the history of capitalism.

Following these changes, eighteenth- and nineteenth-century cities in Western Europe experienced a population explosion of unprecedented proportions (McKeown, 1976). Table 2.1 illustrates some of this change. Between 1800 and 1900, for example, the population of London went from 861,000 to 6,480,000, while that of Berlin went from 172,000 to 2,424,000, although seaports, such as Naples, grew much less.

TABLE 2.1
Growth of Cities in Europe, 1700 to 1990
(*population in thousands*)

City/Metro Area	1700	1800	1900	1990
London, England	550	861	6,480	9,170
Paris, France	530	547	3,330	8,709
Naples, Italy	207	430	563	2,960
Lisbon, Portugal	188	237	363	2,396
Amsterdam, Holland	172	201	510	—*
Rome, Italy	149	153	487	3,021
Madrid, Spain	110	169	539	4,451
Vienna, Austria	105	231	1,662	2,313
Berlin (unified), Germany	—*	172	2,424	3,022

*Unavailable from comparable sources.
Sources: Adapted from T. Chandler and G. Fox, *3000 Years of Urban History* (New York: Academic Press, 1974), pp. 321–341; *Statistical Abstract of the United States, 1991*, U.S. Department of Commerce, Economics and Statistics Administration, Bureau of the Census, Table 1437, pp. 835–836.

Occupations became specialized, and the division of labor grew ever more complex as capitalism developed. Aided by emergent nation-states, the political and legal relations of capitalism began to dominate the countryside in Europe. Capitalism required the legal sanctification of private property, and this resulted in the "commodification" of many aspects of society. All this buying and selling meant that markets were formed and prospered, providing people with even more ways to make money.

Land, for example, which was once held only by the nobility and the church, became commodified and available for purchase by anyone with money. A real estate market emerged that cut up and parceled out land for sale. A second market, this one for labor, emerged as the serfs, who were bound by feudal traditions to their masters, were freed only to become commodified wage laborers. As feudal relations of dependence and reciprocity were broken down by capitalism and the pursuit of monetary accumulation, immense numbers of people were forced out of the rural, farming areas and into the cities, where they looked for work by selling their labor for a wage on the labor market.

With the coming of the industrial revolution, this "urban implosion," or shift of population from rural to urban places, reached truly astounding proportions. According to Lewis Mumford (1961), the cities of the late eighteenth century contained relatively few people, numbering fewer than 600,000 (see Table 2.1). By the middle of the nineteenth century, capitalist industrialization had created cities of a million or more all across Western Europe. The most dramatic changes were experienced in England and Wales, because it was there that the scale of industrialization and capitalist development was most advanced. According to Geruson and McGrath (1977:25), urban counties in Britain grew by 30 percent between 1780 and 1800 and again by approximately 300 percent between 1801 and 1831. Commercial and industrial counties experienced a net population increase of 378,000 between 1781 and 1800 and an additional 720,000 between 1801 and 1831. At the very same time, agricultural counties *lost* 252,000 people during the first period and lost 379,000 between 1801 and 1831.

Census figures at the time of the nineteenth century were not always accurate. Nevertheless, Braudel (1973:376) suggests that around the turn of the century, several regions in Europe tipped their population balance from rural to urban, especially in England and the Netherlands, a truly momentous occurrence. In short, for the first time in history, several nations changed from populations that were predominantly rural to ones dominated by urban location, and this is why the urbanization process in Western Europe after the 1700s was so significant.

By the middle 1800s, Western Europe possessed many industrialized cities. What was life like in them? The cities that emerged in the nineteenth century, unlike the ancient places, were not conceived according to some overarching symbolic meaning, such as religious or cosmological codes. Development was a haphazard affair. Individual capitalists did what they willed, and real estate interests operated unchecked by either legal code or cultural prescription. Land was traded like other goods. About the only clear pattern that emerged involved the spatial separation of rich and poor. The industrial city of Western Europe became the site of a clash of classes: the workers against the capitalists.

BOX 2.3   LEWIS MUMFORD ON THE INDUSTRIAL CITY

Competition for space by poor unprotected immigrants had the same effect on seventeenth-century Paris or Edinburgh as on eighteenth-century Manchester and nineteenth-century Liverpool and New York: the ground rents rose and the living quarters worsened. . . . Who benefited by that advance? Not the occupants. Whose income kept pace with it? Not the workers'. . . . With appropriate variation, this condition held throughout Europe, and in the more prosperous seaports of North America. From the standpoint of the working classes, the period was one of increasing exploitation, and with regard to their quarters, one of increasing dilapidation and constriction. . . .

By the seventeenth century destitution had been accepted as the normal lot in life for a considerable part of the population. Without the spur of poverty and famine, they could not be expected to work for starvation wages. Misery at the bottom was the foundation for luxury at the time. As much as a quarter of the urban population in the bigger cities, it has been estimated, consisted of casuals and beggars; it was this surplus that made for what was considered, by classic capitalism, to be a healthy labor market, in which the capitalist hired labor on his own terms, or dismissed workers at will, without notice, without bothering as to what happened to either the worker or the city under such inhuman conditions. In a memorandum dated 1684 the Chief of Police of Paris referred to the "frightful misery that afflicts the greater part of the population of this great city." Between forty and sixty-five thousand were reduced to outright beggary. There was nothing exceptional about Paris.

When Herman Melville, as a boy, visited the prosperous city of Liverpool in the eighteen-thirties, he found, as he describes in "Redburn," a woman with two babes at her breast dying in a cellar opening under the sidewalk. Despite his efforts to obtain aid, no one would succour these creatures. They were removed only when their dead bodies stank.

Observing the excesses of the time and the utter devastation visited on working-class life by the factory regime of capitalism, Karl Marx (1967) recognized that class struggle would become the driving force of history. It was left for Friedrich Engels (1973), Marx's close friend, to document in graphic terms the pathological nature of uneven development characterizing urban growth under capitalism in his classic account, *The Condition of the Working Class in England.* In fact, several books were written in the nineteenth century cataloging the hardships caused by industrialization, including Henry Mayhew's *London Labour and the London Poor* and Charles Booth's *Life and Labour of the People in London.* These works, and many more, described what Booth called "the problem of poverty in the midst of wealth." Lewis Mumford writes of living conditions in the industrial city of the nineteenth century in Box 2.3.

BOX 2.4 TWO POETS VIEW THE CITY

London
by William Blake

I wander thro' each charter'd street,
Near where the charter'd Thames does flow,
And mark in every face I meet
Marks of weakness, marks of woe.
In every cry of every Man,
In every Infant's cry of fear,
In every voice, in every ban,
The mind-forg'd manacles I hear.
How the Chimney-sweeper's cry
Every black'ning Church appalls;
And the hapless soldier's cry,
Runs in blood down Palace walls.
But most thro' midnight streets I hear
How the youthful Harlot's curse
Blasts the new born Infant's tear,
And blights with plagues the Marriage hearse.

Chicago (excerpt)
by Carl Sandburg

Hog Butcher for the World,
Tool Maker, Stacker of Wheat,
Player with Railroads
      and the Nation's Freight Handler;
Stormy, husky, brawling,
City of Big Shoulders . . .

In the chapters to follow, we will see that many of the ideas associated with modern life have their origins in observations made about industrial cities. The same core problem of uneven development—the graphic contrast between the wealthy and the poor, for example, and the contradictions between progress and misery—remains very much at the center of the urban dynamic in cities around the globe. On the one hand, the city represented hope to all those laboring under meager conditions in the countryside. It was the site of industrialization and the great dream of modernization and progress. On the other hand, the powerful forces of urbanism dwarfed the individual and crushed the masses into dense, environmentally strained spaces. The city rhythm, unlike that of the country, was above nature, and life was worth only as much as the daily wage for which it could be exchanged. These contrasting images of the city are captured by two poems: the promise of urban life by Carl Sandburg and the horror of that same life by William Blake (see Box 2.4).

Were cities in the United States much like their European counterparts? The processes of urbanization and capitalism that created large cities in Europe during the nineteenth century also thrived in the United States at the same time. In many ways, U.S. cities were governed by the same dynamic as in Europe. In some important ways, however, the former cities represent unique cases in the history of urbanism. We will explore this record in the following chapters.

CHAPTER

3

URBANIZATION IN THE UNITED STATES

The United States is one of the most urbanized nations on the globe. Many of its people, however, dislike the large city. Thomas Jefferson (1977) suggested that cities were the source of evil and corruption that would threaten the young democracy's political system. Despite such sentiments, U.S. urban growth has been prolific and continues after 300 years. For much of that history, the everyday life of Americans has been defined in urban terms.

In many respects, development in the United States mirrors the same trends and effects of social forces unleashed in Western Europe. We experienced, for example, the same industrial revolution that England did, and even contributed significantly to its technological breakthroughs. Everyone has probably heard of McCormick's reaper or Thomas A. Edison's lightbulb. Such inventions helped the United States compete with industrial giants like England in the nineteenth century.

Yet, for all its close links to the Old World, the city-building process in the United States exhibits several features that exaggerate aspects of urbanization found elsewhere. These include (1) the lack of walls or fortifications around cities; (2) real estate development as a major sector in the economy of capitalism; (3) the ideology of privatism, which limits the role of the state and emphasizes individual accomplishments as the basis of community; (4) large-scale immigration and population churning on cities; and (5) the regional dispersal of the metropolis. This chapter illustrates these features within the larger context of U.S. urban history.

The Stages of Urban Growth

Many different factors have contributed to urban expansion in the United States. The role of economic forces; transportation, construction, and communication technology;

political changes; immigration policy; and success at wars are but some of the major causes for the development of city building. *The best explanation for urban patterns is found when connection is made between the production of settlement space and the society's political economy.* According to the sociospatial perspective, this does not mean that the clearly defined stages of metropolitan growth are directly correlated to exact stages of economic development; rather, it means only that important features of each period in economic development are associated in certain ways with important factors in the social and political change of metropolitan space (see Table 3.1).

Four distinct stages of urban growth in the United States have resulted in the formation of the multicentered metropolitan region. These are (1) the colonial period, 1630 to 1812; (2) the industrial period, 1812 to 1920; (3) the metropolitan period, 1920 to 1960; and (4) the deconcentration and restructuring of settlement space within the multicentered metropolitan region that has taken place since 1960.

Urban and suburban settlement space within the United States has developed within a free-market economy based on private property and capital accumulation. We know this type of economic system by the name of *capitalism.* As both Adam Smith and Karl Marx emphasized, capitalism is a dynamic system that brings about changes in the social relations and political systems with which it comes in contact. The stages of urban development correspond to growth periods in the development of U.S. capitalism. These stages of development are often referred to as (1) mercantile capitalism, (2) industrial capitalism, (3) monopoly capitalism, and (4) global capitalism. But these periods do not represent an evolutionary theory of development such as that of V. Gordon Childe in the last chapter. Although cities in the United States went through these periods, there is no reason that another society has to pass through exactly the same sequence as in the United States, as indeed other countries' economic transformations also differ from ours. Furthermore, according to the sociospatial perspective, stages in metropolitan growth and in the political economy are only loosely coupled, as mentioned above. Nonetheless, discussion of separate phases of city building is an effective way to organize our analysis of the connection between developments in the U.S. political economy and the forms of settlement space over time.

The Colonial Period: 1630 to 1812

The United States was colonized by European capitalist societies operating according to the political economy of *mercantilism,* an early stage of global capitalism. In this system, the nation-states of Europe organized the expansion of their local economies at a time when manufacturing was *not* industrialized and with the aid of the political apparatus of the nation-state. The wealth of countries, it was believed, depended on

TABLE 3.1
Stages of Capitalism and Stages of Urbanization in the United States

Stages of Capitalism	Stages of Urbanization
Mercantile-colonial period	Colonial period: 1630 to 1812
Industrialization period	Industrial period: 1812 to 1920
Monopoly capitalism period	Metropolitan period: 1920 to 1960
Global capitalism period	Multicentered expansion: 1960 to today

the well-being of commerce or trade, while domestic manufacture was protected from foreign competition by government tariffs. Mercantilist theory called for the colonization of resource-rich but undeveloped areas of the globe accomplished through the state's own military and naval power. Wealth would increase if raw materials could be plundered from the undeveloped colonies, while manufactured articles would be produced exclusively in the home countries. By these arrangements, the maximum amount of work would be given to the nation's own laborers and excess population could be drained off to the colonies.

In the 1700s the cities of the United States were little more than colonial outposts of England, France, and Spain located on the shores of a country with a foreboding and unsettled interior. The attention and the energies of the colonists were directed eastward across the Atlantic Ocean toward the colonial powers and events in Europe. The existence of these cities was guaranteed by the might of the colonial power's navy and military organization.

Colonial cities were port cities. The docks and warehouses and the shipping, insurance, and trading companies constituted the focus of urban development. Farther back from the port facilities merchant and counting houses were located, while behind the port district the beginnings of residential quarters, principally for the colonial businessmen and their families, were located. Artisans of all kinds who engaged in handicraft manufacture of the simple implements required for daily life were also located in the town. Their shops and residences were situated throughout the port district.

As mercantilism developed, it also became a way of relieving population pressures by promoting immigration to the colonies. This, in turn, stimulated a nascent real estate industry in the port cities. Many U.S. cities, in fact, were laid out to accommodate both mercantile economic functions *and* residential real estate speculation. Often single entrepreneurs in England were granted permission by the Crown to set up their own town as just such a speculative enterprise. The case of Philadelphia, founded in the late 1600s by the Quaker entrepreneur William Penn, illustrates the combined mercantile and real estate venture:

> Philadelphia was laid out in 1681 on a plan that was probably the original speculator's design for an American City, a plot that measured one by two miles and was easily divided into lots that might be sold at a distance. (Vance, 1990:265)

Colonial Philadelphia was a mercantile city with extensive docks and warehouses along the Delaware River.

The colonial cities of the United States prospered because of the success of British mercantilism. Each of the largest towns filled an economic function connected with European trade. Boston was the center for colonial provisions; Newport specialized in shipbuilding and slavetrading; New York trading focused on flour and furs; Philadelphia focused on meat, wheat, and lumber; and Charleston was known for the export of rice and indigo. Initially Baltimore had few natural advantages, and it lagged behind the growth of these five cities, but in the later 1700s its businesses specialized in the flour-exporting trade, and it prospered. However, towns such as Williamsburg, Virginia, which were laid out solely as political centers, never grew.

Table 3.2 lists colonial cities with populations of 5,000 or more in 1790. New York City and towns in New York State dominated the colonies. Some cities, such as Philadelphia and Boston, remain important population centers today. Others, such as Stephentown, New York, or Southwark, Pennsylvania, never became metropolises.

By the time of the Revolutionary War, U.S. cities played a crucial role due to their demographic and economic power. The first confrontations, such as the Boston Tea Party, took place in cities. The wealth concentrated in New York, Boston, Philadelphia, and Newport also financed the revolt. Colonial cities became centers of propaganda that disseminated antiloyalist views throughout the colonies. At the time of the revolution, for example, 36 newspapers actively operated in the colonies (not all of which opposed the Crown). Finally, cities played a major role because they nurtured paramilitary

TABLE 3.2
The 20 Most Populated Colonial Cities, 1790

Rank	City	Total Population
1	New York City, NY	32,305
2	Philadelphia, PA	28,522
3	Litchfield, CT	20,278
4	Boston, MA	18,038
5	Northern Libertiestown, PA	9,907
6	Rensselaerwick, NY	8,305
7	Watervliet, NY	7,422
8	Stephentown, NY	7,209
9	Newport, RI	6,744
10	Canaan, NY	6,670
11	Providence, RI	6,371
12	Canajoharie, NY	6,155
13	Fishkill, NY	5,941
14	Frederickstown, NY	5,932
15	Southwark, PA	5,663
16	Marblehead, MA	5,661
17	Gloucester, MA	5,317
18	Amwell, NJ	5,201
19	Washington, NY	5,190
20	Cambridge, NY	5,009

Source: *A Century of Population Growth in the United States, 1790–1900*, U.S. Department of Commerce and Labor, Bureau of the Census, Table 104, p. 1909.

organizations. These organizations became part of the colonial militia when war finally broke out. One example was the Sons of Liberty in the New York Colony:

> Founded in the fall of 1765 as a secret organization, the Sons of Liberty became a public body with meetings announced in newspapers. . . . In addition to communicating with other groups in the New York colony, the Sons of Liberty also kept in touch with organizations in such other colonial towns as Boston, Baltimore, and Newport. The Sons of Liberty armed themselves and became a paramilitary group ready to resist British encroachments. The group also provided an organizing function, marshalling two thousand people in October 1765 to prevent the landing of stamps to be used for tax purposes. (Hoover, 1971:92)

One legacy of colonial dependency was the absence of autonomous government and the concomitant lack of political responsibility among the citizens of the cities. As colonies they were administered by agents of the English king. Precisely this lack of political influence may have contributed to the revolutionary fervor, because the growing wealth and population of the colonies had no democratic recourse in the administration of port cities. In any event, the absence of autonomy, according to the historian Sam Bass Warner, Jr. (1962), fostered a "laissez-faire" economic and social milieu that developed into the culture of *privatism* that so closely characterizes U.S. cities even today (see Chapters 11 and 15).

Privatism, a legacy of our colonial history, refers to the civic culture that eschews social interests in favor of the private pursuit of individual goals. From the very beginning of our urban experience, residents already believed their principal responsibility lay in the pursuit of self-interest. Unlike the citizens of ancient Athens, for example, who were obligated to pledge their indebtedness to the city that gave them birth, residents of the American colonies were not responsible to the city but only to the colonial power. Over the years, this greatly restrained the development of a civic culture that fosters community values and social responsibility. Instead, the limited vision of privatism remains in place. According to Warner:

> To describe the American tradition of privatism is not to summarize the entire American cultural tradition. . . . The tradition of privatism is, however, the most important element of our culture for understanding the development of cities. The tradition of privatism has always meant that the cities of the United States depended for their wages, employment, and general prosperity upon the aggregate successes and failures of thousands of individual enterprises, not upon community action. It has also meant that the physical forms of American cities, their lots, houses, families, and streets, have been the outcome of a real estate market of profit-seeking builders, land speculators, and large investors. (Warner, 1968:4)

A second legacy of colonial dependency was the absence of independent city economic rights. European cities of the late Middle Ages were powerful economic enterprises because they possessed independent charters of governance as well as the legal right to mint their own currency and conduct trade in their name. Colonial America granted no such privileges to its cities, and the cities did not possess chartered rights. There were no city trade monopolies, no special currency, and no city property rights beyond city borders, unlike Western Europe. Trade was organized by the large European conglomerates such as the Hudson's Bay Company. Any individual or group of entrepreneurs could break away from a U.S. city and settle in the hinterland, forming a separate town. The varied reasons for such fragmentation could be religious, political, or economic. What mattered was only the relative ability to split off and set-tle elsewhere under the protective umbrella of the colonial powers. Laissez-faire, pri-vatism, and the ease of settlement characterized city life during the colonial period. Its obverse was the absence of political autonomy characteristic of the urban community as described by Max Weber. Even after the U.S. revolution, cities failed to acquire in-dependent political rights except as far as these were granted to them by the states. Hence, the legacy of the colonial period remains very much with us today in the form of weak city government and limited city political power.

A third legacy of colonialism was the physical absence of city walls. Max We-ber's ideal city of the Middle Ages possessed defensible fortifications or walls. Else-where, forts usually defined the old city center. Thus, the words *Kremlin* in Russian and *Casbah* in Moroccan both mean "fortress." Few U.S. cities built by colonial pow-ers exhibited this trait (although some did have temporary stockades) because the home country provided for the general defense of the region by sustaining a standing army (Monkkonen, 1989). Consequently, unlike the walled cities of Europe in the late Middle Ages, U.S. places provided for immense locational freedom. Land could al-ways be developed at the fringe. To the clean-cut speculators' grid of the colonial port city was added a surrounding fringe that could always grow by accretion and land speculation. This particular pattern remains very much with us today as growth occurs constantly at the fringe of development in a pattern of sprawl.

A final legacy of the colonial city was the role played by land development as a singular source of wealth in the economy. For the residents of the United States, and unlike in Europe, land was plentiful and cheap. Very early in the history of this coun-try, it became clear to enterprising Europeans with money to invest that land develop-ment was a principal way to acquire greater wealth. But the very nature of exploiting this resource requires concomitant locational activities of a group of people and the ul-timate attraction of residential and commercial users. It does little good to stake a land claim, no matter how large, in a wilderness with no friendly residents around, without an attendant scheme for the eventual development of the land, including state protec-tion for the influx of population. Hence, early in U.S. history, land developers adopted the practice of working closely with politicians and colonial authorities to promote the development of select places. This pattern of *boosterism* involving speculators, devel-opers, politicians, and state authorities, or a *growth network* (Gottdiener, 1985) com-posed of varied individuals who are like-minded developers of land, was repeated many times in our history and remains characteristic of development today (see Chap-ter 7). The sheer quantity of undeveloped land presented by the U.S. case represents a graphic contrast to the pattern of urbanization in Western Europe (which has always reined in the interests of developers for the good of the larger society and because of real estate's scarce supply), although it may have parallels in the recent history of countries such as Australia and Brazil that also have abundant land masses.

It is often noted in elementary school lessons that George Washington, our first president, had the occupation of surveyor in his youth. In fact, he and his family were active real estate speculators. Surveying was just one aspect of this work. As one his-

BOX 3.1 CASE STUDY OF COLONIAL PHILADELPHIA

The case of colonial Philadelphia illustrates the way culture in the form of religious attitudes linked with economic interests in the development of land. In the 1680s, William Penn organized a group of fellow Quakers and obtained permission from the king of England to establish a colony in the New World that he called Philadelphia, or "the city of brotherly love." It was located at the confluence of the Delaware and Schuylkill rivers, and in 1683, 357 houses of settlement containing merchants and businessmen were involved in mercantile trade, as well as local artisans and farmers who serviced the growing population.

Plentiful resources of the region supported the colony. Houses were fashioned from lumber or built of red brick, the latter more costly and reserved for the more affluent. Game and fish were staples of diet, along with oysters from the river basin. The Native Americans of the region were friendly and showed the colonists how to raise corn and produce hominy.

In 1710 a visitor to the colony, Richard Castelman, was so impressed with its quality of life that he wrote about it to friends in England:

> A noble, large and populous city . . . here all religions are tolerated, which is one means to increase the riches of the place; here a journeyman taylor has 12 shillings a week, besides his board; and here even the meanest single women marry well, and, being above want, are above work. If the distressed people of England knew the comforts of this colony, and the easy means there is of a livelihood, they would never stay where they are, in a continual scene of poverty and misery. (Repplier, 1898:29)

Letters such as this sent back home to England served to promote the colonies and, because conditions were worse for many in England, prompted people to try their luck in the New World. By 1720 Philadelphia was the center for immigrant entry into the United States and the largest of the colonies, numbering 10,000 inhabitants. By 1775 its population was 23,700.

By the time of the revolution, Philadelphia had long since abandoned its role as a religious center of the Quakers and assumed its status as a money-making mecca. At this time, the civic ideology of privatism was already dominant. Personal achievement was measured in the successful search for wealth, while community interests were defined in terms of likeminded, money-making families (Warner, 1968:3).

torian put it, land, was "the real wealth" of the colonies. Perhaps Washington's crowning achievement was his participation in the booster effort to develop Washington, D.C., as the nation's capital. In the 1780s, the district was nothing more than an inhospitable swamp of worthless real estate. All that was to change through the efforts of newly achieved political power and economic investment in land. According to accounts of the time, "In 1793 George Washington led a procession with two brass bands and Masons in full costume across the Tiber to a barbecue and land auction at which he purchased the first lots of the new capital's undeveloped swampland. . . . Self-promotion, boosterism, and constant attention to the economic main chance soon came to characterize the young nation's cities" (Monkkonen, 1989:63). Box 3.1 about colonial Philadelphia illustrates the experience of life in colonial cities.

The Era of Industrial Expansion: 1812 to 1920

The settlement of the vast U.S. territory following the Revolutionary War constituted a magnificent drama involving individuals representing the very legends of our country itself. As Gary Nash (1974) has observed, this drama was colored in red, white, and black, because it involved a three-way clash among white former colonists, Native Americans, and black slaves. Frontiersmen such as Davy Crockett shouldered hunting muskets and fought the Indian Wars. Native Americans such as the Apache chief Geronimo and his people were driven from their lands, killed in vast numbers, or re-settled to make way for the white people's development of the interior.

Industrialists such as J. P. Morgan and Jacob Astor accumulated vast sums of money in trade, banking, and real estate, only to lose power and wealth to other up-starts, such as Jay Gould, with equally ambitious schemes. Politicians such as Presi-dent Grover Cleveland mingled with the active boosters of growth during a time when corruption was a way of life in government. In the middle of it all, the fate of the na-tion was decided in a civil war. Great spokespeople such as Frederick Douglass articu-lated the pain of suppression under which black people were living as slaves. Eventu-ally slavery was defeated, but so too was the rural way of southern life in a society that shifted from plantation agriculture to industrialized farming and manufacture. Tech-nology, industrialization, city government, and land development took over the stage of urban growth.

It is helpful to think of American capitalism as acting like a large land develop-ment agency in addition to its role as an industrial enterprise. During the period of for-mative growth, entrepreneurs singled out choice locations in the advancing path of ex-pansion and built cities. According to the historian Richard C. Wade (1959), city construction took place in many cases *before* population influx; that is, urbanization in the United States was often land speculation that proceeded with the aid of local gov-ernments. In a sense, the establishment of a town as a political entity harnessed land to the control of growth interests. As a consequence of political reforms during the presi-dency of Andrew Jackson, it was comparatively easy for groups of capitalist land de-velopers to declare their projects incorporated cities. Hence, with the aid of home rule, the expansion westward during the century between 1812 and 1920, when the majority of the U.S. population became city residents, was an urban expansion and simultane-ously an explosion in the number of governments at the local level. By founding towns, developers also used local governments to provide a civic or community struc-ture for people who came there to live.

These real estate projects that opened the American frontier did not proceed in isolation. Entrepreneurs were also merchants or industrialists. Money was invested in commercial enterprises as well as in land. In fact, capital often flowed back and forth

Many of the West's present-day cities were founded by the Southern Pacific–Central Pacific railroad builders. The photo shows two woodburner locomotives in front of El Capitan Hotel, one of the first buildings erected in Merced, California.

between investments in industry and investments in land. This relation will be explained more fully in Chapter 7. Thus, Cyrus McCormick, the inventor of the reaper, made millions in the 1800s from his factory, but his real wealth came from investment of those profits in real estate (Longstreet, 1973).

In addition, the technology of transport became an explicit means through which investors of capital centered in cities competed with one another to build new cities on the frontier. Thus, railroad entrepreneurs such as Leland Stanford were also city builders. Let us consider the era of urban expansion according to these interrelated links among forms of capital, government policies and politicians, and forms of technology.

Land Development and Technology. Prior to the 1820s, the U.S. urban population remained relatively stable at around 10 percent of the total. After that time, a sudden burst of urbanization surfaced that did not abate until the 1930s. By the 1920 census, over half of all Americans were already living in cities. Hence, in the 100 years from 1820, the United States had been transformed into an urbanized nation.

After the War of 1812, hinterland development was consolidated in the Ohio Valley and the Midwest. At this stage, economic interests located within the large East

Coast cities turned an about-face by ignoring the mercantilist needs of trade with Europe, and actively pursued the development of the interior. In all respects, early westward expansion was highly dependent both on the development of transportation technology and on the protection of white settlers by government from attacks by Native American residents. Land was realized as a capital investment only after transportation and communication infrastructure could be put in place. Roads had to be built. Tracks had to be laid. Telegraph lines were installed. In addition, the safety of work crews for all these efforts had to be ensured. Land was being taken from Native Americans, an effort that required organized government activity and military intervention.

Hinterland development did not follow automatically after the application of transportation technology to growth. Local capital had to be organized to bring about development. Often entrepreneurs competed with one another over investments in the interior of the country because at the time, the unity of capital under corporate interests that cut across space and united efforts in different cities had not yet fully matured. Consequently, westward expansion was a characteristic of competitive capital and was often marked by the schemes of single individuals who sought to build up business and build a city at the same time.

For example, the earliest urban rivalry involved local capitalists situated in the important East Coast port cities. Their future fortunes depended on the continuing success of their respective trade routes to the interior, because the latter was the source of goods for export and raw materials needed by local manufacturers.

Just after the War of 1812, the shortest route to the West lay across either Pennsylvania or Maryland. There were two roads—the "national road" out of Baltimore and the "Pittsburgh Pike" out of Philadelphia—but these links were inadequate for handling the heavy agricultural products of the interior (Rubin, 1970:128). Instead, produce was shipped south on the Mississippi River to New Orleans, making that city the most important export center.

New York entrepreneurs saw their city facing decline as the frontier expanded west. In 1817, they began construction of a canal that linked the Hudson River at Albany 364 miles westward to Buffalo on Lake Erie. In a bold stroke, they hoped to create the most efficient link to the hinterland, with Buffalo becoming an inland port for the Great Lakes region of the Midwest. The canal was completed in 1825 and was so successful that it inspired a craze of canal building across the United States. From its inception, New York City competed effectively with New Orleans as an export point for agricultural produce.

As a result of the successful Erie Canal venture, Philadelphia and Baltimore financial interests faced decline, if not extinction. As the historian J. Rubin (1970:131) notes, they responded with their own schemes, aided greatly by government laws and subsidies. Initially Philadelphia interests demanded that the state proceed with a canal to Ohio. However, construction failed in the Allegheny Mountains, and a rail segment was required. This occurred several times, and Philadelphia ended up with a mixed canal and rail portage system that required several transshipments. The route was hopelessly incapable of competing with New York's Erie Canal.

Baltimore interests viewed Philadelphia's problems with trepidation. They saw the difficulty of crossing the Appalachian Mountains via canal. By the 1830s, the steam locomotive had just been perfected in England and, in a venture as bold as the New York effort, they opted for the construction of a railroad line that would connect

Baltimore with the Ohio Valley over the mountains. The line was eventually called the Baltimore and Ohio Railroad, and it was remarkably successful. As a consequence of these improvements, New York and Baltimore prospered while Boston and Philadelphia declined. In addition, the links to the interior in the 1830s helped found the midwestern Great Lakes cities of Chicago, Detroit, and Cleveland, which also prospered because of successful rail and canal traffic to East Coast ports.

In the period between 1830 and 1920, the most significant technological innovation was the joint development of the steel rail and steam locomotive that perfected the long haul for commerce, resources, and people. Of the 153 major U.S. cities existing today, 75 percent had been established after 1840 when the railroad matured as an established infrastructure, and only 9 percent of these same major cities were built after 1910 (Monkkonen, 1989:75). It would be simple to suggest that transportation technology alone caused the explosion of urbanization. This would be misleading, however. Technology became the means of growth, but inception and execution were the result both of the quest for wealth among entrepreneurs and of the desires of politicians in government at all levels—local, state, and federal—that joined these ventures, aiding them with political resources. It is precisely this conjuncture of investors, political power mongers, and the dream of wealth that characterizes the second stage of urbanization in the United States. According to the historians Glaab and Brown, for example,

> Earlier rivalries had been limited by nature—by the location of rivers and lakes. But railroads were not bound by topography, by the paths of river commerce, or by natural trade patterns. Railroads could be built anywhere, creating cities where they chose. Since the building of railroads was dependent to a considerable extent on subsidies from local communities, railroad leaders were willing to bargain with competing towns to obtain the best possible deal in stock subscriptions, bond issues, and right-of-ways. . . . The "boosterism" associated with the midwest and areas further west is largely a legacy of the late nineteenth century era of urban rivalry. (Glaab and Brown, 1967:112)

As we will see as well in our discussion of the last two stages of urban growth, this pattern of capital investment, coupled with government subsidies and competition among separate places, is repeated countless times and characterizes urban growth and change in the United States and possibly elsewhere. As the sociospatial approach suggests, development was a consequence of a combination of economic, political, and cultural factors—the frontier myth and the American Dream of wealth combined with cooperative government officials and venture capitalists to urbanize the nation.

What exactly were the proportions involved in the lure of wealth that accompanied town building? Consider the Illinois Central Railroad. Its promoters were also prolific city builders. In 1850, 10 towns existed in the vicinity of the railroad's route. After expansion 10 years later there were 47, and by 1870 there were 81. When the Illinois Central entrepreneurs could not make subsidy agreements with the politicians of existing towns for their right of way, they just built their own towns nearby. Champaign, Illinois, for example, was constructed directly by the railroad adjacent to the existing town of Urbana.

Another example shows us the size of the profit realized from real estate alone. Kankakee, Illinois, was built by this same railroad in 1855 at a cost of $10,000, and after just one year the owners had already realized $50,000 in lot sales, or a profit of 500 percent, with more city land remaining. As expansion moved west, a similar pattern recurred involving a host of other promoters and their railroads. In San Francisco, which had developed as the premier city of the West Coast during this period, town lots that could be bought for $1,500 in 1850 were worth from $8,000 to $27,000 just three years later in 1853 (Glaab and Brown, 1967:113, 121).

Manufacturing. So far we have fostered the impression that city building involved exclusively land development schemes combining capital, government, and transport technology. During the period between 1812 and 1920, however, the United States became a world leader in manufacturing. Forces of industrialization unleashed with such effect in England during this time had similar results here. During the period between 1850 and 1900, for example, U.S. production of textiles multiplied 7 times, iron and steel increased 10 times, the processing of agricultural products expanded 14 times, and the production of agricultural implements increased 25 times (Hoover, 1971:180).

The very heart of industrialization was the factory, which was the engine that drove the industrial stage of capitalism. But workers and capitalists were not simply disembodied abstractions. They were people who required places to live, raise families, and spend whatever leisure time they had. Industrialization, therefore, produced the factory town or community that contained workers' families and houses, machinery, and energy sources, all within close proximity.

The first American manufacturing city was Lowell, Massachusetts, which was located on the Merrimack River at a site where the water dropped 90 feet and provided the original power source for its factories. Investors chose this place for a complex of cotton mills and struck on the idea of importing a labor force of young women from the neighboring cities, especially Boston, because they would be easy to control as a source of nonunion labor power. The geographer James Vance gives this account of the city:

> In 1845, thirty-three of the large mill buildings ranged along the canals and banks of the Merrimack, making Lowell the largest cotton town in America and one of its few great industrial cities, with a population of thirty thousand. A full third of the population was engaged as operatives in the mills or their workshops, though female employment remained disproportionate with 6,320 females and 2,915 males. (Vance, 1990:347)

Early industrialization in the United States is associated with the names of entrepreneurs who perfected specific products: Singer sewing machines, Yale locks, Armour hams, McCormick reapers, and Remington typewriters are but some of these innovations. Later on, in most cases, the descendants of the originators carried on the family name and its business. In the 1860s, the leading industries reflected early development of manufacturing and the persisting importance of the United States as a supplier of natural resources. Cotton goods, lumber, boots and shoes, and flour dominated. By 1910, according to Geruson and McGrath (1977:68), the major industries reflected the maturation of manufacturing and consisted of machinery, iron and steel, lumber, clothing, and railroad cars, among other products.

Population Churning and Immigration. We have covered several features of the U.S. case so far. One of the most distinctive is the phenomenon of population turnover, or churning, which for a time was quite exaggerated here compared to other countries. From the mid-1800s to 1900s, U.S. cities functioned as giant magnets that attracted

Jacob Riis's phototgraphs of tenement housing in New York City were part of a broader social reform movement to improve living conditions in the industrial cities at the turn of the century.

immigrants from all over the world. Prior to the 1800s, most people came from the British Isles or as slaves captured from Africa. After 1830, many more arrived from Germany, Scandinavia, Central and Eastern Europe, and China. Between 1800 and 1925, over 40 million immigrants entered the United States. Seventeen million arrived during the period between 1846 and 1900 alone (Vance, 1990:359).

These figures, however, do not capture the way cities functioned as entry points for people. In effect, cities such as New York, Chicago, Philadelphia, and Boston processed vast numbers of immigrants from Europe and elsewhere, orienting them to life in America before many made their way into the hinterland. At this time the internal demographic differentiation of cities took on the characteristics commonly associated with their residential patterns, namely, mosaics of little worlds comprising ethnic enclaves of immigrants. The robustness of cultural life found there inspired succeeding generations of urban sociologists in their studies.

The Lower East Side of New York City at the turn of the century.

During the period of urban expansion, population churned throughout the large cities. By one conservative estimate, half of the residents moved each decade only to be replaced by still more immigrants (Monkkonen, 1989). A study of Boston in the year 1890, for example, revealed that with a total population of approximately 450,000 people, at least 600,000 had moved in a decade before, while somewhat more than 500,000 had moved out. In short, the population size of cities during the formative period of expansion is a static figure that disguises the massive movement of people into and out of those cities.

In a subsequent chapter, we will take a closer look at the importance of immigration to American cities. One way to appreciate population churning is to consider the economic and political opportunities created by the phenomenon. Each new immigrant had to be processed by federal, state, and local officials, which meant more government jobs. Schoolteachers were in constant demand, as were settlement house workers, religious functionaries, and the many specialized businesses that catered to the needs of arrivals from foreign lands. City economies thrived not only because of the influx of population but also because it turned over so frequently, making the same services necessary to new people with similar needs as previous arrivals. Above all, the rapid increase in population provided U.S. industry not only with much needed labor power but also with consumers who could use the products being churned out by the factories. Export trade during this period of U.S. history was not as important as the growing domestic market of consumers.

Population influx had a dramatic effect on the internal configuration of cities. Owners of buildings soon discovered that the voracious demand for housing could be met by converting structures to rental units. Later, new buildings called *tenements* were constructed specifically for rental use. These buildings were designed to squeeze as many families together as possible. The increased density made public health crises common. It also increased the risk of fire. On October 18, 1871, for example, the city of Chicago was almost destroyed by a single fire. Other fires at the turn of the century devastated cities such as Boston and San Francisco.

Yet the escalating demand for housing also afforded handsome profits to owners of tenements. According to one estimate, annual returns on rentals could be as high as 40 percent and by 1890 as much as 77 percent of all city dwellers were renters (Glaab and Brown, 1967:160).

The Role of Technology: Building Innovations and Urban Transport. During the 1800s, the spatial organization of the city changed as new forms of building introduced a larger scale to the physical environment, aided greatly by several innovations in construction. The balloon-frame house replaced heavy timber construction in the 1830s and made it possible for building to proceed more rapidly and with greater quantity than in the past. In 1848, James Bogardus introduced the use of cast iron columns and weight-bearing walls supporting the structure of nonresidential buildings, which eliminated the need for heavy masonry construction and opened the internal spaces of buildings so that factories and warehouses could maximize their unimpeded use of floor space. Elisha Otis invented the elevator, and by 1880 its widespread use enabled taller buildings to work more efficiently. Finally, in 1884 William L. Jenny erected the first skyscraper, the 10-story Home Insurance Building in Chicago, which was also the "first building with a fully iron structure carrying the weight of the edifice" (Vance, 1990:471). The city of skyscrapers was not far away after that.

Tall building construction, unimpeded floor space allowing for the efficient placement of machinery, and the remarkable innovation of the elevator transformed the city into an arena of concentrated industry during the last half of the nineteenth century. Mobility of the workforce became a paramount concern at this time. The need for mass transport was met by a series of innovations, starting with the horse-drawn omnibus that carried 12 to 20 passengers (Glaab and Brown, 1967:147). By the 1850s, these were replaced by the horse-drawn railway car, which not only facilitated the movement of people into and out of the "downtown" districts but also provided the means by which the middle class could suburbanize (Warner, 1962). In the 1870s, the horse was finally replaced by the steam-powered locomotive. By 1881 the elevated lines, or "Els," of New York City were carrying 175,000 passengers a day!

Finally, surpassing all these advances, a major breakthrough occurred in the 1870s when Nikola Tesla's discoveries on alternating current were applied to the production of electrical power. The dynamo replaced the battery, and electric trains and trolleys were perfected. Electrification made possible the extensive, nonpolluting trolley system and also the underground subway train. This change was remarkable. As Glaab and Brown observe, "In 1890, 69.7 percent of the total trackage in cities was operated by horses; by 1902 this figure had declined to 1.1 percent, while electric power was used on 97 percent of the mileage" (1967:148).

The result of all these transformations was the diurnal rhythm of city life—masses of workers converging on business districts in the morning, only to disperse at day's end with the same great spurt aided by efficient and safe mass transit. By the 1920s, the United States had successfully integrated millions of immigrants from over 100 countries into an industrial labor force. Its large cities were all built and humming with activity. Industrialization and urbanization had not only settled the frontier but led the country itself to a place among the world's powers. Box 3.2 illustrates the experience of the city of Chicago during this time.

BOX 3.2 A CASE STUDY: CHICAGO IN THE NINETEENTH CENTURY

Chicago was founded in 1779 by a black man, Jean B. P. de Saible, the son of a slave woman and a French aristocrat. The two rivers, the Chicago and the Calumet, intersecting with Lake Michigan gave the area possibilities. In the 1800s, with the mass migrations west and the opening of the Erie Canal, Chicago became a boomtown. It received a city charter in 1837. At this time in our nation's history, the sheer amount of money that was available from East Coast investors and the massive numbers of immigrants looking for work all came together in the new towns and propelled them into greatness with unparalleled energy. One account of the 1850s captures the entire era that we have just examined:

> Hotels and boarding houses were always full, and full meant three in a bed sometimes, with the floor covered besides. . . . All about the outskirts of the settlement was a cordon of prairie schooners, with tethered horses between, interspersed with camp fires at which the busy housewives were ever preparing meals. A fast-writing lawyer could make five hundred dollars a day writing land titles. Everyday millions of dollars in land values changed hands. Farm lots, city frontage sold added up to millions of dollars. Everyone who had wooden stakes, a hammer, and greedy ways could mark out lots, set up in business, make himself plats of towns and cities that existed only in the spinning minds of the promoters. (Longstreet, 1973:26)

Tracts bought in 1833 for $5,500 sold three years later for $100,000. "Gordon D. Hubbard, Indian trader, bought two lots on La Salle Street for $66.66, sold them for $80,000" (Longstreet, 1973:24).

After the land boom, the commercial and industrial capitalists arrived. Marshall Field, a young, enterprising merchant, came to Chicago from New York and opened a large general store in 1872. Later, using the French innovation of the department store, he established Marshall Field's department store, which set the commercial trends for the city. Cyrus McCormick, another entrepreneur from the East, settled in Chicago and perfected his reaper there. In 1847 he opened his first factory, and by 1858 he was earning a million dollars a year selling his famous reapers.

By the 1860s, Chicago had emerged as a railroad hub with nine different lines that ran into the city. The Civil War made its people wealthy. Two men in particular, Philip D. Armour and Gustavas F. Swift, made their fortunes selling meat to the Union Army. Both had come west from New England. They helped build the Union Stockyards, a 345-acre tract on the South Side that became the great slaughterhouse of the nation. Pigs, sheep, and steers were killed and processed there by the hundreds of millions. Armour and Swift became rich, but at the turn of the century, Upton Sinclair, in his book *The Jungle*, exposed the horrors of the meat-packing industry and its deplorable working conditions, which the owners had tolerated for decades.

The historian Edward Wagenknecht (1964:105) considers the reputation of all these men secondary to "the greatest Chicagoan of all," Jane Addams. She possessed a "genius for goodness" and, although not the originator of the settlement house movement, was its driving force at the turn of the century. Hull House, which opened its doors in the fall of 1889, became a center of social intervention in the lives of the impoverished immigrant workers in the town:

> Jane Addams saw the worst sights of her generation; she was familiar with every phase of the sacrifice of human values that is exacted when a great city places a purely commercial valuation upon the impulses of youth. . . . Yet she insisted uncompromisingly on "the very energy of existence, the craving for enjoyment, the pushing of vital forces, the very right of every citizen to be what he is without pretense or assumption of virtue." (Wagenknecht, 1964:109)

Jane Addams was one of the pioneers of the social work movement in this country, which tried to temper the harshness of unfettered capitalism by aspiring to a better life for urban dwellers through proper education, health care, family values, and aesthetic pursuits.

Chicago was not without its spectacular failures as well. On October 8, 1871, a fire was started on the West Side in the O'Leary barn—by some children playing with matches, *not* by the famous cow. It spread quickly through the densely packed tenements, jumping the Chicago River to the South Side. The city went up in flames, and two days passed before the fire was put out. About 15,000 acres of prime urban property were destroyed and, tragically, several hundred lives. Nearly 14,000 buildings were burned to the ground. It took years for the city to recover. In fact, in the years to follow, the first of many recessions afflicted the United States in general and Chicago in particular. Capital dried up and businesses went under. Unemployment rose in the 1870s and with it the popularity of communist and socialist ideas. A young labor leader named Albert Parsons led political demonstrations asking why relief money raised for victims of the Chicago fire was being used to rebuild downtown businesses rather than new homes. After Parsons led a similar protest against the new Chicago Board of Trade building, Marshall Field and other Chicago business leaders vowed they would get even with Parsons.

By the 1880s, an economic depression swept the United States. The businesspeople of Chicago hired a private detective, Allan Pinkerton, and his gang to break up labor meetings, which were being held with greater frequency. Chicago's laborers had become organized, as had workers in other U.S. cities, and they formed the Workingman's Party of the United States. On May 8, 1886, they called for a mass rally to protest the killing of four workers outside the McCormick Reaper plant two days earlier. It was to be held at the Haymarket on Randolph Street. "Two hundred cops waited at the Desplaines Police Station a block from the meeting. They were all issued new revolvers, said a report, and hickory skull-cracking clubs 'extra long.' Scores of detectives dressed as workers, as always, moved out to mingle with the crowd" (Longstreet, 1973:251). Mayor Altgeld had attended the meeting, and gave orders to the police not to interfere with the peaceful assembly. But when the speeches ended and the mayor left, the police moved in to break up the audience, and someone threw a bomb into the police lines. The police fired on the crowd, and in the resulting chaos at least 7 people were killed and some 60 injured. To this day, no one knows who

(continued)

threw the bomb. But in the following days, eight people were arrested and charged with conspiracy in the bombing, although only two had been present at the Haymarket on that fateful day. Albert Parsons had been in Milwaukee giving a speech at another labor meeting but was arrested anyway, along with August Spies, the editor of the German-language workers' newspaper *Arbeitor Zeitung*. Despite international protest over the proceedings, Parsons, Spies, and two others were hung. Marshall Field had gotten his revenge, and the labor movement in Chicago was set back for decades.

By the 1890s Chicago had recovered. It aspired to be a great city again. The business and political leaders decided to organize an exposition to commemorate Columbus's discovery of the New World. It was meant to be a world's fair that would glorify the virtues of civic planning in Chicago. The World's Columbian Exposition opened on May 1, 1893, on 6,000 acres. Classic white buildings of plaster in Greek, Roman, and Gothic revival dominated. But the innovative transportation building designed by Louis Sullivan captured the scene and ushered in a new era of urban architecture using brick construction, intersecting arches, and decorated facades. More than 21 million people passed through the fair, including President Grover Cleveland. Little Egypt, a belly dancer, was the big hit. Chicago captured the focus of the nation.

Columbian Exposition, Chicago, 1893.

CHAPTER

4

THE METROPOLITAN PERIOD IN THE UNITED STATES: 1920 TO 1960

During the period of urban expansion, economic interests located within cities competed with one another and land development in the West made people wealthy. This stage passed as smaller businesses began to be gobbled up by larger interests. The phase of competitive capitalism slowly gave way to a new era, that of monopoly capitalism. In turn, cities grew progressively larger.

City building and population churning slowed down considerably in the United States in the 1900s following a series of economic depressions. This unsettling downturn culminated in the Great Depression of the late 1920s, which lasted to the early 1930s. Urban activity picked up again as government reforms aided economic recovery and the United States mobilized for another world war in the 1940s. During the metropolitan period, cities not only grew larger but also spread out beyond the political boundaries of their local governments. New areas of development became, in turn, new cities; in many cases, urbanization simply engulfed the smaller towns adjacent to the large cities through a regionwide process of suburbanization.

In the metropolitan period, it was becoming necessary to think about the urban phenomenon less in terms of the large city and more in terms of a region consisting of a mix of residential, work, recreational, and shopping places. The U.S. Department of the Census introduced the term *Standard Metropolitan Statistical Area* (SMSA—see Chapter 1) to account for the regional nature of development. Large central cities such as New York and Detroit also assumed vast economic importance far beyond their borders because of the businesses that were centered there, in this case finance and cars, respectively. This conjunction of spatial reach and economic might gave the city

Park Avenue, New York City—the grand vision of metropolitan life.

a new name: the "metropolis," or "mother city." Visions of the immense city outgrowing its boundaries began to appear in many countries. The German film *Metropolis* is one such example. Cities such as Tokyo, London, Paris, Berlin, Rome, Rio de Janeiro, and Calcutta all reached an unprecedented scale of size and population.

The metropolitan pattern of increasing size and geographical territory became characteristic of many cities in the United States. Following the Great Depression, urban scientists became interested in the phenomenon of the metropolitan region, and many studies were carried out to discover its social, political, spatial, and economic characteristics (McKenzie, 1933; Schnore, 1957; Bollens and Schmandt, 1965). Research revealed that two processes contributed most to regional growth: greater differentiation of the system of cities, expressed as changes in spatial, functional, and demographic differentiation, and the process of suburbanization.

Spatial, Functional, and Demographic Differentiation of the City

According to the sociospatial perspective, metropolitan development and change do not occur because of technological factors alone but are also dependent on political and cultural relations. Economic activities, for example, require a workforce and certain community services, such as adequate schooling and health care, for businesses and their labor pools to survive over time. When there is a proper mesh between the human tissue of family and community life and associated economic activities requiring particular skill levels, both businesses and neighborhoods prosper. In short, the relations among the economy, political structure, and culture are reciprocal.

Accommodations between the social fabric of community life and the needs of business produced the early factory towns, such as Burlington (Vermont) and Birmingham (Alabama), during the early period of family capitalism. One characteristic of this phase was that sources of employment and the labor pool were close together and both were tied to the general fate of the city itself. As the structure of capitalism changed in the 1930s, this equilibrium was shattered, and upheavals in the community paralleled those in business. Neighborhood relations changed when people were thrown out of work after plants closed or businesses altered their skill needs. New demands were placed on school systems, city budgets, and families to aid in the adjustment. In many cases, the success or failure of new ways of doing business depended on how well the community, local government, and families adapted to change. Thus, while economic alterations affect the social fabric, the latter in turn can also affect the well-being of the local economy.

Consequently, each time new economic priorities are put in place, they affect the composition of territory and alter community life. The social organization of a particular place—the way it is organized according to locational choices of business, the scale of community, the flows of commuters, definitions of city service districts, the pace and structure of family life, and so on—is affected by the reciprocal relation between the local economy and the social fabric. In this chapter, we will discuss the changes brought about by the depression restructuring of the 1930s. They involve a process of *horizontal integration* of business activity coupled with metropolitan regional expansion. In the next chapter, we will consider equally important changes that have occurred since 1960.

Changes in Spatial Differentiation

Following the Great Depression, the economic system of the United States changed from a comparatively competitive form of industrial capitalism with a relatively large number of firms in each industry to a concentrated form called "monopoly capitalism" (Baran and Sweezy, 1966) where ownership was consolidated in a few hands. One distinguishing characteristic of the new form was the growth of monopolistic (one firm) or oligopolistic (a select few firms) control of major industries. For example, automobile production prior to the 1930s involved a host of firms such as Studebaker, Hudson, Tucker, and De Soto, along with Ford, Pontiac, and Chrysler. These companies were scattered across much of the United States, and their fates were often intertwined with specific cities and communities. After the 1930s, production of automobiles was essentially in the hands of the Big Four—General Motors, Ford, Chrysler, and American Motors (today it's down to the first three). While these companies also maintained branch plants across the country, their operations were national in scope and their headquarters were no longer tied to the places where they had their major factories. The Detroit area in particular became the headquarters for much of the auto industry, and decisions made there affected towns across the country. This change in the horizontal integration of large businesses to a more dispersed pattern, coupled with greater concentration of ownership, was also repeated in other industries, including steel, the production of consumer durables (such as electrical appliances), and even the consolidation of retailing outlets by giant department stores following branch marketing schemes (such as Sears, Roebuck and Montgomery Ward).

The changes in the scale of economic organization had spatial effects, especially on local community life, and several classic sociological studies documented them (Vidich and Bensman, 1960; Lynd and Lynd, 1937). Concentration of wealth and ownership led to greater horizontal integration of business activities and changes in the spatial relations among community, work, and region. That is, prior to the Depression, most companies had all their functions located together and generally in the same city. These firms were replaced by companies with divisions in any number of locations, which used dispersal in space to advantage to cut costs, especially labor costs. For example, a large company that was part of an oligopoly in one industry might have its headquarters in a center such as New York, where it would be close to the headquarters of the other oligopolists in the same industry. It would also be close to banking and related services necessary to the command and control function of business administration. Its specialized needs would stimulate the local community to supply laborers with adequate training for the jobs that were created. This same firm might have a branch plant for production located in Newark, a central distribution facility in Philadelphia, and so on, each with its own impact on the local community and labor force. Such a pattern of related functional differentiation and spatial or horizontal integration was replicated in many industries.

Ford Motor plant in Detroit, Michigan. Note the full barges and active factories (1950s).

Changes in Functional Differentiation

As a consequence, after 1930, a new, functionally differentiated system of urban places had emerged in the United States; that is, different cities were the homes of different aspects of industry or commerce. Instead of competing with one another, as was the case during the previous period of competitive capitalism discussed in Chapter 3, local capital was now organized and integrated by a national system of concentrated wealth. This pattern was not a product of the city itself, but was attributable to the powers of institutions and social actors whose activities were deployed *within* the cities that were linked to the national corporations producing most of the country's wealth. Thus, horizontal integration and functional differentiation were two related outcomes in the restructuring of social organization after the 1930s. We call this interlinked complex of functionally differentiated activities located within urban places a *system of cities* (McKenzie, 1933; Berry, 1972; Bourne and Simmons, 1978). In studying this system, it is always important to keep in mind that functional differentiation is a feature of the particular complex of economic activities that are located within a city rather than a characteristic of the city itself. Furthermore, the diverse activities across the nation are horizontally integrated by large corporations that possess "command and control" headquarters.

Table 4.1 illustrates the pattern of functional specialization for 11 of the largest U.S. cities in 1990. We can see that in 1990, virtually all cities had substantial sectors

TABLE 4.1
Functional Differentiation of 11 Major U.S. Cities, 1990*
Percentage Employment in Major Industries by Sector†

City	Manufacturing	Trade	Service	Other
Baltimore, MD	12.3	17.6	58.0	12.1
Boston, MA	9.9	16.6	64.6	8.9
Jacksonville, FL	9.4	22.7	52.4	15.5
Los Angeles, CA	18.4	20.1	50.3	11.1
New Orleans, LA	6.8	20.8	59.8	12.5
New York City, NY	11.4	17.2	60.3	11.0
San Diego, CA	13.9	21.7	53.9	10.6
San Francisco, CA	9.2	20.9	58.3	10.7
San Jose, CA	31.3	19.3	38.6	10.8
Seattle, WA	13.3	20.3	55.9	10.5
Washington, DC	4.3	11.9	74.8	9.0

*Other major cities did not have complete data for 1990.
†Functional categories consist of the following census categories:
1. Manufacturing, nondurable goods; Manufacturing, durable goods.
2. Wholesale trade; Retail trade.
3. Communications and public utilities; Finance, insurance, and real estate; Business and repair services; Personal services; Entertainment and recreation services; Health services; Educational services; Other professional and related services; Public administration.
4. Agriculture, forestry, and fisheries; Mining; Construction; Transportation.
Source: Census of Population and Housing 1990, U.S. Department of Commerce, Bureau of the Census, Summary Tape, File 3A (CD-ROM).

of service employment. Not surprisingly, Washington, D.C., is functionally specialized in this type of activity. In contrast, San Jose, at the heart of the high-tech industry
located in Silicon Valley, retains a functional specialization in manufacturing. Some
cities, such as Los Angeles, Baltimore, and Seattle, also have significant manufacturing sectors despite a large service sector. Table 4.1, which does not contain a comprehensive list of all large cities, does indicate considerable variation in the percentage of
employment among the functional sectors of manufacturing, trade, and service. A
more detailed study of these differences would require exploring the kinds of businesses that comprise each sector within each city. Thus, while Boston seems functionally specialized in services, with 64.6 percent of its employment in that sector, we
might also wish to know what *kinds* of services are provided and their respective
shares of the total. In addition, we might also ask just how many headquarters are located in that city in order to place Boston within the hierarchy of command and control centers. In short, variation in the breakdown of employment among the sectors of
the economy within cities provides a great deal of information on how local, national,
and global business activities concentrate in particular places.

By the 1960s the U.S. urban system consisted of a select group of large cities
with populations ranging from several hundred thousand to over 7 million (see
Table 5.1 on page 82). This pattern represents *balanced urbanization* that is characteristic of the older industrialized countries such as England (see Chapter 12 for a
contrast with less developed countries). Several studies have documented the structure of the urban system in the United States (Pred, 1973; Chase-Dunn, 1985). It is
arranged across two different dimensions. On the one hand, cities seem to be distinguished by concentration of business in either manufacturing or services, with the
larger cities less specialized. On the other hand, there is specialization in finances or
commerce. Furthermore, from 1950 to 1970, the functional specialization of the
cities in the U.S. system remained relatively stable (South and Poston, 1982). Cities
such as New York, San Francisco, Chicago, and Atlanta, for example, were diverse
areas, while cities such as Baltimore, Detroit, and Los Angeles were more concentrated in manufacturing, and Portland, Kansas City, and Minneapolis specialized in
financial activities and commerce. These specializations and rankings are somewhat
different today, as we will see in the next chapter. However, until at least the 1970s
they characterized an urban system that reflected the increasing functional integration of the emergent national economy. Until the 1970s they also showed that important business activity remained concentrated within central cities. That is no
longer as true today.

The immense economic changes bringing about the concentration of capital in
large cities were only one aspect of the metropolitan era. As central cities prospered,
they attracted talented people from all over the nation. Metropolises became centers of
culture and political power as well. They were the sites of important museums, universities, and symphony orchestras. They housed art movements and literary revivals.
With their immense populations, they also wielded great political power. In many
cases, such as Chicago and New York City, carrying the state in a presidential election

meant, in effect, carrying the city. Much of this confluence of economic, political, and cultural centrality was to change rapidly beginning with the 1960s (see next chapter). But perhaps the best example of the world-class metropolis during the period prior to this is New York City (see Box. 4.1).

Changes in Demographic Differentiation

Between 1930 and 1960, the complexion of metropolitan demographics also changed. As the metropolitan, corporate economy kicked in following the Depression and large cities fought for their functional niche in the world, corporations hired a growing number of white-collar professionals. Many more trained workers found employment in the sophisticated service industries that aided the activities of business headquarters. A growing number of these new urbanites were highly educated and well paid relative to the times. In the 1950s and 1960s, many of these corporate employees preferred to live in the city. A study by Leo F. Schnore (1963) in 1960 revealed that metropolitan regions with comparatively newer core cities (those reaching a population of 50,000 after 1920) had higher family incomes, levels of education, and percentages of white-collar employees in the central city than in the suburban ring. This breakdown is no longer the rule today, as we will see in Chapter 5 when we consider the contemporary changes.

In other respects, central cities began to assume the dimensions of ethnic and racial concentration that we find at present; that is, beginning with the 1950s, demographic differentiation of the metropolitan population began to take on the sharp racial distinctions that are characteristic today. Writing in the 1960s, Bollens and Schmandt remark:

> Within the metropolitan area itself, the ethnic colonies are concentrated largely in the central city. . . . Chicago, an urban complex of many nationality groups, furnishes a typical example. The latest census shows that of the approximately 600,000 foreign born living in the SMSA, 73 percent reside in the central city. (1965:96)

Bollens and Schmandt add about African Americans at the time that

> The geographical segregation or distribution of ethnic settlements is even more pronounced when the non-white migrants, predominantly Negroes, are considered. . . . As the non-whites have migrated to urban places, they have tended to gravitate into the central cities of metropolitan areas. By 1960 over one-half the non-white population lived in such communities, a gain of 63 percent over 1950. Among the whites, on the other hand, there has been a continual shift from the central cities to suburbs with the result that in 1960, 52 percent of the whites in the 212 SMSA's lived outside the central cities compared to 22 percent of the non-white. (1965:97)

The migration of blacks from the South involved a mass exodus. Millions left in the 1950s and 1960s. By the time of the 1960 census, only half the black population still resided in the South. Several factors were responsible, including the extensive use of the mechanical cotton picker by the 1940s and the phasing out of the sharecropper

BOX 4.1 NEW YORK CITY IN THE METROPOLITAN PERIOD

By the time of the Civil War, New York City was already the country's most populous city and its banking capital. By the 1920s, New York had replaced London as the financial center of the globe. Its great skyscrapers, such as the Empire State and Chrysler buildings; its museums and cultural institutions, including Tin Pan Alley (28th Street) and Broadway theaters; and its universities made New York the cultural and intellectual center of the United States as well. At this time, the New York Yankees were the best team in baseball and arguably the best team ever. Their home run hitter, Babe Ruth, was so popular that the owner, "beer baron" Jacob Rupert, decided to build a large stadium to showcase the team (Allen, 1990). Yankee Stadium, or "the house that Ruth built," with over a 60,000 seating capacity, was constructed in the Bronx and instantly sold out for many of its games.

By 1930 New York already had over 7 million people, a figure that is slightly less than the population today. The Depression hit the city especially hard. Although many people suffered and manufacturing began its unimpeded decline, the city enjoyed a renaissance under the mayorship of Fiorello La Guardia. An outstanding progressive leader, La Guardia used government to get things done. Parks were cleaned up and renovated, new highways were constructed, the subway system was consolidated and improved, and new housing and commercial construction was promoted. La Guardia built the first international airport for New York (now named after him). His administration peaked with the spectacular New York World's Fair from 1939 to 1940, which was visited by almost 45 million people (Allen, 1990:280).

During the 1950s, New York City became the center for corporate headquarters, if not the monopoly capital center for the globe. Beginning in 1952 with the construction of Lever House on Park Avenue, the new, international-style office building took over the skyline with its glass facades and square, flat roof. Midtown became a mass of high-rise corporate towers. At this time the New York School of Art, including Jackson Pollock,

system in the deep South. Many African Americans went north, west, and east, attracted by the possibility of jobs in the newly booming military industries. Most of these migrants settled in the central cities. Returning to the example of Chicago, Nicholas Lemann notes,

> During the 1940s, the black population of Chicago increased by 77 percent, from 278,000 to 492,000. In the 1950s, it grew by another 65 percent, to 813,000; at one point 2,200 black people were moving to Chicago every week. By 1960, Chicago had more than half a million more black residents than it had had twenty years earlier, and black migrants from the South were still coming in tremendous numbers. (1991b:70)

The metropolitan period began to decline in the 1960s at the time of massive suburbanization, predominantly of the white population. Hence, while central cities retained their economic power, prior to 1960 their populations were already undergoing a remarkable transformation. Cities were becoming more minority oriented and less

Mark Rothko, and William de Kooning, assumed the global standard for modern art, and the city became the culture capital of the world (Walloch, 1988). Arturo Toscanini, one of the greatest orchestra conductors, came to live in the city. The NBC Symphony Orchestra was created just for him, and he appeared on television. The new invention, by the way, had its programming centered in New York City, where all the network headquarters resided. By 1960, when the metropolitan period began its decline, there was still no more dynamic, exciting, culturally stimulating, and prosperous place in the United States.

white middle class in population. Before discussing the changes since 1960 (next chapter), let us consider the process of suburbanization, which is also responsible for the regional growth of the metropolis.

Suburbanization and Regional Maturation

While the presence of suburbanization is not unusual for industrialized countries, the massive scale of this phenomenon in the United States is quite distinctive among most societies, except for places like Australia and Canada. To be sure, many societies have experienced growth beyond city borders, but in the United States this has assumed the form of single-family home construction for the middle class on an unprecedented scale. Suburbanization of the white middle class to single-family homes accelerated its pace after the 1930s, and especially after World War II, but it was always an important aspect of settlement patterns. As we learned in Chapter 2, U.S. cities did not possess walls. Fringe area development occurred as the city itself grew. In Europe, the walls were essentially torn down or overgrown so that these countries also experienced sub-urbanization, but at a slower pace and with a different, more working-class-oriented mix of population that was housed in multifamily or apartment buildings.

Growth beyond city borders was a common feature of industrialized societies as early as the nineteenth century. In fact, the desire to live *outside* the city despite commuting there for work seems to be as old as the city itself. Although we can point to numerous writers who extol the virtues of city living, there has always been an expressed "anti-urban" bias in every urbanized civilization. The biblical prophets, for example, took to the deserts east of Jerusalem to escape the excesses of the city and cleanse themselves. Across the centuries, those who could afford to do so always had a country home to balance against time spent at a city address. The historian Kenneth Jackson offers the following excerpt from a letter written over 2,500 years ago as evidence that suburbanization was a process coextensive with urbanization itself: "Our property seems to me the most beautiful in the world. It is so close to Babylon that we enjoy all the advantages of the city, and yet when we come home we are away from all the noise and dirt" (1985:12).

But the presence of a yearning for the country among city dwellers or some anti-urban bias cannot explain the immense scale of suburbanization that is characteristic of the United States. There is a demand-side view of suburbanization that is instructive. By "demand side" we mean the production of a settlement space pattern through the desires of consumers and businesspeople acting in the marketplace. Demand-side theories of urbanization make the assumption that settlement patterns are the result of a large number of individuals interacting competitively in the market to satisfy desires. Often they are simply aided by innovations in transportation technology. Many geographers, such as John Borchert (1967), and urban sociologists, such as Amos Hawley (1981), suggest this approach as an explanation of urban spatial patterns.

To an extent, the demand-side view helps us understand aspects of suburbanization, especially the desire of U.S. residents for a home of their own. Homeownership is a potent cultural symbol in our society. It provides people with their most important social status. Owning a home also links with other aspects of consumerism that express basic values in U.S. culture (Veblen, 1899).

There is also, however, a "supply-side" view to urban patterns. In this approach, what counts in development is less the desires of individuals than the quests of special interests, especially networks of businesspeople aided by allies in government that promote development to acquire profits. Joe R. Feagin sums up the supply-side view:

> Traditionally most urban analysts and scholars have argued that everybody makes cities, that first and foremost the choices and decisions by large groups of consumers demanding housing and buildings lead to the distinctive ways cities are built. But this is not accurate. Ordinary people often play "second fiddle." In the first instance, capitalist developers, bankers, industrial executives, and their business and political allies build cities, although they often run into conflict with rank-and-file urbanites over their actions. Cities under capitalism are structured and built to maximize the profits of real estate capitalists and industrial corporations, not necessarily to provide decent and livable environments for all urban residents. (1983:8)

The history of suburbanization in the United States is a protracted story of bold quests to acquire wealth through the development of fringe area land and individual or group pursuits of a residential vision that would solve the problems of city living. In other words, an account of this phenomenon must consider supply-side and demand-side factors as intertwined.

In the early 1800s, for example, industrialists who had recently acquired fortunes, such as Leland Stanford in railroads, Andrew Carnegie in steel, and James B. Duke in tobacco (the so-called "nouveaux riches"), sought symbols of their new-found wealth. One practice was to purchase a palatial home with substantial space for manicured lawns and at some distance from the city. According to Thorstein Veblen (1899), who introduced the term *conspicuous consumption,* space in these suburban homes was used as a symbol of "excess" and the ability to afford it. The fronts of houses were given over to large, manicured lawns labored over by a team of hired gardeners, lawns that were used for nothing except the growing of grass. The mansions themselves had many more rooms than were needed to house family and servants. Guests could always be accommodated on the spot with their own individual bedroom; space was simply held vacant. The backyards were devoted to "suburban" leisure—genteel games such as croquet or badminton, lazing in lawn chairs, or simply walking in the garden. Conspicuous consumption, pastoral delights, and the large, single-family house with generous living space became for many Americans the suburban ideal. This cultural value glorifying a particular space fed the economic aspects of demand for homeownership outside the city. In Chapter 9, we will see that other metropolitan lifestyles are also dependent on their own particular spaces for cultural expression.

Traditional explanations for suburbanization stress the importance of transportation technology as its cause (see, for example, Jackson, 1985; Muller, 1981; Hawley, 1981), with each innovation, such as the switch from commuter rail to automobile, signaling a new pattern of land use. Transportation modes, however, served only as the *means* for residential suburban development; they were not the cause. Transport technology was always used to further real estate developer schemes. The demand-side view demonstrates that the desire for the suburban lifestyle may have been active in the minds of urbanites because people emulated the rich and disliked the confines of the large city. But dreams alone did not produce concrete spatial patterns. Rather, suburbanization was generated by the supply-side activities of real estate entrepreneurs and government subsidies responding to and feeding demand-side desires.

Initially suburban development leapfrogged over the urban landscape. Suburban housing was built as a separate town removed by several miles from city boundaries. In the late 1800s, Westchester and Tuxedo Park outside New York City, Lake Forest and Riverside outside Chicago, Hillsborough adjacent to San Francisco, Palos Verdes near Los Angeles, Shaker Heights eight miles from Cleveland, and Roland Park outside Baltimore were all private developments built as towns. Most of these places advertised themselves as extolling suburban virtues, which at the time meant racial, ethnic, and class exclusion in addition to low-density residential living. It was not until the late 1940s that suburban development occurred on a mass scale. Hence, the desire for racial, class, and religious exclusion also added to the complex of cultural factors contributing to the desire to suburbanize.

The early deconcentration of industry followed this same pattern. In the 1800s, owners of large businesses often moved all their operations outside the city by developing a separate town. The classic study of such "satellite cities" was done by Graham Taylor in 1915. Gary, Indiana, for example, was built on sand dunes at the base of Lake Michigan by U.S. Steel in the 1880s. At about the same time, George Pullman pulled his railroad car business out of Chicago and built Pullman, Illinois, a few miles away. In 1873 Singer Sewing Machine relocated from Manhattan to an existing city, Elizabeth, New Jersey, but converted it through its presence into a company town, where the factory remained until 1982 when it closed due to foreign competition.

Taylor (1915) gives two main explanations for the creation of satellite cities. First, the new ventures represented an important investment in real estate as well as an industrial relocation. More space was needed for industrialized plants, hence the need to move out of the congested central city. But the need for space was coupled with the acquisition of real estate. Pullman, for example, expected to make as much money from the development of land he owned in the new city as from the factory itself. Second, industrialists pulled their plants out of cities because the latter were hotbeds of union activity. Workers in any one plant were invariably in contact with workers in other plants and other industries. The city concentrated unions as well as people. During the sequential recessions in the United States, beginning with the 1870s, strikes and worker activism were especially frequent. The decentralization of industry was an important tool for minimizing union influence, according to Taylor (see Chapter 7).

To be sure, transportation technology eventually played a profound role in suburbanization. After the 1920s in particular, the movement of people to the suburbs was aided greatly by the mass production and consumption of the automobile. Prior to that time, regional metropolitan space was organized in a star-shaped form with greatest development situated along the fingers of rail corridors. The private automobile enabled developers to work laterally and fill in the spaces between the mainline tracks. In the 1920s 23 million cars were registered in the United States, and that figure increased to 33 million 10 years later. "By 1940, the U.S. auto registration rate exceeded 200 per 1000 population and the average number of cars per capita (which was 13 in 1920) had fallen to less than 5" (Muller, 1981:39).

Turn-of-the-century suburbanization played a great role in determining the patterns of growth that followed during the years between 1920 and 1960. Trolley lines and tract housing laid down in the previous period provided the material infrastructure, such as right of ways, sewers, and utility lines, for much of the urban growth that was to follow. It is often suggested, for example, that Los Angeles looks the way it does— spread out in a pattern of immense sprawl—because it was built during the age of the automobile. Actually, the formative period of development for Los Angeles took place *prior* to the invention of the auto. Los Angeles was a product of electrified trolley lines and very active, aggressive real estate speculation schemes that capitalized on the ease of home construction in the region (Crump, 1962). Today's freeways in Los Angeles simply follow the transit routes of the major trolley lines that once existed (see Figure 4.1). The fact that the latter were pollution free should not be lost on the present generation suffering from smog, nor should we forget Spencer Crump's (1962) case study showing how automobile, oil, and highway construction companies colluded to sabotage the trolley car transit business.

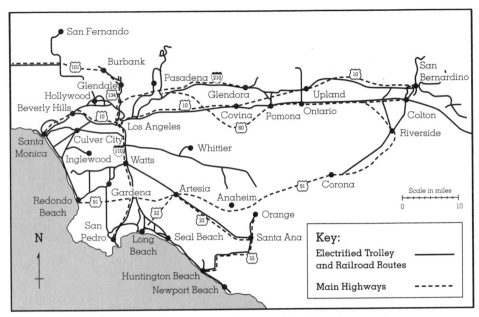

Figure 4.1   Trolley routes and auto highways in Los Angeles

The major thrust of suburbanization in the United States took place after 1920, with a profound acceleration of growth after World War II. Truly it can be said that present-day regional patterns of metropolitan development materialized during this time. Prior to the 1920s, a suburban residence could be afforded only by the more affluent; after 1940, suburbanization became a mass phenomenon. So far in this chapter we have mentioned several supply-side factors contributing to decentralization. On the demand side, we have indicated the profound cultural effect that the style of life associated with affluent suburbia had on the tastes of urban individuals and families. While many Americans may have desired to leave the city, few had the means prior to World War II, especially because of the Great Depression. Here the federal government became crucial in creating a mass housing market because its policies promoted single-family homes.

In the 1930s, the Depression was ravishing the home construction industry. Because a principal asset of banks was (and still is) home mortgages, this economic downslide also had a devastating impact on the banking industry. In one estimate, housing values declined by 20 percent between 1926 and 1932, and by 1933 at least half of all home mortgages were in default (Jackson, 1985:191). The Great Depression altered the nature of U.S. capitalism because during this time, the federal government changed from an indirect participant in the economy to a direct subsidizer of business. In the 1930s, Washington, D.C., attempted a rescue of the housing industry, and at the same time it hoped to save the banks.

In 1934 Congress passed the National Housing Act, which established the Federal Housing Authority (FHA). Briefly put, for qualified houses, the federal government insured buyers' mortgages. For banks, this took the risk out of private loans. It also pumped needed capital into the housing industry. Foreclosures went from

BOX 4.2 PROFILE OF 1950s LEVITTOWN, LONG ISLAND

Prior to the 1940s, most homes were custom built or were renovated farm houses, and most of this suburban housing remained relatively expensive (Gottdiener, 1977). After the war, voracious demand supported by federal government programs made it possible to build housing in large quantities, but construction techniques had not quite been perfected to build single-family homes that were affordable. Abraham Levitt and Sons was one of the nation's largest builders in the 1940s. Work on many military construction projects had given the company the experience necessary to build inexpensive housing on a mass basis. Levitt built the first large-scale, affordable suburban housing development on several thousand acres of converted potato farms in the town of Hempstead on Long Island, adjacent to New York City:

> After bulldozing the land and removing the trees, trucks carefully dropped off building materials at precise 60-foot intervals. Each house was built on a concrete slab (no cellar); the floors were of asphalt and the walls of composition rock-board. . . . The construction process itself was divided into 27 distinct steps. . . . Crews were trained to do one job—one day the white-paint men, then the red-paint men, then the tile layers. Every possible part, and especially the most difficult ones, was preassembled in central shops, whereas most builders did it on site. Thus, the Levitts reduced the skilled component to 20–40 percent. . . . More than thirty houses went up each day at the peak of production. (Jackson, 1985:234)

Levitt was not sure that government subsidies and the GI bill would prove effective in supporting homeownership on a mass basis, so the first houses were offered only for rent in 1947. Soon after, in 1949 and in response to overwhelming demand, they were sold outright. The two-bedroom Cape Cod boxes initially cost $6,990. The community, now called Levittown, eventually numbered over 17,000 houses and contained over 80,000 residents. Levitt's organization feared that if they let in blacks, they would run the risk of failing to sell their homes to the white majority. Consequently the developer carefully screened prospective customers for race. Hence, the blue-collar community, which became a symbol for the postwar American Dream, was not integrated.

Unlike large-scale developments of today (as we will discuss in the next chapter), early suburban projects were marketed with a full complement of

250,000 in 1932 to 18,000 by 1951 (Jackson, 1985:203). The act also established the Federal National Mortgage Association (Fannie Mae), which facilitated the transfer of funds by banks across geographical and political boundaries in the United States. The Fannie Mae program and later Ginnie Mae, or the Government National Mortgage Association, helped restructure the banking community and subsidized mortgage lending on a mass scale.

Subsequent housing acts were passed in 1937 and 1941. Along with earlier initiatives, they established the homeowner's tax subsidy. Homeowners could now community amenities. Builders were obligated to supply a community quality of life, not just construct housing. Levittown came with nine swimming pools, 60 playgrounds, 10 baseball diamonds, and seven "village greens," or minimall centers, within the development (Jackson, 1985).

During the next few years, Levitt and Sons built communities in Pennsylvania and New Jersey. The modular construction process they innovated was duplicated by builders all over the United States, and the mass construction of suburbia began.

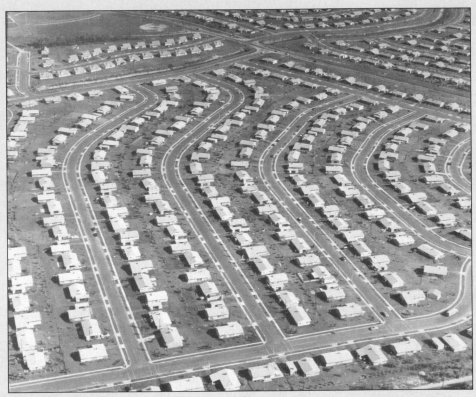

After World War II, William J. Levitt built Levittown, ripping up 5,000 acres of Long Island, New York, and putting up 17,447 homes, all with the same floor plan and all mass produced at a price well below the then-current market level.

deduct the interest paid on mortgages from their taxes. This subsidy quite literally made it cheaper to own a home than to rent. Along with this tax subsidy, the Serviceman's Readjustment Act of 1944 perhaps had the most direct effects on housing. As the war was ending, Congress pledged to support returning servicemen with a package of welfare measures including subsidized education. One provision of this act established the Veterans Administration (VA) guaranteed loan program. Under the plan, GIs could purchase homes with no money down. The mass exodus to suburbia was now guaranteed.

So we see that mass demand for housing was primed by government programs. Most new construction took place in the suburbs. Over 16 million returning servicemen were eligible for benefits under the 1944 act, and a mass market was created. At this time, and due expressly to the war effort, the United States had perfected mass production assembly line techniques that could manufacture vast quantities of goods. All types of consumer durables, including cars, washing machines, vacuum cleaners, toasters, dishwashers, refrigerators, and air conditioners, were being produced on an immense scale after the 1940s. Suburban housing developments featured the new goods, and in the 1950s all aspects of mass production—housing, consumer durables, automobiles—combined to create the characteristic view of suburbia as the epitome of the consumer society. This political, economic, and cultural conjuncture that led to a society *domestically* producing and consuming mass quantities of goods with a large population engaged in assembly line factory work and active union membership is called *Fordism,* and it is a characteristic of monopoly capitalism. As we will see in the next chapter, under global capitalism the structure of Fordism broke apart as manufacturing activity drained from the United States to countries elsewhere.

The beneficiaries of suburbanization were overwhelmingly white. From 1940 to 1960, in two decades, the majority of the white child-rearing middle class left the central cities for the suburbs. In the previous section, we saw that this coincided with a period of mass black migration out of the South. This population transfer of whites and blacks is sometimes referred to as "white flight." Experts on the topic indicate that it is largely a product of the pull factors identified earlier (Frey, 1979). That is, whites did not leave large cities because blacks were moving in or the quality of life was declining; rather, they left because the quality of life was much better in the suburbs and because government programs subsidized them. Racial factors, according to the demographer William Frey (1979), affected less the decision to move than the destination of choice; that is, whites preferred to move to exclusively white areas in the suburbs.

Racism played a more overt role in preventing African Americans from moving to the suburbs themselves. Few were able to make that change in status. Those blacks who did suburbanize could find housing only in other black areas outside the city. The color barrier was strictly enforced by suburban developers. Box 4.2, which contains a case study of Levittown, New York, illustrates both the mass phenomenon of suburbanization after World War II and the racial exclusion on which it was based.

In sum, the following factors contributed to the decentralization of people to suburbs prior to the 1960s. On the demand side: city congestion, urban environmental concerns, the popularity of the suburban lifestyle, and effective transportation choices. On the supply side: active real estate development and speculation at the urban fringe, decentralization of industry, government-subsidized programs, and tax incentives.

The Pattern of U.S. Urbanization: A Summary

The story of city growth in the United States is high drama. European settlers under the protection of global colonial powers confronted Native Americans and took their land away. Immense resources were harnessed by individual "robber barons" and later by corporate interests working collectively with state bureaucrats and politicians. Industry was propelled along by remarkable innovations, especially those that exploited new forms of energy and transformed the industrial process. In the span of a century, the United States became a major industrial power.

Many facets of U.S. urbanization exaggerated in scale of population and territory aspects of metropolitan growth found elsewhere. Cities were built without walls, and both suburbanization and regional expansion were present early in our history and have persisted as characteristics of the metropolitan pattern. Formation of city government and the role of the local state as a service supplier characterized the political economy. To this day, municipal governments in the United States are much less involved in ameliorating the social conditions of existence than are their European counterparts. Alternatively, while other industrialized nations hem in development with extensive land use controls, local governments in the United States are often closely connected to real estate interests. By the 1970s, the United States had become the first nation of the globe with a majority of citizens living in suburbia, and life in this type of settlement space has influenced the culture of society to the present time.

CHAPTER 5

THE RESTRUCTURING OF SETTLEMENT SPACE: 1960 TO PRESENT

In the 1950s, most people still lived in large cities with an economic base grounded in manufacturing. Although suburbanization had commenced decades earlier, this trend could not match the magnitude of central city growth. After 1960, processes of *deindustrialization*—the loss of manufacturing—and *deconcentration*—the movement of people and activities away from the large city—transformed the United States, and a new pattern of sociospatial organization emerged. The growth trends of the present are so powerful that they require special attention.

Since 1970, population growth has been greater for metropolitan areas outside city centers rather than inside them, which reverses the traditional urbanization process of population concentration. This process is known as *population deconcentration*. Commenting on the 1980 census when the trend was first recognized, a demographer noted, "For the first time in well over 100 years, there was virtually no major nationwide population trend in the direction of concentration" (Long, 1981:1). For a brief time in the 1970s, even small incorporated cities lying outside the major metropolitan centers grew faster than the large cities, although by the 1980s that rapid growth had already subsided.

Other demographers are just as astounded by the changes of the last several decades. According to Frey and Speare (1988), most of the trends prior to the 1960s that characterized the U.S. population were altered and, in some cases, reversed during the last 20 years. First, there has always been a progressive drift of people from the East, Midwest, and South to the West. After 1960 this shift accelerated, producing rapid growth in the West. The South also grew remarkably during this period. Second, after the 1970s the South gained more than the West, for the first time, in net population growth. By 1980, the Sunbelt region of the West and South together contained the *majority* of the nation's population—a historical shift indeed!

Third, in the past large cities expanded faster than smaller ones. Since the 1970s this process has been reversed, with growth rates in smaller cities outstripping those of almost all larger ones. In 1970, for example, Phoenix was ranked eighteenth in the country with a population of just over 500,000. By 1994 it was ranked ninth, having grown by an incredible 60 percent. In contrast, with the exception of New York, all large Midwest and East Coast cities *lost* population between 1970 and 1990. In the most extreme case, Detroit lost a staggering 31.5 percent of its people (see Table 5.1).

Finally, the shift of metropolitan residents to suburbia accelerated during this time. By 1970, in fact, more people lived in suburbia than in central cities. If, in 1920, we could say with truth that the United States had become an urbanized nation, today we can say with equal confidence that the United States is dominated by suburbanization. Between 1960 and 1990, the United States went from a society dominated by large central cities in the Frostbelt to a nation with the bulk of its population living in the Sunbelt and in suburbia!

Let us examine these changes according to the sociospatial perspective. Other approaches place too much emphasis on technological changes or the push factors of economic growth. In this chapter we will look at these considerations, but also discuss the roles of government intervention, real estate activities, and the changed spatial arrangements of businesses and people.

How Cities Have Changed

In 1950 the proportion of total employment for manufacturing was 26 percent, with the next largest sector, retailing and construction, accounting for 22.6 percent. By the 1980s, the latter proportion was virtually unchanged but total employment in manufacturing dropped to 22 percent. The largest proportion of workers, or 24 percent, was employed in so-called *nodal services:* transportation, finance, wholesaling, business repair, insurance, and real estate. Cities shifted in 30 years from an economy dominated by manufacturing to one that specialized in services (Frey and Speare, 1988). For the largest cities, such as New York and Chicago, there is considerable evidence that the sector of capital involved in national and global processes of financial investing has taken over the downtown (Gottdiener, 1985; Sassen, 1991). Employment in the sector of finance capital alone has increased dramatically for the categories of investing services, management consulting, legal services, accounting services, and the like.

Observers such as Bluestone and Harrison (1982) have referred to the drastic decline of manufacturing in the United States and other advanced countries as *deindustrialization,* or the closing of factories, the rise of manufacturing unemployment, and the relocation of manufacturing outside the country. Between 1970 and 1980 alone, the United States and Western Europe lost 8 million manufacturing jobs, while other countries, such as Japan and Korea, gained over 6 million (Yago et al., 1984). We will discuss the political economy of these changes more fully in Chapter 7.

A padlock on one of the main gates of the U.S. Steel plant in Youngstown, Ohio, tells the story. Steelworkers attempted, through the courts, to buy the plant and keep it going. A recent court decision was not in their favor and the plant is to be shut down and dismantled. (See Box 5.1.)

Economic and Social Restructuring

In the 1950s, the typical city was an industrial city. Factories filled the air with the smoke of manufacturing activity. Workers in plants lived nearby in so-called blue-collar neighborhoods. Although predominantly white, this population was made up of many ethnic groups—Italian, Irish, Jewish, Polish, Hungarian, German, and Scandinavian. Everyday life was circumscribed by the factory routine for both women and men. A coordinated exodus of workers from their homes converged on the plants in the morning, while children ran off to neighborhood schools at about the same time. Schools provided vocational training for most boys and homemaker or secretarial skills for girls as a means of fitting them into a working-class world with limited aspirations that few thought would ever change. Several generations of working-class families grew to maturity within this milieu.

The Shift from Manufacturing to Service Industries. By the 1980s, this pattern of everyday life had changed. Cities no longer were dominated by manufacturing, and working-class family life based on predictable employment opportunities in manufacturing had largely disappeared, producing attendant changes and crises in education

BOX 5.1 PLANT CLOSURES AT YOUNGSTOWN, OHIO

The sheet steel and tube plant at Youngstown was founded by two local brothers in 1900. For several generations, it provided families in the city with regular employment. In 1969 something happened to the company that is typical of other factories that eventually had to shut down (Bluestone and Harrison, 1982): It was bought out by a conglomerate located in another city, the Lykes Corporation, with interests in real estate, shipbuilding, banking, and ranching (Buss and Redburn 1983:15).

At the time of the purchase, the steel industry was enjoying steady profits because of the war in Vietnam. In the early 1970s, however, it was hit with a crisis that involved many elements, including the rising importation of cheap steel from Europe and Asia. Between 1969 and 1978, the steel industry in the United States lost 95,000 jobs, or 17 percent. Between 1977 and 1980 alone, U.S. Steel shut down more than six plants around the country, Bethlehem shut down two plants, and other, smaller companies folded their operations.

As the steel industry declined, owners of mills faced the dilemma of shutting down or modernizing. As a conglomerate, the Lykes Corporation was able to shift investment to other assets rather than continue to invest in the Youngstown company. In 1977 it shut down the major facilities at one of the plants, laying off 4,000 workers overnight. Eventually over 10,000 jobs in all were lost in the community as the entire operation shut down. According to the case study by Buss and Redburn,

> The Lykeses must bear responsibility for a good deal of the failure at Youngstown Sheet and Tube. From the beginning, they viewed the steel company primarily as an investment; it was never thought of as an operation that young Lykes men might wish to manage. Lykes Corporation decided to cut its losses at Youngstown Sheet and Tube by letting the steel-making operations flounder. . . . Second, Lykes began investing capital needed for renovating the

and job training. The city of Pittsburgh, for example, was once synonymous with steel. In 1930, over 32 percent of its workforce was engaged in manufacturing. By 1980, only 14 percent of the labor force was employed in manufacturing, and steel production engaged only 5.5 percent. In contrast, service employment had risen to 38 percent, thereby dominating the economy (Jezierski, 1988). Pittsburgh had been transformed from an industrial to a nodal service city. In the process, however, it lost 24 percent of its jobs and 37 percent of its population between 1940 and 1980. Between 1980 and 1990, it lost an additional 12.8 percent of its people. Cities have shifted from an economy dominated by manufacturing to one that now specializes in services and retailing, but with a smaller employed labor force and, in many cases, a smaller population than in the past (Frey and Speare, 1988:4). Box 5.1 discusses the effects of deindustrialization on the community fabric of cities.

A second and equally important change beginning with the 1960s was that most central cities experienced slow or no population growth. The child-rearing middle class virtually abandoned the large city as a place to live (see Table 5.1). However, as steel mills into its nonsteel subsidiaries. This accelerated the decline of the antiquated mills. (1983:21)

As a global conglomerate, the Lykes Corporation was different from the family business that started the company in a period prior to monopoly capitalism. With the internationalization of capital, conglomerates can pick and choose among a variety of ways to make a profit. They can also take tax losses on investments that are not profitable. Considerations of community involvement and the responsibility of preserving employment sources for generations of local workers are not at issue. According to Buss and Redburn (1983:22), the way the mills were shut down was outrageous. No advance warning was given. The company did not provide any transition programs for employees: "Workers simply had a job one day and no job the next." The company, which was located in New Orleans, refused to meet with local community leaders to discuss the closure. "Workers didn't just lose their jobs, they lost pension rights, status and other advantages of accrued seniority. All workers, after a brief period, lost their group health insurance coverage" (1983:22).

Studies such as the one by Buss and Redburn have tried to document the effects of massive job loss on communities and individuals (Dooley and Catalano, 1980). The economy of the city will never be the same following the plant closures, although some light industry has returned to Youngstown. Job loss has profound emotional consequences for individuals and families. Buss and Redburn (1983) found that many families pulled together and helped one another out to cushion the effects. The initial period of a few years resulted in personal stress occurring only in a minority of cases, although the long-term effects have yet to be studied. Eventually some of the workers were able to find other jobs. Research discovered that despite the smaller salaries in alternative employment, workers went back to leading productive lives with a minimum of stress. What counts, it seems, for emotional security is simply to have steady employment rather than a high salary. The case of Youngstown, Ohio, was repeated many times across the United States between 1970 and 1990.

with the other shifts, national figures mask the regional nature of this phenomenon, which occurred largely in the cities of the Northeast and Midwest. Between 1970 and 1980, New York City's population declined by 10.4 percent, although currently it is growing slowly again; Chicago declined 10.1 percent between 1970 and 1980 and an additional 7.4 percent between 1980 and 1990. Between 1990 and 1994, population decline slowed but continued. Detroit lost 20.5 percent of its population between 1970 and 1980 and another 14.6 percent between 1980 and 1990, or almost 500,000 people in two decades. Detroit lost an additional 3.5 percent between 1990 and 1994. In contrast, the cities in the Sunbelt actually thrived during this same period. Los Angeles grew by 17.5 percent between 1980 and 1990 and became the second largest city in the country, while Houston gained 400,000 people between 1970 and 1990, becoming the fourth largest. Earlier cities such as Jacksonville and San Jose grew by over 100 percent between 1960 and 1970. Table 5.1 shows the populations for 24 of the largest cities from 1960 and illustrates the regional differences in these population shifts, such as decline in the Northeast and growth in the Sunbelt after 1970.

TABLE 5.1
The 24 Most Populated U.S. Cities, 1970–1994

City	Population				Percentage of Change		
	1994	1990	1980	1970	1990–1994	1980–1990	1970–1980
New York City, NY	7,333,253	7,322,564	7,071,639	7,894,862	0.15	3.5	-10.4
Los Angeles, CA	3,448,613	3,485,557	2,966,850	2,816,061	-1.06	17.5	-5.6
Chicago, IL	2,731,743	2,783,726	3,005,072	3,366,957	-1.87	-7.4	-10.1
Houston, TX	1,702,086	1,630,864	1,595,138	1,232,802	4.37	2.2	29.3
Philadelphia, PA	1,524,249	1,585,577	1,688,210	1,948,609	-3.87	-6.1	-13.4
San Diego, CA	1,151,977	1,110,623	875,538	696,769	3.72	26.8	25.7
Detroit, MI	992,038	1,027,974	1,203,339	1,511,482	-3.50	-14.6	-20.5
Dallas, TX	1,022,830	1,007,618	904,078	844,401	1.51	11.4	11.3
Phoenix, AZ	1,048,949	984,309	789,704	581,562	6.57	24.5	35.3
San Antonio, TX	998,905	935,393	785,880	654,153	6.79	19.1	20.2
San Jose, CA	816,884	782,224	629,442	445,779	4.43	24.3	36.7
Baltimore, MD	702,979	736,014	785,795	645,153	-4.49	-6.3	-13.0
Indianapolis, IN	752,279	731,311	700,807	744,624	2.87	4.4	-4.9
San Francisco, CA	734,676	723,959	678,974	715,674	1.48	6.6	-5.2
Jacksonville, FL	665,070	635,230	540,920	528,865	4.70	17.4	21.7
Columbus, OH	635,913	632,945	564,871	539,677	0.47	12.0	4.6
Milwaukee, WI	617,044	628,088	636,212	717,099	-1.76	-1.3	-11.3
Memphis, TN	614,289	618,652	646,356	623,350	-0.71	-5.6	3.5
Washington, DC	567,094	606,900	638,333	756,510	-6.56	-4.9	-15.7
Boston, MA	547,725	574,283	562,944	641,071	-4.62	2.0	-12.2
Seattle, WA	520,947	516,259	493,846	530,831	0.91	4.5	-7.0
El Paso, TX	579,307	515,342	425,259	322,261	12.41	21.2	32.0
Cleveland, OH	492,901	505,616	573,822	750,903	-2.51	-11.9	-23.6
New Orleans, LA	484,149	496,938	557,515	593,471	-2.57	-10.9	-5.9

Sources: Census of Population and Housing, 1997, U.S. Department of Commerce, Bureau of the Census; Census of Population and Housing, 1990, U.S. Department of Commerce, Bureau of the Census, Summary Tape, File 1C (CD-ROM); Census of Population, Characteristics of the Population, Number of Inhabitants, U.S., U.S. Department of Commerce, Bureau of the Census, Summary, Table 27; 1970 Census of Population, Characteristics of Population, Number of Inhabitants, U.S., U.S. Department of Commerce, Bureau of the Census, Table 28.

Population declines in most cities were also matched by profound racial changes, with minority populations increasing. In New York City, for example, the black population increased from 21 percent in 1980 to 25 percent in 1988, and Detroit went from 43.7 percent to 63.1 percent. Along with the minority influx was a white flight from the central cities, produced largely by the pull of suburbia (see Chapter 4). In many cities, the combined black and Hispanic minorities became the majority, thereby changing the racial balance. The combined black and Hispanic population for our largest cities in 1988 was 45 percent for New York City (by 1990 it was over 50 percent), 44.5 percent for Los Angeles, 53.8 percent for Chicago, 45.2 percent for Houston, 41.6 percent for Philadelphia, 23.9 percent for San Diego, 65.5 percent for Detroit, 55.8 percent for Baltimore, and 25 percent for San Francisco. Over 300 minority mayors were elected in cities across the nation, including Chicago, Detroit, Baltimore, El Paso (Hispanic), New Orleans, New York, Atlanta, and Washington, D.C. (see Chapter 11 for a discussion of minority empowerment).

Shifts in Ethnic Composition. Third, our largest cities have experienced profound ethnic shifts. The waves of immigration from Western and Eastern Europe that gave U.S. cities much of their ethnic character ceased by World War II. Beginning with the 1970s and accelerating in the 1980s, new waves of immigration flowed through our largest cities, increasing the percentages of foreign-born living there. For example, in the Sunbelt cities such as San Diego, much of the 60 percent increase from 1970 to the present reflected a large influx of Hispanic residents. Metropolitan regions on the West Coast have seen a large increase in the Asian population, often with specific groups settling into suburban counties, such as the Filipino communities in Daly City (San Francisco) and Mira Mesa (San Diego, sometimes referred to as Manila Mesa). Metropolitan areas on the East Coast have had an increasing proportion of new immigrants from the Caribbean and Eastern Europe; in New York City, the foreign-born population increased from 5.4 percent of the total in 1970 to 23.6 percent in 1990. In the Midwest as well, the new wave of immigration has resulted in startling changes. The Chicago metropolitan area, once known for its Polish, Italian, and Bohemian neighborhoods and suburbs, now is home to more than 1 million Hispanics, mostly of Mexican origin, making it the third largest Mexican community in the United States (after Los Angeles and San Antonio).

As immigration in the 1990s reached record levels, urban and suburban settlement spaces across the country became more diverse ethnically than at any previous time in the country's history. See Chapter 9 for a more detailed discussion of ethnic changes in American cities.

Uneven Development. The final change that took place in cities links economic shifts with changes in the composition of the population and uneven social development. As we have already discussed, employment growth was located principally in the service sector, especially in *nodal services* that were provided to corporations and banks— legal services, printing, business consulting, financial consulting, and related services in communication and transportation. Early observers of this trend toward specialization in nodal services suggested that they would provide the core industry for economic revitalization of cities following the profound decline in manufacturing

(Noyelle and Stanback, 1984; Sassen-Koob, 1984). It is now clear that no real renaissance has taken place. What has occurred is that robust activity in advanced services has benefited a relatively small and select group of trained professionals who earn high salaries, while leading to modest employment in low-paying service and clerical jobs in activities that aid the work of the highly paid core. The so-called service city actually consists of two layers: a core of nodal services forming the focus of internationally important economic growth that employs highly trained professionals and a second segment of relatively low-paid service workers who clean the buildings and maintain the landscaped areas around the buildings that contain the command and control industries and the relatively affluent professionals they employ.

Manufacturing of a sort has returned to the city. In recent years nonunionized, low wage factory work has appeared, such as fashion industry sweatshops, which often rely on the use of undocumented workers (Davis, 1987). Such industry clashes with the glitz of the much touted "command and control" centers that large cities advertise as being their core economic function. This contrast between affluence and poverty, between "yuppie" professionals and the working poor or undocumented laborers, seems to characterize many cities today. This so-called "dual city" has been the subject of some debate (Mollenkopf and Castells, 1991). Social polarization has occurred in the city, but there are more divisions than the class distinctions between wealthy and poor, and this contrast has graphically increased within large cities in all areas of the world, not just the United States.

In addition, immense numbers of less affluent, immigrant, and marginalized workers have created within the city a large, *informal* economy. The informal economy is defined as the combination of workers who are "off the books," goods produced in unregulated factories with nonunionized and undocumented laborers, goods and services produced and exchanged for barter (i.e., not cash but in kind), and goods and services sold without regulation on the streets. The informal economy in some countries often rivals the formal sector. Everywhere, this aspect of economic activity has emerged as an increasingly important way in which people within urban areas make a livelihood. One example of the informal economy is the illegal drug industry, which runs into the billions of dollars in sales and is an international operation. And in cities such as New York, illegal factories manufacture "faux" designer fashion items, such as fake Rolex watches, and then use recent or undocumented immigrants to sell them on Manhattan street corners for only a fraction of the genuine article's price. Even discounting the major effect of drug dealing, the informal economy in large cities represents a formidable source of jobs and income (see Mingione, 1988). The informal economy is usually not discussed, and its presence clashes with the legitimated image of large cities as centers for multinational business leaders (Boer, 1990).

In sum, cities have changed remarkably since the 1960s. They have more minorities, due in part to a growing immigrant population. Except for these immigrants, population growth in the cities of the 1980s has been slow. Today's large cities possess a transformed economy that is more specialized in nodal services and low-wage manufacturing, with a thriving informal economy of drug dealing and illegal factories that employ immigrants. All of these economic and social processes fuel a growing social disparity between the working poor, the underclass, new immigrants, and street vendors on the one hand and affluent professionals on the other (see Chapter 9).

How Suburbs Have Changed

In the 1950s and 1960s, suburbs were considered places where urban professionals who worked in the city bought homes to live and raise a family. They were called "bedroom communities" for this reason (Jackson, 1985). We now know that this image merely represented an early view of such places. Since the 1960s, suburbs have matured (Schnore, 1963). In many ways they have become diverse culturally, economically, and politically, much like medium-size urban areas (Muller, 1981). Places such as Tysons Corner, Virginia, outside of Washington, D.C.; Costa Mesa, California, beyond the boundaries of Los Angeles; and Dunwoody, Georgia, outside of Atlanta, are all important and developed suburbs.

Researchers have defined suburbs for study purposes as the "outside central cities" portion of the MSA. But this definition *under*estimates the expansion that has created new suburbs and regional development outside the MSA since 1970 (Muller, 1981). A compromise definition counts all the "outer rings" of the MSA as suburban, keeping in mind that this definition still underestimates the extent of deconcentration. In addition, the census has come to recognize that some areas of the country are now fully urbanized despite lying outside the MSA and lacking major city centers. Consequently, in the 1970s the census designated the suburban regions of Nassau–Suffolk Counties on the East Coast (outside the New York City MSA) and Orange County on the West Coast (outside the Los Angeles–Long Beach MSA) as all-suburban, independent MSAs. In the future it is very likely that other counties, such as those outside the cities of Chicago, San Francisco, and perhaps Houston, will also achieve independent MSA status. Therefore, we now recognize that many suburban regions contain as complex a social organization as do cities.

In 1970, the U.S. census noted for the first time that more people were living in suburbs than in other settlement spaces. At that time 37.1 percent of the population was suburban, compared with 31.5 percent that lived in the central city or 31.4 percent in rural areas. By 1990 even more rural areas had been absorbed by suburban growth, and the plurality of that population increased further. According to the figures, 46 percent of the 1990 population lived in suburbia, 40 percent in central cities, and 14 percent in rural areas (U.S. Bureau of the Census, 1990). While virtually all cities suffered from no or slow growth over the past decades, suburban regions remain the most rapidly growing areas of the country.

The change to suburban dominance in population is reflected in comprehensive statistics on economic activity. In many cases, suburbs have outpaced their adjacent central cities in economic importance since the 1970s. Muller cites, in particular, Philadelphia and its surrounding suburbs (1981:19). In the 1980s, the suburbs outside Philadelphia contained 63 percent of the entire region's employment (i.e., including the central city itself); 67 percent of all manufacturing jobs; 68 percent and 70 percent of all wholesaling and retailing, respectively; and over 50 percent of all regional employment in financial, insurance, and business service sectors.

Push and Pull Factors in Suburbanization

Massive suburbanization since 1960 has occurred due to a combination of push and pull factors. Government intervention played a significant role in the development of the immense tracts of land outside large cities after World War II. Most instrumental were the tax laws allowing for the deduction of mortgage interest from income taxes. In effect, this subsidized middle-class housing needs, and because most affordable single-family housing was and still is located in the suburbs, this program also subsidized suburbanization. Since the 1940s, it has literally paid to own your own home.

The home mortgage subsidy is equal to or greater than all other government spending on housing (Feagin, 1983). Subsidization of suburbanization, however, did not stop at housing. During the 1950s, pressure was placed on the federal government to construct a national system of highways. The result was the 1956 interstate highway program, which acted in the name of national defense to subsidize the construction of over 40,000 miles of roads. A gasoline tax was imposed to pay for this construction, and at its height the highway fund amounted to $50 billion (Muller, 1981). This system of interstates carved up the countryside adjacent to cities, opening up the vast U.S. hinterland to suburbanization.

The combined efforts in promoting single-family housing and automobile transportation created a form of suburbanization in the United States that differs from that of other advanced industrialized countries, such as Britain and Sweden. In the latter places, ambitious mass transportation schemes were harnessed to aggressive town planning to produce suburban housing that was accessible and affordable.

In the United States, by contrast, mass transportation systems that had been in place prior to World War II were abandoned and replaced by highways that were the result of the cooperative efforts of automobile companies, highway construction firms, and local politicians (Crump, 1962; Whitt, 1982). The result is a suburban landscape consisting of immense regions of single-family home developments and the hegemony of the automobile culture (Weiss, 1988; Davis, 1986).

One of the most important observations about suburbia from the demand-side point of view is that it is quite a popular place to live. Despite the many criticisms, such as its boring lack of choices and homogeneity, most residents are happy with the suburbs and few miss living in or even visiting the city (Muller, 1981:14). There is some evidence that suburbs are hard on adolescents and the elderly poor, but these groups are not powerful enough to alter either planning priorities of development or federal policies that subsidize suburban growth.

In the suburbs, we seem to have found a happy marriage between middle-class demand-side preferences for housing and living arrangements and supply-side subsidies providing the incentive structure for growth patterns. The landscape that such development has created, however, is very much a product of specific transportation and housing policies. These have sanctified the expensive, single-family home and surrendered regional space to the automobile culture. Without alternatives, the increasing social costs of this pattern of suburbanization become more evident each year.

Suburban Social Characteristics

There is no typical suburb and, just as understandably, no unique suburban lifestyle exists, although there is a typical suburban everyday life associated with single-home ownership, automobile commutation, and low-density neighborhoods that differs from life in the central city. Through much of the postwar era, it was assumed that people who lived in the suburbs would commute to the downtown areas to work and even to shop. In the 1960s and 1970s, human ecologists studied the employment-to-residence ratio, which compared the number of jobs within a suburban community with the number of persons in the labor force. Leo Schnore (1963) was able to categorize suburban communities as bedroom suburbs (perhaps the stereotypical suburb of the era), service suburbs, mixed residential suburbs, and net-employment suburbs. But over the last two decades, the employment patterns of suburban residents have changed greatly. The majority of people who live in the suburbs are now employed at jobs within the suburban region, not in the city. The commute from the suburb to a downtown office has been replaced by the commute to a job in a suburban office complex—or manufacturing plant or shopping mall. While there are important differences among different types of suburban communities, most now represent the mixed residential suburb.

In the main, lower-income as well as more affluent whites have found places in the suburban region to live. Blacks, however, have over the years found it difficult to suburbanize even to this day. They represent around 5 percent of the total suburban population despite being 12 percent of the general population. Typically, black people suburbanize by moving to areas outside the central city that are directly adjacent to their city neighborhoods (Muller, 1981). As we have seen, therefore, blacks are considerably *over*represented in the central city and *under*represented in the suburbs relative to their total population. In other countries that also have a racially mixed society, such as Brazil, large cities such as Rio de Janeiro have the opposite pattern. There the blacks and the poor live in shantytown suburbs, with the affluent ensconced in the city center (see Chapter 12).

While whites have found suburbs open to them, the uniformity of housing price within each subdivision has resulted in graphic income segregation within suburban regions. Wealthier suburbs in particular have been successful in keeping blacks and the less affluent out of their areas through the home rule device of *exclusionary zoning;* that is, local control over land use and building codes enables individual communities to prohibit the building of low- or moderately-priced housing. This perpetuates the value of higher-priced homes, thereby maintaining exclusivity. Years of such practices have made suburban housing increasingly expensive, thus creating a housing shortage in suburbia for first-time buyers.

In sum, suburban regions have taken on diverse socioeconomic characteristics. For the white population there is considerable diversity of community type, although there are increasing class differences and a housing shortage due to the decreasing affordability of moderately priced units. African Americans remain relatively excluded from suburban living except in designated places. Hence, the vast suburban regions are increasingly segregated by class and race. In its own way, this pattern replicates the division of race and class within the central city. Thus, city problems of residential segregation have been duplicated in the suburbs and are now regionwide.

Economic Deconcentration

For the suburbs, economic deconcentration has meant a combined process of both capturing new job growth and decentralizing economic activities from the large central city, as well as the process of their recentralization in minicenters within the suburban region. Let us consider the separate economic dimensions of deconcentration.

Retailing. The total amount of all retailing in the United States is now dominated by malls located in suburban realms of the metropolis. By the time of the 1970 census, the suburban share of MSA sales passed the 50 percent mark for the 15 largest MSAs. According to Muller,

> Steadily rising real incomes, fueled by the booming aerospace-led economy of the middle and late sixties, created a virtually insatiable suburban demand for durable consumer goods. With almost no pre-existing retail facilities in the burgeoning outer suburbs, huge capital investments were easily attracted from life insurance companies and other major financial institutions. Not surprisingly, regional shopping centers quickly sprang up at the most accessible highway junction locations as their builders strived to make them the focus of all local development. (1981:123)

Suburban shopping malls were so successful that their numbers increased more than tenfold from approximately 2,000 in 1960 to over 20,000 in 1980. Over time this success threatened central city shopping areas and bypassed them as the important places to consume. Sizes of suburban retailing centers increased over time to malls and supermalls. Houston's Galleria complex, for example, is modeled after the Galeria of Milan, Italy. It is several stories high and is built around an olympic-size skating rink that is open year-round, a feat of some proportions if you consider the warm, humid climate of Houston. The Galleria has three large department stores, over 200 smaller shops, four office towers, two hotels, over 15 restaurants and cinemas, nightclubs, and even a health club. Its seven-level parking facility has room for over 10,000 cars. Lately the name *Galleria* has become popular for malls in many other places in the United States, and it usually connotes a large and expansive upscale mall.

Lenox Square Shopping Center outside of Atlanta is one of the largest in the South, covering 74 acres. Malls are one cornerstone of regional growth.

This type of spectacular, fully enclosed space for shopping has begun to replace the downtown streets of the central city department store district. As the success of malls has advanced, the scale of their construction has increased. Recently the phenomenon of "megamalls" has emerged as the new suburban focus of retailing. In the summer of 1992 a new, fully enclosed complex was constructed outside the city of Minneapolis that is so large it has room at its center for a seven-acre miniversion of a famous California theme park, Knotts Berry Farm. This "Mall of America," as it is called, contains 2 million square feet of space and enough parking for thousands of cars. Central cities cannot compete with such family attractions in immense suburban spaces.

Manufacturing. We have noted the progressive decline of manufacturing in the United States and its devastating impact on central cities. Over the years suburban areas have changed their bedroom image in part by being the recipients of many new manufacturing industries that have remained active. By the 1980s, the percentage share of manufacturing for the suburban rings of most metropolitan areas nationwide was over 50 percent. Boston and Pittsburgh, for example, have over 70 percent of their manufacturing located in the suburbs; Los Angeles, Detroit, San Francisco, St. Louis, and Baltimore have over 60 percent located in the suburbs.

Suburban developers innovated a form of space called the "industrial park" that is zoned entirely for business, especially manufacturing. Usually local towns or county governments provide significant tax incentives, infrastructure, and other subsidies to

Aerial view of industrial buildings, Silicon Valley, California.

attract manufacturing. The presence of such attractive and inexpensive locations in suburbia is one factor in the progressive deconcentration of manufacturing.

Most recently suburbs have innovated a new form of local space known as a *high-tech growth pole* or "science park." These are more specialized research and development centers that are often linked with manufacturing and are located near university facilities. The most spectacular example is Silicon Valley, adjacent to Stanford University in California. A corridor stretching from the city of San Jose to Palo Alto makes up the spine of Silicon Valley and contains over 800 factories that produce state-of-the-art electronics and computer products. This complex is intimately connected to the research resources of Stanford University, where the transistor was invented and where the largest electrical engineering department is located.

While Silicon Valley remains the best known of the new spaces created by high-tech industries, other examples of growth are Route 128 outside of Boston, the San Diego–LaJolla complex associated with electronic medical technology innovators, the Research Triangle complex located near the Duke and University of North Carolina campuses, and the Iowa-to-Minnesota corridor of high-tech medical firms anchored at the Mayo Clinic in Rochester, Minnesota. The area around Irvine, California, is very typical of the new spaces created by high-technology industries. It is anchored by the University of California at Irvine campus and stretches for miles across what was once ranching and farming land. This region has been the subject of a study (Kling, Olin, and Poster, 1991) arguing that a new social order has developed here that surpasses the stereotype of suburban life and is based on consumerism, suburbia, professional occupations, and an economic base of knowledge- or information-processing industries. In Chapter 13, we will discuss the emergence of similar spaces located in advanced industrial societies around the globe.

The significance of these high-tech growth poles is that they foster industrial development that is completely independent of the central city. Because of their economic success, they often become the principal places in the society that earn money on the global market, thereby leading the country's growth (see Storper and Walker, 1991). In the past, models of industrial development have placed the city in a dominant role by referring to it as "the core," with the suburbs described as "the periphery." Development of society meant nurturing city-based industry. In this model, which better describes urban growth in the 60s and 70s, manufacturing was believed to originate in the city and then migrate out to the suburbs. All evidence now rejects this concept. The city is no longer privileged as the incubator of most industries, although some new manufacturing, such as textiles and light manufacturing, may still start up there. Development begins just as frequently in the suburbs as in the cities, and ". . . suburbia is quickly identified as a major zone of industrial expansion in its own right, in which *self-generated* growth has been primarily responsible for its current eminence" (Muller, 1981:143). Hence, the new patterns challenge the way people once thought about economic development.

In sum, then, the central city has lost its role as the dominating node of a regional economy. In many industries, important businesses are likely to locate in the suburbs and economic development is now a metropolitan regional affair.

Office and Administrative Headquarters. Perhaps the most significant example of the increasing importance of mature suburbs and, conversely, the decline of the central city is the progressive relocation of corporate headquarters to fringe areas. In the past, such headquarters were almost exclusively located in the central city. Today this is much less the case, although many headquarters remain in city centers. During the 1960s New York City, for example, was host to over 130 of the Fortune 500 companies. By the 1980s the number was down to 73, and it is now fewer than 60, or a loss of over 70 corporate headquarters in 30 years.

According to some recent books, large cities have emerged as the "command and control" centers for the global economy (Sassen, 1991; Noyelle and Stanback, 1984). This overstates the case for the economy in general and ignores decentralization to areas outside the city but within the metropolitan region (see Kephart, 1991). As indicated above, the largest cities have become the centers for finance capital activities, while other aspects of capitalism, such as producer services, marketing, and manufacturing, have decentralized. One indicator of this more complex spatial differentiation of functions is the phenomenal 30-year decline in the number of corporate headquarters located in New York City.

We have seen that the city can no longer be regarded as the dominant location choice for manufacturing or corporate headquarters. But the maturation of suburban areas with regard to administrative employment is even more significant. Despite some predictions that, as metropolitan regions grew, central cities would retain their command and control functions (Hawley, 1981), this has not proven to be the case.

In a study of the 21 largest MSAs, Ruth Armstrong (1972, 1979) found that, leaving the special case of New York City aside, administrative functions were evenly distributed between large cities and their suburbs in 1960. During the decades following her study, administrative and headquarter employment decentralized in favor of the suburbs as companies such as Pepsico and General Electric abandoned centers such as Manhattan for the adjacent suburban towns of Purchase, New York, and Fairfield, Connecticut, respectively. Several other studies have verified that this trend is continuing and that command and control centers are growing in the surburbs (Quante, 1976; Pye, 1977). In short, administrative functions, like all other economic activities, have been deconcentrating since the 1960s.

Over the years, then, suburbs have matured, becoming more and more like the diversified urban space of the past. They are autonomous employing regions with diverse populations (except for minority representation). As such we can no longer talk of some city-suburb hierarchy with a privileged city as the dominating center. In fact, for many metropolitan regions, such as the St. Louis or Philadelphia area, the power of the suburbs outweighs the central city itself.

Beyond Suburbia: The Multinucleated Region

By the 1990s, suburban regions in many areas of the United States had so matured that development was occurring in peripheral areas independently of major urban centers. This special and independent mode of regional, multinucleated growth was manifested as the *fully urbanized county,* such as Orange County, California, which is a net employing region with a labor force of over 1 million (Kling, Olin, and Poster, 1991). The most important characteristic of the fully urbanized county is that it does not contain any large cities, yet it functions much like a city by providing jobs as well as housing for its residents.

First studied by Gottdiener and Kephart (1991), the fully urbanized counties appeared in number during the 1980s, although two regions, Orange County in California and Nassau–Suffolk Counties in New York, had already achieved independent MSA status by 1980. Other multinucleated counties lie outside of MSAs. Oakland County in Michigan is typical. It lies adjacent to but outside the Detroit MSA, and had a 1980 population of *over* 1 million people, but its largest city contained only 76,715. It employed virtually all of the people who lived there with an employment-to-residence ratio of .93 in 1980, and grew by 11 percent between 1970 and 1980 (a rapid rate considering, especially, that Detroit itself declined in population). Oakland County's labor force was composed of 26 percent in manufacturing, 30 percent in retailing and wholesaling, and 25 percent in services, as well as other industries; that is, it possessed a balanced, diversified economy. Finally, in 1980 Oakland County had a median family income of $28,407—above the national average—and was 93 percent white.

Oakland County in Michigan was very much like at least 20 other multinucleated metropolitan regions located around the country that were identified as a new form of space because of their urban character and their deconcentrated form (Gottdiener and Kephart, 1991). In short, today our notion of suburbia has been transformed completely from the early pictures of the "bedroom community" to the fully urbanized but multicentered region. Results from the 1990 census suggest that this maturation process is continuing along the lines we have described.

The Shift to the Sunbelt

Without question the population and activity shift to the Sunbelt is the most important historical event of the last half of this century for the United States. The scale of change is quite spectacular. Although variations exist, most analysts define the Sunbelt as 13 southern states—Alabama, Arizona, Arkansas, Florida, Georgia, Louisiana, Mississippi, New Mexico, North Carolina, Oklahoma, South Carolina, Tennessee, and Texas—plus parts of two western states: California (southern counties below San Luis Obispo) and southern Nevada (Las Vegas, SMSA) (see Bernard and Rice, 1983). Between 1945 and 1975, the Sunbelt region doubled its population. In the decade between 1960 and 1970, Sunbelt MSAs received 63.8 percent of the total population increase for *all* MSAs (Berry and Kasarda, 1977:168). Between 1970 and 1980, the Northeast lost 1.5 percent of its population, the Midwest gained only 2.6 percent, but the South grew by 21.5 percent and the West by 22.6 percent, including a natural increase for all regions (Frey and Speare, 1988:50).

Sunbelt cities such as El Paso, Texas, almost doubled their populations between 1970 and 1990, growing from 322,261 to 515,342, and between 1990 and 1994 the increase continued at over 12 percent. Phoenix, Arizona, went from 581,562 in 1970 to 933,403 in 1990, increasing an additional 6.5 percent between 1990 and 1994, and San Diego grew

Phoenix, Arizona, one of the rapidly growing Sunbelt metropolises.

from 696,769 to 1,110,549 during the same period. All of this growth took place while Frostbelt cities stagnated with population decline or limited growth (see Table 5.2).

The phenomenal growth of the Sunbelt region is better illustrated by the metropolitan perspective of Table 5.3. It shows that between 1980 and 1990, the Los Angeles metro area grew by 26.4 percent, Dallas by 32.6, Houston by 19.7, Miami by 20.8, Atlanta by 32.5, San Diego by 34.2, and the Phoenix metro area by 40.6 percent, respectively. Similar increases were experienced during the 1970 to 1980 decade. These increases continued for the period between 1990 and 1995 (see Table 5.3).

Rapid demographic growth was matched by rapid employment growth in the Sunbelt. Between 1970 and 1980, manufacturing expanded by 12 percent in the North but more than double that, or 24.4 percent, in the South. While service employment grew by 11.5 percent in the North, it increased by 44 percent in the South and 47 percent in the West (Frey and Speare, 1988:92). According to one observer, ". . . never in the history of the world has a region of such size developed at such a rate for so long a time" (Sale, 1975:166).

The movement west and southward has been around for some time. Sunbelt states have been receiving a greater share of MSA population than the Frostbelt since the 1920s (Berry and Kasarda, 1977:168). Indeed, the movement of people westward has been a trend in the United States since the 1800s. The shift to the Sunbelt, however, displaces the economic center of gravity in the United States toward the West from the East Coast, and also obliterates what was once a core-periphery relation between a formerly agrarian South and West and an industrialized North and Midwest. Today the

TABLE 5.2
Population Growth for Sunbelt Cities, 1970–1994

City	Population				Percentage of Change		
	1994	1990	1980	1970	1990–1994	1980–1990	1970–1980
Los Angeles, CA	3,448,613	3,348,557	2,966,850	2,816,061	-1.06	17.5	5.6
Houston, TX	1,702,086	1,630,864	1,595,138	1,232,802	4.37	2.2	29.3
San Diego, CA	1,151,977	1,110,623	875,538	696,769	3.72	26.8	25.7
Dallas, TX	1,022,830	1,007,618	904,078	844,401	1.51	11.4	11.3
Phoenix, AZ	1,048,949	984,309	789,704	581,562	6.57	24.5	35.3
San Antonio, TX	998,905	935,393	785,880	654,153	6.79	19.1	20.2
San Jose, CA	816,884	782,224	629,442	445,779	4.43	24.3	36.7
Jacksonville, FL	665,070	635,230	540,920	528,865	4.70	17.4	21.7
Memphis, TN	614,289	618,652	646,356	623,350	-0.71	-5.6	3.5
El Paso, TX	579,307	515,342	425,259	322,261	12.41	21.2	32.0
New Orleans, LA	484,149	496,938	557,515	593,471	-2.67	-10.9	-5.9

Sources: Census of Population and Housing, 1990, U.S. Department of Commerce, Bureau of the Census, Summary Tape, File 1C (CD-ROM); Census of Population, Characteristics of the Population, Number of Inhabitants, U.S., U.S. Department of Commerce, Bureau of the Census, Summary, Table 27; 1970 Census of Population, Characteristics of Population, Number of Inhabitants, U.S., U.S. Department of Commerce, Bureau of the Census, Table 28.

TABLE 5.3
Metropolitan Regional Growth for the Sunbelt, 1970–1995

Area	Population				Percentage of Change		
	1995	1990	1980	1970	1990–1995	1980–1990	1970–1980
Los Angeles–Anaheim–Riverside, CA CMSA	15,362,165	14,531,529	11,497,549	9,980,850	5.7	26.4	15.2
San Francisco–Oakland–San Jose, CA CMSA	6,539,602	6,249,881	5,367,900	4,754,366	4.6	16.5	12.9
Dallas–Fort Worth, TX CMSA	4,449,875	4,037,282	2,930,568	2,351,568	10.2	32.6	24.6
Houston–Galveston–Brazoria, TX NECMA	4,164,393	3,731,029	3,099,942	2,169,128	11.6	19.7	42.9
Miami–Ft. Lauderdale, FL CMSA	3,443,501	3,192,725	2,643,766	1,887,892	7.9	20.8	40.0
Atlanta, GA MSA	3,431,983	2,959,500	2,138,136	1,684,200	16.0	32.5	27.0
San Diego, CA MSA	2,644,132	2,498,016	1,861,846	1,357,854	5.8	34.2	37.4
Phoenix, AZ MSA	2,563,582	2,238,498	1,509,175	971,228	14.5	40.6	55.4

Sources: State and Metropolitan Area Data Book 1991, U.S. Department of Commerce, Economics and Statistics Administration, Bureau of the Census, Table 2; *State and Metropolitan Area Data Book 1986*, U.S. Department of Commerce, Economics and Statistics Administration, Bureau of the Census, Table A; 1997 census.

Sunbelt is more formidable economically than other areas of the country. Between 1970 and 1980, almost three-fourths of all job growth took place in the Sunbelt. By the 1990s, however, the economic recession had hit Sunbelt areas especially hard. California, for example, suffered major job losses, as did Texas. Hence, current patterns of Sunbelt growth reflect a cycle of boom and bust.

Texas serves as an example of the Sunbelt shift. In 1950 its largest city, Houston, was ranked fourteenth in the country. Now Houston is our fourth largest city, just behind Chicago. The latter lost its longtime "second city" designation in 1980 when Los Angeles became more populous and was second in size to the largest city in the United States, New York. Texas, however, not only has one large metropolis, it has several. In fact, in 1990 it had more cities in the top 10 than any other state: Houston, Dallas, and San Antonio. Between 1970 and 1980, the Texas economy grew two and one-half times faster than the nation's economy, and its manufacturing growth from 1975 to 1980 alone was the fastest in the nation (Feagin, 1988).

More recently, explosive Sunbelt growth has turned to bust. Texas in particular was hit hard by the recession beginning in the 1980s. For this reason, the best way to describe Sunbelt development is in terms of boom and bust cycles rather than the once touted vision of unending growth. The case of Houston is illustrative of this pattern. Between 1970 and 1980, the city rode the crest of an unprecedented oil industry boom. Millions of people were drawn to the area and its job creation in manufacturing-related industries. After 1980, however, the boom in oil prices went bust as the price of a barrel plummeted from $30 to $11. Consequently, Houston entered a period of economic depression that was severe in the 1980s. The downturn lasted until 1987, during which time the city lost one in eight jobs and unemployment skyrocketed to well over 11 percent.

At present the economy has improved and a more stable pattern exists. The turnaround has been fueled by a shift from manufacturing dominance to service industries, in particular business, medical, and professional services, including law and engineering. Unemployment in the Sunbelt decreased in the 1990s, although it remains unclear whether the local economy will continue to improve as long as the country remains in recession.

Push and Pull Factors in Sunbelt Development

As we have seen, the Sunbelt had an advantage over other parts of the United States because of its comparative economic potential. This represents a potent pull factor. The region has other advantages as well. Energy and tourism are also exploitable industries. Cheap energy in particular and the warmth of the Sunbelt climate cut home maintenance costs drastically compared to the Frostbelt. Low energy costs are a major locational incentive for business, both now and in the future. Lower home maintenance costs and comparatively lower homeowner tax rates also provide considerable incentives for people to move to the region.

A comparison between Frostbelt and Sunbelt locations reveals advantages for the latter regarding labor costs. Sunbelt places do not have a past history of union organizing, and wages there are comparatively lower for manufacturing industries (although higher for many professional services). Sunbelt cities flaunt what they call a "good business climate." This usually means the absence of unions, tax breaks to business, and a general "hands-off" policy of minimal government regulation.

As in the case of suburbanization, one of the most potent supply-side forces that has developed the Sunbelt as a place to live and work is the operation of government intervention. To the extent that government subsidization of real estate development aided growth, it was instrumental in the population shift to the Sunbelt, where real estate is a major industry. But government involvement goes way beyond this obvious observation. Most of the heavily subsidized government industries in the United States, including agribusiness, energy, and military spending, are pillars of the Sunbelt economy.

Over the years, for example, the heavily subsidized agriculture industry has witnessed an immense shift of population out of farm residence, from over 30 percent in 1920 to around 3 percent today. At the same time, the family farm involved in agriculture has given way to the large land holdings of corporations engaged in agribusiness. Farm production has become more specialized and part of a total conglomerate structure involving the growing, processing, and marketing of food by giant corporations linked to the multinational system of capital (Shover, 1976; Hightower, 1975; Berry, 1972).

An important consequence of the rise to hegemony of agribusiness has been the shift of food production away from the Northeast and Midwest and to the Sunbelt (Sale, 1975; Coughlin, 1979), where large, open tracts of land are being used. According to Sale (1975), the shift to agribusiness in the Sunbelt has made the family farm uneconomical, causing many small farmers to sell their land to suburban developers. Finally, agribusiness remains subsidized on a grand scale by the federal government, whose Department of Agriculture is the second largest bureaucracy after the Department of Defense (Shover, 1976).

A second pillar of Sunbelt growth is the energy industry, which is also subsidized by the government. The Atomic Energy Commission and its government affiliates are among the largest employers in the state of New Mexico. In a case study of Houston, Texas, Joe R. Feagin (1988) shows how state supports underpin the energy industry, while at the same time business leaders espouse the virtues of "free enterprise." Feagin observes that when discussing government involvement, distinction is made between state forms of regulation, which are opposed by business, and state promotion and subsidization of economic activity, which is supported wholeheartedly.

In the case of the alleged "free enterprise" city of Houston, development was aided over the years by active government promotion of projects, while regulation was kept at a minimum. Contrary to the prevailing view of Sunbelt cities as economically backward until recent times, Houston was already a major agricultural center for the Texas cotton industry prior to the growth of the petroleum business. As the latter became the new focus of the local economy, government subsidization went hand in hand with the development of the city through private ventures. The federal government provided funds for the dredging of the Houston ship channel and periodically cleared the important port facility for ship traffic. In addition, oil refining and new petrochemical industries during the 1940s were supported directly by the feds, ranking sixth in receipt of national government plant investment (Feagin, 1988:68). Local businesses were the beneficiaries of these subsidies. As a consequence, Houston developed into the energy capital of the United States, only to be hit by a downturn and restructuring in the 1980s.

The third government-subsidized pillar of Sunbelt growth is military spending. During World War II, 60 percent of the total $74 billion spending effort went to the 15 states of the Sunbelt (Sale, 1975:170). Major industries in Sunbelt states were established during this time. Los Angeles became an aircraft and shipbuilding center. Kaiser Steel was formed in southern California, importing many workers from the East. Petrochemical and energy-related efforts were also subsidized, as we have already seen. Armaments industries and arsenals were expanded in the South and West. Huge military bases were constructed in California, Texas, Georgia, Florida, Alabama, and the Carolinas, among other Sunbelt states.

By the 1970s, the 15 Sunbelt states were receiving 44 percent of all military spending, including over 50 percent of the Defense Department payroll; had the majority of all military installations (60 percent); were employing more scientists and technicians than all the rest of the United States; and received 49 percent of "Pentagon research and development funds—the seed money that creates new technologies and industries" (Sale, 1975:171). All of this effort and money has created a new industrial core in the Sunbelt that is supported by government spending. Because taxes are collected across the United States but differentially spent on military-related activities, the federal government has for decades transferred wealth from all other regions of the United States to the Sunbelt.

Military spending in the Sunbelt region continued to grow throughout the 1980s on an immense scale. In 1975 military spending was approximately $90 billion. By 1987 it had increased to $390 billion, a fourfold change taking place after the Vietnam War (Gottdiener, 1990). Arms sales in particular became a key U.S. industry in the 1980s, prompting one observer to suggest that the nation had switched to a permanent war economy (Mandel, 1975; see also Melman, 1983; Stubbing and Mendel, 1986).

With Sunbelt prosperity so closely linked to the well-being of arms sales, cuts in the military budget have had profound effects, leading to a downturn in the economic fortunes of states such as California. For example, in July 1991, the McDonnell Douglas Corporation announced it was laying off about 1,000 workers from its southern California plant and shifting another 1,600 to its facilities in St. Louis, Missouri. The company cited "defense cutbacks and budget woes" (*Press Enterprise,* July 8, 1991: D-2) for its decision, which benefited the Midwest at the expense of the Sunbelt.

The loss of such military-related jobs has turned the once recession-proof economy of California into another case of Sunbelt boom and bust. Since 1989, California has had economic woes so severe that they are eclipsed only by the days of the Great Depression. In 1991, for example, the state lost more jobs than any other, twice as many as the second-worst state, New York. And there is still no sign of an economic reversal. In that same year and for the first time in California's history, more people canceled their driver's licenses because they had moved to another state than applied for one. In short, the population boom in California related to its economic expansion may be over, although low-wage, illegal aliens continue to flock to the state.

Finally, it is important to note that government military spending is a key support of many suburban regions, even in the Frostbelt, and is not simply a Sunbelt phenomenon. Thus, between 1975 and 1980, for example, Suffolk County in New York and suburban Monmouth County in New Jersey, respectively, had 20 percent and 16 percent of their labor force growth in military-related industries. By 1980, only Santa Clara County (i.e., Silicon Valley) had more military-related expansion—31 percent total employment growth.

Recent Sunbelt Trends

The shift to the Sunbelt is a spectacular example of regional realignment experienced by an advanced industrial country. Some urban scholars (Scott and Soja, 1996) have even argued for a new approach to urban studies modeled on "The Los Angeles School." (See Box 5.2.) As we will see in Chapter 13, there are parallels to the U.S. case in such countries as England, France, and particularly Germany, which have also undergone regional shifts as a consequence of high-technology industrial restructuring. Yet despite these changes, it is possible to overstate the case of Sunbelt prominence. There are at least three reasons to temper the notion that this region is gaining in autonomy and power at the expense of areas elsewhere: the need to place Sunbelt economic activities within a national and global context, the boom and bust cycle of development, and the enormous environmental costs of growth.

Economic Differentiation and the Global Economy. Because the U.S. economy has become more functionally specialized, many of the rapidly growing Sunbelt industries are tied administratively and economically to Frostbelt centers. The latter still retain the majority of corporate headquarters, for example. Banking and finance are still controlled by Frostbelt interests (Gottdiener, 1985). In addition, since the 1970s many U.S. firms have been either bought out or heavily invested in by multinational corporations that have headquarters in other countries. Sunbelt factories, no matter how stable in employment, may be only a part of some larger operation that also includes

Aerial view of Disneyland in Anaheim, California. Theme parks and even theme malls are important to Sunbelt growth.

BOX 5.2   THE LOS ANGELES SCHOOL

Los Angeles has almost always been viewed as an exception to the main-stream of American urban culture. Located on the continental margins, the city conjures up visions of unbridled urban sprawl, inconsequential architecture, freeways, sun, surf, and smog. Such images have been exaggerated by the movies and television that Hollywood has sold to the world. There is, however, a deep problem with the exceptionalist narratives of Los Angeles. They render much of what happens in the city as merely illustrative, a series of quirky set pieces, even staged performances. Yet, at least in appearance, Los Angeles bears a strong resemblance to other emerging "world cities," such as Mexico City and São Paulo, as well as to fast-growing urban centers in the United States, including Atlanta, Phoenix, and Seattle.

During the 1980s, a group of scholars and professionals based in southern California became self-consciously aware that what was happening in the Los Angeles region was somehow symptomatic of a broader transformation taking place in urban America. Just as the Chicago School emerged in the 1930s when that city was reaching new national prominence as the prototypical industrial metropolis, Los Angeles is already imprinted on the minds of a new generation of international urban scholars. The fundamental contrast between Chicago and Los Angeles is this: Los Angeles was from its inception a low-density, polycentric urban agglomeration in which development occurred in a patchwork quilt of mixed uses. The polycentrism of southern California has become more exaggerated with the passage of time, compounded today by the burgeoning multicultural and polyglot character of the population in the sprawling metropolis. The present-day confluence of global changes in economic organization, political structures, and sociocultural practices that southern California is experiencing almost *requires* the development of alternative theories of urban growth. Sometimes these theories overlap and coexist in their explanations of the emerging metropolis. The proliferation of diverse ways of understanding is consistent with the project of postmodernism; it is no coincidence that some hold Los Angeles to be the prototypical postmodern city.

Adherents of the "Los Angeles School" do not argue that the city is unique or that it is necessarily a harbinger of the future, although both viewpoints are at some level demonstrably true. It is simply that at present, an especially powerful intersection of empirical and theoretical research projects has emerged in a particular place at a particular time, these projects have attracted the attention of a critical mass of scholars and practitioners, and the world is facing the prospect of a Pacific century in which southern California is likely to become a global capital. The strength and potential of the Los Angeles School derive principally from the intersection of these events and the promise they hold for the re-creation of urban theory. The southern California prototype, with its emphasis on multicentered, dispersed patterns of relatively low-density growth and multicultural/multiethnic enclaves, may yet become a new paradigm of metropolitan development (Dear, Schockman, and Hise, 1998: x–xi, 1–2).

Frostbelt command and control centers or worldwide organizations. Hence, splits between the regions are *not* autonomous. They reflect instead a growing regional specialization in the United States and the entire world as mutinational interests utilize space and place to improve economic performance.

The Cycles of Growth and Decline. As we have seen, the best way to describe Sunbelt development is in terms of boom and bust cycles that fluctuate relatively rapidly. Sunbelt residents who have been attracted to the region by visions of affluence may have to tolerate a life of feast or famine. At present, the national recession has hit many Sunbelt areas especially hard. The powerful states of Texas and California, once thought immune to downturns, have been in the doldrums since the late 1980s. Unemployment was above the national average for a time. California experienced two straight years of fiscal crises that required cuts in spending, wage freezes, and a reassessment of the state's credit rating. Social services such as education are now besieged due to lack of funds, and the quality of life has deteriorated accordingly.

The characteristic woes of the region are exemplified by Silicon Valley, also known as Santa Clara County, in California. This region was once touted as the exemplary high-tech boom area that even countries should emulate in their development plans. Currently the region is called the "Valley of Gloom" (Smith, 1992) because of the severity of its recession. Much of its heralded job creation has shifted to other places around the globe, and its businesses are besieged because of declining sales, while some have fallen victim to both foreign and domestic competitors. As one newspaper report states,

> Not only has Santa Clara County lost 20,000 manufacturing jobs in the last 18 months, industry analysts estimate that tens of thousands of newly created electronic industry jobs have gone elsewhere in the same period. . . . High tech manufacturing in this area is no longer competitive with other areas of the country or the world. Even if the economy rebounds, we're not going back to the double-digit job growth we enjoyed the last two decades. (Smith, 1992:A-1)

It may be possible that this area will experience a revival much like the one in Houston (see above), and the cycle of boom and bust will start up again. But as the newspaper report indicates, a profound sense of pessimism paints the future in more modest growth terms. Silicon Valley is typical of other high-tech growth poles. Its population is both well educated and diverse—37 percent of those over 18 years have at least a two-year college degree, and 12 percent of its population is foreign born. These residents have been used to several decades of affluence and growth. At present, they are learning to suffer with the rest of the nation during the current recession.

The Environmental Costs of Rapid Growth. Because it has been the site of rapid and largely minimally planned growth, the Sunbelt region has also encountered monumental environmental problems. In fact, as of 1991, we may be poised at a point of immense growth difficulties for many areas of the Sunbelt. The environment has long suffered the initial impact of development. Unique and pristine formations, such as the Tampa and San Francisco bays, have been almost destroyed biologically in the wake of change. Clear cutting of virgin forests, pollution of lakes and streams, fouling of beaches with oil or sewage, and emission of choking smog are but some of the environmental problems already well established in the South and West. After years of uncertainty regarding published accounts of the effects of smog, for example, it was recently reported that constant exposure produces *permanent* lung damage in both children and adults (*Press Enterprise,* May 17, 1992: AA-1). The population of Los Angeles lives in just such an environment, yet the presence of damaging smog has done little to date to stem the otherwise constant stream of new arrivals to the region (see Chapter 14 for a more detailed discussion of the environment and the sociospatial perspective).

In more recent years other effects of population growth have appeared. Crime is a serious problem, for example. New York City is often stereotyped as an unsafe city. Its murder rate was 26 per 100,000 persons in 1989. Houston's rate, however, was 27 for that year, Dallas' was 35, and New Orleans' was 47. Even Los Angeles had a high rate of 25, less than New York but the same as Chicago and much more than Boston (17). Sunbelt cities may just be the most unsafe and violent in the nation, containing 9 of our 10 most dangerous metro areas (MacDonald, 1984)—see Chapter 10.

In addition to crime, overcrowding in schools and declining educational quality are a typical Sunbelt lament. These conditions are expected to get worse as the western and southern states encounter intractable budget crises. In 1991 California suffered its largest budget deficit in its history, and educational spending was the first casualty.

In rapidly growing areas, traffic congestion is so bad that it is fast approaching gridlock. It's not uncommon for commuters in parts of California to travel four hours both ways by car, especially when no other alternatives to commuting are available. Finally, housing prices have soared in the best locations, making first-home purchasing progressively out of reach. But despite these and other constraints, life in the Sunbelt continues to attract new people, especially highly trained professionals who have the ability to find well-paying jobs (Kephart, 1991). It is expected that the 15 states of the Sunbelt will continue to grow in the future. Estimates are that this region will contain half the nation's population by the year 2000.

Since the 1960s, the relationships among people, spatial living, and working arrangements have profoundly changed. Gone is the highly compact industrial city with a working-class culture and labor-influenced, democratic politics. In its place, everyday life now transpires in multinucleated metropolitan regions across the country. Development is dominated by the population shifts to the suburbs and the Sunbelt, while the vision of unending growth and affluence has been tempered by the experience of living through rapid cycles of boom and bust. These changes have been explained by the sociospatial perspective, which emphasizes the pull factors of economic and technological change (as do other approaches) but also the importance of government intervention, real estate, and the restructuring of sociospatial arrangements in business and residential activities.

CHAPTER

6

THE RISE OF URBAN SOCIOLOGY

A special inquiry devoted to urban phenomena was the premier achievement of early U.S. sociology. During the 1890s, the University of Chicago started the first sociology department in the country, headed by Albion Small. Almost immediately a prominent role was given to a former journalist, Robert E Park. Small and Park had something in common. They had both gone as students to Germany, in particular to take courses with Max Weber. At that time, the early 1900s, only France and Germany had professional sociologists, and Max Weber was acknowledged as the leading social thinker of his day, although a second sociologist, Emile Durkheim, had accumulated a growing reputation in France.

Early sociologists were concerned with the impact of urbanization on European society. The political revolutions of the 1800s brought an end to earlier ideas that the social and political order reflected a divine plan—but what exactly would the new social order created by widespread changes in the economic and social structure look like? In the wake of the French Revolution, questions about how social order itself could be maintained were not simply a matter of idle speculation.

Ferdinand Toennies (1855–1936) is one of the early German social philosophers who addressed these questions (see Box 6.1). In *Gemeinschaft und Gesellschaft* (published in 1887 and often translated as "community and society," although "community and association" more accurately reflects the original meaning), Toennies sketched out an evolutionary view of the development of human society. The great period of industrialization that transformed European societies beginning in the late 1700s signified a change from community to association. His ideas are often used to highlight differences between village life of the preindustrial period and urban life of the industrial period, and between small-town life and that of the large city more generally. Toennies saw that the transition from community (where individual families have long histories, individuals interact with one another on a personal basis because they often work together

BOX 6.1 FERDINAND TOENNIES ON *GEMEINSCHAFT* AND *GESELLSCHAFT*

The very existence of *Gemeinschaft* rests in the consciousness of belonging together and the affirmation of the condition of mutual dependence which is posed by that affirmation. Living together may be called the animal soul of *Gemeinschaft*, for it is the condition of its active life, of a shared feeling of pleasure and pain, of a shared enjoyment of the commonly possessed goods, by which one is surrounded, and by the cooperation in teamwork as well as in divided labor. Working together may be conceived of as the rational or human soul of *Gemeinschaft*. It is higher, more conscious cooperation in the unity of spirit and purpose, including, therefore, a striving for common or shared ideals, as invisible goods that are knowable only to thought. Regarding being together it is descent (blood), regarding living together it is soil (land), regarding working together it is occupation (*Beruf*) that is substance as it were, by which the wills of men, which otherwise are far apart from and even antagonistic to each other, are essentially united (Toennies, 1971:69).

The city is typical of *Gesellschaft* in general. It is essentially a commercial town and, in so far as commerce dominates its productive labor, a factory town. Its wealth is capital wealth which, in the form of trade, usury, or industrial capital, is used and multiplies. Capital is the means for the appropriation of products of labor or for the exploitation of workers. The city is also the center of science and culture, which always goes hand in hand with commerce and industry. Here the arts must make a living; they are exploited in a capitalist way. Thoughts spread with astonishing rapidity (Toennies, 1957:227–28).

or are related to one another, and all jobs are interdependent on one another) to society (where individuals often interact with others whom they do not personally know and work at jobs that are seemingly unrelated to one another) resulted in a weakening of social ties and a shared sense of belonging to a meaningful community.

Emile Durkheim (1858–1917), who was appointed to the first chair of sociology at the Sorbonne in Paris in 1883, also wrote about the changes brought about by industrialization. In his work *The Division of Labor in Society,* Durkheim discussed many of the same issues presented earlier by Toennies, this time under the labels of *mechanical solidarity* and *organic solidarity.* In the preindustrial village, individuals were held together by the mechanical bonds of kinship and social interdependence—mechanical because they were predetermined and could not be changed as long as the individual remained within the local village. In the industrial city, individuals were no longer bound by the mechanical bonds of kinship; instead they could work at new types of jobs and have greater opportunities for interaction with a wider range of people. These were organic bonds that flowed naturally from the increased social differentiation brought about by the division of labor. If these terms seem to be used backwards (we often think of cities and of work in factories as being mechanical), it is important to realize that Durkheim was convinced that the new industrial economy was an improvement over the limited opportunities of feudal society, and may have deliberately chosen words with a positive connotation to represent the modern city. Durkheim was certain that the new industrial order would replace the earlier ways of life: "with the coming of the industrial economy, village society has disappeared, never to come again."

A contrasting view to that of Durkheim was the perspective of German sociologist Friedrich Engels (1820–1895), who lived in England in the mid-1800s. Engels wrote a classic study, *The Condition of the Working Class in England* (1973), which devoted a chapter to what he called "The Great Towns." According to Engels, the evils of industrialization and capitalism were intensified by the space of the city. This is a perspective to which we will return in the next chapter.

The most influential European in U.S. urban sociology at the beginning was Georg Simmel (1858–1918). He viewed the city in cultural terms and was concerned with the way urban life transformed individual consciousness. For Simmel, everyday existence within the city altered the way people thought and acted compared to traditional society. Both Park and Small took this "interactive" perspective back home with them. In the United States, the work of the early Chicago School that followed was less concerned with historical and comparative studies in the manner of Weber and more focused on social behavior and interaction within the urban milieu in the manner of Simmel.

Any good discussion of American urban sociology must begin with explaining an important distinction. There are really *two* distinct organizing topics in the field: urbanization and urbanism. *Urbanization* refers to the city formation or building process. It studies the way social activities locate themselves in space and according to interdependent processes of societal development and change. Its analysis is often historical and comparative. Urbanization charts and tries to understand the rise and fall of great cities. Many of the discussions in the previous chapters were about urbanization.

Urbanism, in contrast, takes the city formation process as given and seeks instead to understand the ways of life that transpire within this container. Urbanism deals with culture, with meanings, symbols, patterns of daily life, and processes of adjustment to the environment of the city, but also with conflicts, with forms of political organization at the street, neighborhood, and city levels.

While both Max Weber and Friedrich Engels stressed the relation between the historical nature of the city and its ways of life, Simmel was more concerned with the latter. Early U.S. urban sociology followed Simmel most closely and focused on patterns of activity within cities rather than addressing the topic of U.S. urbanization or city formation. Yet for Simmel, the study of life within the city was not meant as an "urban sociology." Simmel was concerned with *modernity,* or the transition from a traditional society characterized by social relations based on intimacy or kinship (known as "primary" relations), by a feudal economy based on barter to an industrial society situated within cities and dominated by impersonal, specialized social relations based on compartmentalized roles (known as "secondary" relations), and by a money economy based on rational calculation of profit and loss. For Simmel, the subtle aspects of modernity were displayed most clearly within the large city or metropolis and through consciously directed behaviors. Simmel gives us a social psychology of modernity that Robert Park took to be the sociology of urbanism, or "urban sociology."

Simmel on the City

What was it like to confront modernity; and why was Simmel so impressed with the city as the vehicle for change? Consider, if you will, a German farmer from Bavaria. His life was tuned to the daily rhythms of agriculture. Nature and his own physical labor provided the boundaries within which the farming endeavor was framed. The regime of labor on the land was early to bed, because darkness meant little work could be done, and early to rise, because it was necessary to use every second of daylight for work—even dawn and twilight. This farmer was immersed in a social world of primary, kinship relations. His principal contacts were members of his family, both immediate and extended. Perhaps several generations and families lived together in the same location and worked the land. Beyond this primary network, the farmer would interact with individuals who aided his enterprise. Most typically he visited a local service center, perhaps a small town. There he was surely involved in a network of people who knew him well. In this kind of traditional society, it was entirely possible that no money changed hands while farm produce and needed commodities were exchanged. Barter, credit, and informal agreements among known persons characterized the social relations of this world.

As Simmel might suggest, suppose this individual—call him Hans—lost the farm and his family in some personal tragedy. With a small amount of money, he now traveled to Berlin to begin a new life. He went to this modern city precisely because it offered him an alternative to the rural, traditional existence of farming. Karl Marx, writing in the nineteenth century, would have focused on Hans's conversion to an industrial worker. He would have taken us into the factory with Hans and described his encounter with abstract capital (the machine), with the relations of production (the assembly line, the factory building, and the daily schedule of work), and with class relations (interaction with the workers and the boss). Simmel virtually ignored this entire domain of the factory, which could be termed the *immediate* environment of capitalism, and focused instead on the larger context of daily life, the *extended* environment—namely, the city.

Hans stands on the corner of a large boulevard in Berlin teeming with daytime auto traffic. He has to dodge the steady stream of pedestrians just to stand still and watch, since everything else is in constant motion. At first shock, Hans would be paralyzed by the "excess of nervous stimulation," according to Simmel. Haven't we all had a similar experience upon visiting a large city? Loud noises from traffic, people in the crowds calling after one another, strangers touching him as they passed without an acknowledgment, and more—noise, noise, and noise. Hans would find himself in a totally new environment that *demanded* an adjustment and a response.

According to Simmel, small-town life required Hans to develop strong, intimate ties to those with whom he interacted. Here in the city, the excess of stimulation requires a defensive response. These are the characteristics of urbanism noted by Simmel. Hans would (1) develop what Simmel called the "blasé" attitude—a blurring of the senses, a filtering out of all that was loud and impinging but also irrelevant to Hans's own personal needs. Emotional reserve and indifference replace acute attention to the details of the environment.

Georg Simmel. Simmel was author of "The Metropolis and Mental Life."

Hans would require the satisfaction of his needs. Yes, he would encounter capitalism and, no doubt, sell his labor for a wage, as Marx had observed. Simmel agreed with Marx about the necessity of that transaction. It would (2) *reduce the quality* of Hans's capabilities simply to *the quantity* of his labor time—the time he spent at work, for a wage. It would make his work equivalent to a sum of money, no more, no less. That sum of money exchanged for Hans's labor time would be all the employing capitalist would provide. Hans would quickly see that absolutely no concern for his health-related, spiritual, communal, sexual, or any other type of human need would be involved in his relationship with his employer. In short, the world of capitalism was (3) an *impersonal world* of pure monetary exchange.

Simmel, unlike Marx, showed how the impersonal money economy extended outside the factory to characterize all other transactions in the city. Hans would use his paycheck to buy the needs of life, but in these transactions, too, impersonal or secondary social relations prevailed. Unless he went to a small store and frequented it every day, he would simply be viewed as (4) an *anonymous* customer being provided with mass-produced items for purchase. As a city dweller, he might find himself more frequently going to a department store where (5) a mass *spectacle* of consumption would be on display.

In all these transactions, Hans would have to be very careful. His weekly paycheck could go only so far. He would have to count how much each item cost and then budget himself accordingly. This (6) *rational calculation* would be at the heart of his daily life. Everything would be measured by him, just as costs were carefully measured at the factory. Rational calculation of money would require knowledge and technique. If Hans mastered it successfully along with gaining mastery over the consumer world of the city, he could look down at his country-bumpkin cousins. City life, for Simmel, was a life of the intellect, and everywhere the relation between the money economy and the rational calculation needed to survive in the world of capitalism prevailed. Those in the city who could not master the technique of money management—of profit and loss—would surely be lost.

We are not finished with the example of Hans. In the traditional society of the country, the rhythm of life was provided by nature. The city environment requires adjustments to (7) a *second nature*—the orchestration of daily activities as governed by clock time and as played out within a constructed space. All life in the city follows the schedule of capitalist industrialization or modernity. If Hans didn't own a watch before coming to the city, he now needed one. Time and money constitute the two types of calculation necessary for survival in the second nature of the urban milieu—the built environment of concrete, steel, and glass that is the city.

Finally, Simmel also commented on the qualitative value of an experience like Hans's. He did not see the transformation as something that was necessarily bad. Hans would be cast in a calculating and impersonal world, but he would also be (8) *freed* from the restrictions of traditional society and its timebound dictates. Hans would be free to discriminate about the types of friends he chose, about the job he took (within strong constraints, mind you), and about where he lived. To Simmel, modernity meant the possibility of immense individual freedom in addition to constraint.

For Simmel, the freedom of the city meant, above all else, that Hans would be free to pursue and even create his own individuality. Provided he had the money, of course—an occurrence that Marx would doubt—Hans could cultivate himself. He could dress according to some distinct fashion, develop hobbies he could share with others, perhaps take up the violin and join a neighborhood string quartet; he could enjoy a certain brand of cigar or shoes, or attend night classes at the university—even Simmel's own lectures. Could Hans and Simmel have eventually met? The city allowed the possibility of attaining such cultural freedom, and the signs of individual cultivation—the clothes, cigars, friends, lovers, discussion groups, opera, art, novels—were collectively the signs of modernity that we may also call urbanism.

Robert Park and the Chicago School of Urban Sociology

Robert Park (1865–1944) may well be the most interesting figure not simply in the development of the Chicago School of urban sociology but in the history of American sociology more generally (see Box 6.2). Born at the end of the Civil War, Park at-

BOX 6.2 ROBERT PARK ON INVESTIGATING HUMAN BEHAVIOR IN THE URBAN ENVIRONMENT

In an early essay published in the *American Journal of Sociology*, Robert Park outlined a series of research questions for studying the metropolis. These questions would allow students to study the "neighborhoods, racial communities, and segregated city areas, existing within or on the outer rims of great cities." Among the questions he posed were the following:

What are the elements of which these communities are composed?
To what extent are the communities the product of a selective process?
How do people get in and out of the social group formed in the local community?
What are the relative permanence and stability of the populations of these communities?
What are the age, sex, and social composition of the people in the community?

Some of the questions clearly reflect the social theory of the day: "What is there in the subconsciousness—in the forgotten or dimly remembered experiences—of this neighborhood which determines its sentiments and attitudes?" Other questions demonstrate Park's personal interest in the mass media and the urban press: "What does the community regard as a matter of fact? What is news? What is the general run of attention? What models does the community imitate and are these within or without the group?" Above all, the questions reveal Park not simply as a master teacher but as an acute observer of life in the modern metropolis: "What is the social ritual, i.e., what things must one do in the neighborhood in order to escape being regarded with suspicion or looked upon as peculiar?" (Park, 1915: 577–612)

tended the University of Michigan and began his career as a newspaper reporter, first for the *Minneapolis Journal* and later for the *New York Journal*. He was assigned to a "police beat" where he would have to pound the streets of the city to develop leads and check facts for his newspaper articles. He later became city editor for the *Detroit Tribune* and drama critic and reporter for the *Chicago Journal*.

Park decided to go to graduate school, and studied first at Harvard University and then at Heidelberg University in Berlin, where he attended lectures by Georg Simmel. He returned to the United States in 1903 and met Booker T. Washington, the most influential African American leader of the day and the founder of the Tuskegee Institute. For the next decade Park would serve as Washington's personal secretary, revising papers and speeches. Park used his spare time to investigate lynchings and write about race relations in the United States. In 1912 Park organized a conference on race relations at Tuskegee, and he was approached by W. I. Thomas, who recently had been hired at the University of Chicago. Thomas wanted to know if Park would come to the university and join other scholars in the newly formed department of sociology—the first of its kind in the United States (Blumer, 1984; Mathews, 1977).

In 1913, at age 49, Park joined the faculty of the University of Chicago. Park's approach to the sociological study of the urban environment was clear: He urged his students to "get the seat of their pants dirty" by getting out into the neighborhoods of the city, studying the many different groups of people who had come there. While Park worked on his own study of the development of the immigrant press in the United States, he and Ernest Burgess conducted undergraduate classes and graduate seminars that required students to go into the community, collect data from business-people, interview area residents, and report back with their information.

The members of the sociology department at the University of Chicago became uniquely interested in their city and were inspired to study the great human drama transpiring outside their windows. During the 1920s, there were already several efforts to monitor the characteristics and needs of the urban population. The settlement house movement and people such as Jane Addams (see Chapter 4) were concerned about urban problems. They conducted some of the earliest surveys in the United States and planned schemes of intervention to aid the large numbers of working poor.

Robert Park and his associates at the University of Chicago were less concerned than was Simmel with the city dweller's encounter with modernity and more involved in detailed study of the specific Chicago milieu. They were responsible for a number of important conceptual advances in the field of urban sociology.

From the very first, the Chicago School urbanists adopted a conceptual position that we call *human ecology*—the study of the process of human group adjustment to the environment. While European thinkers such as Weber, Marx, and Simmel viewed the city as an environment where larger social forces of capitalism played themselves out in a human drama, Chicago School urbanists avoided the study of capitalism per se, preferring instead a biologically based way of conceptualizing urban life. For them urban analysis was a branch of human ecology. Their ideas brought them closest to the work of the philosopher Herbert Spencer, who also viewed society as dominated by biological rather than economic laws of development. Economic competition, in this view, was a special case of the struggle for survival. All individuals in the city were caught up in this struggle and adjusted to it in various ways.

According to Robert Park, the social organization of the city resulted from the struggle for survival that then produced a distinct and highly complex division of labor, because people tried to do what they were best at in order to compete. Urban life for Park was organized on two separate levels: the "biotic" and the "cultural." The *biotic* level refers to the forms of organization produced by species' competition over scarce environmental resources. The *cultural* level refers to the symbolic and psychological adjustment processes and to the organization of urban life according to shared sentiments, much like the qualities Simmel also studied.

In Park's work, the biotic level stressed the importance of biological factors for understanding social organization and the urban effects of economic competition. In contrast, the cultural component of urban life operated in neighborhoods that were held together by cooperative ties involving shared cultural values among people with similar backgrounds. Hence, local community life was organized around what Park called a "moral order" of cooperative, symbolic ties, while the larger city composed of separate communities was organized through competition and functional differentiation. In Park's later work, however, the complex notion of *urbanism* as combining competition and cooperation, or the biotic and the cultural levels, was dropped in favor of an emphasis on the biotic level alone as the basic premise of urban ecology. This led to some of the earliest critiques of the ecological perspective, faulting it for ignoring the role of culture in the city, or what Simmel would call the important influence of modernity, and for neglecting the basis of community (Alihan, 1938), which was social and not biological.

Other members of the early Chicago School translated the social Darwinism of Park into a spatially attuned analysis. For Roderick McKenzie, the fundamental quality of the struggle for existence was position, or *location,* for either the individual, the group, or some city institution such as a business firm. Economic competition, or the struggle for existence, affected spatial position. Groups or individuals that were successful took over the better positions in the city, such as the higher ground, the choicest business locations, or the preferred neighborhoods. Those less successful were relegated to less desirable positions. In this way the population, under pressure of economic competition, sorted itself out within the city space.

McKenzie explained land-use patterns as the product of competition and an economic division of labor, which deployed objects and activities in space according to the roles they played in society. Thus, if a firm needed a particular location to perform its function, it competed with others for that location. The patterns resulting from that process were studied by ecologists.

Ernest Burgess's Model of Urban Growth

Ernest W. Burgess developed a theory of city growth and differentiation based on the social Darwinist or biologically derived principles that were common in the work of Park and McKenzie. According to Burgess, the city constantly grew because of population pressures. This, in turn, triggered a dual process of central agglomeration and commercial decentralization; that is, spatial competition attracted new activities to the center of the city but also repelled other activities to the fringe area. As activities themselves located on the fringe, the fringe itself was pushed farther out from the city, and so on.

Thus, the city continually grew outward as activities that lost out in central city competition were relocated to peripheral areas. This sorting led, in turn, to further spatial and functional differentiation as activities were deployed according to competitive advantages. In Burgess's theory, the city would eventually take on the form of a highly concentrated central business district that would dominate the region and be the site for the highest competitive land prices, while the surrounding area would comprise four distinct concentric rings (1925:51; see Figure 6.1).

Ernest Burgess of the Chicago School.

The importance of Burgess's model cannot be overemphasized. First, he explained the pattern of homes, neighborhoods, and industrial and commercial locations in terms of the ecological theory of competition over "position," or location. In short, competition produced a certain space and a certain social organization in space. Both of these dimensions were pictured in the concentric zone model. Those who could afford it lived near the center; those who could not arranged themselves in concentric zones around the city center. Such a model required, among other things, that the center have the most jobs and social activities and, hence, that it be the most desirable location. This view was challenged in the models of Hoyt (Figure 6.2) and Harris and Ullman (Figure 6.3), which we will discuss shortly.

Second, Burgess's model explained the shifting of population and activities within the space of the city according to two distinct but related processes: *centralization* and *decentralization*. His theory explicitly related social processes to spatial patterns—a most important link for all theorizing about the city that was to follow and a view that is quite compatible with the aims of the new urban sociology.

Finally, Burgess revealed that the characteristics of the social organization of the urban population were *spatially* deployed. A gradient running from the center to the periphery characterized the attributes of the urban population. Individual traits such as mental illness, gang membership, criminal behavior, and racial background were found to be clustered along the center/periphery gradient of the city. Cutting across the urban form from the Central Business District (known as the CBD) to the outskirts, Chicago

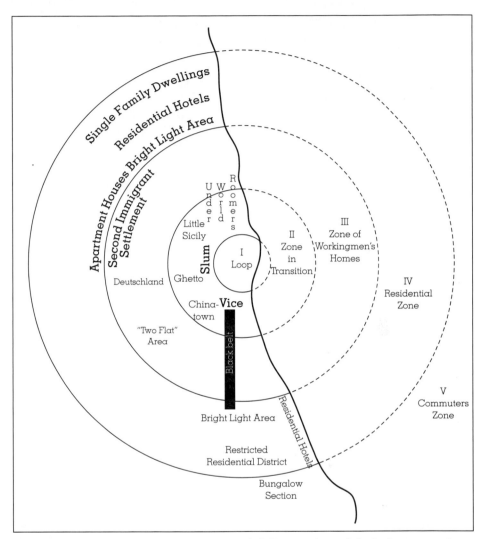

Figure 6.1   Burgess's concentric zone model. Burgess's model of urban growth included ethnic neighborhoods and geographic features of the city of Chicago in the 1920s.

School researchers, using census data, found that the incidence of social pathology decreased while homeownership and the number of nuclear families increased. The inner zones, therefore, were discovered to be the sites of crime, illness, gang warfare, broken homes, and many other indicators of social disorganization or problems.

In practice, however, research on the internal structure of cities contradicted Burgess's view of concentric zones. Two other models of the city were proposed that argued that cities had multicenters rather than a single focus. The first critique of Burgess's model was proposed by Homer Hoyt (1933) and was called "sector theory."

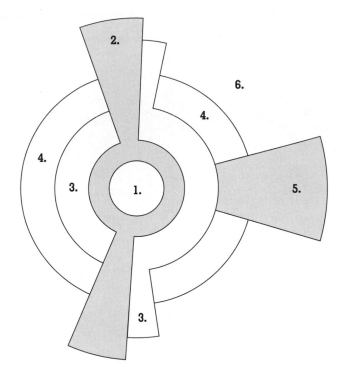

1. Central Business District **4.** Middle-Class Housing
2. Industrial Manufacturing **5.** Luxury, Upper-Middle- and Upper-Class Housing
3. Working-Class Housing   **6.** Commuter Zones

Figure 6.2   Homer Hoyt's sector model emphasized the tendency for activities
such as manufacturing and retailing to concentrate in different sectors.

Hoyt suggested that cities were carved up not by concentric zones but by unevenly
shaped sectors within which different economic activities tended to congregate together, that is, agglomerate (see Figure 6.2). Hoyt suggested that all activities, but especially manufacturing and retailing, had the tendency to spin off away from the center and agglomerate in sectors that expanded outward. Thus, the city grew in irregular
blobs rather than in Burgess's neat circles.

The idea of multiple nuclei as the shape of the city further developed Hoyt's break
with Burgess and is close to the current multicentered approach used in this book (see
Chapter 1). It was introduced in a classic paper by Chauncy Harris and Edward Ullman
(1945). They suggested that *within* any city, separate functions and their particular
needs require concentration within specific and specialized districts (see Figure 6.3).
Thus, within cities, similar activities often locate in the same area, forming agglomerations, or minicenters. Cities often grow asymmetrically around these multiple nuclei.

A common assumption of all of these models is that the city remains the central
place that dominates all other areas. In recent years this way of thinking about urbanized areas has declined, and a focus on the individual city has given way to the re-

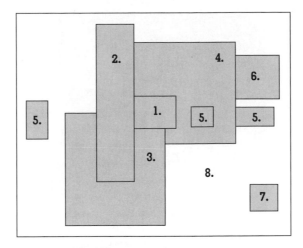

1. Central Business District
2. Manufacturing District
3. Working-Class Houses
4. Middle-Class Housing
5. Luxury, Upper-Middle- and Upper-Class Houses
6. An Outlying Central Business District
7. A Suburban Industrial Park
8. Commuter Zone

Figure 6.3   Harris and Ullman's multiple nuclei model. Harris and Ullman's model emphasized the development of multiple centers for different urban functions

gional metropolitan perspective, which stresses the relative independence of multiple centers, as we have discussed in previous chapters.

While ecologists were concerned with location and with thinking of social activities as located in space, their biologically based explanation for perceived activities and spatial patterns has been rejected in recent years in favor of the new urban sociology (see Gottdiener and Feagin, 1988).

Despite its limitations, under the leadership of the Chicago School pioneers, a large body of research was produced whose hallmark was the connection between social processes of city living and a specific location in urban space. That location, furthermore, was perceived as a consequence of competition over scarce resources, of which one was space itself. Hence, place and space saturate the conceptions of the early Chicago School.

Louis Wirth: Urbanism as a Way of Life

A short time after Park, Burgess, and McKenzie worked in tandem to discover the forces creating patterns of daily life within the city, another Chicago School sociologist, Louis Wirth, defined a different theory of urban space. Other ecologists viewed spatial patterns as caused by powerful social factors such as the struggle for survival. The phenomena they observed were the outcomes of social forces operating within the city. Thus, Park and his associates viewed urban space as a *container,* some built environment that encloses the action. Wirth's idea was different. He wanted to know what it was about the city itself that produced unique behaviors that might be called an "urban way of life." In

Louis Wirth of the Chicago School.
Wirth was the author of "Urbanism as a
way of life," one of the best-known
essays in urban sociology.

this emphasis, Wirth returned to Simmel. However, while Simmel (and Weber and Marx) attributed much of the city way of life to the influence of larger systemic forces, especially capitalism and its money economy, Wirth aimed for a generalized theory that ignored forces having origins outside the city. He studied the characteristics of people in the city and how life there might produce a distinct "urban" culture. Hence, "urbanism," or an urban way of life, became the *dependent* variable to be explained.

Wirth settled on the isolation of three factors. Urbanism was produced in *relatively large* (population size), *densely* populated settlements containing heterogeneous people (different backgrounds); that is, urbanism was a product of large population size, density, and heterogeneity. Wirth's approach was an important advance because he provided a set of factors that could be analyzed statistically according to their effects. Hence, it was a theory with true predictive power. Given a sample of cities, the higher each one scored on the three factors of size, density, and heterogeneity, the more we could expect it to house a true urban culture.

Wirth's theory was very impressive for his time (the 1930s) because of its predictive potential. Problems arose when he tried to define what precisely an urban culture would be like. Recall the example of Hans. Simmel gave us a detailed picture that contained both negative and positive aspects. Essentially, Simmel viewed the city as simply *different*. In his formulation, Wirth stressed the dark side of Simmel's vision: Urbanism as a culture would be characterized by aspects of social disorganization. Most central to Wirth's view was the shift from primary to secondary social relations. Wirth tended to see urban anonymity as debilitating. More specifically, the effects of the three factors on social life can be expressed as a series of propositions, as indicated in Box 6.3.

BOX 6.3 WIRTH'S PROPOSITIONS

Size Propositions
1. The larger the population, the greater the chances for diversity and individualization.
2. Competition and formal mechanisms of social control would replace primary relations of kinship as a means of organizing society.
3. The larger the population, the greater the specialization and functional diversity of social roles.
4. Anonymity and fragmentation of social interaction increase with size.

Density Propositions
1. Greater density intensifies the effects of large population size.
2. Greater density creates the blasé attitude and the need to tune out excessive stimulation.
3. Greater density produces greater tolerance for living closely with strangers, but also greater stress.
4. Escape from density produces development of the fringe and greater land value in suburbia.
5. Density increases competition, compounding the effects of size.

Heterogeneity Propositions
1. The greater the heterogeneity, the more tolerance among groups.
2. Heterogeneity allows ethnic and class barriers to be broken down.
3. Individual roles and contacts become compartmentalized according to different circles of contacts. Anonymity and depersonalization in public life increase.

In the years following Wirth's work, his theory has been exhaustively tested, mainly because it was so clearly stated (Fischer, 1975). Unfortunately, the core assertion that size, density, and heterogeneity cause behaviors considered urban has not been borne out. If we look at the propositions above, many of the assertions seem true of the big city, and hence they help to provide a more detailed picture of what urbanism as a culture is like. However, while the theory contains some truth, we cannot say along with Wirth that the factors he chose produce such results. The large city merely *concentrates* the effects of societal forces producing city culture. Surely we know that rural areas are just as afflicted by crime as is the central city, although the types of crimes and their intensity may vary.

In other examples, studies of social pathology such as mental illness find that rural areas score higher in some cases than do many cities. Other indicators of social disorganization, such as high divorce rates, are ubiquitous in the society. Density causes stress, but urbanites have been very resourceful in finding ways to alleviate the potential stress caused by crowding, and many suburbanites live in apartment complexes which are more densely concentrated than many urban residential neighborhoods. In short, we should not discard the assertion that different aspects of social organization or disorganization are dispersed in patterns of a spatial nature in our society. However, we can question whether those patterns are related to the difference that cities themselves make (see Fischer, 1976).

Finally, Louis Wirth held strongly to the view that the true effects of urbanism would occur as a matter of evolution as cities operated on immigrant groups to break down traditional ways of interacting over time. He did not see the larger city acting as an environment to bring about immediately the change he predicted. These things would take time, perhaps a generation. In Chapter 8, we will return to the topic of urbanism and continue discussing the refinement of Wirth's ideas up to the present.

In the main, Wirth can be remembered as showing us a *style* of doing urban research that differed from Chicago School field work. While others took to the streets to record the everyday life found in cities, Wirth inspired a subsequent generation to plow through census data and derive statistical regularities of urban living. Much urban research is like that to this day. In Chapter 10 we will return to the theory of urban culture and find aspects of Wirth's theory itself that are still useful as well.

The Chicago School: Studies

The work of the early Chicago School should never be forgotten. For about a decade, beginning with 1925, a veritable flood of work poured out of the sociology department. Counting some of the books alone (i.e., ignoring masters and Ph.D. theses produced at that time), the following list samples their accomplishments. All these books were published by the University of Chicago press: F. Thrasher (1927), *The Gang;* Louis Wirth (1928), *The Ghetto;* Ruth S. Cavan (1928), *Suicide;* Clifford S. Shaw (1930), *The Jackroller;* Harvey W. Zorbaugh (1929), *The Gold Coast and the Slum;* E. Franklin Frazier (1932), *The Negro Family in Chicago;* Paul G. Cressey (1932), *The Taxi-dance Hall;* Walter C. Reckless (1933), *Vice in Chicago;* Norman Hayner (1936), *Hotel Life;* and then later, St. Clair Drake and Horace R. Cayton (1945), *Black Metropolis.* Regarding this list, it can also be said that while gender issues were not well articulated at that time, women were involved in the Chicago School. The issue of race, however, was clearly drawn, as was the issue of black family life, and three of the above authors were, in fact, African American, although the entire question of racism seemed undeveloped.

This marvelous output was produced with a similar stamp. It took an important social phenomenon, such as suicide, and located the distribution of its incidence in the space of the city. Chicago researchers then analyzed it in terms of the relation between the individual and the larger social forces of integration/disintegration. Most often this meant that phenomena were explained as products of social disorganization, particularly the breaking up of primary social relations through city living, as Wirth's theory suggested. As a result, the Chicago School was eventually criticized for reinforcing a negative view of city life.

Despite their limitations, we can also appreciate the positive aspects of these early efforts. First, Chicago School researchers explicitly connected social phenomena with spatial patterns; that is, they thought in *sociospatial* terms. Second, they took an *interactionist* perspective. Individuals were studied in interaction with others, and the *emergent* forms of sociation coming out of that interaction were observed closely. Finally, they tried to show the *patterns of adjustment* to sociospatial location and developed a rudimentary way of speaking about the role of individual attributes in explaining urban phenomena. It *was* true that they focused almost exclusively on social disorganization and pathology; the breakup of family integration, for example, was given much more attention than questions of race or class.

The principal reason, however, for this ideological slant was that Chicago School sociologists were deeply concerned with improving life in the city. In their time, they rejected radical prescriptions for change and believed instead that *reformist* efforts prevail. Well-done reports produced by professional sociologists were viewed as one element in this reformist struggle. Perhaps the best example of an academic/reformer was Louis Wirth himself. Wirth not only contributed to the output of the Chicago School on theory and ethnography but left a sizable body of material addressing the issue of urban planning. He devoted considerable time to trying to improve city planning and saw government intervention as a means of elevating the urban quality of life. This reformist, practical side of Chicago Schoolers such as Wirth is often ignored in discussions of their work.

Another way to appreciate their achievements is by returning to their original case studies. A particularly vivid ethnography is Frederick M. Thrasher's 1927 study, *The Gang*. Thrasher spent eight years tracking down the youth gangs of Chicago and in the end was able to identify 1,313 of them. Today media coverage tends to associate gangs with black or Hispanic teenagers in the inner city and lament their violent ways, as exemplified by such films as *Boyz N The Hood* and *Colors*. Thrasher brings us back to the city of some 70 years ago when gangs were as much of a problem, but they were almost all white. Thrasher's study is described in more detail in Box 6.4.

Roderick McKenzie and the Metropolitan Community

Roderick McKenzie, a student of Park and Burgess, sought to apply the principles of human ecology not just to the city but to the broader metropolitan region. McKenzie saw the development of the metropolitan region as a function of changes in transportation and communication that produced new forms of social organization. These stages of development were the pre-railway era (before 1850), the railway era (1850–1900), and the motor transportation area (1900 to present). McKenzie considered technological change as the key variable in producing spatial patterns in urban society, as he states in his introduction to *The Metropolitan Community:*

> . . . formerly independent towns and villages and also rural territory have become part of this enlarged city complex. This new type of super community, organized around a dominant focal point and comprising a multitude of differentiated centers of activity, differs from the metropolitanism established by rail transportation in the complexity of its institutional division of labor and the mobility of its population. Its territorial scope is defined in terms of motor transportation and competition with other regions. (1933:6–7)

McKenzie's ideas were recognized as a significant contribution to the field at the time. In some respects, his approach may be viewed as a precursor to the general concept of the multicentered metropolitan region emphasized by the sociospatial approach.

BOX 6.4   CASE STUDY: GANGLAND CHICAGO, 1927

The population of gangs in the 1920s was composed principally of recent immigrants to this country. Of the total gang census taken by Thrasher amounting to 25,000 members in a city of 2 million, roughly 17 percent were known as Polish gangs, 11 percent were known as Italian, 8.5 percent were Irish, 7 percent were black, another 3 percent were mixed white and black, 2 percent were Jewish, and so on, with the largest percentage of *all* gangs composed of "mixed nationalities" known exclusively for their territory, not for their ethnicity (1927:130). According to Thrasher, roughly 87 percent of all gang members were of foreign extraction! The gang phenomenon was explained in part by the lack of adjustment opportunities for immigrants, in part by the carryover of Old World antagonisms, and also by the need to defend territory against "outsiders."

Thrasher's study demonstrates sociospatial thinking. As Robert Park (Thrasher, 1927:vii) comments in his introduction.

> The title of this book does not describe it. It is a study of the gang, to be sure, but it is at the same time a study of "gangland," that is to say, a study of the gang and its habitat, and in this case the habitat is a city slum.

Note Parks's grounding of the study in a biological metaphor by his use of the word *habitat*. Today we would use the sociospatial perspective and say *territory* or *space*. Gangland is the city space where gangs lived. Their influence was felt all over. What Thrasher did was locate gangs in their space. In fact, he found "three great domains" of gangdom—the "northside jungles," the "southside badlands," and the "westside wilderness." Using Ernest W. Burgess's map of Chicago (see Figure 6.1), Thrasher provided details for each of these areas and the gangs they contained (see Figure 6.4). Within gangland, "the street educates with fatal precision" (1927:101). The northside covered an area directly north of the downtown, or the "loop" on the Burgess map, and behind the wealthy neighborhoods that lined the shore of Lake Michigan. It was home to the "Gloriannas," the site of "Death Corner" and "Bughouse Square," and a gang so threatening that Thrasher disguised its real name.

The westside was the most extensive slum area producing gangs, and it encompassed the west past downtown, spreading out both northward and southward. The westside was home to the "Blackspots," the "Sparkplugs," the "Beaners," and the "hard-boiled 'Buckets-of-Blood'" (1927:9). On the southside of Chicago are located the stockyards and miles of railroad yards. Most of the blacks settled there, but the area remained dominated by Poles

But McKenzie did not have a great influence on later sociologists, and he is sometimes overlooked even by contemporary human ecologists. It is interesting to speculate on the reasons for this oversight. In the 1950s a new field of study, regional science, began investigating metropolitan regions from the perspective of economic geography, an approach with less appeal to urban sociologists. McKenzie's focus on the metropolitan re-

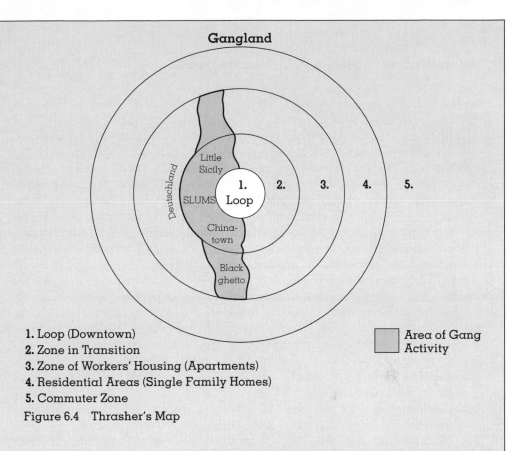

Gangland

Little Sicily

Deutschland

SLUMS

1. Loop

2.

3.

4.

5.

China-town

Black ghetto

1. Loop (Downtown)
2. Zone in Transition
3. Zone of Workers' Housing (Apartments)
4. Residential Areas (Single Family Homes)
5. Commuter Zone

Area of Gang Activity

Figure 6.4   Thrasher's Map

and Italians. The latter gangs were known as the "Torpedoes" or the "So So's." Black gangs of the time were the "Wailing Shebas" or the "Wolves."

As a territorially divided area, the city of Chicago and its environs pulsed with the give-and-take confrontations among the various gangs. Only the relative scarcity of killing weapons such as handguns kept the constant confrontations from erupting into the type of carnage characteristic of many cities today. For students of contemporary urban sociology, there can be no better example of spatially sensitive research than Thrasher's original study. It is doubtful, too, that in today's urban environment anyone could carry out the kind of exhaustive census on street gangs that Thrasher did. Certainly his study is now outdated. But like the pyramids, it remains an inspiration across time.

gion conflicted with the more general tendency of urban sociologists to focus their research and writing, as well as field work, on the central city. A serious consideration of his regional perspective would have led urban sociology out of the city and into the suburban region, something that would not happen for several decades but is a central focus of this text.

From Human Ecology to Urban Ecology

In 1945, Walter Firey published a study of land use in Boston titled "Sentiment and Symbolism as Ecological Variables." He noted that large areas of land in downtown Boston were reserved for noneconomic uses. Parks and cemeteries, as well as a 48-acre area in the center of the city that had formed the original "commons" of the community, had never been developed. In addition, an upper-class residential neighborhood known as Beacon Hill retained its privileged position as a home to wealthy and established Boston families despite its location near the downtown area. Each of these observations runs counter to the concentric zone model. Firey suggested that "sentiment" and "symbolism" are important ecological factors that influence spatial patterns of development in urban space (Firey, 1945). Although other sociologists offered little systematic elaboration of the ideas Firey presented in this important piece of research, his work is often referred to as the "sociocultural school" of human ecology.

After World War II, the ecological approach enjoyed something of a renaissance because ecologists paid careful attention to the census of population and how demographic locational patterns had changed. By 1950, it was found that the U.S. population had matured and spread out across metropolitan regions. In addition to altering population dispersal, the war years had changed the locational patterns of U.S. industry. Many plants dispersed to the countryside during the 1940s. As a result of the war effort against Japan, heavy industry was also decentralized and relocated west. Los Angeles in particular became both a focal point for the burgeoning aerospace industry and an important port for trade with the Pacific Rim markets. All of this restructuring and change called for new research that would chart the emergent patterns.

Working with descriptive tools, urban ecologists produced many studies on the differentiation of social activities across the United States. A great deal of refinement went into statistical analyses of census data that enabled new descriptive models of U.S. metropolitan growth to be devised. Much of this effort followed the style of the Chicago School: an emphasis on spatial location, functional differentiation, and the use of census data to pinpoint population differences as they are deployed in space.

Social Area Analysis

Social area analysis is associated with the work of Eshrev Shevky and Wendell Bell (1955). This method of urban analysis ranked areas within a city or metropoloitan area on the basis of the social characteristics of the population, including social status (education, occupation, and income) and family status (number of children, whether the mother worked, and type of dwelling unit). Areas that scored high on social status and family status (typically suburban communities) could be compared with areas that scored low on the same measures. Social area analysis produced detailed maps showing the location of class and ethnic groups in the San Francisco Bay area, as shown in Figure 6.5; especially noticeable in this mapping are the minority neighborhoods in Richmond, Oakland, and San Francisco, as well as the upper-class suburban neighborhoods in the foothills of the East Bay. But as a more general contribution to human ecology and urban sociology, social area analysis was found to be lacking. It was a descriptive methodology, this time with a visual application, but it did not provide an analytical model that could explain why particular groupings of sociological variables

Figure 6.5   Shevky and Bell's social area analysis of the San Francisco Bay region. This map contrasts areas of high social status (light areas) with areas of high urbanization (darker areas). E. Shevky and W. Bell, *Social Area Analysis; Theory, Illustrative Application, and Computational Procedures* (Westport, CN: Greenwood, 1955).

(ethnicity, social class, and family status) might be mapped in one area of the metropolitan region and not in another.

Factorial Ecology

The development of new computer technologies brought sweeping changes to the field of human ecology. Urban sociologists no longer had to limit their research to field studies of urban communities; now they could assemble data for entire cities and look for associations among, for example, the educational levels, incomes, and employment status of urban and suburban residents. *Factorial ecology* made use of these techniques and, through the 1950s and 1960s, produced a large number of studies that greatly increased our knowledge of the structure of cities, not just in the United States but across the world.

In the usual model, data concerning the social, economic, and family status of urban residents are examined for commonalities among households living in different areas of the city. Each census tract or community area has specific information as to the educational levels, incomes, and employment status of area residents (economic status), the age, marital status, and presence of children (family status), and racial and ethnic characteristics (urbanism), and a computer-generated analysis of this information reveals the structure of urban areas. The factorial analysis of data for American cities and their suburbs indicated that economic status is the most important determinant of residential location, followed by family status and then social status. Because of their increasing focus on these variables and an associated decrease in the field research and community studies, which employed a very different sort of research methodology, urban sociologists working in this tradition became known as *urban* ecologists rather than *human* ecologists.

Having examined the ecological structure of urban areas in the United States, it was only a matter of time before urban ecologists turned their attention to the structure of cities in other areas of the world (see Schwirian, 1974). In a sense, they were out to prove a very important point: that urban ecology was in fact a research paradigm that could be applied to human settlement spaces across time and across space. They believed this model could explain not only the structure of cities in Europe (which had evolved out of a feudal mode of production and with a physical structure very different from that of American cities) but also that of cities in developing nations. According to this theory, residential dissimilarity and segregation among groups (based on religion, ethnicity, caste, or occupation) is universal, and modernization or industrialization will have no effect on this pattern (Mehta, 1968).

Although the evidence from studies of cities in India, Finland, and Egypt was sometimes inconsistent, urban ecologists still believed they had discovered a universal model of urban structure. In "The Factorial Ecology of Calcutta," Brian Berry and Albert Reiss (1969) presented an "integrated model of land use" that combined the concentric zone, sector, and multinuclei models of the past and stated their belief that once the additional effects of local geography or history had been taken into account, their model could be applied to *any* city to explain where any group or business activity is located.

Conclusion

All theoretical paradigms are beset with potential problems and contradictions. Theoretical models borrow concepts and models from other fields of study; they are creatures of the concerns and beliefs of sociological scholars at a particular historical moment. Robert Park borrowed from models of plant ecology to formulate a model of human ecology. He incorporated the idea of conflict among competing land uses and competition among population groups, although it is unlikely that he envisioned the particular forms of conflict among class, ethnic, and racial groups that beset American society at the present time. Later ecologists incorporated new methods of analysis and answered new and even more challenging questions concerning urban life than the early Chicago sociologists could have imagined. But human ecology and its offspring, social ecology and urban ecology, confront numerous obstacles when studying the complexities of the multicentered metropolitan regions that now characterize urban society in the United States and across the globe.

The human ecology paradigm gives undue prominence to one factor—technological innovation—in explanations of urban growth and change. As noted earlier, Roderick McKenzie viewed changes in the metropolitan region as the product of shifts in transportation technology. This approach created problems for other human ecologists who followed McKenzie. Amos Hawley, for example, was interested in explaining two aspects of change in the postwar period: the massive growth of suburbanization and the restructuring of central city areas away from manufacturing and toward administration. In explaining these changes, he dropped the early ecologists' concern for space itself. He viewed social organization as fundamentally produced by the technologies of communication and transportation. As the technology of these means of interaction changed, so did the patterns of social organization. Any theory that takes as its principal source or cause one factor, such as technology, can be considered a form of reductionism. Choosing technology specifically produces a technological reductionism.

The issue of suburbanization is critical to understanding the maturation of settlement space in the United States. After World War II, several demographic studies noted the impact suburbanization was having on the nation's cities. In 1956, Amos Hawley published a paper claiming that while decentralization of the urban population had been around for some time, it was only with the mass introduction of the automobile that suburbanization took on significant proportions whereby the "outer rings" of the city grew faster than did the center. Hawley's argument tried to account for fundamental settlement space changes through technological determinism.

While census data show that suburbs grew more quickly than central cities from 1950 onward, the theory itself depended on fixing the precise time of rapid suburbanization. Ecologists reexamining the data all arrived at the same conclusion: Results were distorted because they did not account for the ability of cities to annex suburban land. Leo Schnore (1957) and subsequently Brian Berry and John Kasarda (1977) set the argument in new terms by correcting census data for annexation. Once annexation is controlled for, it becomes clear that suburbanization has *dominated* urban growth since at least the beginning of this century, that is, since 1900! Their results are shown in Table 6.1. As Berry and Kasarda note:

> Thus, while the street car, electric trains, and automobile may be credited with lowering initial density levels in cities that developed during those vehicles' respective technological eras, they were not responsible for "emptying out" or reversing concentration within existing central-city boundaries. (1977:193)

TABLE 6.1
City and Suburban Growth Rates by Decade

	Decade						
All Areas of U.S.	1960–70	1950–60	1940–50	1930–40	1920–30	1910–20	1900–10
All MSAs	16.3	25.0	21.3	8.3	27.1	24.8	31.1
Cities	0.0	0.8	10.0	4.3	19.7	22.4	29.6
Suburbs	32.5	59.6	41.1	16.0	43.7	30.2	34.5

Source: Adapted from Berry and Kasarda (1977).

In the end, and allowing for the effects of annexation, Berry and Kasarda showed conclusively that there is no evidence that suburbanization *outside* central city limits is correlated with innovations in transportation technology. It is because of studies such as this that urban sociologists in the 1970s and 1980s recognized that they needed a more comprehensive theory of metropolitan growth and change.

The ecological perspective remains active in urban sociology. Its core biological metaphor has been retained, as well as its central view that social organization should be understood as a process of adaptation to the environment. As we have seen, ecologists avoid any mention of social groupings such as classes or ethnic, racial, and gender differences. They see life as a process of adaptation rather than competition over scarce resources that often brings conflict. They have a limited conception of the economy, which they conceive principally as the social organization of functions and division of labor—a conception that neglects the dynamics of capitalism and the global system. Although they emphasize ecological location, they ignore aspects of the real estate industry and its role in developing space. Finally, ecologists seem to ignore the political institutions that administer and regulate society, and affect everyday life through the institutional channeling of resources. Their emphasis is on the push factors or the demand-side view, which neglects the powerful supply-side causes of growth and change in the metropolis. We will examine the factors responsible for the development of the multicentered metropolitan region in the next chapter as we explore the new urban sociology.

CHAPTER

7

CONTEMPORARY URBAN SOCIOLOGY: The Sociospatial Approach

At the beginning of this text, we discussed several conceptual changes that are the hallmark of the new urban sociology. These include a shift to a global perspective on capitalism and the metropolis; the inclusion of factors such as class exploitation, racism, gender, and space in the analysis of metropolitan development; an attempt, when possible, to integrate economic, political, and cultural factors of analysis; special attention to the pull factors of real estate investment and government intervention; and the shift to a multicentered, regional approach to cities and suburbs. In the preceding chapters we have used these concepts, which we call the *sociospatial* approach.

In addition to a change in perspective, the new urban sociology involves important theoretical changes in the way human environments are analyzed. The previous chapter discussed classical and current urban sociology of a traditional kind. This chapter considers the new theoretical ideas that have recently invigorated the urban field.

Since the 1970s, a great deal of creative work has been accomplished by numerous writers who have challenged orthodox ideas of city development. One of the most interesting observations about this effort is that much of it has been carried out by people in other fields and even in other countries. Only recently has U.S. urban sociology been affected by new theories. Second, regardless of the international scope and intellectual diversity, most of the new ideas have their origin in the application to city environments of the ideas of Max Weber, Karl Marx, and Friedrich Engels regarding the analysis of capitalism. This chapter concerns this "political economy" approach. While this perspective represents a considerable advance over those discussed in the previous chapter, mainly because the latter simply ignore the important role of economic and political interests, it has its own limitations. Sociologists have tried to tailor the approach of political economy to the needs of their discipline. In the concluding sections of this chapter, we will discuss such attempts, especially the growth machine perspective and the sociospatial approach of this text.

Political Economy and the City

Marx, Weber, and Engels

The classical sociologists Karl Marx and Max Weber turned to historical analysis to explore their ideas regarding the general laws of social development. Both understood that societies were organized around integrated systems of economics, politics, and culture. Marx emphasized the dominance of economic considerations in analysis, while Weber sought to show how cultural and political factors also affected individual behavior and social history along with economic activity. The two approaches served to complement each other.

While Marx wrote extensively about the new social classes (proletariat and bourgeoisie) created by industrial capitalism, he did not believe there were only two social class groups, as is commonly thought. In his analysis of the failure of the 1848 revolution in France, Marx identified *seven* social class groups and discussed why each group supported (or opposed) a new government. Industrial workers and small shopkeepers in the cities might support the revolution, for example, because their economic and political interests would benefit from a change in the government, whereas farmers in the countryside and large merchants in the cities might oppose it because their economic and social interests were dependent on maintaining the current government (Marx, n.d.). In this sense, Marx's view of social classes may be seen as a precursor to modern-day thinking about interest groups competing within the political arena.

Marx also recognized that the interests of capital and labor are not one and the same—a radical departure from modern-day economic theory and the idea that "a rising tide lifts all boats." Because profit results from the difference between the costs of production (raw material, machinery, and labor) and the price for which a commodity can be sold in the market, capitalist producers will look for any way possible to reduce the costs of production (Marx, 1967). Marx's analysis is as relevant for the monopoly capitalism of the present day as it was for the industrial capitalism of his time; in just the last several decades, we have seen the displacement of workers by automation, a dramatic increase in immigration, and the movement of manufacturing to Third World countries—all of these the consequence of corporations seeking to lower their labor costs, and all having a tremendous impact on the people and the built environment of urban and suburban settlement space across the world.

Marx wrote very little about the city in his classic *Capital* (1967; originally published in 1867), while Weber included some passages about the nature of the city in a much larger text, *Economy and Society* (1968; originally published in separate pieces beginning with the 1880s). For Marx, the early history of capitalism was a struggle between social relations located within urban areas and those situated in the countryside within feudal manors. For Weber, the city developed because of its political powers—

Friedrich Engels, the author of *The Condition of the Working Class in England*.

in particular, the independence of city residents and their local government from feudal relations of authority. In both cases, Marx and Weber showed how modes of social organization, such as feudalism or capitalism, work through a form of space—the city—and social relations situated within that spatial form. It is this perspective that informs the approach of political economy to settlement space.

For example, Weber argued that during the feudal period in the European Middle Ages, traders and craftspeople set up towns and bargained for protection from the king against the activities of local feudal lords. In these towns, capitalism began to thrive through trade in goods and eventually overtook the feudal economy. Thus, as capitalism became a dominating force in Europe, it also created the modern city. The political economy perspective studies social processes within urban space and links them to processes occurring at the general level of society.

While Marx and Weber had comparatively little to say about the industrial city of capitalism, Friedrich Engels devoted some time to the topic. We already mentioned his study of the working-class situation in nineteenth-century England and his field observations of the "great towns," Manchester in particular. For Engels, the large industrial city was the best place to study the general aspects of capitalism as a social system, just as the factory itself was the best place to study the specific details of the relationship between capital and labor. Engels picked the city of Manchester because it was built up as capitalism developed in England, as opposed to other cities, such as London, which had a longer history.

Engels observed several aspects of capitalism at work within the urban space. First, he noted that capitalism had a "double tendency" of concentration: it concentrated capital investment, or money, and also workers. This centralizing process made industrial production easier because of the large scale and close proximity of money and people. Second, Engels noticed that as Manchester developed, investment moved away from the old center and extended farther out to the periphery. Unlike Burgess, but very much like Harris and Ullman and the sociospatial approach, Engels pictured growth as a multiplication of centers. For him this followed no particular plan, and he observed that capitalism unregulated by government planning produced a spatial chaos of multiplying minicenters.

Third, among other important observations, Engels focused on the social problems created by the breakdown of traditional society and the operation of capitalism. In Manchester, he noticed examples of extreme poverty and deprivation: homelessness, orphan beggars, prostitution, alcoholism, and violence. For him this misery was the result of exploitation at the place of work, which went largely unseen in the factory itself, along with the failure of capitalism to provide adequate housing for everyone. He thus connected conditions in the workplace with those in the living space, or what Marxists call the *extended conditions* of capital accumulation, which involve the reproduction of social relations that ensure the continued use of the working class across the generations. For example, if problems such as poverty and homelessness become too severe, they can threaten the ability of working-class families to produce new generations of workers. This would then threaten the future of the capitalist system. Hence, neighborhood or living-space relations and the quality of daily life are just as important to the survival of capitalism as are relations at the place of work.

In addition to the problems of poverty, Engels observed that the city of Manchester was a segregated space. Rich and poor lived in segregated neighborhoods. Engels concluded that capitalism produces this spatial isolation of the classes. The sum total of all these social problems is described by the term *uneven development,* which conveys both the disparity between rich and poor and their segregation in space by capitalism. We will use this concept frequently in subsequent chapters.

Uneven Development

Urban and suburban settlement spaces grow and develop because of capital investment. The ebb and flow of money determines community well-being. Not only are jobs created, but economic activity also generates tax revenue. The latter is used partly by local government to fund public projects that improve the quality of community life. But spending, both public and private, is not uniformly distributed across metropolitan space. Some places receive much more investment than others. Even within cities there are great differences between those sections that are beehives of economic activity and those that seem scarcely touched by commerce and industry.

Within any given business, there are also great disparities between workers who are well paid and those who get the minimum salary. Wages are carried home to neighborhoods, and a significant portion is spent in the local area. Hence, the well-being of a place depends not only on the amount of investment it can attract but also on the wealth of its residents.

In the metropolitan region, the variation in the affluence of particular places is called *uneven development*. It is a characteristic of our type of society with its economic system of capitalism, but, as we will see in Chapters 12 and 13, it is also characteristic of other societies, some of which have communist rather than capitalist economies. People with money seek to invest in places and enterprises that will bring them the highest rate of return. Profit drives the capitalist system. But this profit making is usually expected to occur in a short time period and with the largest return possible. Consequently, investors look carefully at opportunities and always try to switch to places where money will achieve its greatest return. This process also causes uneven development. As capital becomes increasingly mobile, it can shift money around more easily with corresponding effects on the quality of life. At present, capital is more mobile than ever before in history and has the ability to move operations from one country or region to another in search of the lowest costs or highest profit margins. This process, of course, can have immense consequences for individual places.

The changes since the late 1960s in Silicon Valley, the high-tech showcase of California, illustrate this pattern. In the 1960s, when the printed circuit industry was first expanding, all operations, including manufacturing, research and development, and marketing, were located within Silicon Valley. By the late 1960s, one of the leading manufacturers, Fairchild, transferred its manufacturing operations to plants in Mexico, leaving thousands of U.S. workers jobless. Soon after, other electronic assembly plants followed the Fairchild lead, and by the 1970s most of the manufacturing operations of Silicon Valley had been transferred to other countries with cheaper labor. By that time, too, owners of corporations had discovered that operating in Mexico was not as cheap as production in the Orient. Hence, many plants were shut down and work was transferred to Hong Kong, South Korea, and Singapore, then to Malaysia and Indonesia, and more recently to Sri Lanka. In Chapter 5 we saw that, today, Silicon Valley residents lament the rapidity with which the boom and bust cycle played itself out in that region. But other areas of the world are caught in a similar process because of the increased mobility of capital.

Silicon Valley residents are well educated, and they hope that eventually a new round of investment will occur in their space by companies seeking their skills. At that future time, their area of the country may once again prosper. When a place is poor, however, such as an urban ghetto, and its people have limited educations, it is highly unlikely that capital will come there and invest, especially when cheaper wages are available in other countries. This remains so even for "small" capital ventures, such as grocery stores. Ghetto areas, such as the Watts section of Los Angeles, have comparatively few places where residents can provide for their needs. Most often, they must travel out of their community to shop because local convenience stores charge excessive prices.

As a result of the inherent desire not to invest in places that are already depressed and offer little incentive for profit, uneven development usually becomes more acute over time. This pattern increases the polarization between those places that are poor and those that are thriving. But places are made of people, so the spatial disparities result in different life chances for metropolitan residents. As Engels observed in Manchester, inequities create a problem of social justice as the less affluent members of the working class find it difficult to raise families that will acquire a reasonable, productive status in society.

Because of uneven development, the society would degenerate into a two-tiered structure, with a select group of people and places that are well off while surrounded by a sea of poverty, except that government in the United States has stepped in with a safety net of programs that tries to prop up the bottom stratum. Unemployment insurance, welfare, and job training are but a few of the ways government agencies use tax revenues to fight the inherent tendency of capitalist activities to produce uneven development. Over the years, however, despite periods of prosperity, the problems of the poor have been little affected by government programs (Jencks, 1992). New techniques of public policy therefore are sorely needed.

Metropolitan areas today are besieged by the uneven nature of capitalist development. Job security and planning for the future are jeopardized for people in communities across the nation. Extremes of poverty and wealth characterize metropolitan life. This clash between rich and poor in the city was also observed over 100 years ago by writers in the industrial towns of England. What is new and different today is the global extent of such uneven development and the way the cyclical nature of growth affects people and places across the world.

The Revival of Urban Political Economy: Henri Lefebvre

In the late 1960s and early 1970s, the Marxian tradition was revived in social science. Urban analysis was affected minimally at first in this country, but greatly affected in France by the philosopher Henri Lefebvre. Lefebvre is without question the seminal source of new thinking on the city from a critical and Marxian perspective (Lefebvre, 1991). His accomplishments can be broken down into four areas:

1. He went back to the work of Marx and Engels on the city and extracted from their writing an urban political economy. That is, Lefebvre showed how it was possible to use economic categories such as capital investment, profit, rent, wages, class exploitation, and uneven development in the analysis of cities. In effect, he argued that the city development process was as much a product of the capitalist system as anything else—the production of shoes, for example. The same operation of the economy applies in both cases.
2. Lefebvre showed how Karl Marx's work on the city was limited. He introduced the idea of the circuits of capital, particularly the notion that real estate is a separate circuit of capital. For example, we often think of economic activity as involving the use of money by an investor of capital, the hiring of workers, their production of products in a factory, and the selling of the goods in a market for a profit, which can then be used for more investment. Automobile production would be a good example of this circuit. Lefebvre called all such industrial activity the "primary circuit of capital."

   Much of the wealth created in a capitalist society is of this type. But for Lefebvre there was a "second circuit of capital," real estate investment. For example, the investor in land chooses a piece of property and buys it; the land either is simply held on to or is developed into some other use; it is then sold in a

Henri Lefebvre, the great French philosopher of
daily life, died in 1991 at age 89.

special market for land, the real estate market, or developed as housing for a profit.
The circuit is completed when the investor takes that profit and reinvests it in more
land-based projects. Lefebvre argued that the second circuit of capital is almost
always attractive as investment because there usually is money to be made in real
estate, although at present a recession is occurring in all economic sectors. As we
have seen in the development of the United States, investment in land was an
important means for the acquisition of wealth. But in addition, it was investment in
real estate that pushed the growth of cities in specific ways.

3. Lefebvre also introduced the idea that real estate is a special case of the dynamics
of settlement space. For Lefebvre, all social activities are not only about interaction
among individuals but about space as well. Social activities take place in space.
They also produce a space by creating objects. The city-building process, for
example, creates a certain space. When we visit a city, we experience particular
attributes of the space that was created in that area. Other city spaces may be
different, although places produced by similar social systems tend to resemble each
other, such as the close resemblance of suburbias in California and Virginia or
between the United States and Australia.

Lefebvre therefore introduced the idea of space as a component of social organization, as we discussed in Chapter 1. When people discuss social interaction, they are implicitly talking about behavior in space as well. Space is involved in a dual sense (see Chapter 1): as an influence on behavior and, in turn, as the end result of construction behavior because people alter space to suit their own needs.

4. Finally, Lefebvre also discussed the role of government in space. The state uses space for social control. Government places fire stations and police departments in separate locations across the metropolis in order to respond to distress relatively quickly. The state controls a large amount of land and utilizes it in its administration of government. It dispenses resources and collects taxes according to spatial units such as cities, counties, individual states, and regions. Government also makes decisions and relays them to individuals across the network of administrative units, that is, from the national level back down to the separate regions, individual states, counties, cities, and ultimately neighborhoods.

Lefebvre argued that the way capital investors or businesspeople and the state think about space is according to its abstract qualities of dimension—size, width, area, location—and profit. This he called "abstract space." In addition, however, individuals use the space of their environment as a place to live. Lefebvre called this interactively used space of everyday life "social space." For him the uses proposed by government and business for abstract space, such as in the planning of a large city or suburban development of new houses, may conflict with the existing social space, the way residents currently use space. Lefebvre said that the conflict between abstract and social space is a basic one in society and ranks with the separate conflict among classes, but is often different. With this view, he also departed from Marxian analysis because the latter stresses class conflict as the basic force in the history of capitalism.

In sum, Lefebvre is responsible for a large number of the ideas that inform the sociospatial perspective used in this text. He also heavily influenced a number of critical and Marxian urbanists to develop ideas of their own. In the following sections, we will discuss some of the most contemporary urban approaches and indicate how the ideas of Lefebvre in some cases or those of the classical thinkers Marx, Engels, and Weber in other cases have influenced new theories of urban development.

Class Conflict Theories: Gordon, Storper and Walker, and Castells

A class conflict approach to urban development was introduced by the economist David Gordon (1977, 1984). He suggested that the locations chosen by capitalists for factories were affected not only by economic needs but also by the desire to remove their workers from areas of union organizing. According to Gordon, owners of businesses prefer to locate in places where workers are not as militant as they are in cities with a long labor tradition.

To prove his point, he studied a period in U.S. history when workers were especially militant: the latter part of the 1800s to the 1900s. He calculated the number of workers engaged in strikes during those years and matched it with the number of times owners of factories decided to relocate to the suburbs or to more isolated cities. The matchup was significant for the years between 1880 and 1910. Hence, the need to control labor conflict by relocating to the outlying areas of large cities was a very early reason that urban development assumed a regional, multicentered form, because it led to the suburbanization of factories (see Chapter 4).

Two geographers, Michael Storper and David Walker, have expanded Gordon's approach (Storper, 1984; Storper and Walker, 1983). They view labor force considerations as the principal locational variable. By doing so they argue against the received wisdom of traditional location theory asserting that businesses choose to locate in a specific place because of marketing and production costs (including transportation), a view that is similar to that of urban ecologists (see the last chapter). Walker and Storper's "labor theory of location" argues that the commodity, labor, is unique. Its quality depends not only on the physical attributes of the worker but on his or her training and interest in being a part of a union, that is, in organizing against capital for rights and benefits.

For example, studies of the shift in manufacturing to Asia note that it is caused predominantly by labor force considerations (Peet, 1987). These include not only the presence of cheap labor but also the particular qualities of the workers. In the case of the electronics and garment industries in Asia, the workforce is overwhelmingly female, young, and unmarried. These laborers are advertised by development officials as providing a docile, easily controlled workforce (Fuentes and Ehrenreich, 1987). According to one Malaysian government brochure, "The manual dexterity of the Oriental female is famous the world over. Her hands are small, and she works fast with extreme care" (Fuentes and Ehrenreich, 1987:205). Reports on the condition of these women describe a world where they are kept bound by the conditions of work from living productive family and social lives.

According to the class conflict approach, then, any given nation has regions that vary with regard to the quality of labor. In part, the quality of schools and training facilities is responsible for this. However, the presence of a union tradition in the local area is also considered. Finally, particular cultural conditions, such as extreme patriarchy that subjugates women workers, are also important for creating a docile labor force.

Storper and Walker use these ideas to explain the shift of industry to the Sunbelt in the United States, which occurred because the southern and western regions of the country have weak or nonexistent unions. They also suggest that their approach is applicable to the entire globe and that location decisions of multinational companies follow what has been called the "international division of labor" (Frobel, Heinrichs, and Krege, 1980); that is, multinational corporations decide where to locate their activities by choosing places around the globe that specifically have cheap and compliant labor. In short, for these theorists, the qualities of labor are the determining factors in industrial location.

In broadest terms, the contentions of class conflict theorists have merit, especially for the case of shifts in the location of manufacturing in recent years. Since the 1970s, the advanced industrial societies have lost over 8 million manufacturing jobs. At the same time, Latin American and Asian countries have experienced a 6-million-job growth (Peet, 1987). During this period, the average hourly earnings for the United States was $8.83, for Mexico $1.59, for South Korea $1.35, and for India 40 cents.

These wage differences provide considerable incentive to invest global capital in less advanced countries. Regions with low class struggle and with a docile labor force are also attractive.

Class conflict theorists make a mistake common in traditional Marxian analysis: They try to explain *everything* by economic factors alone. In the previous chapter we saw that some traditional ecologists, such as Amos Hawley, commit the fallacy of technological reductionism; that is, they explain everything in terms of changes in technology. Similarly, traditional Marxists such as Storper and Walker are economic reductionists. Thus, while class conflict may indeed explain many of the moves owners made to outlying areas during periods of intense union strikes, it cannot explain relocations during other periods, and there are certainly additional reasons for such moves, such as the pull factors we already discussed in the case of suburbanization: cheap land, low taxes, and other government incentives that subsidize capital.

There is no doubt that labor force considerations are a major reason for the transfer of manufacturing activity to less developed countries such as Mexico or Malaysia. This approach, however, cannot explain why many multinationals continue to build plants and offices in places such as the United States, Germany, and Japan, which have comparatively high wages. Factors including relative government stability and the desire to remain close to markets are also important considerations. For example, Japanese companies such as Honda and Mazda have recently opened up plants in the United States. Most of the popular models from these two companies are made in Ohio and Michigan, respectively, where they are close to the important U.S. markets. These factors also play a role in the well-being of places within a global economy. (We will discuss some of this behavior in Chapters 12 and 13.) Thus, while the cost and quality of labor count for much in location decisions, other factors are also relevant.

An interesting variation on the conflict perspective was devised by the European sociologist Manuel Castells (1977, 1983). He was familiar with some of the work of Lefebvre since they both lived in Paris, but Castells broke with him and followed the ideas of more orthodox Marxists. Castells suggested, however, that traditional Marxian analysis was limited when dealing with social movements in cities. In particular, advanced countries had highly developed welfare states; that is, the national government supported a variety of social programs for all workers, such as unemployment insurance and subsidized housing, that sustained people's quality of life. Most often welfare programs were administered by local, that is, city governments. Struggles for resources by residents of the city therefore often took the form of conflicts aimed at local government rather than the capitalist class.

For Castells, the unique aspects of urban sociology as a special field of inquiry were defined by the issues arising from city government's administration of worker subsidies, such as housing, mass transportation, education, health, and welfare. This created the conditions for a special kind of conflict that did not fall into the traditional Marxian category of disputes between labor and capital. Yet state-supported resources were necessary for the reproduction of the working class; that is, state intervention provided for the "extended conditions" of capitalism, as we discussed in the case of Engels. Thus, urban struggles were a new form of conflict (Castells, 1983) produced by the modern form of capitalist social organization—namely, welfare capitalism. Such social movements are highly significant for the study of urban sociology.

Castells is well known among urbanists, and his ideas have been influential. His approach, however, has become increasingly limited over the years. When he wrote in the 1970s and early 1980s, many advanced industrialized countries possessed welfare states of the kind he envisioned. Since that time, however, financial problems have caused societies to cut back and in fact dismantle their welfare states (see Chapter 11). Consequently, local city governments do not engage in as many activities subsidizing the quality of life as they once did. In turn, local conflicts are much less concerned with disputes between citizens and government and more focused on economic or general social needs, such as the fight against racism or the desire for jobs. Instead of the specific "urban question" asked by Castells (1977), critical urbanists today ask a more general and farther-reaching "social question" that relates to regional issues and the well-being of the *entire* society. Hence, Castells' work, like that of other conflict theorists, is limited to pushing a single aspect of city life rather than a more comprehensive view.

Capital Accumulation Theories: Harvey and Scott

When sociologists discuss economics, they usually think in general terms and focus on individuals such as wealthy businesspeople who own companies. Class conflict theories go beyond individuals to discuss group behavior—particularly, the clash between the capitalist class of owners or investors and the class of workers who sell their labor for a wage. In this section we consider other urbanists who use economically based ideas to explain city development, but with a great deal more detail than traditional sociologists.

David Harvey, a well-known geographer from England, started out as a mainstream member of his field, concerned with mathematical modeling techniques. During the late 1960s, however, he was greatly influenced by events in the United States, such as the ghetto riots, and by the writings of Henri Lefebvre. In the 1970s, he wrote a book and a series of articles that applied Marxian economic analysis to the condition of the cities. He was especially influenced by the earlier writings of Lefebvre on the urban analysis of Karl Marx and Friedrich Engels. See Box 7.1 for an example of his work.

Harvey, like Lefebvre, systematically applied the categories of Marxian economic analysis to the study of urban development. He asserted four things. First, he stated that the city is defined in the manner of Engels as a spatial node that concentrates and circulates capital. Second, he applied a conflict perspective to discuss the way the capitalist and the working classes confronted each other in the city (1973, 1976). According to Harvey, and unlike the general way sociologists usually speak about classes, this basic conflict takes many forms as both the capitalist and working classes split up among themselves into various groups or factions as a consequence of protracted struggles for advantage. The capitalist class, for example, can be divided among financial investors (finance capital), owners of department stores and other marketing assets (commercial capital), and owners of factories (manufacturing or industrial capital). Workers can also be split—for example, among factory laborers, white-collar salespeople, and professional financial analysts, all of whom still work for a wage. Each of these factions may

BOX 7.1   DAVID HARVEY'S CASE STUDY OF BALTIMORE

David Harvey asks how returns to the ownership of land or property can be understood when "the distinction between capitalist and landlord has blurred concomitantly with the blurring of the distinctions between land and capital and rent and profit" (1985:65). Harvey defines a specific category called "class-monopoly rent" as the return on property owned in cities. He suggests that the ability to earn this money is contingent on a combination of factors involving both a variety of financial institutions and government subsidies. Hence, the process of earning money from real estate is quite complex and varies from location to location.

To demonstrate this point, Harvey divided Baltimore City into eight real estate submarkets. Each of these submarkets had its own dynamic of investing and selling. Harvey used data for 1970 and obtained the following results:

1. The *inner city* was dominated by cash and private loan transactions with scarcely a vestige of institutional or governmental involvement in the used housing market.

2. The white *ethnic areas* were dominated by homeownership financed mainly by small, community-based savings and loan institutions that operated without a strong profit orientation and which really did offer community service.

3. The black residential area of *West Baltimore* was essentially a creation of the 1960s. Low- to moderate-income blacks did not possess local savings and loan associations, were regarded with suspicion by other financial institutions, and in the early 1960s were discriminated against by the FHA. The only way in which this group could become homeowners was by way of something called a "land-installment contract" (where a white middleman bought the home first and rented it to blacks for a profit until a loan could be secured).

4. The areas of *high turnover* were serviced mainly by a combination of mortgage banker finance and FHA insurance. . . . In the high turnover submarkets created by these programs there were plenty of opportunities for the speculator to realize a class-monopoly rent.

want different things from urban development, so that conflict and coalition building are always a part of urban life. However, the basic struggle is still between capital and labor, as Gordon, and Storper and Walker, also suggest (see pp. 134–37). As Harvey suggests, "Labor, in seeking to protect and enhance its standard of living, engages in a series of running battles in the living place over a variety of issues that relate to the creation, management and use of the built environment" (1976:268).

Third, Harvey discusses how the volatile urban mix of economic interests brings about government intervention as a means of quieting things down so that planning can take place and capitalists can get back to their principal task of profit making (1975, 1976). As Harvey suggests, "capital, in general, cannot afford the outcome of struggles around the built environment to be determined simply by the relative powers of labor, the appropriators of rent and the construction fraction" (1976:272). Therefore, the capitalist class requires government to intervene and aid the profit-making process within cities.

5. The *middle-income* submarkets of Northeast and Southwest Baltimore were typically the creation of the FHA programs of the 1930s. By the 1960s homeownership was being financed conventionally by federal savings and loan institutions and by some of the smaller ethnic savings and loan institutions. . . .

6. The more affluent groups made use of savings and commercial banks to a much greater degree and rarely resorted to FHA guarantees. Such groups usually had the political and economic power to fend off speculative incursions. . . . (1985:72–78)

Several important observations can be made from the above material. First, urban development is not some monolithic process of growth (as the growth machine perspective suggests). The second circuit of capital is composed of a variety of arrangements, each with its own set of social factors, conflicts, and possibilities in determining the level and quality of investment in real estate.

Second, the second circuit of capital consists of a combination of private financial institutions, community banks, and assorted government programs that support housing in different ways. Real estate is not a pure case of private enterprise but involves the government in direct ways. Speculators, developers, homeowners, and renters react differently in these separate environments, and while some people are simply interested in owning a home, others are out to make money any way they can.

Third, the housing market in the United States discriminates against blacks and the poor. Inner-city blacks have it the worst. They must finance most of their transactions by cash payment. Banks will not lend to them. Poor white ethnics also have trouble obtaining bank support, but they have managed to establish community savings and loans that help them out. Only the middle and upper classes have free access to loans, with fully 75 percent of such households obtaining bank financing.

Finally, the discrimination against poor and/or black people is also revealed in the data on government-sponsored insurance. Inner-city and ethnic areas cannot obtain such support. However, more affluent sections have no trouble getting FHA or VA insurance. In short, the real estate market not only works through a complex assortment of combined public and private resources but also reinforces the inequities and uneven development of the society.

Sometimes, however, investment simply will not flow into districts of the city because they are so run-down or unattractive economically. In such cases, Harvey argues, government must step in to make the areas profitable again. Usually this form of state intervention involves the tearing down or destruction of existing buildings to make way for new construction, such as in the example of government-supported urban renewal programs (see Chapter 15). According to Harvey, "under capitalism there is, then, a perpetual struggle in which capital builds a physical landscape appropriate to its own condition at a particular moment in time, only to have to destroy it, usually in the course of a crisis, at a subsequent point in time" (1982:14). For Harvey this process of boom and bust, or new construction and urban decay, is basic to urban change in a capitalist system.

Finally, Harvey took a detailed look at the capitalist class and how it made money within the space of the city. He borrowed the concept of circuits of capital from Lefebvre and elaborated on the latter's ideas. In particular, Harvey argued that capitalists involved in the first industrial circuit are principally interested in location within the urban environment and in reducing their costs of manufacturing. Capitalists in the second circuit hold a different set of priorities relating to the flow of investment and the realization of interest on money loaned or rent on property owned. These differences are reflected in the different ways capital investment circulates within the two circuits. Harvey illustrated these differences in his case study of development in the city of Baltimore during urban renewal (see Box 7.1).

While investment in factories is often located in places with cheap housing, capitalists in the second circuit often refuse to invest in poorer areas and seek out only the higher-rent districts of the city. As a consequence, areas of the city can become run-down and abandoned not because of the actions of industrial capital, the faction that we usually think of as determining city fortunes, but because of actions taken by investors in real estate, as the sociospatial perspective suggests. In the Baltimore study, both suburbanization of the population and central city decay were linked to the priorities of the second circuit of capital as assisted by government programs. Harvey's work bears out the importance of Lefebvre's ideas on the real estate industry, and also Engels' central insight into the production of uneven development under capitalism.

Allen J. Scott, another influential geographer from England, has gone even further than Harvey in one sense by detailing the production process and its impact on space. For Scott, all things are explained by the needs of industrial manufacture (1980, 1988). In this case, Scott is also a reductionist, but unlike Harvey, he is not a Marxist. Rather, Scott is a follower of the nineteenth-century economist David Ricardo, who argued that all profit making, and hence the dynamics of capitalism, can be explained by the process of production rather than capital circulation as Harvey would have it.

Scott says little about the factions of classes, the political context of development, the role of real estate, and the pull factors of government intervention because they are not particularly relevant to the production process per se. Instead, Scott (1988) gives us a detailed picture of the spatial impacts of changes in production processes, which, he argues, explain changes in the form of cities.

Allen Scott's approach cannot explain the production of the built environment, despite his claims to the contrary. The missing ingredients to his analysis of changes are the roles of the real estate industry and the action of state government, as the sociospatial perspective suggests (see the last section). Nevertheless, his approach is extremely helpful in understanding the new relations between the location of business and the global economy.

In Chapter 4, we saw that social life is organized around a combination of working, shopping, and community service relations. Although changes in each of these *sociospatial* dimensions can affect the organization of everyday life, the structure of the local economy is most important. In Chapter 4, we saw that during the metropolitan phase of growth, U.S. corporations lost their purely local character due to the concentration of ownership under monopoly capitalism. Their operations shifted to a national network of manufacturing, marketing, and administrative functions that were *horizontally integrated* by the same company but spatially dispersed across the country.

Scott (1988) suggests that after 1970, additional changes occurred in the sociospatial relations of business. These can be best characterized by the phenomenon of *vertical disintegration.* In this process, large corporations sell off or abandon many of their activities that supported production, such as the manufacture of parts and materials or the supply of inputs to the production process. Instead, they contract out to suppliers for such inputs and acknowledge the lowest bids. Competition among suppliers results in much lower costs to the firms than producing parts and materials themselves. Because the burden of supply is carried by subcontractors rather than by the manufacturing company itself, the inventory stocks of the company and thus its costs are also lowered.

This arrangement of vertical disintegration in production is coupled with the horizontal integration of manufacturing, marketing, and administration across the globe in the command and control centers of transnational corporations. The new organization of business is a major reason for the success of both new firms and new competitors of Western countries, such as Japan, especially in the areas of electronics and automobile production. It is also one reason large cities have shifted to business service employment (Sassen, 1991).

Vertical disintegration has a number of drawbacks that must be overcome. For one thing, subcontracting the supply of parts and materials reduces the need for large inventories by manufacturers, thereby reducing costs, but those inputs must be available when needed. The Japanese technique of "just-in-time" supply is used to make sure that inputs are at the factory when needed. Often this means that a single supplier will sign on as responsible to the larger company, with the prospect of going bankrupt if performance is not adequate and the contract is not renewed. But it also means that around any large factory may be found a complex of small subcontractors in a complex industrial space offering a variety of employment opportunities. Second, when manufacturers give up producing their own inputs, problems can arise in the coordination of production. This limitation is overcome with the introduction of computerized manufacturing systems or CAM (computer-assisted manufacturing), which is able to keep track of all needs. Electronic information processing has revolutionized the manufacturing process in this manner. It has also created new job skills and made new, more sophisticated demands on both workers and their educational systems. All these changes have effects on the local community and the process of the extended reproduction of the workforce.

For Scott, the end result of vertical disintegration is the ability of large companies to carry out businesses on a global scale. They can locate manufacturing, administration, and marketing in a host of places across the world. Suppliers of "just-in-time" parts can also be almost anywhere. This makes capital extremely mobile. It puts a great pressure on individual places and individual communities of workers to be productive and attractive for capital investment. When capital is dissatisfied with existing arrangements, it is comparatively easy, according to Scott, to relocate.

In sum, both the class conflict and capital accumulation approaches of the new urban sociology provide impressive improvements over more traditional perspectives. The world today is a volatile one where the predictable accommodations of work, shopping, and residential living characteristic of the industrial city have been shattered. Economic factors such as the ebb and flow of real estate investment and the changing structure of manufacturing in a global system affect the sociospatial features of daily life. So do the activities of workers involved in the struggle lying at the heart of the capital/labor relationship, and the residents of communities who are concerned about maintaining their quality of life. Each of these aspects helps determine the pattern of sociospatial organization.

Until the development of the new urban sociology, the effects of special, powerful interests (such as transnational corporations) on the pattern of growth were ignored by the traditional approach that emphasized biological factors of species competition over territory. But the work of geographers and Marxian analysts places greater importance on economic than on social factors in sociospatial arrangements. As we have discussed, there are several limitations to both the class conflict and capital accumulation approaches. In recent years, therefore, sociologists have added to the new perspective on the city by showing how social factors are also important in the production of settlement space.

The Growth Machine

This approach is most closely associated with the work of Harvey Molotch and his recent collaboration with John Logan (Logan and Molotch, 1987). Molotch was dissatisfied with the traditional ecological approach to urban development and highly influenced by new work carried out among French urbanists inspired by Lefebvre and Castells (Pickvance, 1976). Molotch was especially taken with the studies by the Frenchman Lamarche (1976) on the role of property development in the city. The focus of urban change involves the activities of a select group of real estate developers who represent a separate class that Marx once called the "rentiers." It is this class that both prepares land for new development and pushes the public agenda to pursue growth.

For Molotch, the intentions of the rentier class mesh well with the needs of local government. This is so because government is in constant need of new tax revenue sources. As increasing numbers of people enter an urban area, their demand for services strains fiscal budgets. Without new sources of revenue, city governments cannot maintain the quality of life, and the region is threatened with a decrease in prosperity. Property development is a major source of taxes. New people also bring in new demands for city goods and services, which aids the business community and, in turn, increases revenues to local government. In short, according to Molotch, cities are "growth machines" because they have to be. Pushed from behind by demands for community quality and pulled from the front by the aggressive activities of the rentiers, city governments respond by making growth and development their principal concerns.

Molotch's approach might be considered the exact opposite of the one advocated by Allen Scott. For Scott, spatial development is explained by the internal workings of the production process. For Molotch, industrial production has little to do with urban change. Both perspectives focus on only one aspect of the more complex development process. Logan and Molotch (1987) use the growth machine to explain the dynamics of urban development, but they also recognize that the global context of capitalism accounts for many of the changes occurring in cities. In addition, they have qualified their one-dimensional emphasis on development to acknowledge that the pursuit of growth does not always proceed smoothly. At times, members of the community who are not part of the rentier class may perceive further growth as threatening their own quality of community life. For example, people in a quiet, well-tailored suburban neighborhood might resent the construction of a nearby mall and multiple-family rental apartments. Or residents of a central city area may dislike the tearing down of affordable housing to build new, luxury condos. In these and other cases, the pursuit of growth is tempered, and perhaps blocked, by splits in the community supported by groups that oppose growth. Hence, local politics often becomes a battleground for pro- and antigrowth factions.

The Sociospatial Perspective

Real Estate and Government Intervention

How can we make sense of the various ideas offered by new urban theories? This text adopts the sociospatial perspective (SSP), which takes what is best from the new ideas while avoiding the endemic reductionism characteristic of both traditional ecology and recent Marxian political economy. It does not seek explanation by emphasizing a principal cause such as transportation technology (Hawley), capital circulation (Harvey), or production processes (Scott). Rather, it takes an integrated view of growth as the linked outcome of economic, political, and cultural factors. At one time, it might have been suggested that such an integrated view derives from the tradition of Weber. However, since the 1950s, even Marxists have looked for ways to advance an integrated perspective (see Althusser, 1971), and this is especially important for the understanding of space (see Lefebvre, 1991).

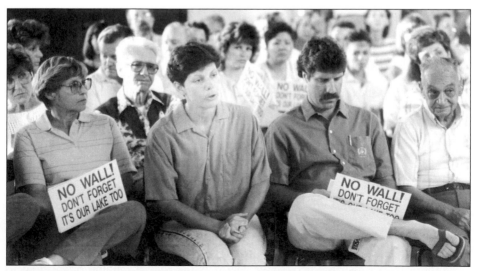

A woman speaks out at a homeowners' association protest against new construction in Lake Forest, California.

The failure of traditional urban sociology to explain urban unrest, such as in Watts (Los Angeles) in 1965, provided an incentive to develop a new approach.

The sociospatial perspective is inspired by the work of Lefebvre as applied to the needs of urban sociology by Feagin (1983, 1988) and Gottdiener (1977, 1985) and their collaboration (1988). The SSP can be distinguished from other approaches by the following characteristics. First, it considers real estate development as the leading edge of changes in the metropolitan region. While other approaches tend to focus only on economic changes in industry, commerce, and services, the SSP adds to these important dimensions an interest in the way real estate molds metropolitan growth. Second, the sociospatial perspective considers government intervention and the interests of politicians in growth as a principal factor in metropolitan change. Traditional urban ecology and the newer approaches of urban political economy either ignore completely the role of government in channeling growth or treat the state as simply derivative of economic interests. The SSP considers the state as relatively autonomous—that is, with officials having interests of their own—and, more specifically, considers politics as being highly linked to the concerns of property development (Gottdiener, 1986).

Third, the sociospatial perspective considers the role of cultural orientations as critical for an understanding of metropolitan life. Because of the importance of this subject, culture will be considered in more detail in Chapters 8 and 9.

Finally, the SSP takes a global view of metropolitan development. The most local areas today are tied to the activities of multinational corporations and banks. Changes in the way they invest affect each of us. By emphasizing global economic changes, however, the sociospatial perspective also seeks to understand how local and national factors interrelate with international links. All spatial levels of organization are important in understanding metropolitan development. In the following section, let us review some of these features while keeping in mind the differences between the SSP and other sociological perspectives discussed in the previous two chapters. In particular, we will see how the sociospatial perspective is a much more sophisticated and useful approach than either the growth machine or traditional ecology.

Real Estate Investment as the Leading Edge of Growth. From the earlier chapters on urbanization in the United States, we have seen that interest in real estate profits played a central part in urban development. George Washington not only was the first president of the country but also participated in the innovative scheme to develop the swampland that became the site of the nation's capital. During the 1800s, great profits were made by businesses as the country industrialized, but they were also made through investment in land. Cyrus McCormick earned millions from the manufacture of his famous reaper, but millions more from his activities in real estate. Railroad tycoons competed with one another by building the infrastructure that opened up the great landmass of the United States to development, but they also established towns and developed real estate as they went along. Finally, over the last few decades, we have seen that the shifts to suburbia and the Sunbelt were fueled in part by the phenomenal expansion of the single-family home industry and the development of lands outside the large central cities of the Northeast and Midwest.

The sociospatial perspective argues that other perspectives have neglected the important role played by investment in real estate in the process of regional development. Traditional urban sociology or ecology, for example, overemphasizes the push factor of technology as an agent of change. Marxian political economy pays special attention to the activities of capitalists and the way changes in industrial investment patterns affect local spaces. The SSP acknowledges push factors such as changes in economic production and transportation innovations, but also highlights the role of pull factors such as government intervention and the action of real estate—the second circuit of capital—as crucial to explanations of metropolitan growth. Both demand-side and supply-side dynamics are studied in their details.

The sociospatial perspective stresses the human dimension along with structural arrangements. It wants to know who the actors are and how they behave, not just the facts or figures about aggregate levels of growth and change. Activities involve people acting as part of social classes and class factions, or of gender, racial, and ethnic interests. How people come together to struggle over the patterns of development is an important question for the SSP (see Chapters 11 and 15); but this is not viewed as a machine.

Feagin (1983), for example, discusses specifically the variety of ways real estate developers and speculators create development projects and channel money to real estate investment. Agents of growth include *financial conduits* such as commercial banks and trust or pension funds, savings and loan associations, insurance companies, mortgage companies, and real estate investment trusts; *real estate brokers* and chamber of commerce members; and *public utilities* and other relatively immobile public service agencies that must work to maintain the attractiveness of specific places. Real estate, therefore, is composed of both individual actors and a structure of financial conduits that channel investment into land.

Gottdiener (1977) also demonstrates how both structure and agency are important for an understanding of real estate activities. A case study of suburban Long Island, New York, identifies the following types of social roles assumed by investors in the built environment:

1. Land speculators who purchase land or buildings simply to be sold at a later date for a profit.
2. Land developers who purchase land with or without housing and then develop it by constructing housing or other built structures such as factories or malls. To this type can be added developers who restructure the uses of land and buildings, such as those who convert rental into condominium units, single-family into multifamily dwellings, and residential housing into office space.
3. Homeowners and individuals who invest in property as part of an overall scheme for the protection of income and not just to acquire shelter.
4. Local politicians who are dependent on campaign funds from the real estate industry, and lawyers or other professionals who make money from government-mandated requirements that necessitate legal services.
5. Individual companies or corporations that do not specialize in real estate but develop choice locations for their respective businesses, such as office towers or industrial plants, and a host of financial institutions, such as savings and loans, that channel investment into land.

The preceding list of institutional and private interests involved in the development of the metropolitan region reveals that growth is not simply determined by economic "push" factors of production, as both the class conflict and capital accumulation perspectives maintain, or by a special class of people called rentiers, as the growth machine approach emphasizes. Development is caused by the pull factor of people's activities involved in the second circuit of capital, real estate. This sector is not simply a select group of investors, as the growth machine believes, but is composed of both *actors* interested in acquiring wealth from real estate and a *structure* that channels money into the built environment. The latter consists of a host of financial intermediaries such as banks, mortgage companies, and real estate investment trusts, which allow a large variety of people to put their money in land.

Because the second circuit of capital enables anyone, even individual homeowners, to invest money in real estate for profit, it is wrong to separate the people in society into a select few who seek to make money in real estate (exploiting its exchange value) and a majority who seek only to enjoy the built environment as a staging ground for everyday life (the exploitation of space's use value). Instead, space can be enjoyed for its uses and for its investment potential by both business and local residents. In fact, that's what makes the relationship of society to space so complicated. The latter is *simultaneously* a medium of use and a source of wealth under capitalist commodity arrangements.

Because developing the built environment involves so many different interests, growth or change is always a contentious affair. This criticism has vital theoretical and empirical implications for the study of urban sociology, especially the role of the state, as we will see next.

Government Intervention and Political Agency. The sociospatial perspective suggests that metropolitan growth is the outcome of negotiations and contending interests, rather than the product of some well-oiled machine without conflict. Developers, for example, must negotiate with government planners and politicians, citizen groups voice their concerns in public forums, and special interests such as utility companies or religious organizations also interject their stakes and culturally defined symbolic visions in metropolitan growth. The end result of these negotiations is a built environment that is *socially constructed,* involving many interests, and also controlled by the quest for profit.

The absence of a separate class of growth mongers means that the conceptualization of local politics by the growth machine perspective is limited. Feagin (1988) shows how powerful economic interests use the state to subsidize growth; hence development often reflects the direct interests of industrial and financial capital rather than some select, separate class of rentiers. Gottdiener (1977, 1985) indicates how local politicians are intimately involved with development interests. The purpose of this alliance is not growth and increased public revenues per se, as it is viewed by the growth machine, but *profit.* In this sense, growth interests represent both factions of capital involved in the accumulation process and also community interests concerned about growth and the quality of life. It is this melding of profit taking and environmental concerns that is most characteristic of settlement space development, and it involves a second source of complexity in the society/space relationship.

The interests aligned around issues of change in the built environment should be seen as *growth networks* rather than as the monolithic entities suggested by the concept of a "machine" (Gottdiener, 1985). The idea of networks captures the way alliances can form around a host of issues associated with development, often splitting classes into factions. The concept of network captures the diversity of people who may join, often only temporarily, to pursue particular growth paths. What counts is not necessarily the push for growth, but both the way different community factions perceive the form growth will take and how they evaluate their own environmental needs. There is a rich complexity of people and interests involved in metropolitan growth and change which is captured neither by ecological or political economy perspectives, because they ignore particular agents, nor by the growth machine approach, which reduces conflict to a simple dichotomy of pro- and antigrowth factions.

For example, each community group may have its own interests which are manifested in local politics. They often join in coalitions to push for some version of growth while opposing other coalitions that have their own vision of the future. Growth is not the result of single-minded efforts by some machine. Rather, development is a contentious process involving many groups in society that push for a variety of forms: rapid growth, managed growth, slow growth, no growth, and so on. Local social movements arise not just because of economic needs, but because of racial, religious, ethnic, and community interests concerned with the quality of life.

Development or change is a constant occurrence of the American landscape. Local politics consists of the clashes between all these separate interests as they play themselves out in the second circuit of capital and within the forum of local government. We will discuss this process as it relates directly to metropolitan politics more fully in Chapter 11.

The Global Economy

Finally, the sociospatial approach agrees with all other perspectives that acknowledge the important role of the global economy, the new mobile or "flexible" arrangements in production, and their effects on the restructuring of settlement space. It argues, however, that the push factors of capital mobility and considerations regarding the international division of labor, discussed earlier, are not the only ones determining growth. Often perspectives identified with the "new" urban sociology simply stress the effect of the global system as the key determinant of metropolitan change (see Smith and Feagin, 1987; Palen, 1991). The pull factors of state policies and the second circuit of capital are also important, particularly as manifested at the local, regional, and national levels.

Hence, the sociospatial approach has a more integrated view of push and pull factors associated with growth. The influence of the global system does have a profound effect on the fortunes of place, but unlike other approaches (see Logan and Molotch, 1987; Sassen, 1991; Smith and Feagin, 1987), the SSP does not believe that it has a sole determining effect.

This feature was illustrated in Chapter 5 with the discussions of suburban and Sunbelt development. At that time, it was pointed out that while the U.S. economy had become integrated into the world system, development patterns of deconcentration to suburbs and Sunbelt regions had been going on for many years, even prior to the 1960s when the restructuring of the global system began to be felt. The shifts to the suburbs and the Sunbelt are the two *most* important sociospatial changes in U.S. history, but neither can be said to have been produced by the power of the global economy. They have their roots in growth trends that have been going on for years and that involve important aspects of both government intervention and the phenomenal draw of real estate investment.

For example, in Chapter 5 we studied the nature of suburban development after recognizing that the majority of Americans live in suburbs, not central cities. Suburbanization in the United States has been going on since the turn of the century. Development accelerated after World War II when the government initiated special loans to veterans and consolidated the income tax subsidy to homeowners, providing families with a cash incentive to invest in real estate. Suburbanization was also promoted by a variety of federal housing acts passed since the 1930s that revitalized the real estate industry and by the Interstate Highway Act in the 1950s, which promoted the construction of freeways. All of these factors fell into place long before the advent of global economic effects.

We have also seen how the Sunbelt prospered as a consequence of government programs and real estate activity. Government military spending during World War II and later during the Cold War propped up the Sunbelt economy by transferring billions of dollars in tax money from the Frostbelt to this region. Real estate investment found riches in a host of Sunbelt schemes for the development of housing and industry. Other factors, such as the prosperity of agribusiness, also helped growth. In short, the most important spatial changes experienced by the United States are the consequence of many factors operating at all spatial levels, as the SSP suggests, rather than at the global level alone.

Of course, since the 1970s, changes in the global economy have had a profound effect on the built environment. The decline of manufacturing in the United States and the transfer of many production activities abroad have wiped out the traditional relation between central city working-class communities and their capitalist employers. The economy of our largest cities has restructured away from manufacturing and toward specialization in advanced services and information processing, particularly those business services required by the finance capital faction that coordinates investment activity for the global economy (Sassen, 1991). The record high of the stock market and record low in unemployment through the 1990s have not altered this longer-term trend of restructuring of the urban economy and increasing economic polarization of urban space. All these changes affect the nature of the local labor force and alter living and working arrangements. We will discuss some of these effects on the people of the metropolis in Chapters 8 and 9. Other effects of the restructuring initiated within the context of a global economy will be considered in Chapters 10 and 11 when we look at metropolitan problems and policies, respectively. Finally, in Chapters 12 and 13, we will discuss the effects of global restructuring on Third World cities and settlement spaces in European countries and Japan.

The sociospatial changes produced by the global economy have also been important because of the new spaces that have appeared in recent years. Prior to the 1970s, neither Santa Clara County nor the peripheral areas around the city of Boston were significant employment centers. During the last two decades, they proved to be world-class economic spaces, becoming Silicon Valley and the Route 128 high-tech corridor, respectively. These new spaces produced by high-technology industries earned disproportionately large sums of money on the world market for their employment size. At one time, these results prompted analysts to suggest that other countries follow suit and promote their own export-oriented high-tech corridors as the key to future prosperity (see Chapter 13). Today Silicon Valley and Route 128, along with other such spaces, are experiencing a severe recession. The global economy is now shaky as recession hits worldwide. According to the SSP, alterations and development of new spaces of production and consumption will be produced not by investment directed at the global level alone but also by the logic of real estate development and by other pull factors, such as the quality of government intervention, in addition to factors that operate locally, regionally, nationally, and globally—that is, at all sociospatial levels.

Summary

The sociospatial perspective involves ideas that distinguish it from previous sociological approaches. First, it incorporates a number of different factors, instead of emphasizing one or two, that can account for development and change. It particularly seeks to provide a balanced account of both *push* and *pull* factors in metropolitan and re-gional growth. Second, it considers the role of real estate in development as the com-bined activities of both agency and structure. Investment in land is a sector of capital accumulation with its own factions and cycles of boom and bust. The categories of po-litical economy, such as profit, rent, interest, and value, are just as applicable to metro-politan development as to any other part of the economy.

Third, the sociospatial perspective strives for a detailed view of politics that em-phasizes the activities of individuals and groups in the development process. The SSP focuses on the activities of certain *growth networks* that form coalitions interested in choices that must be made over the direction and effects of change.

The sociospatial perspective considers cultural factors such as race, gender, and the symbolic context of space just as important as economic and political concerns (see the next chapters). It also deals specifically with the special qualities of spatial forms and their role in the organization of society. At present, metropolitan life is played out within the context of an ever-expanding multicentered region. We have dis-cussed the historical significance of this form of settlement space in previous chapters and will discuss its signficance for daily life in chapters to come.

Finally the sociospatial perspective, along with other approaches, adopts a global view of development, but does not claim that the world economy alone is responsible for the restructuring of settlement space. Global changes are particularly relevant for an understanding of how cities, suburbs, and regions have been affected by the econ-omy in recent years. New spaces of industry, commerce, and services have helped re-define settlement patterns as multicentered regional development. Historically, how-ever, the pull factors of government intervention and investment in real estate have also played an essential part in the restructuring of space.

In the remaining chapters we will examine the role of culture in metropolitan life, address the issues of politics and problems, and then turn our attention to other coun-tries to compare the U.S. experience with growth and restructuring elsewhere.

CHAPTER

8

PEOPLE AND LIFESTYLES IN THE METROPOLIS

In previous chapters, we studied the growth and development of metropolitan regions. The next two chapters concern the people of the metropolis and explore the relationship between everyday life and local territory. The sociospatial approach to metropolitan life asserts that diversity in lifestyles and subcultures exists not just within the city but throughout the metropolitan region. This is especially the case since 1980 as suburban settlement spaces have matured. In this chapter we consider the interplay between the social factors of income, gender, age, and race and the spatial patterns of population concentration or dispersal across the metropolitan region.

A basic tenet of the sociospatial approach is that social factors determining the patterns of population dispersal are also linked to particular spaces. Class or gender relations, for example, are conducted through spatial as well as social means. Lifestyle differences are externalized in a specific environment: the ghetto, the street corner, the mall, the golf course. Furthermore, these places are always *meaningful*. Interaction is shaped through the signs and symbols of sociospatial context. In this chapter we will consider the effect of class standing on lifestyles, gender differences and everyday life, racial and minority distinctions, and new patterns of ethnic formation and immigration. The effects of class, gender, and race are so powerful in our society that we will also consider them in Chapter 10 when we discuss social problems. We will see how differences in sociospatial factors affect the way people live, their interactions with others, and their use of space.

Class Differences and Spatial Location

Class Stratification in the United States

The sociologist Max Weber believed that an individual's class standing is important because it helps determine the life chances that could be expected in the future, that is, the possible opportunities or constraints for future achievement open to any individual. He also suggested that economic factors of class status, such as the type of occupation or monetary resources that an individual possesses, are not the only determining factors of overall social status. Standing in the society's hierarchy also depends on particular cultural attributes, such as prestige or symbolic differences, and on the possession of political power. Thus, life chances differ according to economic, political, and cultural factors, but material wealth, as Karl Marx maintained, clearly is the most important of all social variables.

The United States is a stratified society. This means that individuals and households are located within a social hierarchy that determines their access to resources. Stratification is often pictured as a pyramid of social standing. Those at the very top control most of the society's resources; they also enjoy the most symbolic prestige and political influence. Those below are the most numerous and have the least power. The United States, despite an active ideology that preaches equality, in fact has the most unequal distribution of wealth of any industrialized nation (Philips, 1988). The top 1 percent of the population control over 70 percent of the wealth, and the top 5 percent control over 90 percent. Status considerations such as driving an expensive car, living in a large home, taking fabulous vacations, and wearing expensive clothing are greatly influenced by the media images of affluence and what life is supposed to be like at the top of the stratification diamond.

Most research on the American class structure divides our society into at least five different groups. Judgments for these divisions are based on what social scientists call *SES,* or *socioeconomic status,* which is a particular combination of wealth, occupation, education, gender, and race, among other factors (see Robertson, 1987). The five groups are the lower class, the working class, the lower middle class, the upper middle class, and the ruling class. Only the ruling class controls enough wealth to be considered independent from economic needs. Thus, the middle class in particular remains caught in the social relations of class stratification despite its relatively high SES standing (Ehrenreich, 1990).

These SES standings also involve the ability to sustain a residence in a particular place. Thus, socioeconomic status is also about living in a certain space. In our society, due to stratification differences, the choice of residential location is not always voluntary. Restrictions of wealth, race, and gender are particularly potent sifters of population across the metropolitan regions. SES differences and the system of social stratification therefore manifest themselves both as differences in individual lifestyles and as differences in neighborhood living or local space. Let us consider some of the distinct ways stratification is reflected in this interaction between social relations and territorial practice, as the sociospatial perspective suggests.

The Wealthy

The upper classes always had the advantage of several homes because they could afford it. Former President George Bush, for example, has for many years maintained residences in Houston, Texas; Washington, D.C; and Kennebunkport, Maine. Many wealthy people alternate among townhouse, suburban estate, and rural recreational home. In the city, the wealthy are associated with the more fashionable districts such as Nob Hill in San Francisco, Beverly Hills in Los Angeles, the Gold Coast near Lake Michigan in Chicago, Beacon Hill in Boston, and Park Avenue in New York City. Their activities, in short, take place within a certain space.

One important way the wealthy manifest their power is by isolating themselves as much as possible from the rest of the population. Their segregation is voluntary. In the city, this is accomplished by living in ultraexpensive housing with security guards and controlled entrances. While taxis are available, the wealthy often utilize private, door-to-door limousine services. Shopping and recreation are all located in heavily policed areas. In the city, such isolation remains somewhat of a constant chore that taxes the resources of surveillance and control. In the suburbs or at country homes, however, the benefits of isolation are more readily enjoyed. Box 8.1 details one of the very few sociological studies done on the wealthy, by E. Digby Baltzell (see also Fussel, 1983). This study indicates that while the wealthy require their own segregated space, the areas they choose for their voluntary isolation vary over the years.

The upper class is not confined to city residence. One of the earliest studies of the affluent in suburbia was Thorsten Veblen's *Theory of the Leisure Class* (1899). Although wealth was behind their behavior, the most important characteristics of the lifestyle were symbolic or cultural. Veblen coined the concept *conspicuous consumption* to refer to this particular aspect of the affluent style of suburban life. This concept refers to an outward display of consumption that demonstrates wealth and power through the wasting of resources and the symbols of upper-class membership. The suburban homes of the wealthy, for example, were endowed with excess. Houses were

A large suburban home in Westchester County, New York.

BOX 8.1 THE PHILADELPHIA GENTLEMEN

Perhaps the best study by a sociologist of the upper-class lifestyle is E. Digby Baltzell's (1958) *Philadelphia Gentlemen*. The author distinguishes between the elite and the upper class. The former are "those individuals who are the most successful and stand at the top of the *functional* class hierarchy. These individuals are leaders in their chosen occupations or professions" (1958:6). Baltzell's book is not about the elite but about the upper class, which he defines in contrast as the

> group of *families* whose members are descendants of successful individuals one, two, three or more generations ago. . . . [Individuals in this social grouping are] brought up together, are friends, and are intermarried one with another; and finally, they maintain a distinctive style of life and a kind of primary group solidarity which sets them apart from the rest of the population. (1958:7)

According to Baltzell, the upper class in Philadelphia restricted itself to a particular location in the city and tried to remain out of sight. Over the years, however, its choice of location varied; that is, it usually did not stay in the same neighborhood generation after generation, but tended to be subject to the same forces of deconcentration and regional drift as were other individuals in the metropolis. Most American cities have a pattern similar to Philadelphia of once fashionable districts that have declined as the wealthy shuffle around the metropolitan region in search of secure enclaves for their lifestyle. As Baltzell remarks,

> In Philadelphia, the rise and fall of upper-class neighborhoods can be divided, with some overlapping of course, into three periods: (1) during the colonial period and through the first part of the nineteenth century, fashionable Philadelphians lived in what is now the downtown business district around Independence and Washington Squares; (2) after the Civil War, and until World War I, the upper-class center of gravity, as it were, became the Rittenhouse Square district; (3) after World War I, the center of society moved west once again out to the suburbs along the Main Line and in Chestnut Hill. At the same time, of course, many of the wealthier families had country places even as early as the eighteenth century. (1958:179)

The most characteristic area of upper-class life was the Main Line, which stretched westward from the central city of Philadelphia on the commuter railroad to the suburbs of Overbrook, Merion, Wynnewood, Ardmore, Haverford, Bryn Mawr, Rosemont, and other towns out to Paoli, Pennsylvania. As Baltzell observes,

> Exploited in the literature and by the popular press, the famous Main Line is the most popular elite suburb in Philadelphia. Each Sunday, Philadelphians read all about upper-class social life in the Philadelphia *Inquirer*'s popular society column, "The Mainliner." (1958:201)

Baltzell notes that the upper-class lifestyle consisted of a withdrawal from civic affairs and the concentration on business by the males, while females were expected to stay close to home minding the household and entertaining when necessary for the husbands' needs. In addition, however, women were expected to be involved in philanthropic enterprises outside the home, such as organizing charity balls or fund-raising activities for the arts. Children were sent to exclusive private schools, and social life meant interacting only with other members of the upper-class *Social Register*. Family time for these people was divided between town and country residences. In this way, the upper class maintained its spatial and social isolation from other segments of the society.

huge, over 5,000 square feet or more, with many more rooms than were necessary to service the immediate family. Estates had large front and rear lawns that were landscaped and attended to by a staff of gardeners. Conspicuous consumption was symbolized by the landscaping of yards precisely because land was allowed to lie uncultivated as a resource—the lawn was just for show.

The wealthy practically invented the stereotypical suburban lifestyle (see Chapter 4). As a sign of conspicuous consumption, it is focused on leisure activities; that is, symbols of leisure mean that people do not have to work. An important affluent social institution is the country club, which is costly to belong to and restrictive in its membership. The fees usually run into the tens of thousands of dollars, thereby automatically keeping the working class out. In many parts of the country, clubs such as the Everglades Country Club in Florida prevent African Americans and Jews from belonging even if they can afford membership fees. The leisure activity of choice for the affluent is golf, and in recent years this game has come to symbolize suburban wealth and leisure itself, because golf is most often played at country clubs. A second important recreational pursuit is tennis, which also requires outdoor maintenance when played at the country club, although tennis is also played in the city. In a wealthy area such as Palm Desert, California, located about 100 miles east of Los Angeles, a considerable amount of the town land is devoted to golf courses, which require immense amounts of water and daily care. Because Palm Desert is located in the desert, the presence of so many golf courses is indeed a luxury.

At present, wealthy suburbanites maintain their isolation through mechanisms similar to those utilized in the city, such as the high price of homes, surveillance and control by private security forces, gate-guarded and enclosed communities, and the sheer separation that comes from spatial dispersal itself. Whether we are dealing with the city or the suburbs, the wealthy tend to use topography to their advantage. Their homes are located at the greatest heights. In the suburbs, this often means that estates are built on the high ground, on hillsides or escarpments. In the city, this "god's eye view" is acquired with apartments higher up in luxury buildings.

In short, the wealthy possess a distinct lifestyle founded on class privilege and symbols of high social status. Their daily life manifests itself in space through unique molding of the environment to create isolation and exclusion. The wealthy also overcome the limitations of space by owning several residences, each with its own locational advantages. Whether living in the city or the country, their lifestyle, like any other, is sociospatial; that is, it is organized around expressive symbols (Fussel, 1983) and particular spaces.

Yuppies, Buppies, Dinks, and the Suburban Middle Class

A large proportion of central city residents are not members of the upper class but do have money by virtue of occupation and family choice. Since the 1970s, as manufacturing has declined in the city, there has been a phenomenal increase in service-related jobs (see Chapters 5 and 12; also, Sassen, 1991). Many of these are professional positions created by the information-processing economy of the city, such as the financial and legal institutions associated with corporate headquarters. In previous chapters, we discussed how certain kinds of economic activity create or help reinforce lifestyles,

The Soho area of Manhattan, where gentrification reflects the upscale urban lifestyle.

community relations, and expressive symbols. Recently the shift to information-processing professional services has also affected metropolitan settlement space by reinforcing certain upper-middle-class patterns of behavior.

The term *yuppies,* or young, urban professionals, has acquired a derogatory connotation, but it is a very useful way to describe relatively young (late 20s to early 40s), middle-class professionals who live in the city. The same can be said for the term *dinks*—double income, no kids—which describes yuppie couples without children. We should note that yuppies and dinks represent urban subpopulations characterized by their income, occupation, and lifestyle; they are *not* identified by ethnicity or race. In the 1980s, the term *buppie* was used to identify young, black, urban professionals as large numbers of African American college graduates entered the labor force. Only recently have such components of the middle class achieved the kind of numbers that have attracted attention. According to Sassen (1991), yuppies were responsible for gentrification and the upgraded housing and renovation of older loft buildings in New York and other cities (Zukin, 1989); their culinary demands spurred the opening of many new and often exotic restaurants; and their more specialized everyday needs, such as last-minute food shopping, health and fitness requirements, and reading and cinema tastes, have opened up new sectors of employment for a host of immigrant groups and working-class urban residents looking for entry-level service positions. Box 8.2 details some of the characteristics of the urban professional lifestyle.

BOX 8.2   THE UPSCALE URBAN LIFESTYLE

Market researchers have studied yuppies in detail because they spend so much of their income on consumer products. They identify characteristic yuppie areas as located in the more affluent sections of the central city (Weiss, 1988). Many live in high-rise buildings in areas of high population concentration and in newly gentrified housing in suddenly fashionable areas of the inner city. According to one report:

> Almost two thirds live in residences worth more than $200,000, decorating their living rooms according to *Metropolitan Home*, buying their clothes at Brooks Brothers, frequenting the same hand-starch Chinese laundries. In Urban Gold Coast, residents have the lowest incidence of auto ownership in the nation; these cliff-dwellers get around by taxi and rental car. (Weiss, 1988:278)

Market researchers also note the peculiar, service-dependent nature of yuppie consumer behavior. For the sake of last-minute convenience, they will spend more to eat out or purchase items at close-in grocery stores that charge more than large supermarkets. Convenience is prized by people whose high salaries often require them to devote extra hours to their work. According to Weiss:

> Residents usually eat out for lunch and dinner, and their forays to grocery stores mostly yield breakfast items: yogurt, butter, orange juice and English muffins—all bought at slightly above-average rates. Compared to the general population, residents buy barely one-fifth the amount of such pedestrian treats as TV dinners, canned stews and powdered fruit drinks. Where these consumers do excel is at the liquor store: they buy imported champagnes, brandy, beer and table wine at twice the national norm, possibly to take the edge off stress-filled urban living. (1988:281)

The novelist Jay McInerney (1984) has captured the mindset of individuals who live alone, have high-paying jobs, and haunt the central city gentrified districts, which contain an implosion of various cultural influences from around the world. As his novel's character, a yuppie writer living in New York City, observes:

> You're dressed and out of the house before ten. The train pulls in just as you make the platform. . . . The car is full of Hasidim from Brooklyn—gnomes in black with briefcases full of diamonds. You take a seat beside one of them. He is reading from his Talmud, running his finger across the page. . . . At Fourteenth Street three Rastafarians get on, and soon the car reeks of sweat and reefer. Sometimes you feel like the only man in the city without group affiliation. . . . The *Post* confirms your sense of impending disaster. There's the Fiery Nightmare on page three—an apartment blaze in Queens; and on page four a Killer Tornado that ravaged Nebraska. In the heartland of the country, carnage is usually the result of acts of God. In the city it's manmade—arson, rape, murder. (1984:56, 57)

In the early 1980s, the leaders of many cities believed that the two-pronged explosion of jobs and spending related to the expansion of the business service sector would replace manufacturing as the key growth industry of urban areas. Indeed, places such as Pittsburgh (Jezierski, 1988) managed to change from centers of industry to focal points for global banking and investment. Restructuring of the financial and corporate business sectors with a consequent decline in the growth of jobs, however, occurred in the mid-1980s, cutting short this expansion. Especially significant were the changes occurring after the October 1987 "crash" of the New York stock market, which led to greater computerization of financial transactions, the reining in of risky ventures such as junk bonds, and the failure of several investment firms (Minsky, 1989). Throughout the 1990s, corporate downsizing led to the loss of tens of thousands of white-collar jobs in cities across the country. Hence, despite what was once believed, the place of yuppies in the revitalization of central cities may be overrated.

Most of the middle class do *not* live in the city. Years of white flight to a suburban location for the majority of people who can afford to buy their own home have emptied the central city of much of its middle class. The majority of middle-class Americans have spread out and prospered across the vast expanses of developed housing tracts located in suburban settlement space throughout the metropolitan region.

Middle-class suburban living might be thought of as the upper-class lifestyle within a more modest budget. Symbols of status abound in this kind of environment as well. The typical suburban home is a scaled-down replica of the estate. It consists of a frontyard that is strictly ornamental and a backyard reserved for leisure. In the warmer parts of the country, the desirable backyard may contain a built-in swimming pool, which usually is no more than 30 feet long. The 1990s may be known as the decade of the backyard deck; most new middle-class homes have decks in the backyard where children play and adults cook on the gas barbecue, and home improvement chain stores have spread across the suburban landscape. While the upper-class estate involves a team of gardening and maintenance people, the middle-class homeowner is a "do-it-yourselfer." Indeed, a stereotyped activity of the suburban male invariably involves fighting crabgrass on the lawn, repairing roofs, and maintaining homeowner appliances. Women in suburbia also have a unique lifestyle, as we will discuss more fully later when we consider the relationship between gender and space.

For suburbanites, leisure activities are confined to the weekend, when there is some free time. In many developments and municipalities, tax monies have been devoted to acquiring the kind of public facilities that the affluent enjoy in private. These include public golf courses, swimming pools, tennis courts, and parks. In areas close to the ocean or a lake, suburban municipalities often build and service public marinas for boating and other water sports. Suburban life is family life. Box 8.3 details everyday life in suburbia.

The Working Class and the Working Poor

Traditional urban settlement space is associated with the large numbers of workers employed in manufacturing. In the nineteenth century, the city was invariably dominated by factories. Modest working-class housing was constructed in grid-pattern rows

BOX 8.3 THE MIDDLE-CLASS SUBURBAN LIFESTYLE

A picture of middle-class suburban life was drawn by the geographer Peter Muller:

> The needs and preferences of the nuclear family unit shape modes of social interaction in middle-income residential areas. The management of children is a central group-level concern, and most local social contact occurs through such family-oriented formal organizations as the school PTA, Little League, and the Scouts. However, despite the closer spacing of homes and these integrating activities, middle-class suburbanites . . . are not communally cohesive to any great degree. Emphasis on family privacy and freedom to aggressively pursue its own upwardly mobile aspirations does not encourage the development of extensive local social ties. Neighboring (mostly child-related) is limited and selective, and even socializing with relatives is infrequent. Most social interaction revolves around a nonlocal network of self-selected friends widely distributed in suburban space. (1981:72)

This relative isolation of individuals in suburbia and the exclusive autodependency of the spatial arrangements is particularly hard on teenagers. Ralph Larkin makes these observations about suburban teenagers in a place he calls Utopia:

> The most serious complaint among Utopia High School students is boredom. They are restless. Many complain of having nothing to do. They are forced to compete with each other for grades, sexual attractiveness, hipness, and all the other minutiae that are involved in the status race. Since everyone else is struggling for the same, somehow scarcer rewards, friendship has a hollow quality to it. It is a gloss on a relationship in which vulnerabilities are hidden so they won't be capitalized on by others. (1979:60)

In his pioneering study of the suburban shopping mall (1984), Jerry Jacobs discussed how teenagers fight the boredom of their lives by converging on a certain space, the fully enclosed shopping mall. Jacobs took one particular teenager, Julie, as typical and detailed her activities within this environment as follows:

> First and foremost she and her friends spend "a lot of time" at the (video game) arcade. They often stop in at the "Gift Horse," a shop featuring "jewelry and design shoelaces and calendars and mugs." They might on these walks stop to visit "The Old Erie Coffee House." Ironically, this is not a place to drink coffee although coffee, tea, and their accoutrements are sold there. However, on these jaunts, Julie and her friends usually have a different agenda in mind, and go there to look at "cute stuffed animals, the little animal farm, animals, mugs and stuff, cards and pins." From there they might move on to "Sweet Temptation" and get some "gum or something." By then, it would be approaching lunchtime and they would go to the "T. J.'s" (a hamburger place not unlike McDonald's) where they would get a large french fries and a coke and sit and talk about a variety of topics. . . . (1984:98)

nearby. Weekly schedules were centered in this space, which included the few amenities available to the working class—the pub, the association football park (soccer) or
the local baseball diamond, and the streets themselves, which served as playgrounds
for children (Hareven, 1982).

In the period immediately after World War II, U.S. cities contained a prodigious
density of such working-class districts. Since the 1960s, however, this pattern has been
in decline. One reason is that many factory workers attained middle-class status with
the ability to purchase single-family homes in the suburbs (Berger, 1957), often with
liberal government-sponsored veterans' benefits. A second, more drastic cause was the
decline in manufacturing itself. When the factories closed, working-class life became
all the more precarious.

Although working-class families have suburbanized in large numbers since the
1960s, many still remain residents of large cities. They are often referred to as the
"working poor" because their standard of living is declining as cities themselves have
become expensive places to reside. The quality of life of the working class is dependent on the public services provided by local government. They require mass transportation, for example, which is becoming increasingly expensive. The level of medical care for this less affluent group is precarious and dependent on city-supported
hospitals because they work at jobs that do not provide adequate, if any, health insurance. In fact, the Health and Hospitals Administration of New York City, which runs
that city's medical facilities, has a yearly budget of about $1.5 billion, as much as the
entire budget of several small countries.

Because so much of their standard of living depends on city services, the working
poor are often at odds with public administrators. City politics involves clashes between this public and the municipal administration over the quality of services. Since
the latter 1970s, declining fiscal health of cities has made this political conflict worse
because of budget crises and cutbacks (as we will see in Chapter 11). The working
poor and their advocates in the city fight a running battle with the mayor over the declines in education, fire and police protection, sanitation, highway maintenance, health
care, and recreational amenities.

The Underclass

The "underclass" consists of the most isolated elements of the poor who have little
prospects of employment, are residents of husbandless households, and whose lives
are besieged by crime and drugs. This segment of the population was first called to our
attention by Ken Auletta's (1983) journalistic account and later analyzed by the
Chicago sociologist William J. Wilson (1987). In recent years, the term *underclass* has
been dropped because it has assumed the characteristics of a buzzword that blames the
victims of racial and economic deprivation rather than, as originally intended, highlighting the causes of extreme poverty and isolation. To avoid the negative connota-
tions of this term, this text refers instead to the *ghettoized poor* (see Box 8.4; see also
Chapter 10 for a more detailed discussion).

According to Wilson, the plight of the ghettoized urban poor arises from the loss of
jobs in the inner city. They have become so isolated and concentrated in specific areas of

BOX 8.4   THE GHETTOIZED POOR

Sociologists Terry Williams and William Kornblum studied poor inner-city areas in four cities: Cleveland, Ohio; Louisville, Kentucky; Meridian, Mississippi; and New York City, New York. A common stereotype is that all members of the underclass are poor. While many are, others have made fortunes off of the drug-centered economy within ghetto areas. Williams and Kornblum contrast two individuals living in the same place. Much of daily life revolves around a particular space, the local "candy store" and the street corner on which it is situated. As they observed:

> The neighborhood once was flooded with junkies, but it is changing slowly. The candy store is one of the last institutions in the area to serve this particular consumer group. In fact, the store operates on several levels. It's a hangout for kids, number runners, drug dealers, and winos. The kids can buy reefer; adults can buy wine under the counter; boosters (sellers of stolen goods) sell their wares to customers and managers alike. . . . Seventh was the avenue of the big-time hustlers. There they sported their fine cars and pretty women. . . . The names of infamous street hustlers who made it into big time are given legendary status.

> C. C. has a long way to go if he wants to make it to the big time. Right now all he can do is talk big. Wearing a floppy hat that he claims is a Christian Dior, a fur-type vest, sneakers, and khaki trousers, he takes a perverse pleasure in shouting obscenities at his peers. As one of them, Zero, dressed in a grey hooded jacked [sic] zipped up to the neck, passes to go into the store, C. C. looks at him. "Yo, what you wearing all of that shit for? This ain't the north pole—you look like a motherfucking polar bear. . . ." Zero gets to the door, steps in for a second, then comes out, grabs C. C. around the neck, and proceeds to twist his head around. As he twists he mumbles something like "I-done-told-you-to-stop-fucking-with-me-ain't-I?" (1985:48–49)

Williams and Kornblum identify C. C. as "among the losers of the street world," but there are also what they call "winners," such as Darryl:

> Darryl's expensive tastes are evident in his wardrobe—a mink coat, several pairs of three-hundred-dollar boots, a closet filled with silk shirts, and a diamond ring—in addition to his four cars: a 450 SEL Mercedes Benz, a 633 CSI BMW, a Cadillac Seville, and a Volkswagen Rabbit. He also owns two three-story brownstones and is, in the words of the teenagers, "coming off strong." Darryl has been a dealer in heroin and cocaine for ten years. When he was nine years old he already controlled a crew of kids who sold joints at school. Today, at nineteen, he is a veteran. (1985:49)

the city that their needs fundamentally outstrip the available municipal resources aimed at alleviating the condition of poverty. As a result, they are doomed to raise children with few prospects for a better life unless they turn to criminal activity. Box 8.4 details aspects of the poverty-stricken ghetto resident's lifestyle. Thus, the so-called "underclass" phenomenon is really caused by a combination of sociospatial factors—such as poverty and racial exclusion—and the spatial concentration of large numbers of poor people within specific areas of cities and suburbs, rather than by individual failings (see Chapter 10).

The life of the ghettoized poor is subjected to an almost unending list of pathological consequences of city living, including public health crises such as AIDS, child

A central city area of poverty-stricken street people, Portland, Oregon.

abuse, tuberculosis, dropouts from education, juvenile crime, drug addiction and the bearing of addicted babies, juvenile motherhood, murder, rape, and robbery (see Chapter 10). The crime and pathology associated with poverty-stricken ghettos make city living difficult for everyone and are largely responsible for the high murder rates in urban areas.

Women, Gender Roles, and Space

The issue of gender roles and settlement space is a vast topic on which urban sociologists have largely been silent. As recently as the 1970s, one well-known geographer wrote a book entitled *This Scene of Man* (Vance, 1977) and, not to be outdone, in 1989 an equally famous urban sociologist published a study of Chicago entitled *The Man Made City* (Suttles, 1990). Feminist scholars would indeed agree that the city is man-made because women had little to do with its planning and even less to do with its construction.

As a result, the built environment reflects men's activities, men's values, and men's attitudes toward settlement space. Yet the lives of women are a critical component of urban and suburban activities. Increasingly, with the prodding of feminist observers, we are gaining greater insight into the role of women, and their needs, in everyday metropolitan life (Hayden, 1981).

Women and the Urban Political Economy

During the nineteenth century in the early stages of industrial manufacturing, it was common for entire families to labor; 10 and even 12 hours a day, 6 days a week, were the norm. Home life was second to the needs of the factory, and even children were pressed into the service of wage labor in textile mills and other industries (Hareven, 1982). Over the years, conditions in these Satanic Mills, as Karl Marx (1967) called them, changed. Child labor laws were passed at the turn of the century in the United States prohibiting school-age youth from full-time employment. Many women continued to work, but the growing number of middle-class families during the 1920s enabled people to copy the upper-class lifestyle with married women remaining at home. This effect of class, which occurred because of successful economic growth beginning this century, resulted in the redefinition of the middle-class woman's role to that of housewife (Spain, 1992).

Over the years, further changes in class standing and in the economy altered the relationship of woman to both the family and the larger society. Status differences were caused by the effects of male social dominance, which dictated women's life chances, and by the effects of the economy. For example, among the middle class during the 1920s women were expected to remain housewives. During World War II, however, many women returned to full-time occupations, including manufacturing, as in the image of "Rosie the Riveter." After the war and especially during the suburbanization of the 1950s, middle-class women were once again expected to remain home as housewives. But in the 1970s, real wages in the United States began to decline, and participation in the middle-class lifestyle has grown increasingly expensive. Owning a home in the suburbs typically requires more than one income, and it is common for both spouses to pursue full-time employment. A majority of all adult women now work outside the home, whether single or married.

Recent statistics from the U.S. Department of Labor illustrate the phenomenal changes in the labor force participation of women since the 1950s. In 1950 roughly 30 percent of women worked outside the home, but by 1986 the figure was 55 percent. In 1950 it was relatively rare for married women with children to be employed. Only 28 percent of women in this group with children between ages 6 and 17 worked, but by 1986 the figure had jumped to 68 percent (see Hochschild and Machung, 1989).

In contrast to the cycles of middle-class gender role differences, working-class women have always had to secure employment outside the home, even if limited to part-time work. Minority women, for example, have always worked, and many are the main sources of income for families due to employment discrimination against males. Certain industries, such as garment manufacturing, depend almost exclusively on the exploitation of female labor in factories. In Chapter 7 we discussed the role patriarchal norms of domination play in the global economy. Women in Asia and Latin America, in particular, are exploited as the source of labor for the electronics and garment industries in countries such as Mexico, Singapore, and South Korea (see Chapter 13). As one scholar suggests (McDowell, 1991), male domination of female roles is an integral part of the global economy and a major reason for the success of recent restructuring that has shipped manufacturing jobs to developing countries. In short, female gender roles are dictated in part by patriarchal social conventions and in part by the needs of the economy.

Domestic labor is unpaid and has low status. In fact, housework is usually not a family topic of importance. Yet the well-being of the family depends on the cooking, cleaning, nurturing, and monitoring of the household. In most societies, it has been women's lot to bear the responsibility for these tasks. Even when women work outside the home, men expect them to complete a "double shift" of cleaning, cooking, and child care when they return home. According to a classic study of this burden (Hochschild and Machung, 1989), married women who work outside the home still do an average of 3 hours a day of housework compared with 17 minutes for their male spouses. As one group of observers note:

> As women it is assumed that we will be ultimately responsible for the upkeep and general maintenance of our homes whether we have another job or not. . . . Even when others contribute to this work, the primary responsibility remains with the women. We are conscious of its demands at all times; responsibilities cannot be shut off by retreating into a "room of one's own." (Matrix Collective, 1984)

Domestic or unpaid labor supports child rearing and family life. While these activities are necessary in all societies, the tasks themselves are the primary responsibility of women, who for the most part labor alone. Urban sociologists refer to these activities as the *social reproduction of the labor force,* because household work along with education and health care combine to nurture children until they themselves enter the labor force. The socialization of women to accept the role of domestic laborer in our society therefore is an essential and necessary component of the economy.

As discussed above, the participation of middle-class women in the formal economy has been cyclical. Since the 1970s, women have entered the paid labor force in record numbers. As a result of economic restructuring—that is, with the decline in manufacturing and the rise of service industries (see Chapter 5)—new opportunities have been created for women. Women have responded by moving into the professional service sector. One consequence of this shift has been a change in the way both men and women view household tasks, with a greater willingness among middle-class men to share in domestic labor, especially a growing percentage of men who "mother" (Lamb, 1986; Grief, 1985). Another consequence has been the multiplication of service-related jobs created by working mothers. Many of the pressing household tasks have been farmed out to specialized service workers for a fee. Child care, housecleaning, shopping assistance, and lawn care are but some of the services that have taken the place of unpaid domestic labor. In addition, fast foods, restaurants, and take-out shops have expanded their operations greatly over the last 25 years. All of these new economic activities have changed the texture of space in both cities and suburbs. Specialty shops and services spring up everywhere to cater to those families with double incomes. Supermarket and giant merchandising stores such as Wal-Mart make shopping more efficient for the consumer although they have other negative consequences for local business. Along with malls retailers also redefine metropolitan space through the construction of minicenters across the region.

The sociospatial relations of the modern, global economy have as much to do with gender roles and patriarchy as they do with economic and political factors. When women stayed at home and engaged in full-time but unpaid labor, they were responsible for keeping up the appearance of the neighborhood. Once middle-class women in the United States were encouraged to change their social role, although still expected to do a "double shift," energies and resources were transferred to service industries that catered to domestic needs. Neighborhoods changed to accommodate fast-food and take-out places, restaurants, laundries, and dry cleaners, and supermarkets and malls made shopping progressively more convenient.

Houses in the suburbs required at least two-car garages because both spouses commuted to work, and teenagers required their own vehicles for work, school, and leisure activities. In both urban and suburban settlement spaces, day care and extended child care programs changed the place where children went to play—from city streets supervised by mothers to indoor group play areas supervised by paid day care specialists. Elsewhere in the global economy, young girls comprise the bulk of the manufacturing labor force in electronics and garment industries because patriarchal relations make them docile and low-paid workers. The control of women's bodies is as essential to the sustenance of Third World countries as it is to the "first world" patriarchal societies. Everywhere, then, the nature of gender roles has a direct effect on sociospatial relations, as can be seen from the comparison of Sweden and the United States in Box 8.5.

Women and the Environment

The concluding remarks of the last section can be expanded to explore more specific relations between settlement space and gender. These relations extend from the home to the community to the larger metropolitan region. The home, for example, is the one space in the environment where people can be themselves. It is the private and intimate space. Due to the family division of labor, women have been assigned the main task of decorating the home. Through this activity they express their own individuality (Matrix Collective, 1984). Housing has several meanings, as we will see (Chapter 9), and it is a signifier of status. But for women, their control over the environmental space of the home has meant an opportunity for self-expression. It has also meant, for the middle class, a restricted domain within which women are allowed to influence their environment.

If the home space can be viewed in this way, it is partly because women have been socialized into the role of responsibility for shelter maintenance. Spatial relations therefore play a great role in the perpetuation of female socialized roles in our society. However, if the female gender role assigns a certain power to women through control of the home environment, the opposite is the case for the larger physical environment of the city and metropolis. Once out in public space, women have to beware. They are subject to harassment and, quite often, danger. Women living in large cities must acquire "street smarts" early if they are to successfully negotiate public space. As one commentary noted:

> Whether you wear a slit skirt or are covered from head to foot in a black chador, the message is not that you are attractive enough to make a man lose his self-control, but that the public realm belongs to him and you are there by his permission as long as you follow his rules and as long as you remember your place. (Benard and Schlaffer, 1993:390)

In contrast to men, women are situated in a constrained space and do not enjoy the same freedom of movement. For example, women are cautioned not to go out alone at night, and with good reason. If they walk or jog around the neighborhood, they usually

BOX 8.5 GENDERED SPACE IN THE BUILT ENVIRONMENT

The sociospatial approach asserts that urban and suburban settlement spaces influence individual behavior; however, this influence is mediated by gender, class, and other individual characteristics. In this way, the meaning of space and the built environment may differ for men and women. Consider the ways in which the structure of settlement space in Sweden and that in the United States have very different consequences for the daily activity and well-being of women.

Suburban developments in the United States usually consist of single-family homes located some distance from the urban center. Local zoning restrictions require that suburban settlement space be low-density (not simply single-family homes instead of apartments, but also lot sizes of between one and three acres). Land-use plans also require physical separation of residential areas from business and commercial development. The federal government has spent billions of dollars constructing a highway system for private automobiles, and public transportation is limited.

In Sweden, suburban developments are of moderate density, usually garden-type apartments located in mixed-use districts where stores and businesses are located within walking distance. Extensive public transportation connects suburban settlement space to the city core, and child care and other services (provided through the public sector) are available within the local community (Popenoe, 1977).

The effects of these two very different built environments on women's lives could not be more dramatic. In the United States, women who live in suburban housing developments are comparatively isolated from friends, relatives, their place of employment, and health and other public services. A second family automobile is needed for women to take their children to day care, go grocery shopping, or travel to their jobs. Then there is the cost of travel time to and from each of these destinations (separated from one another by zoning). In Sweden and other Scandinavian countries with similar welfare state structures and urban planning, women in suburban developments are more likely to live near friends, relatives, and their place of employment. If they do not, public transportation is available, eliminating the need for a second automobile. Because day care and other family services are funded by the state and located in the new planned suburban communities, they are readily available. And because friends and even relatives may live within walking distance, it is easier to pool resources to arrange for other family needs (Popenoe, 1980).

The arrangement of suburban settlement space in Scandinavian countries encourages women to become fully integrated into the metropolitan community and to build strong social networks with others in the community. In contrast, the structure of suburban settlement space in the United States—where homes, workplaces, schools, and shopping areas are separated from one another—places a significant burden on suburban women's time needs (Fava, 1980) and isolates them from employment opportunities and daily activities within the metropolitan region.

do so only in secure places. The women's movement has been particularly attentive to the needs of females for safe places, such as "Take Back the Night" rallies. The constricted and confined safe places for women in our society are another form of oppression. By patterning what activities are allowed, what are isolated, what are considered safe or dangerous, and what are connected to other activities, such as the combination of child care and shopping found in the mall or the gender segregation of children in elementary schools (Thorne, 1993), space plays a role in gender socialization.

The secondary status of women is also reinforced through spatial design. Community planning invariably assigns the major portion of open space to traditionally male-dominated activities, such as sports. Places for mothering are rarely considered at all, and often are restricted to playgrounds. Creating safe environments for children and mothers requires some planning. In Columbia, Maryland, one of the totally planned New Towns in the United States, pedestrian and automobile traffic are separated by the segregation of space. This feature of Columbia makes it easier for mothers to protect children at play. It is not so easy to suggest ways the home and community environments can be improved by taking the needs of women more into account, although some progress through feminist activism has been made in sensitizing planners and architects to the specific needs of women (see Matrix Collective, 1984). In sum, current gender role changes and new demands of family life may affect our environment in the years to come (see Chapter 14 for an extended discussion on environmental and planning concerns).

Ethnicity and Immigration

Ethnic formation is the consequence of government policy and intergroup competition within an ethnically diverse society (Omi and Winant, 1992). In relatively homogeneous societies, lifestyle differences may exist, but they usually are not expressed as ethnicity; class, gender, religious, subcultural, and age differences may be more important. When indigenous people, such as mainland Chinese, immigrate to another country that contains people from many different origins, such as the United States, subcultural differences may take on the dimensions of ethnic differences. These are almost wholly "semiotic" or symbolic in nature (see Chapter 9). In particular, ascribed characteristics and inherited beliefs may make individuals with foreign heritages uniquely different. What counts for the dynamics of ethnicity is the extent to which those symbolic differences clash with those of the dominant society or of other ethnic groups in a diverse society.

In the United States, ethnic lifestyles are closely connected to the waves of immigration from abroad. Our understanding of immigration should include a spatial perspective that acknowledges the important role of the globalization of capital as well as the push and pull factors that most often are used to explain why people left their land of origin in the first place. Three distinct waves of immigration to the United States have occurred. The first two waves are discussed in this section, and the third wave, or "new immigration," is discussed in the following section of this chapter.

First Wave

Many thousands of years ago, Asians immigrated to the Western Hemisphere over a land bridge to Alaska. Beginning with Columbus's fateful voyage in 1492, Western European settlers from the British Isles, Spain, Holland, and France confronted the Native Americans. These European settlers arrived as a consequence of official state policy. Some were convicts taking advantage of an alternative sentence to debtors' prison in their homeland. Others signed on with the promise of free land and other resources. Still others, such as the Puritans who founded the Massachusetts Bay Colony and William Penn and his Quaker community, came in search of religious freedom. At the time of the American Revolution, some 95 percent of immigrants to the United States were Northern European, and nearly 70 percent came from Great Britain (Steinberg, 1996).

During the 1840s, the potato famine in Ireland forced many people from that country to immigrate. The Irish people were the first large group of immigrants who were not Anglo-Saxon Protestants, and they confronted extensive discrimination because they were Catholic (Higham, 1977). By the time they arrived, the earlier groups had entrenched themselves as the ruling class. Many of them, such as John Rockefeller (from Scotland), Cornelius Vanderbilt (whose family had come from Holland), and Leland Stanford (of English origins), had made fortunes in the burgeoning industrial economy of the United States. The Irish were considered less valuable than the African slaves of the South, and they were used for dangerous tasks, such as the building of the railroads, or as the first proletarian factory workers in the northern cities where slavery was not allowed.

Second Wave

By the 1800s, industrialization was in full bloom and the cities of the United States were expanding. At about that time a second, substantial wave of new immigrants arrived here from the countries of Central and Eastern Europe. Most second-wave immigrants made their homes in the city. Many had come from rural backgrounds and had to make adjustments to the urban way of life (Handlin, 1951). As we noted in Chapter 3, the cities of the time were overcrowded. Housing for most immigrants lacked the basic necessities of sanitation and sewage. Public health crises and crime waves were quite common (Monkkonen, 1986). The quality of urban life went into decline. In addition, they found most jobs in the factories of the largest cities, and they had to accommodate themselves to the industrial daily schedule.

It wasn't long before antagonisms developed between immigrant groups organized as workers, and city officials and factory owners. Both the Irish who had arrived somewhat earlier and the second wave of Central and Eastern Europeans were viewed by established residents as threatening to the American way of life. Some second-wave immigrants had already been exposed to radical labor movements in Europe, and these groups, such as the Industrial Workers of the World (IWW), started up in the United States. Because of the large majority of Catholics among the foreigners, particularly the Irish, Italians, and Poles, a popular antiurban sentiment was that large cities were centers of "Rum, Romanism, and Rebellion."

It may be difficult for us to imagine today, but the older, first-wave immigrants, especially those among the elite of the country, propagated racist ideas about the Irish, Italians, Poles, and Jews in the late 1880s. Among the books published was Josiah Strong's (1891) racist diatribe that blamed the white foreigners for diluting the "American Race" and for spawning the crises of the city. In another case, during the 1920s, many outspoken anti-Semites operated in the open, including Henry Ford, who would not allow Jewish workers in his factories and financed a successful reprinting of the virulently anti-Semitic forgery, *The Protocols of the Elders of Zion*—a racist book that is still circulated today.

To a great extent, such racist and anti-Semitic attacks appeared alongside others accusing the new immigrants of harboring communist and anarchist or anticapitalist ideas. Thus anti-immigrant racism was a strong weapon used to call immigration itself into question. Around the turn of the century, reaction to the second wave of arrivals was so strong that it eventually led to a restriction of immigration from Eastern and Southern Europe. This was accomplished in a succession of federal acts that established quotas favoring first-wave, Western European, and Northern European countries. These quotas actually lasted until the immigration reform bill of 1965.

Fighting between employers and workers was not the only conflict of the time; conflict also took on a spatial manifestation. Areas in the city were marked off by ethnicity, class, race, and religion. For example, most large American cities historically have had two separate Irish neighborhoods—one for Irish Catholics, the other for Irish Protestants. These groups competed with each other over territory and access to public resources. Employers would also pit workers from different ethnic groups against one another in a largely successful effort to prevent union organizing and keep workers' wages low. Thrasher's study of Chicago gangs, discussed in Chapter 6, provides an excellent example of how these "defended neighborhoods" that are a sociospatial phenomenon of ethnicity came into being.

Theories of Immigrant Adjustment

The image of the American city as a mosaic of ethnic neighborhoods emerged at the turn of the century as a consequence of competition for settlement space within the industrial city. Early studies described the adjustment of ethnic groups in terms of Robert Park's *race relations cycle,* which included stages of contact, conflict, accommodation, and assimilation. And in keeping with the analogy of a biological model from the natural sciences, Park, and later Roderick McKenzie, would describe population changes within urban neighborhoods as part of a cycle of invasion–succession (McKenzie, 1944). This "ecological" metaphor was criticized early on as being too mechanical a view for the complicated process of neighborhood change (Alihan, 1938). Today we know that the turmoil of population turnover in the city had more to do with competition for jobs within a labor market segmented by race and ethnicity and the operation of the real estate market and the competition for housing among large numbers of immigrants than it did with some innate biological contest over territory among separate ethnic groups. However, this now outdated "ecological" metaphor was notable for its appreciation of the role of space in the action of social groups. That is, in the conflict among different economic, residential, and commercial interests, control of space was one very important feature, especially for cultural reasons.

The most powerful theory of immigrant conflict and accommodation in the United States was the "melting pot" view. It was believed that change would occur gradually and, in some cases, over successive generations as the children of arrivals eventually assimilated into the American way of life. Immigrants might find the United States a strange country and experience certain difficulties upon arrival, such as having to learn English. As a consequence, they would invariably seek out enclaves of their own kind within the city, thus perpetuating the ethnic character of the neighborhood. Over time, however, the melting pot theory suggested, their children would become familiar with U.S. culture and language. They would leave the enclaves and mix, or "melt," with the children of others. Melting pot theorists asserted that the forces operating to bring about such changes were the free-market economy, the public schools, and the institution of democratic politics, all of which allowed for active participation and public life. Adjustment to the United States would occur, according to this view, over several generations with assimilation the end result (Glazer and Moynihan, 1963; Gordon, 1964; Sowell, 1981; Lieberson and Walters, 1988). Implicit in this view was also the notion that the United States was a land of unbridled opportunity and mobility. The widely believed "American Dream" fostered the idea that any immigrant who worked hard and lived a responsible life could become a successful U.S. citizen. Beyond this variant of the American Dream was the belief that success in the United States depended principally on individual self-worth, or human capital. That is, having certain skills and the desire to work hard (human capital) became all that was needed for success because the opportunities themselves were there for the taking.

Lieberson (1980) and Morawska (1990), among others, have recently challenged this melting pot theory. They suggest that while individual attributes are important to future success, there are also institutional impediments that may prevent immigrants from realizing their full potential, such as economic and political constraints. In particular, mobility and success are often a function of business cycles. When economic times are rough, newly arrived residents have an almost impossible task of improving themselves. But when the economy itself is expanding, as it was for much of the period between 1840 and 1920, immigrants may indeed find golden opportunities.

Third Wave

Earlier ideas about race and ethnicity and the immigrant experience are being challenged by the newest, third wave of immigrants that has arrived since the 1970s. Changes to immigration laws enacted in 1965 replaced the earlier quota system (which had been designed to keep Asians and other non-European groups out of the country) with a preference system based on occupational characteristics. Supporters of the immigration reform legislation could not have anticipated the unprecedented response across the globe. Between 1968 and 1990, some 10 million people immigrated to the United States. Further reforms passed by the Bush administration limited immigration to some 540,000 persons each year. But after intense lobbying from the U.S. Chamber of Commerce and other business groups, this number was increased to 650,000 legal immigrants each year. This rate has not been observed here since the last great wave of immigration at the beginning of the twentieth century. And just as in this earlier period in

A Hispanic neighborhood in New York City. Travel agencies are important
because of frequent visits back to countries of origin.

our history, increased immigration is supported by business as a way to increase the
labor pool—and thereby to keep wages from increasing.

The composition of the third wave of immigrant groups is very different from
that of earlier periods. During the first and second waves, 75 percent of the arrivals
were from somewhere in Europe. Today the same percentage are coming from Latin
America and Asia. Each year since 1970, more than 55,000 Mexicans and 50,000 Filipinos have immigrated to the United States. In California, for example, 22 percent of
new immigrants came from Asia and 43 percent from Mexico during the 1970s (Espiritu and Light, 1991). Also striking is the fact that the majority of new immigrants to
the United States are female—and this is true even from countries such as Mexico and
the Philippines, where women are often thought to be less independent. As a consequence of this new immigration, the United States of the twenty-first century will be
more culturally diverse—and more Asian and Hispanic—than at any time in its history. To understand just how significant these changes will be, consider the fact that
Hispanics will outnumber African Americans as the largest minority group in the
United States early in the twenty-first century, and that even if immigration were
halted completely, the U.S. Hispanic population will still double within the next
20 years, from some 14 million to more than 30 million.

A third distinct characteristic of the new immigration is that it is economically diverse as well as culturally contrasting. Many of the newer arrivals exhibit the classic

BOX 8.6   THE ETHNIC ENCLAVE

Ethnic neighborhoods have a long history in the United States, from the Chinatowns and Irish communities of the mid-nineteenth century to the "Little Italies" and Poletowns of the twentieth century. Within the ethnic ghettos, new immigrants could live alongside others from their home countries and quickly build social networks that allowed them to find housing and employment. In the post–World War II period, many older European ethnic neighborhoods began to disappear as the third- and fourth-generation families moved out to the suburbs. In many cities, urban settlement spaces occupied by older ethnic groups have been replaced by new immigrants.

As the new immigrant communities in Chicago, Los Angeles, Miami, New York, and many other cities have continued to expand, ethnic entrepreneurs have started businesses that employ other community residents. These include food stores, restaurants, clothing and textile stores, and other retail stores, as well as repair (auto, plumbing, electrical) and personal services (travel agencies, legal services). Urban sociologists have been studying these *ethnic enclaves* for many years. We know that the ethnic enclave provides an important service for new immigrants—a place where they can find housing and employment opportunities with others from their home countries. Min Zhou (1992) reports that new immigrants in New York City's Chinatown found access to inexpensive housing and employment opportunities that allowed them to become upwardly mobile.

But others are concerned that ethnic enclaves may have negative consequences for new immigrants. Because most ethnic business enterprises are small, family-run stores, wages are lower than in other companies, and opportunities for advancement are few. Although new immigrants may be able to get by within the ethnic enclave simply by speaking their home language, their lack of English-language proficiency will limit their ability to interact with others outside the community and their opportunities for higher-paying jobs in stores and businesses outside the ethnic enclave economy. Also, new immigrants, especially illegal immigrants, are sometimes exploited within the ethnic enclave by their own compatriots (see Lin, 1998). Undocumented (or illegal) immigrants have been found working in unsafe conditions and being paid below the minimum legal wage at restaurants and factories in the Chinatowns in New York and Los Angeles and in the large Mexican enclaves in Chicago and Los Angeles.

characteristics of the past: limited education, rural backgrounds, and limited resources. A large number, however, are the exact opposite. These well-endowed immigrants are educated—many have college degrees—they are former city dwellers, and they often come with enough personal financial resources to start their own businesses. In their home countries of India, Korea, the Philippines, and elsewhere, this loss of a young and highly educated population is referred to as the "brain drain." Thus, many third-wave arrivals have achieved success in the United States in a relatively short time. According to Portes and Rumbaut (1990), in the decade between 1980 and 1990, professionals and technicians accounted for only 18 percent of the U.S. labor force but represented 25 percent of the immigrant population.

Noodle samples are cooked for shoppers at a Japanese supermarket located in suburban Costa Mesa in Orange County, California.

This "bimodal" distribution—that is, having *two peaks:* one high income, one low income—of immigration is a consequence of uneven development in the global system of capitalism. In the 1960s and 1970s, many countries underwent crash modernization programs that were not entirely successful. On the one hand, large numbers of the middle and working classes received technical and professional training. But upon graduation, their economies had not expanded fast enough to offer them work. On the other hand, agricultural reform programs and development of interior places forced many impoverished and uneducated rural residents into the cities. They too took the chance on immigrating rather than waiting around in their home countries for work (Espiritu and Light, 1991).

Some of the recent immigrants have not only been successful; they have realized opportunities in new ways. For example, a suburb outside Los Angeles, Monterey

Park, became a focal point for new Chinese immigration. Between 1960 and 1988, the population went from 85 percent white to 50 percent Chinese, with other Asians also in residence. Consequently, the city is known as the first "suburban Chinatown" (Arax, 1987; Fong, 1991), and it provides an excellent example of why we can no longer consider large cities as the prime site for ethnic subcultures. Recent arrivals have invested over $1 billion of their own money in the suburb, and it is estimated that the Chinese own at least 66 percent of all business and property there (Espiritu and Light, 1991:43). Other areas of the country report a similar phenomenon of immigrant suburbanization, where in many cases new arrivals bypass the large city entirely (see Box 8.7).

Current immigration to the United States (and other developed nations) reflects changes in the global system of capitalism in another respect. Following the breakup of colonial systems after World War II, many European countries saw an increase in immigration from their former colonies—Caribbean blacks and Muslim and Hindu Indians in England, Indonesian and other groups in the Netherlands. At the end of the Second Indo-Chinese War, the United States admitted 300,000 Southeast Asian refugees, and the death squads and political conflicts in Central America in the 1980s brought another 500,000 refugees, despite efforts of the Reagan administration and the Immigration and Naturalization Service to prevent them from entering the country. And as noted earlier, each year some 50,000 people immigrate to the United States from the Philippines, our former colonial outpost in the South Pacific.

The new immigration already has had a profound effect on settlement spaces within metropolitan regions across the country. Some groups have moved into older ethnic neighborhoods, greatly expanding their numbers and size. In Chicago, for example, the Mexican neighborhood in 18th Street/Pilsen has expanded across the 26th Street/Little Village community into suburban communities, while the older Chinatown area near the Loop has seen extensive redevelopment that has doubled the number of business establishments and dwelling units. In these and other ethnic communities across the metropolitan region, local residents have constructed new settlement spaces rich with symbolic meanings—from Mexican storefronts identical to those found in Monterrey or Aguascalientes, the primary sending areas in Mexico for immigration to Chicago and the Midwest, now reproduced in *suburban* settlement space, to new commercial malls and housing designed by a Chinese American architect. The city of Chicago is developing a new riverfront park in this new Chinatown, designed by a Chinese American landscape architect, which will reproduce traditional Chinese design elements in this new *urban* settlement space.

Ethnic Settlement Space in Cities and Suburbs

The multicentered metropolitan region contains a diversity of settlement spaces. While it is commonplace to speak of differences between urban and suburban communities, in fact most such differences have disappeared (if in fact they ever existed). For many years, sociologists spoke of ethnic communities and racial ghettos in the central city as if ethnic and racial groups lived only in these sorts of urban neighborhoods. But the history of ethnic settlement patterns has long been one of diverse neighborhoods and movement to the suburbs. While most American cities have had

BOX 8.7 FAREWELL TO CHINATOWN

Ask Torontonians how to get to Chinatown and most will give directions to the corner of Dundas Street and Spadina Avenue, a bustling neighborhood filled with the sites and scents of Asia. With its gritty feast for the senses and rapid pulse of street-level energy, this neighborhood is the archetypical North American Chinatown.

But for someone seeking the largest Chinese community in the city, the directions would be different, and surprising: They would lead straight to suburbia. In a long-overdue transition, Toronto's Chinatown is moving up-town to cleaner and roomier surroundings. After a century of isolation and discrimination, Chinese-Canadians in Toronto are at last moving into the broader community. This Chinatown is in the north end of Scarborough, one of Toronto's sprawling suburbs, and it is far bigger than the one downtown. Rosa Chan, a librarian and president of Scarborough's largest Chinese community group, rarely goes back to downtown Chinatown. Now it feels dirty and cramped to her: She prefers the new houses, clean malls, wide streets and open spaces of suburbia. Besides, she can find all the Chinese goods she needs close to home. Only the older generation prefers down-town, she says: "It's more the traditional way of Chinese living—people are crowded together, like in Hong Kong."

For the Chinese community—an estimated 350,000 of the 3.9 million people in Metropolitan Toronto and its adjoining municipalities—downtown Chinatown is becoming a sort of colorful false front. Most live, work, shop, and play in the suburbs. The new neighborhoods have none of Chinatown's street life. The car is king and people drive to the Chinese plazas along four- and six-lane thoroughfares. The suburban communities are spread through-out large housing tracts, with stores and services scattered among dozens of widely spaced shopping centers and strip malls. The tens of thousands who have embraced the suburban lifestyle are still a distinctive group, with their own unique activities and problems. But for many of them, the idea of an isolated "Chinatown" is as much a relic as the archaic ponytail.

There is a nagging remnant of racism against the Chinese community. Chinese-Canadians fear it may get worse if rising unemployment increases hostility toward newcomers who appear to be prospering. Hate literature, saying Chinese people are dominating and corrupting the city, was recently distributed in Scarborough. Chinese employees are still kept out of most management and executive positions in non-Chinese companies.

Some Chinese-Canadian suburbanites worry that their culture is grad-ually weakening amid the malls and fast-food joints. There is some turbu-lence under the placid surface. Clashes can be expected between parents accustomed to traditional ways and children who want to adopt the freer North American lifestyle. Still, for most Chinese-Canadians, Toronto offers a broadening range of opportunities and improved chances to make a good life. The transition into the suburbs symbolizes the start of a new era for Toronto's Chinese community. "Both sides were afraid," Wong says. "The non-Chinese were afraid of change, and we were afraid of the new envi-ronment. I think this dispersal is a great thing." (Gorrie, 1991) notable German, Polish, Italian, and other ethnic neighborhoods, the ethnic ghettos typically contained only a small proportion of all immigrants from each group. Most Germans, Poles, and Italians lived in other neighborhoods across the city and early on began to make their way into suburban communities. Massey and Denton (1993) note that it probably was the early work of the Chicago School that misled urban sociologists into thinking that inner-city ethnic neighborhoods were the focal point of immigrant life. Immigration occurs across metropolitan regions and affects all regions of the country, as the figures in Table 8.1 show.

African Americans. Unlike other ethnic groups, African Americans were forcibly removed from their home countries and brought to the United States as slaves during the 1700s. In 1990, their descendants constituted 12.4 percent of the total population. Until the twentieth century, the overwhelming majority of blacks, more than 90 percent, lived in the South, and most were located in rural areas. Since the turn of the century, however, there has been a steady movement of African Americans to the North in general and to cities in particular (Lemann, 1991b).

In the 1800s, many slaves fled the South for freedom. Using such routes as the "underground railroad," they arrived in the cities of the North, and some even made it as far as Canada. By the end of the Civil War, several communities of African Americans were already established in northern cities. As a result of discrimination against blacks, however, these areas soon became segregated. A similar pattern of ghettoization occurred in the making of black communities in Chicago (Spear, 1967), Philadelphia (W. E. B. DuBois, 1899), and New York (Drake and Cayton, 1945).

During the turn of the century, the mechanization of agriculture, coupled with the immense increase in industrialization with its job opportunities, both pushed and pulled blacks off southern farms and into northern factories. This process accelerated as a consequence of World War I, fell off during the Great Depression, and resumed with full intensity during World War II. As a result, by the 1950s African Americans were almost as urbanized as were whites, with over 60 percent of their total population living in cities. After 1950 a large percentage of whites began an exodus from the cities to the suburbs, which at the time were almost overwhelmingly closed to black migration. As a result, the percentage of African Americans living in central cities rose. By the 1980s, cities such as Los Angeles, Chicago, Atlanta, and Detroit had black mayors, and in the 1990s the list grew to include New York and others.

As we have seen, racial discrimination is still a potent force that prevents African Americans from integrating into society. For blacks, segregation into distinct ghetto areas of most cities still persists despite their large urban numbers. During the last two decades, a growing number of blacks have achieved middle-class status (Wilson, 1987) and now live alongside white families in downtown high-rise apartment buildings, upscale city neighborhoods, and a wide range of suburban communities across the metropolitan area. However, much of the African American population remains highly segregated; in Chapter 10, we will discuss the immense problems this segregation poses for the quality of urban life. The sights and sounds of poverty and discrimination and the symbols of political struggle mark racial ghettos from other urban settlement spaces.

TABLE 8.1
Destinations of Major Immigrant Groups in Selected Years

Nationality	Year	Number	As Percentage of Total Immigration	Percentage in Top Three Destinations	Most Common Destinations		
					First	Second	Third
Mexican	1979	52,096	11.3	17.3	El Paso	Los Angeles	Houston
	1984	57,557	10.6	27.9	Los Angeles	Chicago	El Paso
	1987	72,351	12.0	33.0	Los Angeles	El Paso	San Diego
	1993	126,561	14.0	31.4	Los Angeles	Chicago	Houston
Cuban	1979	15,585	3.4	59.1	Miami	New York	San Juan
	1984	10,599	1.9	51.8	Miami	Jersey City	New York
	1987	28,916	4.8	86.0	Miami	New York	Tampa
	1993	13,666	1.5	81.5	Miami	Jersey City	Tampa
Dominican	1979	17,519	3.8	80.6	New York	San Juan	Bergen-Passaic
	1984	23,147	4.3	78.7	New York	San Juan	Bergen-Passaic
	1987	24,858	4.1	76.0	New York	San Juan	Bergen-Passaic
	1993	45,420	5.0	71.1	New York	San Juan	Boston
Filipino	1979	41,300	9.0	17.8	San Francisco	Los Angeles	Honolulu
	1984	42,768	7.9	28.1	Los Angeles	San Francisco	Honolulu
	1987	50,060	8.3	30.0	Los Angeles	San Francisco	San Diego
	1993	53,457	7.0	26.0	Los Angeles	New York	San Diego
Total	1979	460,348		25.5	New York	Los Angeles	Miami
	1984	543,903		29.8	New York	Los Angeles	Chicago
	1987	601,516		33.2	New York	Los Angeles	Miami
	1993	904,292		30.9	New York	Los Angeles	Chicago

Source: U.S. Immigration and Naturalization Service, *Statistical Yearbooks* (Washington, D.C.: U.S. Government Printing Office, 1968, 1976, 1980, 1985, 1988, 1994).

Mexican Americans. Much of the Southwest, including parts of California, Arizona, New Mexico, and Texas, once belonged to the country of Mexico. Over time these lands were taken over by the United States. As a result, a significant Mexican population was included within our borders, and the places in the Southwest bear Mexican names. Mexican Americans suffered discrimination at the hands of the "Anglos," or non-Hispanic Americans. Due to the language barrier, they also found it difficult to achieve mobility. Settlement in most of the Southwest was confined to specific ghettos or *barrios,* which literally means "neighborhood" (Moore, 1976).

In 1990, Hispanics accounted for over 8 percent of the total population and Mexicans constituted roughly 60 percent of all Hispanics (Bean and Tienda, 1987). Between 1980 and 1990, the Hispanic population as a whole increased by over 50 percent. This figure underestimates the total number of Hispanics, because many are illegal aliens. Mexicans continue to cross over to the United States in record numbers, and the community will retain its rapid growth rate in the future. Most settle in the border states of California and Texas. Often overlooked are the long-time urban populations of midwestern cities such as Chicago and Detroit, where Mexican and Mexican American workers were recruited to work in the steel mills, auto assembly plants, and meat-packing houses in the 1920s. Chicago's Mexican neighborhoods now contain the third largest Mexican population in the United States (Hutchison, 1998), and the Chicago metropolitan region includes spillover suburban communities adjacent to the city and new barrios in the manufacturing suburbs, as well as third- and fourth-generation suburban families in the northern Indiana area.

In the Southwest, some barrio areas are known for gang-related activities and a high rate of murder, principally caused by gang violence (Moore, 1978; Vigil, 1988); others are simply areas where Mexican American families can find housing. Recently, however, Mexican Americans have achieved a certain level of mobility and have entered the ranks of the professional middle class. For example, Denver had the first elected Mexican American mayor; Tomas Rivera served as a chancellor of the University of California; and several Mexican Americans are now members of Congress and the president's cabinet. As language barriers are overcome, and with their increasing numbers, this group is expected to play a greater role in U.S. society.

Puerto Ricans. In 1898, the United States defeated Spain in a war of "manifest destiny" and acquired the former Spanish colonies of Cuba, Puerto Rico, Hawaii, and the Philippines. Since that time, Puerto Rico has been governed as a trust, or dependent territory, of the United States; while the island does not have statehood, Puerto Ricans are citizens of the United States and vote for a representative in the House of Representatives. Like other Caribbean countries, most of the population of Puerto Rico is mestizo—a racial mixture of various European and African ethnic populations—but with large white and black populations as well. For many years there was a small Puerto Rican presence in the United States, largely limited to Miami and New York, but in the decades after World War II this would change dramatically.

In the 1950s, labor shortages led the U.S. government to recruit workers from Mexico and the Caribbean. The Puerto Rican communities in Chicago, Philadelphia, and other cities were formed around this earlier migration of laborers from the island

Migration of a People. This mural provides a narrative of Puerto Rican immigration to Chicago, beginning with colonial labor on sugar plantations, the migration of families to the U.S. mainland, and employment in industrial jobs.

(as shown in the mural *Migration of a People*). Although Spanish Harlem in Manhattan (New York City) may be the best-known area of Puerto Rican settlement in the country, in the 1960s there was a large increase in Puerto Rican populations in many cities, especially in the Northeast. Like other ethnic groups, Puerto Ricans often settled into older neighborhoods in the central city. Because most Puerto Ricans are part-black, some believe they confront greater discrimination in employment and housing than other Hispanic groups; in fact, Puerto Ricans rank alongside African Americans on many measures of poverty, unemployment, and family disruption.

In the 1980s, sociologists began to study the return migration of Puerto Ricans from the urban centers of the North to the home communities of their parents on the island (Alicea, 1990). Although the Puerto Rican population on the mainland has continued to grow from both natural increase and migration, many households and individuals have chosen to return to the island (a decision prompted by both a loss of basic employment in American cities and the discrimination that darker-skinned Puerto Ricans may confront). While we often read of the "problems" of immigrant adjustment for ethnic groups arriving in the United States (as discussed earlier in this chapter), researchers have studied the adjustment of people returning to the island. Just as bilingual programs are required to teach immigrant children to speak English in public schools across the country, bilingual programs in Puerto Rico teach children coming from the United States to speak Spanish so that they can complete their education and find employment on the island.

Native Americans. The residential settlement patterns of Native Americans are especially interesting. Some Indian tribes continue to live in the same communities that Spanish explorers first visited in the 1500s; indeed, the Twelve Pueblo communities outside of Albuquerque, New Mexico, are the oldest continuously inhabited towns in the United States. Other Indian tribes were forced from their homelands by the Indian Removal Act of 1830. The Cherokees had by this time established permanent towns and schools, but were forcibly removed from their homes in Georgia, Alabama, and Tennessee and relocated to reservation land in Oklahoma. During the 1870s, the United States ceased to recognize these people as belonging to independent nations, and they came under the administration of the Bureau of Indian Affairs.

While we often think of Native Americans as an isolated group living on rural reservations, they too are an urban population. It is estimated that half of the Native American population lives in cities (with especially large concentrations in Los Angeles, Chicago, and Minneapolis), and in several areas of the country Indian reservations are located adjacent to large cities (such as the Salt River and Gila reservations outside of Phoenix) or even within the boundaries of cities (such as the Oneida reservation in Green Bay, Wisconsin). For many years, Native Americans suffered extreme poverty regardless of their residence in cities or rural reservations, and to some degree this is still true. But over the last two decades, many Indian tribes have prospered from economic development associated with casino gambling, although in many ways the patterns of uneven development endemic in the larger economic system have been replicated among Indian tribes across the country.

As we learned earlier, the federal government began cutting funding to states and cities in the 1970s. Instead of raising taxes to cover the additional expense of social programs, many states passed constitutional amendments that allowed them to run state lotteries. As a consequence of this action, Indian tribes (sovereign nations with rights comparable to states) may run the same type of gambling enterprises (such as lotteries) as state governments. The rise of the Native American casino industry is a direct consequence of the fiscal crises of the federal and state governments. Many Native American reservations located close to urban centers have been able to generate substantial revenues from casinos. The actual development strategies used vary greatly from tribe to tribe. In Phoenix the Salt River reservation has leased land to a development company that built and manages the largest shopping mall in the metropolitan area, while in Green Bay the Oneida Indian Nation has used profits from gaming to fund new health clinics and elder housing, purchase land within reservation boundaries lost in previous generations, and diversify into retail businesses and manufacturing companies. Many of these reservations have seen a population increase as tribal members living in cities across the country have returned to employment opportunities that did not exist just two decades earlier. Yet uneven development may still be the rule; while tribes near urban areas have prospered, those in remote areas of the country have been unable to generate revenue from gaming and remain very poor. And within individual tribes, there still is substantial concern over high levels of poverty, family disruption, and low rates of high school completion.

Conclusion

As this summary of settlement patterns for ethnic groups demonstrates, sociospatial relations continue to play a significant role in the lives of minority groups in the

United States. As the example of Wilhelmina Reyes in Chapter 1 demonstrates, some groups have been able to move into the mainstream of American society and have gained access to employment, housing, and the quality of life that we believe all Americans should have. Others remain in segregated social spaces—ghettos, barrios, or reservations—where they may be isolated from opportunities in the larger society.

In the years to come, these new sources of ethnic formation and ethnic identity will influence U.S. culture in ways we have yet to anticipate, just as the formidable influx some 80 years ago once did. At the turn of the century, many people feared that foreign workers would take away the jobs of American workers and dilute or destroy American institutions; yet those foreigners are now a permanent part of the American mosaic. In the last decade, we have had the lowest levels of unemployment in nearly half a century at the same time that immigration has reached near-record levels, suggesting that immigrant workers need not take the jobs of American workers. In a few short decades, the new immigrants of today will become part of an even greater American mosaic, living in ethnic neighborhoods if they choose or alongside other groups across the metropolitan region. As we will discuss in Chapter 11, new immigrants have changed the complexion of metropolitan politics. Only time will tell what form this influence will take, but immigration from Asia and Latin America to the United States will likely continue at its active pace into the twenty-first century.

Years ago it was proper to speak of an "urban mosaic" (a term used extensively by Robert Park) to capture the diversity of people and lifestyles in the city. Today the entire metropolitan region, both cities and suburbs, must be described in this term. As we have seen, urban and suburban settlement spaces are stratified by class, race, and gender. They are also differentiated according to ethnicity, race, age, and family status. Each lifestyle manifests its own daily rhythm within the settlement spaces each group has created within the metropolitan region. The built environment displays the expressive symbols of this interaction between social factors and local territory. But settlement space also directs behavior in certain ways. In contemporary societies, it is likely that gender roles are conditioned as much by the spatial restrictions of the built environment as by patriarchal domination. Sociospatial relations among groups and individuals are also conditioned by class and race distinctions ranging from inclusion in neighborhoods of shared interests to the extreme case of ghetto segregation.

Economic and political forces influence sociospatial patterns by planning and regulating the built environment. But so do cultural features. Class, racial, gender, and ethnic differences are expressed as symbols that imply difference. Images of a large home, an expensive car, certain styles of clothing—all patterns of everyday consumption—are potent signs of status. Racial interaction operates largely through the regulation of appearance and of segregated social space. This semiotic dimension of the sociospatial perspective will be discussed more fully in the next chapter.

The diversity of metropolitan life has been studied in great detail. In fact, such explorations of the everyday texture of urban and suburban life have formed a central focus for the work of urban sociologists since the early days of the Chicago School. A variety of methodological perspectives are employed in the study of everyday life in urban and suburban settlement spaces, including participant observation, interviews, network analysis, and semiotics. Let us consider each of these approaches in the next chapter.

CHAPTER

9

NEIGHBORHOODS, THE PUBLIC ENVIRONMENT, AND THEORIES OF URBAN LIFE

Film directors usually establish a Manhattan location by filming a long shot of some busy street in midtown or the financial district. In it we see a crowd of people pressed together—a sea of bobbing heads hurrying on their way to and from business. To establish the location of Los Angeles, in contrast, filmmakers often take to the air and provide a helicopter shot of clogged freeways, or at other times, shoot from a car moving slowly on palm tree–lined streets.

Different images reflect spatial differences. Locale, or the sense of place, matters. Preparing ourselves for a trip to New York would involve special things such as acquiring a rudimentary understanding of the bus and subway systems. For a trip to Los Angeles, preparations would be somewhat different and would certainly involve, for example, arranging for auto transport and learning something about the freeways. A visit to most suburbs would also be different, yet closer to the Los Angeles experience than to New York City. In the suburbs, we need transportation to shopping or entertainment that is not a short walk away as it is in the city.

Suppose we took a trip to a large city—San Diego, for example. What would we do there? Figure 9.1 lists some of the activities San Diego has to offer.

Every place possesses some distinguishing feature that can be enjoyed, whether it is the picturesque quality and friendly people of the small town, the quiet and spaciousness of the suburbs, or the hustle and bustle of the large city. A resident of the metropolitan region has a choice on any given day whether to experience the cultural

---

Population (1995): city: 1,151,977; metropolitan region: 2,644,132

Museums: San Diego has many museums—something for everyone in the family. We can study painting and sculpture from the Renaissance to the present day at the San Diego Museum of Art and the Museum of Contemporary Art. The Balboa Park and Casa Del Rey Moro museums feature work by Mexican, Chicano, African-Latin, and African American artists. Or we could visit the San Diego Aerospace Museum and see more than 65 aircraft and spacecraft. At the San Diego Maritime Museum we can tour the *Star of India*, one of the few remaining clipper ships of the nineteenth century.

Music and Theater: We can attend concerts by the San Diego Symphony Orchestra or the San Diego Opera. The La Jolla Chamber Music Society presents visiting orchestras and ensembles during SummerFest La Jolla, a three-week festival held each August. The Tony Award–winning La Jolla Playhouse presents musicals, comedies, classics, and world premieres. There are more than 100 performing arts companies in San Diego County.

Zoo: The San Diego Zoo and Wild Animal Park is world famous. Or we could visit Sea World and watch the fireworks each evening at closing time.

Night Life: There are wonderful ethnic restaurants throughout the city and cozy bistros in La Jolla where you can look out over the ocean. Much of the nightlife in the city is now oriented around the Old Town/Gas Lamp neighborhood and Seaport Village in downtown San Diego.

Scenery: San Diego is one of America's most beautiful cities—and you can see it best from the Cabrillo National Monument and Point Loma lighthouse, with a spectacular view of San Diego on one side and the Pacific Ocean on the other. A visit to the Hotel Coronado in the middle of San Diego harbor is a must for every visitor. Just a short drive up the coast will take us to the Mission of San Juan Capistrano. And a visit to Black's Beach in La Jolla is often the highlight of summer travel to the city!

Sports: See the professional sporting events of your choice: the San Diego Padres (baseball), the San Diego Chargers (football), the San Diego Clippers (basketball), as well as semiprofessional and collegiate teams in these sports and more!

Figure 9.1   What to do in San Diego.

amenities of urban or suburban life. These opportunities are a function of the activities or features found in particular places, such as cities or suburbs, rather than arising from the particular environment of a city or suburb itself. But many urban sociologists insist that the nature of space does produce differences in behavior on its own so that the city—any city—would influence behavior in specific ways.

The arguments, both pro and con, regarding whether urban and suburban settlement spaces have the ability to change behavior constitute the focus for the study of metropolitan culture. Investigations of urban and suburban ways of life comprise a large part of research work by urban sociologists. In Chapter 6 we studied the early contributions of

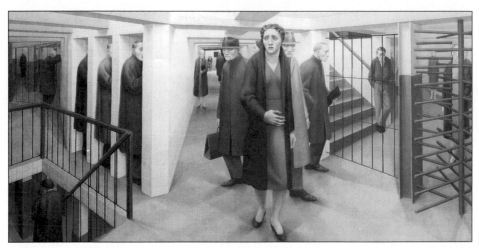

A Vision of Urban Anonymity by Richard Tooker. Contrast this with the photo on page 198.

sociologists to the study of urbanism, particularly those associated with the Chicago School, which focused exclusively on the city. In this chapter we will consider more contemporary studies exploring the relationship between spatial location and social interaction for all communities in the metropolitan region, including suburbs and cities.

Does Space Affect Behavior? The Search for Community

Early urban sociologists in the 1920s and 1930s were preoccupied with whether urban settlement space produced differences in behavior, specifically when contrasted with the rural way of life. Hundreds of thousands of people left the farms and small towns of America and moved to the large industrial cities looking for work. At that time, sociologists worked with an idealized image of small-town life and were suspicious of the city. They believed that small towns offered people a sense of community resulting from primary or intimate ties in social relationships. In contrast, early researchers viewed cities as destroyers of intimacy, forcing secondary or anonymous relations on individuals, with a consequent loss of community feeling. In contrast to the "friendly" rural town, city people were believed to be unfriendly, rushed, uncaring, suspicious, and hard to get to know.

As we also saw in Chapter 6, Louis Wirth, of the Chicago School, believed that living in large cities resulted in forms of social disorganization such as increased crime, divorce, and mental illness because of the decline of close community ties (see Chapter 10). For Wirth it was the city itself, operating through demographic factors such as size and density of population, that produced urban behavior. When we go to a store in a city, we do not have, nor do we seek, a close relationship with the salesperson. We simply want service and wish to get what we want to buy as quickly as possible. Rural area residents,

in contrast, are likely to already have established primary relationships with the employees and even the owners of local businesses. The same contrast applies to relations with
neighbors in the city and rural areas. The domination of secondary relations in the city,
Wirth believed, would result in negative effects such as crime and other problems. This
assertion is known as the *social disorganization* thesis of urban life.

Field Research on Community

Following World War II, a number of sociologists decided to challenge Wirth's theory. Studying local neighborhoods within the larger cities, these sociologists discovered communities with strong primary relations among the residents (Whyte, 1955;
Gans, 1962). In the 1960s and 1970s, a series of community studies contradicted the
social disorganization thesis of the early Chicago School. Researchers discovered evidence of vital, healthy primary relations and an active community life in urban neighborhoods. Ulf Hannerz's (1969) remarkable study of an inner-city ghetto area in
Washington, D.C., exemplifies the case study approach to community. This fine-
grained analysis depicts ghetto residents as multidimensional human beings, trapped in
the ghetto by racism and poverty. Hannerz could not find a single "characteristic"
ghetto resident. Rather, he discovered a typology of behavioral patterns reflecting differences in individual character and family organization as each person dealt with
racial and economic adversity in his or her own way. These results have been replicated in Elijah Anderson's (1978) ethnographic account of a black neighborhood on
Chicago's South Side titled *A Place on the Corner.*

To the outside observer, densely populated inner-city neighborhoods seem chaotic.
One sterling accomplishment of field research has been to document the order created
out of urban chaos by city residents. Herbert Gans's (1962) classic field study of
Boston's East End challenged the view that the area was a "slum" and discovered that
life in this working-class community was highly organized around peer groups. Adult
males spent leisure time with other males, adult females with their female friends, and
so on. Once the form of social organization of the community was understood, it became a familiar place. As explained in Box 9.1, the insights for Gans's conclusions
were obtained using the methodology of field research or participant observation.

Other field research carried out in the 1950s and 1960s showed that primary relations and an intimate community life could be found in suburban settlement space.
One of the earliest studies of suburban communities was William H. Whyte's *The Organization Man* (1956). Whyte depicted the classic suburb of the time as a place where
nuclear families were housed in single-family, detached homes; where women did not
work but spent their time in housekeeping chores and chats over coffee with neighbors; and where men commuted into the city to corporate, professional jobs. For more
recent examples, see Baumgartner (1988), Jackson (1985), and Fishman (1987).

While city-based analyses tended to choose the working classes or "ethnics" with
extended familial ties to kin and neighbors who lived in close proximity (see Box 9.1),
suburban studies concentrated on the middle-class nuclear family and its communal
relations among friends. This division of labor, which follows from Burgess's model
of urban growth as well as Wirth's description of urban life, gave the false impression

BOX 9.1 FIELD WORK METHODOLOGY

The methodological approach known as *field work* always situates observations within a particular space and time. A distinguishing feature of field work is that investigators get to know residents intimately because they often live among them for an extended period of time. They also get to know the space well and often supplement observations of behavior by describing the space in which it occurs. Field work is based on the systematic writing of notes that describe in as much detail as possible the day-to-day experience of participant observation. All descriptions, examples, impressions, and conclusions of research must be based on these extensive notes, which the researcher guards carefully as the record of investigation.

Herbert I. Gans's (1962) study of a poor Italian neighborhood is a classic. Before Gans's study, the common conception of such areas was that they were slums and that the people living in them needed the aid of middle-class professionals to overcome their problems. Such conclusions were reached from afar. Gans, in contrast, actually lived in a so-called slum area, which is what field work is all about. His perception of the "slum" changed quickly from the initial impressions of an outsider to those of one who is intimately familiar with the environment. During his field experience Gans learned that our "outsider's" view of such areas is misguided:

> My first visit to the West End left me with the impression that I was in Europe. Its high buildings set on narrow, irregularly curving streets, its Italian and Jewish restaurants and food stores, and the variety of people who crowded the streets when the weather was good—all gave the area a foreign and exotic flavor. . . . Looking at the area as a tourist, I noted the highly visible and divergent characteristics that set it off from others with which I was familiar.
>
> After a few weeks of living in the West End, my observations—and my perception of the area—changed drastically. The search for an apartment quickly indicated that the individual units were usually in much better condition than the outside or the hallways of the buildings. Subsequently, in wandering through the West End, and in using it as a resident, I developed a kind of selective perception, in which my eye focused only on those parts of the area that were actually being used by people. Vacant buildings and boarded-up stores were no longer so visible, and the totally deserted alleys or streets were outside the set of paths normally traversed, either by myself or by the West Enders.
>
> Since much of the area's life took place on the street, faces became familiar very quickly. I met my neighbors on the stairs and in front of my building. . . . In short, the exotic quality of the stores and the residents also wore off as I became used to seeing them. (Gans, 1962:12)

that social classes had become stratified within urban and suburban settlement spaces. Bennett Berger's (1960) study of working-class households in suburban Richmond, California, was an important milestone, arguing that working-class individuals who moved to the suburbs did not automatically change their behavior and attitudes and become middle class; instead, they preserved their working-class way of life in this new environment. Throughout the 1970s and 1980s, urban ecologists were busy discovering the diversity of social classes and ethnic groups in the suburbs. They concluded that while individual suburbs were internally homogeneous, the suburban region was heterogeneous. We know now that the entire metropolitan region is in fact quite diverse, and this is true not just of urban settlement space but also within and between suburban settlement spaces, as discussed in Chapter 8.

The sociospatial perspective suggests that there are no *unique* differences in social life between urban and suburban settlement spaces. After several decades of comparative field work, it is clear that cities and suburbs are home to a variety of lifestyles, which are more a function of the complex interplay among class, ethnicity, race, and gender than a result of living in a particular environment. Does this conclusion mean that location has no effect whatsoever on personal behavior? Field research tended to debunk the social disorganization thesis of urban life, but another method, network analysis, discovered conditions under which location did play a specific role in people's lives. Let us consider this research tradition next.

Network Analysis: Does Location Matter?

In the 1970s, Claude Fischer (1975) claimed that while most of the differences among individuals in the metropolis were caused by background factors such as class and race, certain attributes of behavior differed among people according to their location. Because of the size of urban populations, residents of the large city had the opportunity to act in ways that rural residents would ordinarily find more difficult. According to this *subcultural perspective* on urban life, city dwellers have a greater opportunity to establish relations with a greater variety of people than do persons in places with smaller populations. It is these relationships, or *networks,* that sustain differences in lifestyles observed between city and rural dwellers. Hence, according to Fischer, the subcultural diversity of cities created by large population size does produce differences between urban and rural behaviors.

Following the subcultural perspective, Fischer (1982) documented the effect of location on the quality and structure of personal networks. He found that individuals in the city differed from rural counterparts because they had fewer kin or more unrelated intimates in their personal networks. However, Fischer also discovered that the effect of place alone, when controlling for all other factors, *was quite small.* The single most important predictor of nonkin networks was education: the more years of education, the more nonrelatives in an individual's personal network. A second important factor was income, which also contributed to independence from relatives. Thus, while location within urban and suburban settlement space does influence behavior, it is not as powerful as the *compositional* factors related to education, income, and other social considerations that we discussed in Chapter 8. Box 9.2 examines the network methodology used by Fischer and others to show the differences location makes in lifestyle patterns.

Network analysis has uncovered a second important aspect of urban community relations. As the metropolitan environment of cities and suburbs has matured, people now organize their lives across a greater spatial distance than in the past. Among other things, this means that one's intimate relations may involve people at some distance. Network researchers who have studied this more mature phenomenon of U.S. settlement spaces

BOX 9.2 SOCIAL NETWORK ANALYSIS

The study of social networks in urban sociology originates in the work of two British social anthropologists. J. A. Barnes described social networks as groups of persons interconnected by friendship and kinship relations (Barnes 1954). Elizabeth Bott's (1957) study of working-class and middle-class households in London was the first study to apply the ideas presented in Barnes' work. She found that the working-class households had overlapping and densely connected family and social networks, while the middle-class households had less dense networks. Network analysis uses personal interviews to discover the links among people—whom they interact with on a daily or weekly basis, how many people an individual knows, and so on. This method was compared to a chain letter by the anthropologist Ulf Hannerz:

> We are probably all familiar with chain letters. You receive a letter from somebody instructing you to send something—money, a picture postcard, or whatever—to the person at the top of a given list, then remove that name while adding your own at the bottom of the list, and finally pass the new list with instructions along to some number of persons whom you choose yourself. If everything worked according to plan, the chains would rapidly branch out, so that for your trouble you would in due time get a sizable number of responses from others, perhaps people personally unknown to you. But frequently . . . you get nothing at all, because somewhere along the line there are people with no wish to participate. (Hannerz, 1980:163)

Barry Wellman, a sociologist at the University of Toronto, interviewed urban and suburban residents of the Toronto metropolitan area to determine where their friends and relatives lived and how frequently they visited with each of them. This information allowed Wellman and his colleagues to discover systematic differences in the social networks of urban and suburban residents, and of male and female respondents in both settlement spaces. Wellman (1988) noted that social networks need not be confined to the local neighborhood. In fact, for many urbanites, social networks reach far beyond local settlement space to include friends and coworkers from across the metropolitan area—evidence of the existence of "community without propinquity." With the advent of internet mail lists, Wellman and other social network analysts have expanded upon this earlier work to examine how community and social networks are constructed across cyber space.

therefore have redefined our understanding of community, because in the past, people assumed you were most friendly with those who lived near you as neighbors. According to Wellman (1979, 1988), the concept of community must be rethought to emphasize the nonneighborhood basis of personal ties. People's communities consist of networks that are not spatially distinct but are dispersed across the metropolis and the country.

Current research using network analysis on community relations suggests that while spatial location matters, its effects are *not* large. Other factors, such as class, education, gender, and race, are most important when explaining urban behavior, as we saw in Chapter 8. Because network researchers look at the role of space in only a very specific way, they miss important influences of the built environment. The *sociospatial*

189

perspective conceives of the influence of space in a broader, more general way while acknowledging the central role played by social factors. In the following section, we will consider the role of space in social interaction to highlight how urban and suburban settlement spaces interact with compositional factors. We will discuss the new theory of urbanism and illustrate it with a look at several issues in which spatial or contextual factors count heavily in our understanding of urban and suburban behavior.

Does Space Affect Behavior? A New Theory of Urbanism

The Sociospatial Approach to Metropolitan Culture

The findings of earlier research on "communities" and "urbanism" are clearly related to the historical conditions of the time. Wirth observed the city of the 1920s and 1930s when the United States was still experiencing a large rural-to-urban migration. Fischer (1976) made his claims about city/rural differences when that distinction still mattered (prior to 1970) and when suburbs were only recently maturing, a condition that has changed today.

In Chapter 5, we saw that suburbs have steadily matured and possess patterns of life very much like those of the large city. Fischer's subcultural theory still argues for something unique about cities and neglects large suburbs. The suburban region of Orange County, for example, possesses as varied a subcultural life as is true of any large city, although 20 years ago it may have been less developed than the city (Kling, Olin, and Poster, 1991). Furthermore, the suburbanization of Asian families in Monterey Park, California, and of Mexican families in Berwyn and Cicero, Illinois (see Chaper 8), have produced ethnic enclaves outside of the city, thereby adding to the subcultural diversity of suburban life.

While it is true that city residents enjoy more choices than do people living in lower-density areas with regard to their respective circles of friends, this effect is explained best by income differences, because an individual must be able to afford to sustain a network of friends outside the immediate area. Hence, the effects of urbanism that are attributed to subcultural differences are also closely intertwined with the compositional effects of social factors, such as level of income, education, and race.

Today all areas of the metropolitan region exhibit tremendous diversity. Instead of discussing lifestyle differences as a function of urbanism, it makes increasingly more sense to adopt a metropolitan perspective and relate social differences to locational differences in the region. We suggest that lifestyles within the metropolitan region are explained best by a combination of compositional or social factors and the action of the environment. While the population size and density of cities do play a role in producing distinctive lifestyles, this effect works through the effects of settlement space as well as through demographic factors. The quality of the environment conditions the opportunities available for distinctive lifestyles.

For example, Manhattan in New York City is known for its active street culture. Over 1 million inhabitants are squeezed onto an island that is less than 20 square miles in area. One aspect of Manhattan street behavior involves a strong emphasis on fashion and appearance as a way of judging other people (we will discuss the phenomenon of fashion later). Consequently, New York subcultures possess a highly developed sense of clothing differences. In contrast, Los Angeles dress is notoriously casual. It is not uncommon to see people appearing at fancy restaurants in the least formal attire. Los Angelenos stress the importance of cars in everyday life, and several subcultures have developed around the use of the automobile as an expressive symbol, such as the Chicano lowrider cults. The city of Los Angeles encompasses almost 1,000 square miles, and public transportation is limited. Consequently, it is understandable to find cars playing so important a role in daily life. Manhattan is a pedestrian town, while Los Angeles is notorious for its reliance on the automobile, and this helps to explain some of the cultural differences between the two places, although there are also other reasons, such as historical and demographic differences.

Second, in addition to the influence of spatial environment on behavior, people's actions are organized according to how they view particular places. Urban and suburban settlement spaces, like other objects in society, possess a social *meaning;* that is, place or location has a symbolic value that counts in determining behavior. For example, Hummon's (1986) comparative study of big-city, suburban, and small-town residents, using a questionnaire and interview method, found that individuals in each location possessed different imagery by which they reinforced their own positive feelings about where they lived and negative feelings about alternative locations. For the most part, residents of big cities, suburbs, and small towns each participated in the construction of positive images of place rather than all subscribing to some antiurban bias or some universal desire to escape the city for either the suburbs or a small town. Box 9.3 illustrates this third method for studying settlement spaces, interviews or questionnaire analysis.

Third, while all individuals possess a distinctive lifestyle that is based in part on their collectively held symbolic values, they are also constrained by material factors, such as income, in determining where to live or locate economic activity. People in cities and suburbs selectively locate in different areas of the metropolitan region according to both their symbolic and material needs. While some portion of their decision is *voluntary,* where they choose to live may be determined by where they can afford to live or even where they are allowed to live. As we saw in Chapter 8, residential location may also be the consequence of *involuntary choice* dictated by ethnic or racial factors.

In the last chapter, we demonstrated the importance of symbolic factors to the patterns of metropolitan life. Let us analyze in more detail how symbolic processes and the sense of place are related to people's behavior in cities and suburbs. We will examine three aspects of the semiotics of space: mental maps, the spatial context and behavior in public, and the sense of community.

Mental Maps and the Semiotics of Place

Mental Maps. Cities and suburbs are not only spaces where people organize their lives; they are also physical environments that are *meaningful.* People impute distinct meanings and associate specific emotions with places. Often a single space, such as the New York City skyline, can invoke an incredible variety of such meaningful associations from individuals. The signifier *home,* for example, is attached to your place of

BOX 9.3 QUESTIONNAIRE AND INTERVIEW METHOD

David Hummon (1986) wanted to test the images of place in different communities. He chose a large city, San Francisco, and three other places in the same area of northern California, including a middle-class suburb, a working-class suburb, and a small town. It was necessary to study a variety of communities to obtain a comparative analysis. Hummon chose an equal number of households at random in each of the four cities from lists using census tract data and field observations to ensure diversity of classes. Because most of the communities were white, he excluded black neighborhoods within the central city to control for race. As he states:

> This ensured that urban residents did not differ significantly in minority background from suburban and small-town residents. Households were sent a letter describing the research; up to four call-backs were made to locate residents and this led to slightly over half of the selected households.
>
> The interview focused on issues of community belief and sentiment and utilized open- and closed-ended questions. The former were emphasized to ensure considerable spontaneity, complexity, and richness in responses. Interviews typically lasted one hour and fifteen minutes and, with the permission of the respondents, were taped and transcribed for analysis. (1986:6)

Hummon classified his responses according to whether the interviewees were "pro-urban," "ambivalent or indifferent about where they lived," or "antiurban." His results are given in Table 9.1, adapted from this study.

In Table 9.1 interviewees were asked several questions regarding preference for locations—the city, the town, and the suburb. The results suggest that where you live *does* influence in a positive way how you feel about your location. The majority of small-town residents reflected antiurban feelings; residents of a large city (San Francisco) were very pro-urban; while suburbanites were as ambivalent about the city as they were anti-urban. If Hummon were concerned with pursuing a cultural analysis of these results, he could have gone further in understanding them. In particular, people probably value where they live because that place has important, personal meanings. Thus, attachment to place involves both social and spatial factors, as urban semiotics shows (see Box 9.4).

TABLE 9.1
Sentimental Posture toward City by Place of Residence

	Place of Residence		
Posture	Large City	Suburbs	Small Town
Pro-urban	62	15	0
Ambivalent	31	42	25
Antiurban	8	42	76
Total	101%	99%	101%

residence, but it can also signify the block where you live, your neighborhood, or a section of the metropolitan region where your particular living space is located. The feelings of comfort, security, and familiarity associated with your house or apartment may be experienced by returning from a trip outside the neighborhood and glimpsing the familiar objects of the local environment. Sociologists and other urbanists who study the role of meaning and cognition in space use the method of mental mapping and semiotics. Box 9.4 gives examples of mental mapping.

People negotiate through a metropolitan space of familiar neighborhoods, known workplaces, leisure and consumption places, and unfamiliar gray areas of little specific meaning. Known places are pictured in great detail by the mind's eye. In between them are gray areas that are not distinctly detailed. These gray areas are negotiated by direct travel routes so that residents pass through them in the least amount of time possible. Consequently, these zones remain undistinguished. All people, in short, carry with them a "mental map" of their weekly routines that varies in its detailed knowledge of space. We use these maps to negotiate through space and to assign meanings to different places. Often these maps are a function of power and class differences, or social stratification.

The study of mental maps helps to augment our understanding of how individuals relate to metropolitan environments containing large numbers of people and differentiated activities. Kevin Lynch (1964), an urban planner, discovered that variation exists among individuals regarding how they depict a space, but also that places themselves vary in their ability to invoke detailed mental images. Thus, a city with an impressive skyline or distinguishing statues and buildings produces an image that is remembered by visitors and residents alike. In contrast, many places seem so ordinary that their physical appearance is hard to recall even after repeated visits.

Lynch's discovery of the importance of *imageability* implied that some spaces were *better* designed than others because they were more legible; that is, they were easier to understand as built environments. Imageability therefore facilitated movement or use. For example, Lynch contrasted the mental maps of residents in two cities—Jersey City, New Jersey; and Boston, Massachusetts. He found that residents of Jersey City had a much less detailed mental image of their space. It was more difficult for them to visualize the features of places they often passed or went to during the week's routines. Lynch's discovery has important consequences for city planners, architects, and landscapers, as we will see in Chapter 14.

The Semiotics of Place. Mental maps assign meaning to space. But the meanings of objects also come from the various ways we use them as symbols. Material forms, such as particular buildings and constructed spaces like plazas and freeways, all possess meanings that are ascribed to them by social use. They are known to us by their functions, as the study of spatial semiotics suggests (Barthes, 1986). Hence, the phenomenon of the mental map is but a special case of the more general semiotics of settlement space. Malls, theme parks, architectural forms, and neighborhood places all work to orient our behavior and provide us with a sense of place by conveying certain meanings through objects that act as signs of their function as places of business,

BOX 9.4   THE METHOD OF MENTAL MAPS

The technique of mental mapping is used to discover how residents of any given place conceive of their environment. They are asked to draw their own local neighborhoods and fill the picture in with as many details as possible. Studies are done by obtaining mental maps from a sample of residents. In all cases, the conception of place will vary from person to person. Researchers then study the causes of such variation by comparing individuals and groups with one another. We know, for example, that the way children draw mental maps of their environment differs from adult maps.

One of the more common results from mental map research is the discovery that differences in both the conception and meaning of a local place are correlated with differences in class status (Golledge and Rushton, 1976). In general, differences in the conception of space reflect social stratification or the perceived differences regarding power and class in society. Researchers have uncovered racial differences in the way people conceive their local settlement space. One study of the Mission Hill area of Boston, which contains a housing project inhabited primarily by low-income African Americans surrounded by a white community, discovered that the black residents' view of their environment was greatly restricted, while comparable white residents held a much more expansive image of their surroundings (LaGory and Pipkin, 1981:119).

Two of the maps from this research project are shown here. In the first map, Ernest shows the location of the housing project in which he lives at the bottom of the map, and the wide street emphasizes the dividing line between the white and black neighborhoods. In a personal interview, the author discovered that Ernest had never ventured across Parker Street. The second map was drawn by Ralph, a student at a prestigious private school. Ralph's map is much more detailed and includes a number of schools and even colleges in the area; his "action space" within the neighborhood environment is much less restricted (Ladd, 1967:47–48). Ernest's map indicates how minority status may confine people within urban spaces because of anxiety about venturing beyond racially mixed areas. This kind of territorial anxiety is also felt by women in large and small cities, as we discussed in Chapter 8, and by people in general because of the increase in random street crime (see Chapter 10).

Ernest's Map   Ralph's Map

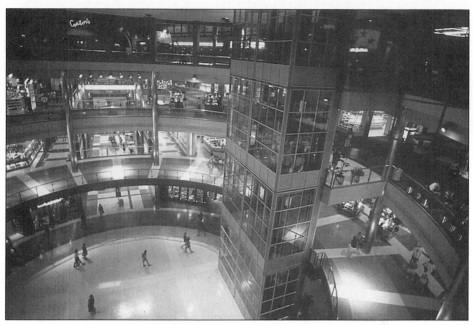

Shopping malls provide a controlled environment and skillful use of corporate symbols and signs.

recreation, amusement, shopping, and the like. Instead of strangeness and disorientation, the signs of space create order and familiarity, which is helpful both in reducing the stress of daily living within giant, metropolitan regions and in enabling residents to *use* the built environment effectively.

For example, the suburban shopping mall is a successful adaptation of architectural form to the needs of commercial interests. Malls are the counterpart in low-density suburbia of the higher-density city center shopping district. The mall works because of its skillful use of symbols and signs coupled with environmental forms. Malls are designed with large parking lots and blank external facades that make customers respond to the overarching meaning: "for shopping-related activities, enter here." This technique, known as *introversion,* is meant to discourage prospective customers from dawdling in the mall parking lot. Additional semiotic devices control shoppers once they are inside. Shopping malls feature atriums, "food courts," and even amusement rides for children. Often they are designed with images that invoke city living—avenues with artificial street lamps and small, neatly spaced trees and benches. And because all shoppers are on foot, they provide shoppers with a taste of the typical urban street crowd.

Corporate product signs, or "logos," are also important in the mall. Each store has its own symbolic and functional associations that are the consequence of advertising and of what customers know about its price range. Product signs, or brand name logos, also take advantage of the fact that people have already been conditioned by advertising to associate certain products with store signs. These internalized associations are then used to advantage in the mall by directing people's attention to specific stores or

BOX 9.5 SHOPPING MALLS AND THE DECLINE OF PUBLIC SPACE

The image of the public marketplace has been appropriated by the builders and promoters of modern shopping malls. Their corporate owners frequently refer to malls as the new "medieval marketplaces" and "town squares." [But] the mall as marketplace is the exact opposite of the medieval market square. Rather than being an integral part of a larger urban tapestry, in order to succeed, malls must keep the actual city at bay.

The environment of malls is meticulously regulated to ensure absolute predictability. Each type of mall is defined by its matrix of shops, design features, and clientele. There are festival markets, such as James Rouse's Faneuil Hall in Boston; malls that concentrate on exclusive, upscale, high fashion stores; malls that cater to the "typical" middle-class family; and major brand discount malls. For every region of the country and from city to city, within these themes the activities, the mix of exhibits, the tenant stores, atmosphere, and customers are remarkably uniform. A suburban mall in Alabama will have basically the same stores as one outside San Diego, with perhaps a nod in the direction of regional tastes and preferences in gift and curio shops and restaurants. Rouse's Union Station in St. Louis will seem familiar to anyone who has been in Boston's Faneuil Hall.

Of course, what is excluded from malls is as important in creating an ambience as the particular mix that defines them. "Undesirable" characters and activities are prohibited—no pawn shops, liquor stores, beer halls, or second-hand stores here, and no going-out-of-business, bankruptcy, or damaged good sales either. Bell-ringing Salvation Army Santas and their Christmas kettles are not considered the right kind of image and are barred from many malls. Obvious noncustomers, such as bag ladies, the homeless, or in some cases teenagers, will be asked to move on or will be thrown out.

Teenagers, who represented a growing $56 billion market in 1990, present a revealing dilemma for mall management; some of them are customers, and their parents are surely customers, but they pose a potential threat to the mall's controlled atmosphere. Most malls have instituted policies designed to limit the contact between adult customers and free-roaming teenagers, and some have gone farther. Park Fair mall in Omaha has banned all persons under 18 years of age. Almost all malls have increased security measures targeted at teens.

Mall managers are particularly militant about forbidding any activities that call attention to social issues. The East Town Mall in Madison, Wisconsin, permitted military recruiters to set up displays of military vehicles but refused to allow the anti-nuclear dance troupe, Nu Parable, to perform. In Arizona, mall owners sued a group of citizens who gathered petition signatures for the recall of Governor Evan Mecham. In 1988, a 71-year-old man received a 1-year prison sentence for entering a mall and distributing leaflets that urged world peace. Virtually all malls display notices that "public activities" are not necessarily protected in the mall: "Areas . . . used by the public are not public ways, but are for the use of the tenants and public transacting business with them. Permission to use said areas may be revoked at any time."

Source: Dennis Judd, "The Rise of the New Walled City," in H. Liggett and D. C. Perry, *Spatial Practices* (Newbury Park: Sage Publications), pp. 144–166.

products. They hold such power only because consumers have already become familiar with them in their daily lives, so they respond to their stimulus and are oriented in their journey through the mall.

Customers are able to "read" the space of the mall and make their way through it with ease so that shopping is as stressless as it can be. But shopping malls are not public spaces, and they may not be open to all persons, as described in Box 9.5.

Behavior in Public Space

For many years, urban sociologists have been aware that the large city with its dense crowds offers special challenges to residents. They have studied the way people negotiate this particular environment, and have found that the techniques of accommodation that are used comprise much of what we might identify as uniquely *urban* behavior. Yet this interaction, which takes place in *public* space where strangers as pedestrians encounter others in places such as malls, department stores, and bars, also occurs in suburbia. For this reason, the study of behavior in public space can take place throughout the metropolitan region and can involve the interaction of people as pedestrians or as drivers/passengers in cars.

Behavior in public depends on the proper expression, interpretation, and negotiation of signs between people interacting with one another and with the built environment. This semiotic aspect of city and suburban living is quite essential to daily life, as the sociospatial perspective suggests. According to Anderson, for example, interaction in the public space of a large city requires "street smarts":

> One gains street wisdom through a long and sometimes arduous process that begins with a certain "uptightness" about the urban environment, with decisions based on stereotypes and simple rules of public etiquette. Given time and experience, the nervousness and fear give way to a recognition that street life involves situations that require selective and individualized responses—in this complicated environment, applying broad stereotypes simply will not do. (1990:6)

Social psychologists who have studied this interaction in public insist that *all* behavior is interpreted according to the particular spatial context; that is, we interpret someone's action based on the space where it occurred (Karp, Stone, and Yoels, 1977). Hence, behavior is a combination of social and spatial factors. If we saw two men fighting each other in a park, we would be concerned and might call the police. The very same action placed inside a boxing arena would be considered entertainment. Thus, we decide how to interpret the behavior of others, which is essential to determining our own behavior, in part by interpreting space as a context for action. In short, spatial context has a very powerful role in the patterning of behavior in public.

Spatial context also determines how individuals behave toward one another. In a classic study, the sociologist Erving Goffman (1963:36) observed that when ordinary situations become extraordinary, interaction rules among complete strangers in the city change, and they might begin to act intimately. Thus, if a subway train gets stalled, the normally silent passengers might suddenly talk to those strangers sitting next to them about the incident. A study on bystanders (Darley and Latane, 1970) discovered that urbanites are not by nature blasé about other people's troubles on the street. But when

A crowded street in the Wall Street section of Manhattan, New York.

an incident occurs, the more bystanders who witness it, the less the likelihood that any single one will intervene. Because of the density of city crowds, social responsibility is spread so thin that bystanders may choose not to get involved even when they witness a serious breach of behavior. This phenomenon sometimes makes us wonder about the perceived weakness of social links among people living in large cities. It also suggests that the social disorganization perceived by Chicago School researchers may have been a temporary or short-term product of spatial context rather than an innate or permanent change in people's behavior produced by the move to the city.

Darley and Latane (1970) applied this insight to explain the behavior of bystanders in the now infamous Queens, New York, case of Kitty Genovese, who was stabbed to death despite her repeated screams for help that were heard by 38 of her neighbors. According to this study, no one intervened because of the spatial context, that is, the large number of bystanders who all felt that others bore a greater responsibility for responding to crime.

The most distinctive aspect of city life involves interaction with large numbers of strangers. Whom to trust and whom not to trust, how to act in a crowd, how to react to people you do not know, and how to interact with strangers in shops, restaurants, museums, and on the street constitute a major aspect of the metropolitan resident's set of behaviors, whether living in the city or the suburbs. As in other cases, signs and meaningful clues make a difference in the way people feel about and act in public space. Some researchers, for example, have studied interaction with strangers as a problem that can bring unattractive consequences from poor judgment in "reading" the sociospatial context. For example, J. Henslin (1972) studied cab drivers in a big city and discovered that their lives might depend on the way they size up a prospective fare. They do not stop for everyone. Experiencing this, many African Americans find it difficult to get cabs at night regardless of how wealthy they may be. Also, because many taxi drivers will not travel to ghetto areas or accept fares that do not possess the proper appearance, unlicensed or "gypsy" cabs have appeared as an alternative industry that has become the ghetto resident's taxi of last resort. Gypsy cabs are part of the informal economy of the city (see Chapter 5), and they involve some risks because they usually have no insurance and do not have to comply with industry regulations.

Appearance and fashion have always figured prominently in the types of judgments people make when dealing with strangers, especially in public space. Goffman (1963) regards the way we look as providing the most concise and meaningful cues to guide the interaction of others in the city (but we can add the suburbs, too!). In dealing with strangers, fashion provides us with a way to "read" such things as class standing, lifestyle interests, and even whether or not an individual poses a threat to us. As discussed earlier, in large cities with dense pedestrian environments, people are more attuned to fashion than in places where automobiles dominate, such as Los Angeles, although there may be several reasons why this is true.

The spatial context is just as important in the organization of life within suburban settlement space as it is in the city. Instead of subways or buses, suburbanites contend with cars and carpools, which involve people who are acquaintances who share driving to work, shopping, school, and recreational activities. Unlike individuals riding in city mass transportation, people in carpools feel compelled to be friendly. It is the sociospatial context and not the proximity of one commuter to another that makes the difference. Yet for carpoolers, being friendly at 6:00 A.M. with little sleep and a full day of work ahead may be a difficult chore. Consequently, carpools have never been as popular as they could be. A novelist described the hell suburban mothers go through while chauffeuring children around town to and from schools, doctors, shopping, and friends: "With three children in three different schools, she [the heroine of the novel] lives most of her life now in her Honda hatchback. There is no one to talk to but her slobbering dog, which resides in the back seat, and she longs for a drive-in window at the local psychiatric hospital" (Lawson, 1991:C-1).

Neighboring and Community

Neighboring is often said to be the most characteristic behavior of suburbia. Yet this is a phenomenon of the city as well. Only when we speak in generalities can we say that dwellers in large cities know fewer of their neighbors than do residents of smaller places. Neighboring and community involvement are strongly related to life cycle—whether individuals are single or married, childless or with children. Most neighboring tends to be done by people raising families. The stereotypical image of suburbia as a place of neighboring may be the result of the fact that families with small children prefer to live there. But the spatial separation of families in suburban housing developments may be less conducive to visiting with neighbors, whereas medium-density city neighborhoods with local businesses may facilitate social interaction among community residents. When we look more closely at the city, we can find instances of intense neighboring, such as in the ethnic communities studied by Herbert Gans (1962) and others (see Box 9.1).

Neighboring studies are important because they are related to the issue of community and territory. There is a conception of everyday life that places individuals within a nurturing neighborhood of friends and relatives. This conjunction of a certain space with an intimate circle of primary relations became the classic image of the community.

In a previous section, we saw that network researchers such as Wellman (1988) have called this image into question. Community is less dependent on territory and more a function of a network of friends and relatives dispersed in space. According to Fischer (1982), there is some variation in the extent to which local or dispersed networks exist for residents of cities. The territorial reach of friendship networks depends on the presence of *competing commitments;* that is, if an individual is relatively isolated and has few outside involvements, that person will most likely be dependent on neighbors—it's all that's available. However, the more outside involvements an individual possesses, the less likely the person will be tied to immediate neighbors. In short, according to the network perspective, neighboring and close ties to community space are a kind of residual effect produced when other, more attractive alternatives are not available.

Fischer's analysis pinpoints how choice of location affects individual network ties, but it is also remarkable for the way it de-emphasizes the effects of class, age, and gender as they are deployed in space—a relationship that is important to the sociospatial perspective. For example, elderly people living in the city are not physically capable of traveling long distances for companionship or help. They are dependent on their local community, but they may also prefer things that way. Not everyone assertively seeks the most compatible network of people across the metropolitan region. In other cases, people may have an extensive network but also retain a need for a local community. For example, single career women living in a large city may possess a robust network of friends living throughout the metropolis, but they find it uncomfortable to travel or dine alone. They too, along with others, may find the need for a close-at-hand network of neighbors.

In reevaluating neighboring studies according to the sociospatial perspective, it is clear that middle-class males are more likely to be involved in social networks that are not grounded in settlement space—the "community without propinquity." In contrast, the poor, the elderly, some women, and most certainly segregated minorities have closer ties to their immediate neighbors. They may be the ones to whom community and the local territory of friendship relations matter most.

Other neighborhood researchers have remarked on the factors neglected by the network perspective. Susanne Keller (1968) indicates that community relations can be a function of class. She found that middle-class people have more casual acquaintances, while working-class individuals are more dependent on their neighbors. Another observer, Ida Susser (1982), carried out an important field study that clearly indicates the differential roles of class, race, and gender in fostering neighborhood ties. As the sociospatial perspective suggests, these factors operate symbolically and within a specific territory to make behavior meaningful.

Susser lived in and researched an industrial area of Brooklyn, New York. She makes the important point that many studies of neighboring networks aim for some universal results, while the role of community in people's lives very often depends on historical and social circumstances that are specific to places and local economies. The Greenpoint section of Brooklyn, for example, was a traditional working-class community containing several factories. Residents were very attached to their local space, which provided them with ethnic and religious resources such as Italian restaurants and churches with Polish-Catholic congregations. As with other communities of this type, the locals engaged in robust neighboring and mutual aid. Everyday life was organized within this particular space with the aid of expressive symbols of ethnic, racial, gender, and community status.

In addition to these historical circumstances, Susser describes how the economic decline of New York City affected neighboring within the community. In the 1960s and 1970s, New York, like other larger industrialized cities, was afflicted by the steady decline in manufacturing that we studied in Chapter 5. New York City also experienced a terrible fiscal crisis in the 1970s when it almost ran out of money and credit (see Chapter 10). Adjusting to this dilemma required drastic declines in the city budget, with corresponding cutbacks in city services. As a result of the financial crisis, "municipal workers were laid off . . . city services were drastically cut, tuition was imposed at the City University of New York, and transportation fares were hiked 43 percent" (Susser, 1982:11).

The changed social conditions increased the dependence of neighbors on one another. This was especially the case for women and minorities. Family life suffered as men were laid off from jobs. While it is true, as the network researchers might observe, that close ties to place were exhibited by those with limited "competing commitments," in this field study of Brooklyn we can see just how selective the effect of "competing opportunities" (see Fischer, 1982) can be with regard to class, race, and gender. Mothers with small children, poor people unable to afford transportation costs, and minorities trapped in ghetto areas were the least likely to take advantage of acquaintances outside the area—if, indeed, they had any. Instead, Susser observed how these besieged residents relied more heavily on neighbors for support.

This form of community involvement was intensified as individuals fought to protect their quality of life in the face of severe city service cuts due to the fiscal crisis of the city. Active mutual aid among neighbors gave rise to community political action. As Susser observes:

> Relying on community ties between neighbors and relatives, the working-class people I observed were constantly involved in local holding actions as they tried to influence political decisions that would affect their living standards. The formation of block associations, sit-ins to protest inadequate day care, and the occupation of buildings in reaction to the reduction of city services were frequent forms of political expression. (1982:6)

General observations about neighboring that downplay attachment to local territory may disguise the specific needs of the poor, of women, and of minorities for strong communities. They may also obscure the actions taken by such groups to *create* strong communities, an interest that is very much a part of both city and suburban politics, as we will discuss in Chapter 11.

The semiotic perspective aids our understanding of metropolitan culture by explicitly demonstrating the links between behavior and sociospatial context. All interaction is meaningful. People use expressive symbols to organize their daily lives. The range of signs includes spatial organization, or context, as well as the use of the common objects of our culture. As an ensemble, the collection of signs helps us to understand behavior in public space and aids in our own orientation to the built environment. It is on this meaningful foundation that all interaction among people within the metropolitan milieu is based. The specific cultural mechanisms of sociospatial behavior that we have explored include mental maps, the use of the built environment as expressive symbols, the mechanisms of interaction in public, and particular attachments to community or neighborhood territory.

This relationship among meaningful social interaction, community life, and the spatial context of the built environment has been studied most closely by researchers examining variation in the types of neighborhood relations among people living in cities and suburbs. In comparative studies of neighborhoods, we learn about the significant ways that the meanings attached to place interact with social or compositional factors of class, race, and gender. Let us now turn to these studies.

Types of Neighborhoods and Community Interaction

Albert Hunter (1979:269) defines the neighborhood as a "uniquely linked unit of social/spatial organization between the forces and institutions of the larger society and the localized routines of individuals in their daily lives." As we have already seen, you do not have to be neighborly to belong to a neighborhood. For Hunter, typologies of neighborhoods can describe local community life, but they neglect to indicate connections to the larger society. Good case studies of neighborhoods, in contrast, provide a glimpse of the links to sociospatial organization in the larger society, an approach very much in keeping with the perspective of this text. As Hunter remarks, "If one does not view the neighborhood within its [social] context, in short, one ends up with description, not explanation" (1979:269).

Studies of neighborhoods or communities note great variation in the degree to which local residents are attached both to the area and to one another. To analyze this variation, researchers have constructed typologies of different communities based on local attachments. They suggest that in addition to rural, suburban, or urban location, there are considerable differences among *all* localities regarding the quality of neighborhood interaction.

Rachelle and Donald Warren (1974) have done the most extensive work on the sociospatial aspects of neighborhood typologies. They studied the ways in which communities vary with respect to *identity, interaction,* and *linkages.* By combining information on these three dimensions, they identified six types of urban communities: integral, parochial, diffuse, transitory, anomic, and stepping-stone (see Box 9.6). Other sociologists have sought to identify those forces that might draw people together to

BOX 9.6 TYPES OF NEIGHBORHOOD INTERACTION

After studying dozens of cities and suburbs in the Detroit metropolitan area, Rachelle and Donald Warren (1974) concluded that residential areas vary according to three dimensions:

1. **Identity:** How strong is the sense of connectedness to place? How much do people feel they share with their neighbors?
2. **Interaction:** How strong are the interactive ties to neighbors? Do they visit often?
3. **Linkages:** Are there ties between the local neighborhood and the larger community? What is the nature of these ties?

On the basis of these dimensions, the Warrens identified six specific types of communities, five of which are described below. These community typologies may also be identified with important community case studies in urban sociology to illustrate how neighborhood interaction varies across settlement spaces:

- The *integral community* scores high on all three dimensions. There is a cosmopolitan as well as a local center; individuals are in close contact and share many concerns. They participate in community groups and citywide groups. It is represented by a variety of studies of suburban communities, such as Seely, Sim, and Loosley's (1956) *Crestwood Heights*.
- The *parochial community* scores high on identity and interaction but low on linkages with the outside. A strong sense of shared ethnic identity exists; the neighborhood is self-contained and independent of the larger community. This is similar to the ethnic neighborhood studied by Herbert Gans (1962) in *The Urban Villager*, as well as Eliot Liebow's *Talley's Corner*.
- The *diffuse community* scores high on identity but low on linkages and interaction. Residents have many things in common, but there is little local involvement with neighbors and few connections to the larger community. Examples range from public housing projects (such as *There Are No Children Here*) to new suburban communities.
- The *transitory community* scores high on interaction but low on identity and linkages. Residents in these neighborhoods are highly mobile and do not form attachments to the community; there is little collective action or community organization. Morris Janowitz (1956) called this the *community of limited liability*. It is also represented in Elijah Anderson's (1999) *Code of the Streets*.
- The *anomic community* has low identity, interaction, and linkages; there is no internal cohesion and great distance from the outside world. The anomic community is characteristic of poor neighborhoods where there is little connection among residents. It is represented by William Julius Wilson's (1995) study of poverty neighborhoods in Chicago, *When Work Disappears*.

create a feeling of shared community. As Georg Simmel recognized, social conflict is one of those factors that draw individuals and groups together. In urban sociology, we can identify this process in the *defended neighborhood.*

In the defended neighborhood, there is a heightened sense of community identity and increased social interaction as a consequence of political action. At times this may be temporary, but some communities manage to maintain the strong links to outside city agencies even after mobilization has declined. The example of the Greenpoint neighborhood in Brooklyn, New York, discussed earlier illustrates this phenomenon. According to Gerald Suttles (1972), the defended neighborhood closes itself off as a consequence of some external threat (such as an attempted move by a different racial or ethnic group into an area) or a city agency plan to modify the environment in some way (such as the construction of an incinerator or garbage dump). Defended neighborhoods usually attempt to forge strong links with city government in an effort to use political influence (Susser, 1982; Castells, 1983).

Summary

In the previous chapter, we surveyed the diversity of metropolitan life. We saw that lifestyles are a consequence of the interaction between compositional social factors, such as class and race, and specific territorial relations that assign particular individuals to particular places within the metropolitan region. In this chapter, we considered how living and working arrangements foster types of community. Many of the discussions about ways of life have suggested that spatial location can influence behavior. Thus, while Chapter 8 considered how people are organized into places, this chapter deals with the question of how places influence behavior. Such balanced considerations are in keeping with the sociospatial perspective, which claims that space operates in this dual way as both a product and a producer of behaviors in society.

According to the arguments of urban sociologists, spatial location per se has little effect on lifestyles, which are better explained by compositional factors. Even one's sense of community has much more to do with one's network of intimate friends and kin than with where one lives. Yet the degree to which a community without place characterizes people's lives varies according to compositional factors such as class and gender, age and race, and ethnicity and religion. Hence, the localized, territorially specific community remains important to the way people organize their daily lives. This holds equally for single, middle-class professional women alone in the city, for poor black men who are disadvantaged because of racial oppression, and for aged central city dwellers, all of whom need the sustaining resources of local neighborhoods and vital community relations.

Space affects behavior in other ways. We orient ourselves in particular places by assigning meaning to space. All objects are meaningful to us. The meanings of space and the objects of the built environment help us organize our everyday lives. This sociospatial process utilizes particular mechanisms in ordering public interaction. We recognize the cues of behavior and acquire street wisdom by repeated use of public space. Our interpretations of behavior require an understanding of spatial context. Spatial context, in short, is a principal component of meaning.

Finally, we have discussed how the metropolitan region is diversified not only with regard to the individuals who live there (Chapter 8) but also with regard to the types of neighborhood ties and commitments to community that can be found in particular settings. Sociologists have produced a long list of studies that document the diversity of neighborhood types and community relations in both urban and suburban settlement spaces. An understanding of such differences helps us overcome stereotypical thinking about the people of cities and suburbs.

While the richness of social life across the multicentered metropolitan region was examined in some detail in the last two chapters, metropolitan life also has its problems and challenges. The next chapter considers how metropolitan problems result from a combination of social and spatial factors.

CHAPTER

10

METROPOLITAN PROBLEMS:
Poverty, Racism, Crime, Housing, and Fiscal Crisis

On October 12, 1962, Ruby moved into a large housing project in Chicago with her four children, all of whom had been born out of wedlock. Her new husband had a job in a nearby factory, and their rent was subsidized. Three years later, her husband abandoned her and Ruby had to go on welfare to support her family, which had grown to seven children.

Over the next decade one son was murdered, another was sent to prison, and two daughters went on welfare to support children of their own. The two daughters live in the same project, raising the third generation on welfare. Only one son managed to escape the inner-city projects and move to a middle-class neighborhood by keeping a steady job. For years Ruby was trapped in the projects, which experienced rising crime, deteriorating maintenance, large-scale drug use, and gang-related activities. In 1979, Ruby left her children and returned to the South to live near her relatives (Lemann, 1991a).

Ruby's family provides a good example of the types of problems that Americans associate with large cities. Ever since the founding of this nation, the city has been depicted first in short stories and novels and later in television and movies as the corrupter of morals and family life. Theodore Dreiser's well-known novel *Sister Carrie* (1900) describes the misfortunes of a young woman who comes to Chicago to work and in the end is corrupted by life in the city. In one Gallup Poll (1982), more than one-third of all residents of cities with a population of over half a million stated that they would prefer to move out. There is, in short, an *antiurban* bias in American culture that persists in viewing the large city as the source of social disorganization.

Early images of the city feature overcrowding: immense traffic jams of primitive Model T automobiles mixed in with horse-drawn carts, tenements teeming with immigrants, and crowds of children swarming across city streets. For almost a century, city life in this country was plagued by frequent public health crises such as cholera outbreaks, high infant mortality rates, alcoholism, family violence, street gang activity, and crime. At around the turn of the century, a wave of murders set an all-time record that was not broken until quite recently. For much of our history, then, city life has virtually been synonymous with social problems. Yet we know that these same problems—crime, disease, family breakup—are really experienced everywhere, not just in large cities.

The early sociologists of the Chicago School believed that the move to the city brought with it social disorganization. While subsequent research showed that this perception was inaccurate, people in the United States still rank small and middle-size cities as providing the highest quality of life. The negative perception of the large city provides the basis for varying mental images of place (see Chapter 9). Yet we have also seen that there are a good many positive aspects of urban living and that the early belief in the loss of community among migrants to the city was unfounded.

In previous chapters, we have been developing the themes of the sociospatial approach and, in particular, we have tried to show that problems that appear to afflict individuals such as Ruby and her family are caused in part by factors that we cannot readily see. In Ruby's case, she is a victim not only of poor family relations, personal limitations, and bad luck, but also of racism and poverty, which severely hinder the life chances of black and poor people in the United States. Consequently, explanation for the social disorganization of Ruby's life lies in the particular combination of adverse social conditions, personal circumstances, and the specific effects of spatial segregation and uneven development. This chapter applies the sociospatial approach to metropolitan problems. One purpose of our discussion is to explore whether or not large cities in particular and metropolitan regions in general possess unique features that might propagate specifically "urban" problems.

Theories of Urban Problems

Early observers of city life saw immigrants from rural areas with stable family traditions turning to alcoholism, robbery, child abuse, and prostitution. Something about living in a large city, it was suggested, created social disorganization—broken families and broken lives—and this in turn led to all sorts of urban problems.

Several theories explaining the link between urban living and social disorganization have been proposed over the years, including the breakdown of primary group relations, the compositional approach, and subcultural theory (see Box 10.1). All these theories are derived from Louis Wirth's essay "Urbanism as a Way of Life" and subsequent interpretations of this classic work from the Chicago School of urban sociology. As discussed in Chapter 6, Wirth believed that primary group relationships

BOX 10.1 FOUR THEORIES OF URBAN PROBLEMS

Breakdown of the primary group: Urban living breaks down primary relationships and replaces them with secondary relationships, which produce anonymity and competition. Secondary relations eventually lead to family breakup, alcoholism, crime, and other negative outcomes.

The compositional approach: Differences between city and suburban behavior are the result of class, age, race, educational level, and lifestyle orientation. The urban environment does not produce crime or other social problems; these are the consequence of the composition of particular neighborhoods and areas within the city.

The subcultural view: Unique modes of social interaction in cities create criminal subcultures. Individuals in the city are more likely to be exposed to these subcultures because a larger number of individuals support these behaviors.

The sociospatial perspective: Social problems are ubiquitous across urban and suburban settlement space within the metropolitan region. Family disorganization, street gangs, and drug use are found in suburbs as well as in cities. There are no *unique* differences between city life and life in other developed places such as the suburbs.

(among family and kin, for example) are replaced by secondary group relationships (among neighbors and coworkers) in urban society. Secondary relationships are based on temporary, superficial, and impersonal social interactions. As a consequence, urban life produces anonymity and distance among urban dwellers, who rarely get to know even those people with whom they interact daily, such as shopkeepers, fellow commuters, coworkers, and even neighbors. Wirth believed that secondary relations eventually lead to family breakup, alcoholism, crime, and other negative aspects of urban life (Wirth, 1938).

Herbert Gans (1968) argued that the urban environment does not have a major effect on people's lives. Instead, differences between city and suburban behavior can be explained by differences in class background, age, and lifestyle orientations of city and suburban residents. So-called urban problems are really the consequence of the demographic characteristics—the *social composition*—of the population, such as class, marital status, age, income, race, and educational attainment. There are no innate qualities of urban life that cause specific problems such as divorce or drug use.

Claude Fischer (1975) claimed that the compositional view neglected the special role cities play in social interaction. Life in the city intensifies local cultures and subcultures (as we saw in Chapter 8). While there is no intrinsic reason that urban life should produce social problems, cities might have a negative effect on individual behavior. All forms of deviance flourish within urban environments because there are more individuals who support these subcultures. Urban life does not automatically lead to social disorganization, but it does increase the opportunities to be exposed to deviance and negative effects on one's behavior.

The Sociospatial Perspective

Social problems are ubiquitous across the metropolitan areas of the United States. Cities do not have an exclusive hold on divorce or family violence, and suburbs are now almost as likely as cities to be afflicted with family disorganization, deviant subcultures, drug use, and gang activity (Barbanel, 1992). Many suburban areas have crime rates comparable to those of the central city. As the suburban settlement spaces have matured, differences in poverty levels, crime rates, and other measures of social disorganization have become more similar. If it appears clear that urbanism by itself is not a generator of social problems, it is also clear that the subcultural approach no longer can identify unique differences between city life and life in other developed places.

This book emphasizes the sociospatial approach, according to which the spatial environment plays a role in human interaction, provided it is understood that compositional or social factors are equally important. The variety of lifestyles found across urban and suburban settlement spaces result from social factors such as race, class, and gender. Social problems in particular are caused by poverty, racial exclusion, gender differences, and the uneven development within settlement space that results in differential access to resources and life chances. On the other hand, spatial forms still matter. Environments intensify or dissipate these compositional effects of uneven development. In short, ways of life result from an interaction between social factors and spatial organization.

Cities are not unique in having acute social problems, but the spatial nature of large cities and densely populated suburbs makes the uneven development resulting from the inequities of race, class, gender, and age particularly severe. According to the sociospatial approach, the following factors are the most significant.

First, the principal effect of the city as a built environment is that it *concentrates* people and resources (Lefebvre, 1991; Engels, 1973). Thus, social problems such as drugs and poverty have a greater impact in large central cities and densely populated suburbs than in less dense areas. In confined urban space under the jurisdiction of a single municipal government, it is the sheer numbers that tend to be involved, such as the frequency of murders and rapes or the number of "crack babies," that make social problems grave concerns.

Second, over the years urban populations have been disproportionately affected by the internationalization of the capitalist economies. For example, large metropolitan regions such as Los Angeles or New York are the destinations of choice for most immigrants from poorer nations who have left their own countries in search of a better life. With the flow of immigrants comes specific problems, such as the need for bilingual education, that affect these areas more than other places.

Changes in the global cycles of economic investment also affect metropolitan regions because of the scale of activities in the largest places. For example, after Wall Street stocks took a plunge in October 1987, over 100,000 trained professionals were laid off from brokerage and financial service firms in Manhattan alone, and throughout the 1990s staggering job losses occurred in many areas due to economic restructuring as U.S. companies sought to increase their profits and earnings. Job loss on this scale presents a particularly acute problem for cities.

Finally, social problems are caused by the allocation of resources, which may be accentuated in dense, built environments. For example, large cities are major centers of the global economy. Extreme wealth is created within their boundaries, and the signs of that money are highly visible in the city, such as expensive restaurants, upscale department stores, luxury housing, and limousines. Close by, in the concentrated space of the city, are also people who suffer the most terrible consequences of abject poverty, such as homelessness, malnutrition, and chronic unemployment. Because this contrast is so visible, the issue of uneven development is particularly oppressive to inhabitants.

In summary, problems that can be considered uniquely *urban* derive from the concentrated nature of metropolitan space and the scale of changes in compositional factors. In this chapter, we will consider some problems usually associated with urban life, including racism and poverty, crime and drugs, fiscal problems such as declines in educational quality, infrastructure problems, housing inequities, and homelessness.

Racism and Poverty

Racism

The most extreme effects of racism have been felt by African Americans, who have been systematically discriminated against in employment and in the housing market. As a consequence, their social mobility has been severely constrained. The most powerful indicator of institutional racism in the United States is population segregation. In Chapters 12 and 13, when discussing cities around the globe, we will also encounter the phenomenon of population segregation. But nowhere is the racial nature of this sociospatial effect as clear as in metropolitan areas across the United States.

The classic study of segregation is by the Taeubers (1965). They compiled statistics on American cities with regard to the relative locations of whites and blacks. To measure segregation, they constructed a very useful concept, an "index of segregation." If a city had a 30 percent African American population as a whole, they expected, in the absence of segregation, that the black population would be evenly distributed across space. The index of segregation refers to the percentage of African Americans who would have to move in order for all neighborhoods to reflect the 30 percent black composition of the entire city. If a neighborhood were 90 percent black, 67 percent of the black population would have to move, resulting in an index of .67.

On the basis of Taeuber and Taeuber's study, all U.S. cities were discovered to be highly segregated, that is, with indexes above .50 for African Americans. The Taeubers replicated their study in the 1970s and found little change in the degree of black population clustering. Some of the most segregated cities during the 1970s

BOX 10.2   HYPERSEGREGATION IN AMERICAN CITIES

Douglas Massey and Nancy Denton (1993:74–77) identify five distinct dimensions that may characterize the spatial arrangement of ethnic communities across a metropolitan region:

1. **Unevenness:** African Americans may be distributed so that they are overrepresented in some areas and underrepresented in other areas.
2. **Isolation:** African Americans may be distributed so that they have little interaction with other groups.
3. **Clustered:** Black neighborhoods may be tightly clustered to form one contiguous enclave, or they may be scattered about in checkerboard fashion.
4. **Concentrated:** Black neighborhoods may be concentrated within a very small area, or they may be settled sparsely throughout the urban environment.
5. **Centralization:** Black neighborhoods may be spatially centralized around the urban core, or spread out along the periphery.

These five dimensions together define geographic traits that social scientists think of when they consider segregation. A high score on any single dimension is serious because it removes blacks from full participation in urban society and limits their access to benefits. As segregation accumulates across multiple dimensions, however, its effects intensify. The indices of unevenness and isolation we have discussed so far cannot capture this

were Detroit, Michigan; Chicago, Illinois; Buffalo, New York; Cleveland, Ohio; and Birmingham, Alabama.

Some have argued that not all of the segregation observed in American cities is the consequence of *involuntary* segregation; the spatial cluster of population groups can also be *voluntary*. In the case of African Americans, however, we know that the urban ghettos were created by a form of racism and violence designed to prevent blacks from moving into "white" settlement spaces, federal housing policies that concentrated public housing in the inner city while subsidizing "white flight" to the suburbs through construction of the interstate highway system and home mortgage loans, and other factors. Bullard and Feagin (1991), for example, discuss various techniques used by housing-related institutions to prevent blacks from locating where they prefer, thereby fostering involuntary segregation. This is an example of *institutional racism*.

Rental and real estate agents also use a variety of methods to prevent blacks from locating in white-owned areas. One mechanism is called *steering*. When an African American couple comes to a rental or real estate agent, the agent will steer the couple to areas of the city populated by blacks. Agents will also simply refuse to divulge the existence of housing opportunities in white areas. Despite gains in family income earnings by a growing number of middle-class blacks, racial segregation remains a fact of life for the majority of African Americans. One report observes:

multidimensional layering of segregation and therefore understate its real severity in American society. Not only are blacks more segregated than other groups on any single dimension of segregation, but they are also more segregated on all dimensions simultaneously; and in an important subset of U.S. metropolitan areas, they are highly segregated on at least four of the five dimensions at once, a pattern that we call *hypersegregation*.

Thus one-third of all African Americans in the United States live under conditions of intense racial segregation. They are unambiguously among the nation's most spatially isolated and geographically secluded people, suffering extreme segregation across multiple dimensions simultaneously. Black Americans in these metropolitan areas live within large, contiguous settlements of densely inhabited neighborhoods that are packed tightly around the urban core. In plain terms, they live in ghettos.

Typical inhabitants of these ghettos are not only unlikely to come into contact with whites within the particular neighborhood where they live; even if they traveled to the adjacent neighborhood they would still be unlikely to see a white face; and if they went to the next neighborhood, no whites would be there either . . . No other group in the contemporary United States comes close to this level of isolation within urban society. U.S. Hispanics, for example, are never highly segregated on more than three dimensions simultaneously, and in 45 of the 60 metropolitan areas examined, they were highly segregated on only one dimension. Moreover, the large Hispanic community in Miami (the third largest in the country) is not highly segregated on any dimension at all. Despite their immigrant origins, Spanish language, and high poverty rates, Hispanics are considerably more integrated in American society than are blacks.

The analysis of 219 metropolitan areas shows that despite gains by some, black segregation remains the most extreme and enduring of any group in the nation—a wall of poverty and isolation that remains despite the country's attempts to legislate racial understanding. The depth of white resistance to desegregation has remained so great that even the salve of money has failed to heal the differences. Middle-class and affluent blacks are only slightly more likely to live next door to whites than poor blacks. (*USA Today*, 1991:2)

The sociospatial effects of racism on African Americans are also illustrated by comparing their position with that of other minorities. In metropolitan areas where minorities were at least 20 percent of the population—that is, where they were present in sufficient numbers to perhaps overcome prejudice—Hispanic Americans were highly segregated in only 2 of the 33 metropolitan areas. In contrast, "blacks are highly segregated in 31—two-thirds—of the 47 metro areas where they make up at least 20 percent of residents, including Detroit, Chicago, Miami, Birmingham, Ala." (*USA Today*, 1991:2).

Since the time of the Taeubers' study, researchers of spatial segregation have developed more precise measures of population clustering. The most sophisticated of these studies combine several different measures to arrive at overall estimates of segregation. Douglas Massey and Nancy Denton (1993), for example, used five different measures of population clustering in their study of the causes and consequences of racial segregation in Chicago and other cities (see Box 10.2). Harris and Weinburg (1992) used 19 different indexes of residential segregation for four groups (African

Americans, Asians, Hispanics, and Native Americans) across all 254 metropolitan regions in the United States. This is one of the relatively few studies to incorporate a regional perspective, using the metropolitan area rather than the central city as the unit of analysis. They found that segregation levels had changed very little from 1980 to 1990, replicating the results of the Taeubers' studies for the 1960–1970 period. While they found a very slight decrease in the segregation levels for blacks in some northern cities, segregation of Hispanics, Asian Americans, and Native Americans increased slightly in most metropolitan areas.

From the information presented in these and other studies, it is clear that the major determinant of racial segregation is not income, social class, or length of time in the United States, as suggested by the assimilation model, but racial background. African Americans confront the highest levels of segregation, while Asian Americans have the lowest levels. Racial background is also important in determining segregation for various ethnic groups within these categories: Puerto Ricans are more segregated than Mexicans, for example. Cultural factors such as language and religion are associated with the level of segregation for particular ethnic groups. For example, Filipino immigrants are likely to speak English and are familiar with American schools and government, and are much less segregated than other Asian American populations.

Racial segregation is not restricted to urban settlement space but is region-wide. Taken as a whole, suburban settlement space may be even more segregated than central cities. Institutional racism, including government policies and the actions of developers and real estate companies, has effectively ensured that most suburbs remain racially distinct. As noted in Chapter 4, the first mass suburban community, Levittown, New York, took special precautions to exclude prospective home buyers who were African American. Many studies have shown that when African Americans do acquire suburban residence, they are most likely to find housing in older, industrial suburbs and in inner-ring suburbs adjacent to an expanding urban ghetto. This is referred to as a *spillover* from the central city, and for many years it was argued that black suburbanization simply resulted in the formation of *suburban ghettos*. Since World War II, a significant number of African Americans have achieved middle-class status, and the rate of increase for blacks in the suburban ring has actually exceeded that of whites for many decades. Thus, this group is likely to live in a wide range of suburban communities, although these numbers are still small and disproportionate to their total population in the metropolitan community as a whole.

One effect on U.S. culture of these arrangements is that increasingly whites learn about blacks and blacks learn about whites only from the mass media, because they have little direct contact with each other. Styles of dress and language among teenagers, in particular, are highly influenced by the media and the mass marketing of youth-related fashions in clothing, cinema, and music. In the 1990s, an urban style of ghetto dress among black teenagers that is associated with rap music and inner-city dance styles was marketed nationwide. Many youths in suburbia copy the style that is marketed to them through television and films. At the same time, suburban fashions associated with active leisure wear, especially influenced by southern California, such as skateboarding and beachwear, are also marketed through the media nationwide. Teenage culture represents a battleground of these and other spatially generated lifestyles that are diffused across the country by the mass media (Chambers, 1986), and it is here, in popular culture, that urban African American culture has had its greatest impact on whites.

Poverty

The issue of poverty is not confined to urban settlement space alone. People throughout the metropolitan region suffer from the effects of this problem. Poverty is caused by the uneven development of the economy. In the 1950s, despite growing affluence, large numbers of Americans were poor, with some living in appalling conditions (Harrington, 1962). At that time, it was recognized that there were poor people in rural areas as well as urban places. As a result of government antipoverty programs such as the War on Poverty, the poverty rate declined to about 12.1 percent in the 1960s. In the 1970s and 1980s, however, the rate rose again and reached levels comparable to Depression-era statistics; roughly 20 percent of the total population was living at or below the poverty line in the 1980s (Wilson, 1987).

Although poverty rates were held constant over the 1990s, we must consider two aspects of the poverty problem in the United States. First is the meaning and measurement of poverty. For most of the last decade, the poverty level has been defined as $16,400 for a family of four. It is difficult to figure a family budget at just $1,400 per month, particularly for families living in urban areas with high rents and food costs. Second, despite the near record low unemployment of the 1990s under the Clinton administration (and the record high level of corporate profits as reflected in the stock market), the relative number of persons with incomes below the poverty line has remained the same.

Poverty can be considered an urban problem because of concentrated poverty neighborhoods in large cities, as the sociospatial perspective suggests. The number of central city poor people climbed from 8 million in 1969 to 12.7 million in 1982 (a 59 percent increase). Consequently, the city as a spatial form concentrates the poor in record numbers. As William J. Wilson has observed, "to say that poverty has become increasingly urbanized is to note a remarkable change in the concentration of poor people in the United States in only slightly more than a decade" (1987:172).

Furthermore, the demographic profile of the poor is also cause for alarm. In 1989, 39 percent of young children were living in poverty; among all age groups, 30.7 percent of African Americans and 26.2 percent of Hispanics were below the poverty line. Because the minority population of the United States is overwhelmingly urban, these figures imply a concentration of poor minority group members in the large central cities and represent a *major* problem for the entire society, not just for those living in central cities. As one report suggested:

> As the problems of the urban poor become more toxic to those inside [the city], their immediate impact on most Americans is becoming more distant and elusive. But even

though elusive, the effects of urban poverty can be far-reaching. They strain big-city budgets, produce criminal behavior that is altering urban life, poison race relations and threaten to spawn an undereducated work force that could haunt the nation for decades. (Applebome, 1991:A20)

Economic Restructuring and the Problems of the Poor

While poverty is a phenomenon of uneven development, the last two decades of deindustrialization and manufacturing decline have contributed greatly to the numbers of poor people. During the 1980s, many cities were transformed by the new realities of global location decisions (see Chapters 7, 8, and 13). Manufacturing jobs declined drastically, and central city economies retooled into service centers. These changes created positions for highly trained professional workers, especially in information processing and banking, along with a limited number of low-skilled, poorly paid jobs in the service sectors of food, tourism, and delivery systems, among others. As job opportunities dried up during the recession-plagued years of the 1980s and 1990s, unemployed workers among the less affluent and less educated found it increasingly difficult to make ends meet, and both poverty and crime increased.

The new conditions of poverty, however, are not just confined to the large cities. Deindustrialization and economic restructuring have also affected towns and suburbs that have relied on manufacturing. In Chapter 5 we discussed the case of Youngstown, Ohio, which was devastated by the closing of its pipe mill. There have been other such cases since the 1980s. The decline of manufacturing has resulted in the crushing of communities and a rise of poverty among working-class populations across the country. For example, Homestead, Pennsylvania, near Pittsburgh, was once a thriving town of 20,000 people. It was the site of a large steel mill that was typical of the kinds of businesses that failed due to deindustrialization. According to one account (Serrin, 1992), the community was simply abandoned by U.S. Steel Corporation in the 1980s. It is now an impoverished, bleak community of fewer than 4,000 people. The pattern that has been repeated in countless places such as Youngstown and Homestead is one of no planning and no transition phase allowed to workers who suffer job loss due to plant closings. Many communities across the United States have been impoverished, and working-class whites have suffered the most because of this callous process of change.

Poverty and Race

Central city poverty is compounded by the consequences of racial discrimination. Blacks have always been spatially isolated in our society due to racism. Hence, the economic deprivation that they now suffer because of industrial restructuring has forced the quality of life in ghetto areas to decline drastically (Farley and Allen, 1987). The black unemployment rate, for example, has reached more than twice that of whites (except in 1975): from 9 percent for blacks and 5 percent for whites in 1954 to 14.4 percent and 6.5 percent, respectively, in 1984 (Wilson, 1987:65). Today the structurally unemployed (those who have ceased to look for work as well as those recently out of work) among black city residents has skyrocketed to over 20 percent. Many of these inner-city residents are not just poor; they are ill equipped to participate in the economy because of restructuring to services and the decline of manufacturing. They do not have the skills to obtain the jobs they need to rise above poverty. The case of Milwaukee is illustrative. The policy of restructuring in that city has had negative effects on black residents, according to one report:

> It has devastated the city's poor black neighborhoods whose residents thrived in the high wage union jobs of the city's manufacturing heyday, but are now adrift on a rising tide of unemployment, crime and despair. The retooling of factories also hurt unskilled whites, of course. But, the effect was less severe for several reasons. . . . In Milwaukee the result is a city of 600,000 people where black men stand idle on street corners just blocks from the breweries and factories that used to employ them. . . . More than half of all black Milwaukeeans are on some form of public assistance. (Wilkerson, 1991:Al)

In the 1980s, the alarming increase in poverty among inner-city ghetto residents prompted several observers to suggest that there exists an urban "underclass" living in ghetto areas that is afflicted by isolation and deprivation (see Chapter 8). According to William J. Wilson, the *underclass* consists of a relatively permanent population that (1) is concentrated in poor areas of the city, (2) is chronically removed from the full-time labor force, (3) contains a large proportion of teenage and out-of-wedlock births, and (4) has a comparatively long history of welfare dependency (Wilson, 1987:172). The underclass is a problem because forces or institutions that give people economic and social opportunities, such as education, have ceased to function for a sizable pro-portion of the urban poor. As a result, there is no mechanism that might improve the condition of the underclass.

Since Wilson's important study, the term *underclass* has been attacked because of its common usage that blames the victims of poverty and racism rather than the structural causes and profit-seeking corporations that are responsible for the condition in the first place (Feagin, 1992). According to Herbert J. Gans, "While this word can be used as a graphic technical term for the growing number of persistently poor and jobless Americans, it is also a value-laden, increasingly pejorative term that seems to be becoming the newest buzzword for the *undeserving* poor" (Gans, 1990:271). As a consequence, Wilson and other prominent sociologists have recently called for an abandonment of its usage. We suggest the term *ghettoized poor* as closer to the origi-nal intent of the concept. Ghettoization is not just an effect of poverty and lack of skills but an outcome of overt discrimination against minorities.

The spatial effects of concentrating the poor in a few neighborhoods also con-tribute to urban problems. For example, ghetto areas are the sites of the most violent criminal and drug-related activities, so the urban poor are also the most likely to be crime victims and suffer the most from crime (Taylor, 1991). In addition, ghetto areas have worse medical care than do other parts of the city. A study of infant mortality rates in New York found that the rate was almost twice as high in central Harlem and Bedford-Stuyvesant (23.4 and 21 per 1,000, respectively), both well-known black communities, as the city average of 13.3 per 1,000 (the national average was 10 in 1,000 in 1990).

Despite the recent effort to avoid blaming the victim, the increasing hopelessness of limited job opportunities (see Box 10.3) and the decline of ghetto social institutions

BOX 10.3 WHEN WORK DISAPPEARS

Neighborhood social organization depends on the extent of local friendship ties, the degree of social cohesion, the level of resident participation in formal and informal voluntary associations, the density of formal organizations, and the nature of informal social controls. Neighborhoods in which adults are able to interact in terms of obligations, expectations, and relationships are in a better position to supervise and control the activities and behavior of children. In neighborhoods with high levels of social organization, adults are empowered to act to improve the quality of neighborhood life—for example, by breaking up congregations of youths on street corners and supervising the leisure activities of youngsters.

Neighborhoods plagued by high levels of joblessness are more likely to experience low levels of social organization; the two go hand in hand. High rates of joblessness trigger other neighborhood problems that undermine social organization, ranging from crime, gang violence, and drug trafficking to family breakups and problems in the organization of family life.

Consider the problems of drug trafficking and violent crime. As many students have revealed, the decline in legitimate employment opportunities among inner-city residents has increased incentives to sell drugs. The distribution of crack in a neighborhood attracts individuals involved in violence and lawlessness. Between 1985 and 1992, there was a sharp increase in the murder rate among men under age 24; for men 18 years and younger, murder rates doubled. Black males in particular have been involved in this upsurge in violence. This sharp rise in violent crime among younger males has accompanied the widespread outbreak of addiction to crack-cocaine. The association is especially strong in inner-city neighborhoods plagued by joblessness and weak social organization.

The problems reported by the residents of poor neighborhoods are not a consequence of poverty alone. Something far more devastating has happened that can only be attributed to the emergence of concentrated and persistent joblessness and its crippling effects on neighborhoods, families, and individuals. (Wilson, 1996)

have resulted in changes among racially segregated ghetto residents that seem to be a turn for the worse. According to the black urban sociologist Elijah Anderson (1990), ghetto culture possessed a male role model, the "old head," who provided stability and positive values to youth. "Traditionally, the *old head* was a man of stable means who believed in hard work, family life, and the church" (1990:2). He functioned to socialize young men into productive, responsible lives. Anderson continues:

> But today, as meaningful employment has become increasingly scarce for young blacks and as crime and drugs have become a way of life for many, the "old head" is losing his prestige and authority. With the expansion of the drug culture and its opportunities for large sums of quick money, street-smart young boys are concluding that the old head's lessons about life and the work ethic are no longer relevant. (1990:3)

As a car burns in the intersection, marchers fill the streets in the Mt. Pleasant neighborhood of Washington, D.C., on May 6, 1991, after clashing with the District of Columbia police for the second straight night.

According to Anderson, a different role model has emerged over the last two decades:

> He is young, often a product of the street gang, and at best indifferent to the law and traditional values. This "new" old head is in many respects the antithesis of the traditional one . . . he makes ends meet, part time or full time, in the drug trade or some other area of the underground economy. (1990:3)

In sum, the urban problem of the ghetto poor is a product of the sociospatial effects of racism and economic changes due to the restructuring of the global economy and the decline of manufacturing. At present, potential solutions are unclear because even in times of prosperity, underclass areas lack the human resources to capitalize on opportunities; that is, urban poverty does not seem to decline when the economy as a whole improves (Jencks and Peterson, 1991). As Wilson (1987) and others have maintained, special programs are needed to deal with the intractable problems of the poor. In the meantime, the effects of the pathology emanating from poverty-stricken ghetto areas will continue to drain society's resources for years to come.

The potential threat of a large, minority population that is racially and economically deprived has been graphically illustrated many times in the outbreak of violence and riots that often terrorized an entire city. Often ghetto violence of this nature occurs after the police, perceived to be a white racist institution, kill or injure an African American neighborhood resident. Countless times such incidents have occurred across the nation, most recently during the days from April 30 to May 3, 1992. Following a verdict that acquitted four Los Angeles police officers in a case of excessive force against a motorist, Rodney King, rioting broke out on the streets of the south-central ghetto area. As reported in the daily press:

> Violence mushroomed as marauding gangs torched scores of structures and looted dozens of stores despite an all-night curfew and the deployment of the National Guard. Attacks spread to normally tranquil neighborhoods miles away from the city's mean streets, and law enforcement officials dodged bullets. (Wilson, 1992:Al)

All told, at least 53 people were killed and 2,328 were injured in America's bloodiest urban riot. Damage estimates exceeded $1 billion and an extensive area was devastated, including portions of Los Angeles adjacent to the south-central area.

Crime and Drugs

Crime

On the evening of July 31, 1990, John Reisenbach, a 33-year-old advertising executive, left his apartment in the fashionable Greenwich Village section of Manhattan. His phone was out of order, and he had to call an associate. Several feet from the entrance to his building was a pay phone, and Reisenbach stepped in. While talking, he was approached by an African American man of about the same age who demanded money. When Reisenbach refused, he was shot dead. In the following weeks, four children under age 15 were also shot in the city. These innocent bystanders included three-year-old Octavia Brown and six-year-old Kevin Acevedo, who were caught between warring drug dealers.

These tragic stories give the impression that crime is rampant in cities and that cities are unsafe as human environments. When people speak of crime, they usually mean *violent crime*, which includes murder, assault, rape, and robbery. However, a large amount of *property crime*—burglary, larceny, and auto theft—also occurs every year in cities and suburbs. White-collar criminals, for example, such as insider traders on Wall Street and the bankers involved in the savings and loan scandal, are responsible for the theft of billions of dollars. But these crimes are not usually considered an outcome of life in large cities or suburbs. For the most part, the crimes associated with metropolitan areas are of the violent variety or property crimes such as burglary and auto theft. These crimes affect our view of public safety and the safety of our homes.

Table 10.1 indicates the crime rates for the largest cities in the United States in 1990 and 1995. The cities of New York, Los Angeles, Chicago, Houston, Philadelphia, and Detroit all had over 500 murders in 1990. During that same year Houston, Dallas, and San Antonio had over 100,000 property crimes, while New York, Los Angeles, and Chicago had over 200,000. Surprisingly, the murder rate is declining in many cities; see the figures for 1995. With the exception of Phoenix, Baltimore, and New Orleans, the rate has dropped.

Many people think that cities have become more dangerous than they were in the past, but how accurate is that assessment? Table 10.2 shows the changes in the per capita crime rates between 1980 and 1990. While New York City had 2,245 murders in 1990, it was not the nation's most dangerous city; its total crime rate per capita was

TABLE 10.1
Violent Crimes for the 24 Largest Cities, 1990, and 1995

City	Crime Index Total		Violent Crime Total		Property Crime Total		Murder		Rape		Robbery		Aggravated Assault	
	1995	1990	1995	1990	1995	1990	1995	1990	1995	1990	1995	1990	1995	1990
New York, NY	444,758	710,222	115,153	174,542	329,605	535,680	1,177	2,245	2,374	3,126	59,280	100,280	52,322	68,891
Los Angeles, CA	266,204	321,536	70,518	84,792	195,686	237,727	849	983	1,590	2,014	29,134	36,098	38,945	44,714
Chicago, IL	NA	NA	NA	NA	NA	228,829	824	851	NA	NA	30,086	37,156	39,205	41,114
Houston, TX	131,602	184,869	22,260	22,637	109,342	162,232	316	568	837	1,335	9,222	12,921	11,885	7,813
Philadelphia, PA	108,278	114,032	21,972	21,387	86,306	92,645	432	503	773	734	13,612	12,806	7,155	7,344
San Diego, CA	64,235	101,564	11,077	12,047	53,158	89,517	91	135	346	439	3,244	4,331	7,396	7,142
Detroit, MI	119,065	125,325	24,011	27,747	95,054	97,578	475	582	1,104	1,657	10,076	13,010	12,356	12,498
Dallas, TX	98,624	156,267	15,969	24,550	82,655	131,747	276	447	852	1,344	5,899	10,565	8,942	12,194
San Antonio, TX	79,931	116,774	5,178	5,730	74,753	111,044	142	208	658	430	2,345	2,864	2,033	2,228
Phoenix, AZ	118,126	105,779	11,590	10,665	106,536	95,114	214	128	411	512	3,693	3,383	7,272	6,642
Baltimore, MD	94,855	77,989	21,495	17,942	73,360	60,047	325	305	683	687	11,353	9,477	9,134	7,473
San Jose, CA	36,098	38,090	6,649	4,698	29,447	33,392	38	35	387	416	1,209	1,034	5,015	3,213
San Francisco, CA	60,474	70,183	10,903	12,466	49,571	57,717	99	101	304	422	6,469	7,072	4,031	4,871
Indianapolis, IN	36,469	32,635	6,724	6,224	29,745	26,411	99	58	457	541	2,532	1,642	3,636	3,983
Memphis, TN	65,597	60,255	11,039	9,082	54,558	51,173	181	195	785	831	5,779	4,152	4,294	3,904
Jacksonville, FL	61,129	66,618	9,596	11,654	51,533	54,964	86	176	625	704	2,920	3,963	5,965	6,811
Washington, DC	67,401	65,389	14,744	14,919	52,657	50,470	360	472	292	303	6,864	7,365	7,228	6,779
Milwaukee, WI	52,679	58,406	6,737	6,282	45,942	52,124	138	155	370	495	3,650	4,146	2,579	1,486
Boston, MA	52,278	68,057	9,569	13,664	42,709	54,393	96	143	379	539	3,597	6,022	5,497	6,960
Columbus, OH	58,715	62,703	6,624	7,022	52,091	55,681	77	89	636	647	3,329	3,541	2,582	2,745
New Orleans, LA	53,399	61,799	10,876	11,227	42,523	50,572	363	304	487	361	5,349	6,048	4,677	4,514
Cleveland, OH	38,665	46,085	8,150	9,190	30,515	36,895	129	168	689	846	6,224	4,917	3,108	3,259
El Paso, TX	41,692	57,921	4,948	5,111	36,744	52,810	37	34	242	256	1,076	1,381	3,593	3,440
Seattle, WA	55,507	65,053	4,904	7,780	50,603	57,273	41	53	260	481	2,213	2,695	2,390	4,551

Note: Figures for rape not available for Chicago, IL, in 1990 and 1995.
Source: U.S. Department of Justice, Washington, DC, Uniform Crime Reports, 1990, Table 6.

10 percent. Dallas (15 percent), Seattle (13 percent), Detroit (12 percent), San Antonio (12 percent), and Boston (12 percent) all had higher per capita crime rates.

According to Table 10.2, indexes of combined violent and property crimes reveal that between 1980 and 1990, crime declined in only 5 of the 23 largest U.S. cities. In 14 other large cities, total crimes increased. In some cities, the gain was remarkable. Violent crimes increased 43 percent in Houston, 94 percent in San Diego, 52 percent in Phoenix, 99 percent in Jacksonville, and 81 percent in El Paso. Only San Francisco and Cleveland experienced a decline in the violent crime rate. Table 10.2 also shows that there seems to be no relationship between changes in city population and changes in crime rates. Philadelphia, for example, experienced a 6.1 percent loss in population between 1980 and 1990 and an increase in total per capita crimes. In contrast, the population of San Diego grew by 26.8 percent between 1980 and 1990, but its per capita total crime rate also increased.

To understand the nature of urban crime it is necessary to view it as a *spatial* as well as a social phenomenon. The incidence of crimes varies within any given city by neighborhood. Thus, while all cities have become more dangerous since World War II, there are still places that are as safe as any other place in the country. Conversely, certain neighborhoods are scenes of unremitting terror.

Typically, criminal incidents follow the lines of class and racial segregation: The most dangerous places are also the places where the poorest urban residents live. For example, "the typical New York City murder victim is a black man in his late teens or twenties, killed by an acquaintance of the same race with a hand gun during a dispute—most likely over drug-dealing" (Greenberg, 1990:26). In all cities, racially segregated ghettos are the places where violent crimes are committed the most. Furthermore, most incarcerated felons are either black or Hispanic, and virtually all are poor. They come from the ghetto areas of the city, and their crimes usually were committed in those areas. And as the urban environment is partitioned into areas of relative safety and terror, several extreme examples of violent crimes, such as shootings in public schools, indicate that the islands of safety are shrinking in size and availability.

Why Crime Is an Urban Problem: Its Costs

What effect does crime have on everyday urban life? Perhaps the greatest effect has occurred with regard to the use of city space. In less crime-ridden eras, public spaces such as parks, plazas, and streets were enjoyed by everyone. Parks in particular were used by diverse people at all hours of the day and evening. Today the use of public space is limited: People are afraid to venture into parks without friends nearby, and children must be supervised and kept away from strangers. The evening use of public spaces and facilities, such as streets and mass transit systems, has also been negatively affected. People leaving their offices late at night now take cabs or cars rather than public transportation. A few years ago, a young woman out for a jog in Central Park was brutally attacked by a group of teenagers. Beaten within an inch of her life and raped, she miraculously survived, but this urban professional who was employed on Wall Street became a symbol of the toll of crime on the enjoyment of urban space.

Crime pushes up the security budgets of companies and households and results in billions of dollars in unnecessary medical expenses. It can also devastate property val-

TABLE 10.2
Per Capita Crimes and Changes in Violent Crimes for the 24 Largest Cities, 1980 and 1990

City	Per Capita Crime, 1990	Per Capita Crime, 1980	Percent Increase Violent Crime	Population Change 1980–1990
New York, NY	.10	.10	.17	3.5
Los Angeles, CA	.09	.10	.40	17.5
Houston, TX	.11	.09	.43	2.2
Philadelphia, PA	.07	.06	.24	−6.1
San Diego, CA	.10	.08	.94	26.8
Detroit, MI	.12	.11	.19	−14.6
Dallas, TX	.15	.12	.93	11.4
San Antonio, TX	.12	.07	.34	19.1
Phoenix, AZ	.11	.11	.52	24.5
Baltimore, MD	.11	.10	.08	−6.3
San Jose, CA	.05	.08	.24	24.3
San Francisco, CA	.10	.10	−.02	6.6
Indianapolis, IN	.04	.05	.40	4.4
Memphis, TN	.10	.08	.32	−5.6
Jacksonville, FL	.10	.08	.99	17.4
Washington, DC	.11	.10	.17	−4.9
Milwaukee, WI	.09	.06	.90	−1.3
Boston, MA	.12	.13	.10	2.0
Columbus, OH	.10	.10	.37	12.0
New Orleans, LA	.12	.09	.37	−10.9
Cleveland, OH	.09	.10	−.20	−11.9
El Paso, TX	.11	.06	.81	21.3
Seattle, WA	.13	.10	.50	4.5

Note: All figures not available for Chicago, IL. in 1990.
Source: Adapted from U.S. Department of Justice, Washington, DC, *Uniform Crime Reports*, 1990, Table 6.

ues. In areas of the city with high crime rates, the value of property remains low and does not rise during times of prosperity (Taylor, 1991). Thus, innocent households suffer doubly in crime-infested sections because they are victims of crime and because the value of their housing declines. Poor areas remain in poverty because high crime levels chase away prospective investment. Finally, crime makes the city an unattractive place to live, especially for families with small children. Crime chases families away from the city, which compounds the problem of population loss and the inability of the city to increase its tax base.

As mentioned earlier, white-collar crime results in terrible costs to this society but is not associated with the quality of urban life. Rather, it is violent crime that scares people away from the city. In addition to murder, which usually is committed among people who know one another, mugging is a particularly frightening crime, especially armed robbery. The frequency of this type of crime in the cities contributes greatly to the image of danger.

According to studies of arrestees, many robberies and burglaries are committed in association with drug trafficking. In fact, statistics show a disturbing relationship between violent crime and drug use. The National Institute of Justice surveyed arrestees in the 20 largest American cities and found that at least half of them tested positive for the use of illegal drugs. In New York City, as many as 83 percent of males tested positive at the time of arrest. The range for females was slightly lower, but not by much: a low of 44 percent testing positive in St. Louis and a high of 81 percent in Detroit (National Institute of Justice, 1990).

According to this report, the extent of drug use among arrestees varies from city to city, but the use of drugs by people who commit violent crimes is alarming. The most common drug for both male and female arrestees is cocaine or crack. For example, in the family of Ruby highlighted at the beginning of this chapter, one son and one daughter were addicted to cocaine, and that son was a member of a gang involved in the drug trade.

The lack of safety in large cities results from a high crime rate that is compounded by illegal drug use. When city streets are not considered safe, it is difficult for urban areas to attract new residents and businesses. Consequently, the economic life of the city deteriorates further. In addition, when the enjoyment of public space becomes impossible due to crime and drugs, one of the primary enjoyments of urban culture is threatened with extinction.

Street Gangs

One type of criminal activity with a strong sociospatial component involves street gangs. While gangs are not a new phenomenon—Emory Bogardus studied Mexican gangs in Los Angeles in the 1930s—gang activity has grown significantly in many cities over the last several decades. Frederick Thrasher's classic work on street gangs in Chicago noted that gangs were likely to appear in the "interstitial areas" of urban neighborhoods, where there was a lack of institutional structures, and that children from recent immigrant families—Polish, Italian, and other groups from Eastern Europe—were more likely to become involved in street gangs (Thrasher, 1927). Street gang activity of the present day is often concentrated in the same neighborhoods, and children from recent immigrant groups are still more likely to be involved in street gangs. Many of the reasons for gang involvement are likely the same, including isolation from the dominant culture, peer group pressure, family stress, poverty, and the struggle for self-identity that all adolescents confront (Vigil, 1988). In other ways, however, street gangs of the present day *are* different: The children of immigrants are now Mexican and Asian, not Polish and Italian. Because of the loss of employment in the central city, there are fewer opportunities for gang members to "mature out" of the gangs (Hagedorn, 1988). Gang members are more socially isolated from other adolescent groups than was the case in earlier generations (Moore, 1991). And the open availability of both legal and illegal handguns makes street gang activity more dangerous and unpredictable.

Street gangs develop among adolescent groups within the meaningful spaces of local neighborhoods; gangs are often named after the local neighborhood (Logan Heights in San Diego) or street coordinates (18th Street in Los Angeles), and they aim to defend their "turf" from encroachment by other gangs. It is common to refer to

Figure 10.1   Gang graffiti from Chicago shows alliance between Gaylords and Latin Kings, along with their claims to urban space.

"black gangs" or "Latino gangs," but this characterization is very misleading. Street gangs are organized within specific settlement spaces, and because of the high levels of racial segregation, gang members from African American neighborhoods are likely to be black, while those from Latino neighborhoods are likely to be Hispanic. But there is no one-to-one correspondence; one may come across white members of the Black Gangster Disciples or black members of the Latin Kings. Because both gangs and schools are organized around urban spaces, gang activity may carry over into the public schools (Hutchison and Kyle, 1993).

The graffiti produced by street gangs show their claims to particular neighborhoods and alliances with other gangs (Hutchison, 1993)—and here the semiotic analysis of the sociospatial approach is especially informative. The gang graffiti in Figure 10.1 shows the Latin Kings (of Kedzie Street) and Gaylords (of Palmer Street). An alliance between these groups is demonstrated by the Gaylord figure (a hooded figure) wearing the pointed crown of the Latin Kings. Symbols of opposing gangs are inverted, such as the Latin Disciple pitchfork and Imperial Gangster rounded crown. The networking of allegiances and opposition among Chicago street gangs represented by this photograph extends across the metropolitan region, into the public schools, and even within the prison system, where separate wings of the Stateville Federal Penitentiary are allocated to members of the Latin Disciple, Latin King, Vicelord, and Gangster Disciple "nations."

The alliances (and opposition) among street gangs represent a specific ordering of social space within the contemporary city. Street gangs may fight to defend their home

A Decade of Death

The spread of 18th Street's violence is shown by 154 murders linked to the gang from 1985 to 1995. This only plots homicides within Los Angeles where the killers have been tied to the gang.

Source: LAPD

MATT MOODY / Los Angeles Times

Figure 10.2   Homicides commited by members of the 18ᵗʰ Street gang in Los Angeles are not randomly situated in urban space, but instead indicate where gang members have encountered persons from rival gangs

neighborhoods and, in some instances, move into other neighborhoods to extend their power and reputation. A mapping of the 120 gang homicides committed by members of the 18th Street gang in Los Angeles (see Figure 10.2) clearly demonstrates the spatial nature of this gang activity: Many of the homicides are concentrated in the gang's home turf just west of the downtown area, but there also are clusters of homicides along Hollywood Boulevard (to the northwest) and in south-central LA as gang members have come into contact with gangs from other neighborhoods. Maps such as this suggest how important street gangs and gang activity have become over the last three decades. Gang activity no longer is confined to urban barrios and ghettos but has spread across the metropolitan region, and it is not unusual to find "wannabes" and even bona fide gang members among middle-class youth in suburban settlement space.

Suburban Crime

Compared to crime in the large city, little research has been carried out on suburban crime (see Stahura, Huff, and Smith, 1980; Gottdiener, 1982). Most reports on suburban crimes identify the same factors that cause city crimes, that is, racism, poverty, and class conflict. As in the case of urban areas, the rate of suburban crimes has increased dramatically since the 1980s (Barbanel, 1992). However crimes in the suburbs differ in some ways from those in large cities. First, the property crimes of burglary, auto theft, fraud, and larceny dominate suburban crime, although rape is as serious a problem in suburbs as in cities. Thus, while experiencing violent crime in increasing proportion, suburban areas have much less of it than do large cities. In contrast, property crimes are most troublesome.

Second, there is a distinct spatial component to suburban crime that differs from the city. In the latter, high-crime areas are associated with urban ghettos. While suburbs have ghettos, not all of these are high-crime areas. Instead, according to one study of a mature suburban region outside of Los Angeles (Gottdiener, 1982), police in Orange County, California, associate high crime rates with apartment buildings. These stand out because most residential dwellings in suburbia are single-family homes. In large cities, this distinction would not be effective since most residences are in apartment buildings. According to this study, police in suburbs pay particular attention to apartment dwellings and monitor the activities of their residents. Because of the lower density of suburban areas, surveillance of populations is an easier chore than in the large city (see Davis, 1990).

Aside from the above features, however, suburban crime seems very much like that found in large cities, although perhaps not at the same rate per capita. But given the diversity of suburban communities, ranging from declining industrial suburbs to communities with spillover from adjacent urban ghettos, it is likely that many suburban communities are less safe than many city neighborhoods. While overall crime rates in the United States decreased each year from 1993 to 1998, rates of violent crime remained high, as did the public's perception of and fear of crime. Violent crime, drugs, burglary, rape, and street gang activity have become a significant factor in daily life across the metropolitan region, affecting life in both urban and suburban settlement spaces.

The Fiscal Crisis and Public Service Problems

Urban problems are difficult to solve when insufficient money is available to local governments. A *fiscal crisis* starts when the revenues obtained by government fall short of the expenses of running a city. When this occurs, it is necessary to borrow money and incur debt. *Long-term debt* involves borrowing to improve resources and finance public works such as bridges. This form of borrowing is usually considered healthy as long as the projects are well thought out. Long-term debt is considered an investment in the city's future; if it is successful, the city grows and its economy improves, resulting in an increase in revenues.

In contrast, *short-term debt* involves borrowing to pay general operating expenses that revenues and money transferred to the city from higher levels of government cannot cover. Occasionally cities must borrow simply to cover operating expenses, such as meeting a payroll, but this usually happens only in an emergency. However, as a regular practice it can ruin the health of a city by limiting the amount of money invested for future needs.

Fiscal Crisis

The fiscal crisis of the cities has two components. During the 1970s, many cities faced budgetary shortfalls because of rising costs coupled with decreasing revenues caused by the decline in manufacturing and the rapid deterioration of urban economies. These cities were forced to resort to short-term borrowing to cover their costs. Compounding the problem was the flight of middle-class families from the cities to the suburbs (traveling on highways built with federal money to homes subsidized by federal housing policies), taking with them potential tax revenue that the cities desperately needed. The lower-income and new immigrant communities in the cities required relatively higher levels of health care, education programs, and housing services. When New York and other cities appealed to higher levels of government for financial relief, they were rebuked, and this precipitated the urban fiscal crisis. Cities responded to this situation by cutting services and systematically laying off personnel. New York City, for example, almost went bankrupt during 1976 and was placed in the hands of a money management panel appointed by the state to bring expenditures back in line with revenues and limit the amount of borrowing. As a result of the changes caused by this fiscal crisis, New York is unable to offer a full range of services to its residents. The closing of firehouses, reductions in the numbers of police officers and the hours of policing, the shortening of library hours, and layoffs and firings at city agencies are some of the austerity measures enacted in response to the urban fiscal crisis.

In the 1980s many cities, such as Cleveland, which had *defaulted* in 1978, and New York, which was forced into austerity, regained their fiscal health. The banking community renewed its faith in the obligations incurred by municipal governments. Short-term borrowing was controlled, and many cities prospered. For a time, it appeared that the urban fiscal crisis was resolved (Gottdiener, 1986). However, the problem was simply transferred to higher levels of government. At present, many states face a fiscal crisis; New York and California are especially hard hit. These and other states have had to cut back on budgets for social programs in education, health, and other areas, with perceptible effects on the quality of life. Because state governments can no longer aid cities, local jurisdictions must increase taxes or cut back services. Hence, the effects of the state fiscal crisis have been especially troubling for local communities, and with no end in sight for the first decades of the twenty-first century.

The federal government has not been able to help, since it has acquired serious debt problems of its own for the first time in U.S. history. In 1980 the federal deficit was approximately $40 million, which was unprecedented but still manageable. During the 1980s, it rose to more than $150 billion a year. The interest payments on this massive debt made up 14 percent of gross national product (GNP), and the United States became the world's leading debtor nation. Although President Clinton made deficit reduction of the federal budget a priority, little or no effort has been made to restore either programs or funding cut during the 1980s. In places such as New York and California, governments at all levels are suffering cutbacks of services and programs as a result of the fiscal crisis. The damaging effects of these cuts cannot be exaggerated. In Los Angeles, the police department and the district attorney's office blame California's Proposition 13, which froze property tax revenues, for cuts in social programs resulting in an increase in gang activity that has led to Los Angeles becoming known as the gang capital of the United States. Let us consider the current situation as it affects metropolitan areas across the country.

Social Service Cutbacks: Education and Infrastructure

Cutbacks in the services that municipal governments provide, such as firefighting and education, greatly affect the quality of life. Even before the fiscal crisis, however, questions were raised about the relative distribution of such services. Many scholars argued that poorer areas did not get the same level or quality of services that wealthier areas received. Thus, the distribution of city services had a spatial component and the allocation pattern was inequitable. In Chapter 14 we will see how this sociospatial discrimination is reflected in environmental conditions that proportionately disadvantage the poor. The municipal cutbacks since the fiscal crisis of the 1970s have thus made an unfair situation much worse (Susser, 1982).

Studies of city spending by neighborhood uncovered spatial inequities in the provision of money for education (Sexton, 1961; Oakes, 1985), in municipal health care (Alford, 1975), and in police protection (Nardulli and Stonecash, 1981). In many cities, spending per child was greater in wealthier districts than in poorer ones (Sexton, 1961). This violates considerations of equity because all these districts are serviced by the *same* city government. In short, a pattern of *fiscal discrimination* overlies the existing pattern of racial and income segregation in cities.

Some scholars have disputed the suggestion that city governments abet racial and income segregation through their spending practices, stating that private sector mechanisms, such as the cost of rental housing, actually produce these patterns. Lineberry (1977), for example, found that public bureaucracies did not intentionally create inequities in spending but these inequities were caused by the past errors of bureaucrats. Other analysts argue that not all services are equal. Some, such as education, are much more critical to the well-being of future generations than others, such as the availability of parks. Differences in spending per school district constitute a serious problem of equity (Gottdiener, 1986). When the quality of public schools is not maintained, urban problems, such as poverty-related crime and drugs, are projected into the future. Let us consider two critical city services—education and spending on the infrastructure—and the roles they play in maintaining the quality of urban life.

The City Crisis in Education. The crisis of urban education reflects a national crisis in educational quality. Student performance as a whole has declined over the last several decades, and in world comparisons American grade school students do poorly in science and math. But throughout the metropolitan region, the quality of local schools is a function of where one lives. For the most part, the better schools are located in the wealthier areas. Even inner-city school systems that historically have functioned at a relatively high level, despite the poverty of their pupils, have had to contend with both a prolonged fiscal crisis and a recession, which have combined to cut into the quality of education. Today the pupils attending urban public schools are predominantly poor minority group members with low educational attainment.

There are all too many indicators of the growing crisis in public education in the United States. In large city school districts across the country, fewer than half of the students who start high school will graduate in their senior year. In low-income school districts, a *majority* of teachers are teaching subjects for which they have not been trained or certified. Although all public high school teachers are supposed to be certified to teach, school districts make use of a loophole to allow temporary hiring of non-certified instructional staff; in some schools, a quarter or more of instructors are not certified. When public school teachers in Texas took a required test of general knowledge expected for college graduates, more than a third earned a failing grade. And in Florida, where students who have graduated with degrees in education are required to take similar tests, more than half have flunked (who otherwise would have begun teaching the following year). In this way, the crisis in public education continues at all levels, affecting not just public schools but public universities, most of which are severely underfunded and no longer in a position to deliver the high-quality education expected in the past.

Problems with performance, then, are compounded by the problems of poverty, fiscal crisis, and economic decline. According to one study (Pallas, Natriello, and McDill, 1989), the proportion of American children living in poverty is expected to increase to 27 percent in the year 2020, and the number of children living with mothers who have not completed high school is expected to rise to 21.3 million in 2020. Traditionally, students from such backgrounds do poorly in school. Finally, educational problems are compounded by race. Schools are increasingly segregated in metropolitan areas. The shift of many urban whites to private education accentuates this racial problem. According to one report, "after steady progress toward integration in the 1970s, the 1980s saw as many schools resegregating as desegregating.

At present, a growing number of students in both city and suburban school districts are the children of immigrants, many from non-English-speaking countries. In many large urban school districts, minority students make up more than 50 percent of the student population, and teachers must deal with 30 or 40 different languages spoken by students. In addition to problems of poverty and racial segregation, school systems must struggle with the increasing diversity of American society. The federal government mandates that school districts establish ESL (English as a Second Language) programs if they have students whose home language is not English, but the federal government does not fund these programs. In recent years, many states also have stopped funding the programs, shifting the expense to local school districts.

There has been a failure at the federal level to fund education. Since the 1980s, the budget of the Department of Education as a share of the GNP has declined, and several Republican candidates for president have suggested elimination of this federal office entirely. The federal share of expenditures on elementary and secondary education has declined from 8.7 to 6.2 percent of the GNP. By 1990, states already provided 50 percent and local governments 44 percent of the total costs of education. It is unlikely that they can do more, and because education is an investment in human resources for the future, the urban labor force of the next few decades will not have the same skill levels as in the past. The decline in educational quality poses an increasing threat to our economic well-being in the coming century.

The Infrastructure Problem. One outcome of the decline in government spending has been a progressive deterioration of the urban infrastructure, especially roads, water systems, bridges, public buildings, and streets. Since the late 1960s, total spending on infrastructure as a share of the GNP declined from 2.3 percent in 1964 to 1.7 percent in 1987, while the population has grown. Most of our cities, particularly in the East and Midwest, were built at the turn of the century, and the urban infrastructure of water and sewer systems is now at the end of its expected service life. The problem of infrastructure needs is compounded by the economic and fiscal dilemmas that cities and suburbs face. They have some money to spend, but over the last several decades it has been channeled into economic revitalization. Due to the fiscal crisis, cities simply cannot do everything, and while managing in times of recession, they often sacrifice spending on infrastructure maintenance.

Due to neglect, some spectacular infrastructure failures have already occurred, causing a loss of life. For example, in 1989 an elevated section of the New England Thruway in Connecticut collapsed, killing three people. The highway was closed for almost six months for repairs. Breakdowns in sewer, road, and mass transit systems are now commonplace.

The most recent example of the city infrastructure crisis occurred in Chicago. In February 1992, a cable television company was working in one of the many empty tunnels that exist beneath the streets of downtown Chicago and below the water level of the Chicago River. They found evidence of a small leak and reported it to the city's Department of General Services. On March 13, the tunnel was inspected and a report was filed with the Department of Transportation. On April 2, the city's chief bridge engineer sent a memo to the commissioner of that department who was in charge of infrastructure repairs to attend to the matter of the tunnel leak because it posed an unknown hazard. The engineer estimated that repairs would cost "approximately $10,000" and take two weeks. Yet nothing was done. The Chicago budget was already severely strained from austerity measures. Spending was shunted toward large investment projects aimed at revitalizing the city's economy. But this set of priorities had terrible consequences.

On April 14, the tunnel wall gave way and the Chicago River waters flooded the entire downtown. Buildings had to be evacuated and shut down. An estimated 100,000 office workers were temporarily sent home until repairs could be effected. The chamber of commerce estimated that losses in business and productivity amounted to $150 million each day and that the final bill for repairing the leak and cleaning up the damage could run close to $1 billion. It took several weeks before conditions in the Loop

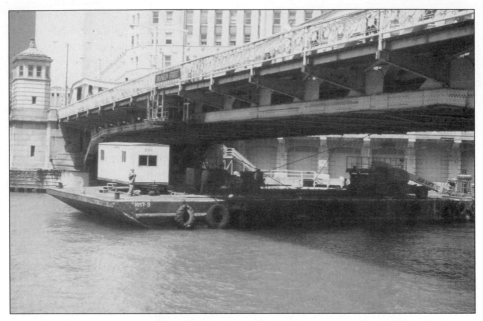

The decaying infrastructure in American cities requires constant repair. Here a construction crew works on a bridge in downtown Chicago.

(Chicago's downtown) returned to normal. The mayor fired the commissioner who had not responded to the need for repairs, but little else could be done (Wilkerson, 1992).

However, most examples of infrastructure decline are not so dramatic. The entire transportation network of highways, railroads, airports, and water and sewer systems must be maintained on a continual basis. In Chicago, this includes 3,500 miles of arterial roads and residential streets, 1,932 bus route miles in the city and three dozen suburbs, and 140 train stations on 222 miles of railroad track. The Chicago Department of Transportation estimates that it would require $855 million each year to upgrade the interstate highways and local streets just to "good" condition, but only $280 million has been available for these improvements in recent years. The Chicago Transit Authority requires $4.1 billion to rebuild an infrastructure now 100 years old, but less than half of that total is expected to be available from federal and state sources through year 2003. Equally pressing is the need to replace the city sewer system, which includes more than 4,000 miles of sewers with a life expectancy of about 100 years. Since many parts of the modern city were built in the 1880s and 1890s, much of the sewer system is now reaching the end of its effective use. But the city's capital improvement project budget includes only some $32 million each year for sewer replacement—enough to replace and reline just 15 miles of sewers each year (Hilkevitch and Kendall, 1999). The problems of infrastructure decline are not unique to Chicago or even to Rust Belt cities; in the next several decades, the sewer systems in Los Angeles, Houston, and other Sunbelt cities will also reach the 100-year milestone.

Housing

In the United States, family well-being depends to a great extent on where one's home is located. Differences in wealth and the location of the family home determine the opportunities available to individuals. Where one lives determines the quality of the school one attends, as we have already discussed, but it also determines the safety of the local streets and how much one's property will increase in value. Over the years, the cost of well-situated housing, either owned or rented, has increased substantially as a percentage of income. Consequently, attractive neighborhoods are now out of reach for many people.

Since 1965, the cost of housing has risen more rapidly than has income. As a result, a growing number of people either cannot afford single-family home ownership or must devote more of their income to housing. In the mid-1950s, an average 30-year-old worker could purchase a median-priced house for just 14 percent of his or her gross earnings. Thirty years later, it would take fully 44 percent of that person's income to purchase the same house (Levy, 1977). Shannon, Kleiniewski, and Cross (1991) illustrated the rapid increase in housing prices. In 1970, the median monthly rent in the United States was $108; by 1985, it was three times as high ($350). The median sales price of new homes went up four times, from $23,000 in 1970 to more than $92,000 in 1986. Price rises were most rapid on both the East and West Coasts, becoming almost prohibitively high in places such as Orange County, California, and Nassau County, New York.

One-third of all households now pay an excessive amount for their housing (i.e., more than 30 percent of their gross salary), and almost one-fourth of all renters are spending more than half their income for shelter. Schwartz, Ferlauto, and Hoffman (1988:10) suggest that since 1975, the average family has not been able to afford an average-priced home. The 1993 Survey of Income and Program Participation found that more than 90 percent of the households living in rental housing could not afford a median-priced new or used house or condominium (U.S. Bureau of the Census, 1993).

Suburban Inequities

Suburban areas of the metropolitan region present a clearer case than do central cities of differentials in the supply of housing. Each suburban municipality offers a bundle of services to prospective residents and, in many cases, a local property tax level that helps to finance the quality of life. Those wishing to live in suburbia choose the level of services and taxes that they can afford by purchasing a house in a particular community.

Forty years of suburbanization in the United States have produced a pattern of clear differences among communities with regard to family income levels and race. There is extreme social segregation in suburbia (Muller, 1981); that is, classes as well as races are spatially separated. Due to the power of home rule, which grants local suburban governments autonomy over land use, several administrative mechanisms have been used to control the racial and economic makeup of prospective residents. Perhaps the most powerful tool is *exclusionary zoning,* which mandates large-lot zoning for residential homes. In general, the larger the lot, the more expensive the home. Moderate-income families are automatically priced out of areas with such zoning.

After a period of development, many communities passed exclusionary zoning ordinances on remaining vacant land precisely to prevent rapid development of affordable dwellings. The result of such practices is income segregation because the less affluent must search for suburban housing in the few communities that make it available.

Exclusionary zoning is a sociospatial problem of the environment that ranks with other environmental issues (see Chapter 14). In recent years, exclusionary zoning practices have been challenged in the courts as unfair because serious equity and social justice questions arise from sociospatial segregation. Perhaps the most famous case involved the city of Petaluma, California. This town is located north of San Francisco in Marin County and, during the 1960s, experienced rapid development. Residents passed a zoning ordinance that mandated large lots for remaining land. They sought to slow down growth and enhance the property values of existing homes. In effect, however, the exclusionary zoning ordinance meant that only a few wealthy families could afford the larger lots, thereby preventing moderate-income families from moving to the community.

The zoning ordinance was challenged by open-housing advocates. They were defeated, and the ordinance was upheld by the Supreme Court in a 1976 decision. The Court ruled that local areas indeed had the right to control their own zoning, despite the issues of social justice that had been raised. Since that time, it has been increasingly difficult to provide affordable housing in all suburban communities, and no less so because zoning has become a tool for the control of growth (see Gottdiener and Neiman, 1981).

Exclusionary zoning means that the quality of local services varies greatly in suburbia. Many states, such as New York, have tried to preserve minimum levels by enacting statewide standards for such things as educational levels. In practice, however, great variation still exists among suburban communities. A typical family moving into a suburban town will immediately be told precisely where the best schools are located, and in most places educational quality varies greatly from school to school. If the education of their children is utmost in importance, the family will try to purchase a home in the best district. Of course, this area will be among the most expensive in the town. In this way, segregation of family income by housing tract perpetuates inequalities of social services, and remains an unfortunate characteristic of suburbia.

Homelessness

One of the first things visitors to the city notice is individuals walking on the street carrying all their possessions. Both disconcerting and pathetic, the sight of homeless people makes us question the well-being of this society as a whole. A recent *New York Times* poll found that about 54 percent of Americans see homeless people in the community or on their way to work (Applebome, 1991).

We cannot say for sure how many homeless people there are at present. We do know, however, that the numbers have not been as great since the Great Depression of the 1930s (Blau, 1992). The homeless are not found in any single place; they are mobile. Their condition also varies. Some days or nights they may be inside charity shelters, and at other times they may have enough money for a room in a single-room-occupancy

A homeless man on the street with his possessions.

(SRO) hotel. In the mid-1980s one estimate was 350,000 homeless "on a given night" (Peroff, 1987), but later estimates have run much higher, to 3 million or more (Flanagan, 1990:320). In addition, the composition of the homeless population, including married couples with children, is more representative of the entire cross-section of U.S. society than during previous periods, such as the Depression.

In Manhattan, for example, the homeless seem to be everywhere, and the city has opened up public buildings such as armories to provide "temporary" shelter to those in need. One report indicated that as many as 24,000 people a day were being housed in this manner (Berak, 1991). The Fort Washington Armory in Manhattan, or "the Fort," is typical. It is a scary place where some men have lived for as long as five years. Roving bands of "jawbreakers" control the shelter, drug use is rampant, noise pierces the night and disturbs sleep, stealing is so endemic that residents must place their shoes under their bedposts at night, and security guards are scarce, unarmed, and poorly paid. It is a place, in short, very much like prison. However, the only alternative is to remain on the street at night, a fate that many homeless prefer to shelter life.

Recent reports indicate that both homelessness and squatting, phenomena once associated with Third World cities, have become increasingly common in European as well as American metropolitan areas (Adams, 1986). There are several reasons for homelessness (Flanagan, 1990; Leshner, 1992). Job loss since the 1970s has taken a terrible toll on families. Economic restructuring, as we saw earlier in this chapter, has caused job loss and community decline. In many cases, a loss of income results in an inability to afford housing; for some families, even rental housing can be hard to obtain with limited financial means. But declines in welfare funding have been a principal cause of homelessness: Fiscal austerity and cutbacks in the federal budget have limited the ability of local communities to support people in need.

Finally, homelessness is also caused by the housing problem and the inequities of the second circuit of capital in the United States. Because the real estate market functions both to drive up the cost of shelter and to foster speculation, units may either be too expensive to rent or own or simply be held vacant as a tax loss. The urbanist Carolyn Adams terms this condition one of "maladjustment" rather than a shortage of housing, because in the United States many housing units remain available. As she suggests,

> The term "maladjustment" is more accurate than "shortage" because in many places the number of existing units is theoretically large enough to house the urban population. Yet many households cannot find housing that is both affordable and suitable for their needs. At the same time, large numbers of housing units stand vacant, awaiting demolition or renovation. The presence of empty housing in cities where large numbers of families and individuals need shelter is an invitation to squatting, and that is precisely what has taken place. (1986:528)

But homelessness is not simply a question of social welfare; it is also a matter of land use issues connected with gentrification, displacement, and the cultural imaginings of what the city should be. Talmadge Wright notes that the "problem" of homelessness in American cities is especially challenging because the homeless, city officials, and other groups have very different visions of how urban space should be used. For low-income persons who cannot afford housing, vacant buildings may be seen as squatter properties. But for most people—including public officials and developers—urban space does not include a place for the homeless (Wright, 1998). This attitude has resulted in the "militarization" of urban space, including such things as concertina wire around dumpsters behind grocery stores and restaurants to prevent homeless persons from obtaining leftover food, park benches specifically designed to prevent people from sleeping, and sprinkler systems in public parks that are turned on during evening hours to prevent homeless persons from sleeping on the ground (Davis, 1990). In Chicago, San Jose, and other cities, homeless populations have mobilized to resist the displacement of their communities, including protests of urban redevelopment projects, squatting activities, and other forms of collective action (Wright, 1998).

Homelessness combines aspects of economic crisis, poverty, and the failures of U.S. health and housing policies. Remedies for this problem require integrated plans that address the root causes. It is clear that with the declining economy, poor people have fewer opportunities to improve their lot, and their relative standing in society is deteriorating.

Housing is a major problem in both urban and suburban areas because the stock of affordable units is on the decline. Due to the relationship between the location of a home and the quality of urban life, the lack of affordability will continue to be an important problem for new families and young couples just starting out in life.

Summary

The effect of differences in the flow of resources to metropolitan communities due to racial and economic problems has created a landscape in which poverty and affluence exist almost side by side. While some individuals and families seem to be doing remarkably well, many are barely holding on to what they have been able to accumulate over years of hard work. Large numbers of Americans now find quality education and affordable housing slipping beyond their grasp or that of their children. In addition, a minority of people do not even have the advantages of this besieged majority. They are mired in an intractable syndrome of isolation and despair. Our central cities are becoming unlivable, with crime and social strife prevailing almost everywhere. In Chapter 14, we will take up other issues involved in social problems, particularly ones that involve the environment and planning. These issues will be related to the process of uneven development that informs the sociospatial approach. In Chapter 15, we will consider some possible solutions and the prospect for a positive urban future.

CHAPTER

11

LOCAL POLITICS:
City and Suburban Governments

Until the 1950s, urban governments in the United States were quite powerful. This is somewhat remarkable because when the political structure of the country was carved out in the eighteenth century, no provision was made for the autonomy of local government. Power under our *federal republic* is shared between the states and the federal government. City governments exist only by permission of the state in which they are located.

In the 1800s, cities were granted specific powers that enabled them to prosper. It was considered beneficial for the entire society if local government could take care of the environmental needs and provide services that supported the quality of daily life. As cities began to grow, they needed *infrastructure,* that is, paved streets, sewer lines, utilities, bridges, and harbors. Cities also needed to provide public services such as garbage collection, police protection, and education.

Through a mutual understanding among the different levels of government, the task of providing for infrastructure improvement fell to the locality. As a result, in the 1800s, states sanctioned the notion of the *municipal corporation,* which provided for city government and its services. In return, those same governments were given limited powers of taxation and, most significantly, control over the regulation of land. Hence, the responsibility for the quality of the local environment fell mainly on municipal shoulders.

From its earliest days, the powers of city government were viewed as a prize, even though their scope was limited. It was understood over 100 years ago that in addition to control over capital and land, control of the bureaucracies and of the decision-making power of government was a separate means of acquiring wealth. The power to tax or regulate both land use and public services gave local government officials significant control over other people's money. Municipalities could, for example, tax the local economy and reap the benefits of growth in the value of land. In addition, city services

239

expanded their domains through various departments or bureaucracies, thereby making the city a major employer. It was this power that made urban administrations central players in the generation and accumulation of wealth throughout the metropolitan period. But the ability of municipalities to influence factors that might affect the accumulation of wealth has largely disappeared with the increased mobility of capital in the era of global capitalism.

In previous chapters we have seen how capital investment operates to produce a built environment. Due to the uneven nature of development, growth brings with it problems of equity and social justice. The struggles involving these issues are carried out in the municipal arena. The government must also intervene to keep capitalists from destroying one another's opportunities in the mad rush for profits. As a result, local government becomes the forum within which issues of growth and change, of the local quality of life, of the demands of citizens for relief from inequities, and of the well-being of local neighborhoods are all addressed. Both conflict and accommodation mark the tenor of community public affairs.

Over the last century, the nature of local government changed dramatically. Unprincipled exploitation of municipal decision-making powers was opposed by a series of reform cycles, some of which were more equitable and enlightened than others. But always, individual city residents and interest groups sought over the years to make local government in the United States function better. Out of that struggle the ethos of self-rule has been fashioned, however imperfect the results may be. The following sections discuss the evolution of these changes and then deal with several important issues surrounding the exercise of municipal authority today—in particular, the decline of democracy in local decision making and the growing power of corporate and banking interests to define the local agenda.

Machine Politics

In the early days of municipal government, political groups that controlled city hall and utilized it to acquire wealth were called *political machines*. One of the most notorious machines was the New York–based Tweed Ring, run by Boss Tweed. His reign made city government synonymous with corruption. A more typical political machine, however, was the one founded by Boss Pendergast in Kansas City (Dorsett, 1968). Jim Pendergast came to that town in the 1880s and opened a popular saloon. It was located in West Bottoms, a typical poor section of the city—typical for any city at that time—with large numbers of low-income working people from a variety of backgrounds, including foreign countries. He entered politics by creating a local Democrats club and quickly extended his influence to adjoining wards within the city. Soon his organization was able to mobilize the majority of votes, and he took control of local government. Boss Pendergast's regime apparently was not corrupt and derived its income from the regulation of saloons, gambling, and prostitution. Its support came from the successful mobilization of the large working-class and other lower-income groups in the city.

After 1910, Jim Pendergast died and his brother Tom took over. In the years to follow, Pendergast remained in control of the city, but increasingly followed the lead of corrupt bosses elsewhere by engaging in fraudulent voting practices and influence

Cartoon of Boss Tweed with his hand in the public till. "I stick my fist in as far as it will go, and pull it out as full as it will hold. I stick to my friends. That's me! There you have Tweed self-painted to the life."

peddling; that is, when business needed some public decision for its own interests, the local political leaders would ask for money in return. Eventually, charges of corruption destroyed this machine as they did so many others.

The principal characteristic of the political machine was that it functioned as a mode of administration rather than one of social change or political ideology; that is, machines did not stand for anything in particular, although most of them ran on the Democratic party line because this group represented new immigrant and working-class groups that had moved to the industrial cities. They worked as organizations that acquired and deployed citizen votes. As Lineberry and Sharkansky (1978:119) note, "Machines are almost never ideological. They are rather broad umbrellas that are large enough to cover every shade of opinion and interest." The members of machines aggressively sought the loyalty of voters, often by promising employment or other favors, a process that has become known as *patronage*. In return, those individuals behind the machine used their political influence to acquire wealth for themselves and their associates in the private sector.

Political machines often were organized efforts of corruption (Scott, 1972). Their power derived from their ability to mobilize large numbers of voters and thereby win elections. Once in power, they had control over the city resources. They helped redistribute wealth to those who really needed it—for example, by employing hundreds of thousands of recent immigrants in search of work. They institutionalized and enlarged city bureaucracies such as health departments. These became useful during times of crisis, such as when epidemics occurred, and they brought order to everyday city life.

Progressive Reforms

The corruption of machine politics was attacked at a variety of levels at the turn of the century. Businesses that had been growing in strength and scope throughout the nineteenth century no longer sought to associate with corrupt regimes. Much of the city infrastructure was also in place across the country by the turn of the century, and there was less for government to do aside from providing services. One remedy used to combat the machine was the movement to change the structure of local government known as *progressivism*. Progressivism attracted large numbers of voters, many of whom had recently attained middle-class status because of economic growth. Eventually the political machines whose base remained within working-class districts were thrown out of office. The control of urban governments was transferred to reformers, many of whom were from citizen and business associations known as "good government" coalitions. Some of the reforms that were enacted involved changing the way local leaders were elected and reorganizing city bureaucracies.

Changes in the Political Apparatus

Under the machines, most cities were carved up into local wards, with each sector able to vote for a councilperson who would sit in the government chamber. Most bosses, such as Pendergast in Kansas City, Cox in Cincinnati, and Tweed in New York, started by capturing a single ward. Machines could use their influence on the voters at the local levels to mobilize support for candidates. One characteristic reform of the progressives involved a switch from precinct to at-large elections in which candidates had to acquire an overall majority of votes across the city in order to win. It was felt that the open glare of publicity and the need to acquire support from all the citizens of the city would act to curb the insider trading and deal making that were characteristic of the ward system.

In short, this progressive reform changed the *structure* of the municipal government apparatus of citizen representation. To this very day, the degree to which various individuals and parties influence city elections depends to a significant extent on the structure of local government. Specifically, it depends on how citizens are represented, in addition to other factors such as their desire for change. For example, at-large elections require consensus building that cuts across particular interests, while the ward system favors champions of local constituencies with their specific concerns. We will return to this point when we discuss power structure studies.

Reforming the City Bureaucracy

The reform discussed above refers to changes in the apparatus of *representation*. A second important progressive reform involved bringing apolitical, professional expertise into local government; that is, the progressives also changed the apparatus of *administration*. Because mayors often represented special interests, and because city bureaucracies were often staffed by cronies of the machine holding patronage positions, progressives sought to eliminate such abuse. They instituted "civil service" structures in bureaucracies, which then hired people according to their professional qualifications and ensured job security, especially immunity from being fired after a change in political leadership. Work in city agencies became a *career* as a result.

In place of an elected mayor, many cities turned to a councilmanic structure of government with elected officials serving on a council and the head of government appointed as a "city manager." This manager was chosen on the basis of professional background and experience, thereby bringing technical expertise into city government. To this day, the extent to which professional careerists and city managers are involved in local government or the apparatus of administration constitutes a *second* independent source of political effects in the running of the city in addition to the structure of representation discussed above; that is, the relationship between elected and appointed career officials represents an important source of variation in the relative success of local government.

For example, city managers are usually career civil servants and have considerable control over the day-to-day budget. When their level of expertise is low, they may be responsible for severe fiscal problems through the mismanagement of finances. Unsound fiscal management has contributed to many of the problems cities now face. Over the past two decades, professional managers have responded to the fiscal problems of cities by improving their ability to aid local government (Matzer, 1986). Several management techniques have been developed, including (1) trend monitoring systems, which enable financial forecasting and trend analysis; (2) fiscal impact analysis, which predicts how future changes will affect people; and (3) creative capital financing, such as floating capital improvement plans for public investment. In short, professional city managers can make a positive difference in the fight against fiscal distress and budget problems.

To summarize, while the machine embodied a vote-for-favor ethic, progressive reforms restructured the representative and administrative apparatuses of government so that influence operated according to general interests expressed in terms of overarching values that were often ideologies. We cannot say unequivocally whether one system was better than the other, although the serious excesses of machine politics were cleaned up by the progressives. The machine, while flawed, did champion the needs of the masses, while the progressives tended to represent the middle-class business community. What we can stress is that explorations into the nature of political power and influence at the local level must consider the independent effects of structures of representation on the one hand and the role of city bureaucrats on the other, in addition to factors related to competition over votes.

The above discussion has demonstrated the importance of structure for understanding the role of local government. Much of politics, however, is high drama and involves constant interactions among various individuals and groups over the satisfaction of respective needs. Politics involves the way these actors utilize power to get what they want. In the following section, we will examine a number of theories of politics that address this important issue of the nature of power.

Theories of Local Politics

Whether we consider city or suburban governments, the central feature of the local state—its ability to acquire wealth and channel social resources—has meant that organized interests must compete with one another for control. This struggle for control over urban and suburban settlement space provides the drama of local politics.

BOX 11.1 THE PLURALIST THEORY OF COMMUNITY POLITICS

Robert Dahl, a political scientist at Yale University, studied political decision making in New Haven, Connecticut, and concluded that political power in the community was broadly shared among local elites. To identify those persons who were influential, Dahl used a method of study known as *decision analysis* (also called *issue analysis*). The study focused on three political issues that local government had confronted in the 1950s: urban renewal, public education, and political nominations. Through the use of personal interviews, news accounts, written reports and minutes, and personal observation, the researchers identified a specific "leadership pool" associated with each issue—a group of leaders who supported each issue and another group who opposed them. They found that the number of persons involved in decisions in each of these areas was quite large: 435 leaders in the area of urban renewal and 497 in political nominations, with an overlap of just 15 persons between these two groups. Dahl noted that community decision making was spread among different political actors according to their individual areas of expertise, and no one group (older families, wealthy business leaders) had influence in each area. This interpretation supports the pluralist view that decision making in the political arena involves a division of labor among top decision makers, and that important public policy decisions are not made by a small number of powerful individuals. Dahl concluded that resources of influence were highly dispersed and that "virtually no one" in the community was entirely lacking in some way to influence government decisions.

Urban sociologists have made use of three competing theories to explain how the political process in metropolitan regions operates: pluralist theory, elite theory, and state managerialism.

Pluralist Theory

Pluralism represents the dominant theoretical paradigm within contemporary political science. According to the pluralist theory, political influence is exercised by interest groups that are widely dispersed across the political spectrum. These interest groups all compete more or less equally within the political system to influence political decisions. While large corporations might influence decisions by contributing to political candidates, for example, labor unions also contribute to their candidates, and over the long run these interest groups share equally in the decisions made by elected officials. Control of government by any one interest over the long term is not possible.

Robert Dahl (1961) used a *decision analysis approach* to study how the mayor and city council of New Haven, Connecticut, made decisions on important political issues, including public education and urban renewal (see Box 11.1). He found that specific groups of leaders emerged to argue for (or against) particular issues, based largely on

BOX 11.2   THE ELITE THEORY OF COMMUNITY POLITICS

Floyd Hunter studied political decision making in Atlanta, Georgia, and concluded that a relatively small group of wealthy individuals and business elites controlled the city. To identify these people, Hunter used what has become known as *reputational analysis*. He drew up a preliminary list of 175 well-known individuals (potential elites) from the city and then asked a panel of 14 persons with knowledge about Atlanta politics and society to select 10 prominent people who were generally accepted as leaders in the city. The responses were then combined to create a list of just 40 local leaders. Hunter personally interviewed 27 people on this list and asked them for the names of 10 other persons who held leadership roles in the city. Hunter found that 12 names were mentioned repeatedly as an elite core of power holders. While this group included some lawyers, industry executives, and socially prominent families, the majority were representatives of what we now call *finance capital*—the top executives in banking, finance, commerce, and insurance businesses in the city. Even more important, not one of the 12 identified as powerful elites in Atlanta was actually part of the official city administration; in fact, only 4 of the 40 names from the earlier list were part of the government! As one of Hunter's interviewees stated, "There are 'crowds' in [Atlanta]—several of them—that pretty well make the big decisions. There is the crowd that I belong to (the Homer Chemical crowd); then there is the First State Bank crowd, the Regional Gas crowd, the Mercantile crowd, and the like" (1963:77).

their specialized knowledge of each issue. There was little overlap among these groups from one issue to the next. Following the classic pluralist model, Dahl concluded that all groups of people in the community were represented by the local leadership and that no single group had special power or influence in local decision making.

Several other case studies of community decision making have been carried out by other scholars subscribing to this theoretical model. But their results have likely been influenced by their methodology, which focuses only on those decisions decided by elected officials in the public arena. Much of what influences government policy takes place behind the scenes and is never brought up for public deliberation (Bachrach and Baratz, 1962). As we will see later in this chapter, many cities have created redevelopment authorities that have the power to condemn land and use public funds without any public oversight.

Elite Theory

The elite theory of urban politics asserts that there is always a select group of influentials, or a "community power structure," that possesses the controlling interest in a town. The elite structure of power was discovered by Floyd Hunter (1953) in his study of Atlanta (see Box 11.2). The power structure in a community can be identified by using a *reputational analysis approach* to identify the most influential people in a town and those with whom they associate. While not actively involved in all government deliberations, this "elite" group monitors them and intervenes through personal influence when it appears that an impending decision or project may interfere with their interests. Hunter's conclusion that Atlanta was run by a group of powerful individuals, most of whom were not part of elected government, was confirmed some 30 years later by Clarence Stone (1989).

Community power structure case studies are very convincing because they capture the way government and the private sector combine to push development toward specific directions, often in spite of community opposition, but mainly in ways that are never brought to life. One characteristic of elites is that they get together relatively often to establish and reaffirm their *common interests*. In Boston, the elite group known as "the vault" (because they met at a hidden location) consisted of 14 corporate leaders who worked to influence both local and state government for their common interests. Among other things, they succeeded in persuading the legislature to set up a nonelective superagency to promote development—the Boston Redevelopment Authority (B.R.A.). Like all other such agencies, the B.R.A. had minimal community input.

Houston, Texas, to cite another example, has been touted for years as a "free enterprise city." Joe R. Feagin (1988) discovered that despite the label, there was a select group in control that used the local state to improve its private interest. Members were called the "Suite 8F crowd" because they met regularly at a room in a local hotel. The Houston group was very effective in persuading government to enhance its own business interests by pushing for development projects that it preferred. In fact, this group had so much influence that it even got the federal government to fund the dredging of Houston harbor, turning it into a port that made many locals wealthy.

Although most case studies of cities affirm the power elite view, not every city is controlled by a select group of business and political leaders. Detroit, for example, remains a one-industry town—automobiles—but the business leadership chose long ago not to live in the city. Their commitment to Detroit's future remained narrowly focused on the needs of the auto industry itself. As a result, politics was more pluralistic in Detroit. This state of affairs did not prevent General Motors from demanding that an entire section of the city, Poletown, be destroyed to build a new assembly plant during the 1980s. Despite organized citizen opposition, the plans were carried out by an all-too-willing city government. Hence, elite groups can function effectively even from far away to control local politics and do not need to be residents of the city.

State Managerialism

Whenever the day-to-day workings of city hall are examined, it is sometimes difficult to discern whether pluralist or elitist powers are in operation. On the one hand, it often appears that many groups are seeking to be heard and that the mayor must spend a great deal of time with constituents. On the other hand, when big decisions are made, the private sector seems to prevail. Recently a *third* perspective on local government has been proposed that fills in the gaps, so to speak, of these other two theories: the state autonomy or state managerialism thesis.

According to this view, local government itself possesses some autonomy from both community and business interests. The local state also has interests of its own.

For example, since government agencies represent a principal sector of employment, the local state seeks to enlarge its power over the private sector just to generate jobs and justify expanding budgets. Leaders of local government are also aware that they must satisfy the majority of the population to remain in power. Hence, they find highly visible ways of catering to the populace that may on occasion offend individually powerful groups, such as demanding that developers make small but significant concessions to community interests before project plans can be approved.

Several studies (Lipsky, 1976; Hero and Durand, 1985) have confirmed the presence of "relative" government autonomy. In particular, it was found that bureaucrats in city agencies have considerable leeway in responding to the needs of clients. Public satisfaction with government varies greatly depending on personal experiences. Pluralist theory asserts that elected officials function by integrating conflicting demands. While that may be one response, bureaucrats may also choose to lead according to what they perceive is their own expert opinion. As studies of local government have noted, it is very difficult to hold public officials strictly accountable for their actions. We often discover their abuses of power only when scandalous incidents of corruption are brought to light. But the ability of city bureaucrats to act on their own has positive advantages as well. We already discussed in a previous section how greater expertise by city managers in handling fiscal problems has made local governments more efficient and prosperous. The relative autonomy thesis suggests that public bureaucrats' ability to pursue their independent interests is always present.

Which View Is Correct?

Years of community power studies have given us a relatively clear picture of the functions of local government. In sum, we might say that the state and its officials act in a variety of ways depending on how they are viewed and on the methodology used to study the government decision-making process. Most cities are controlled by an elite. This notion is *not* the same as the "growth machine" (Logan and Molotch, 1987). A true growth machine is dominated by real estate interests. In reality, however, city elites are most often composed of corporate and financial interests. Furthermore, the actual composition of elites often changes over time. Historical studies demonstrate that while elites focus on some economic interest, the sources of wealth change as the decades go by (Feagin, 1988). Spencer Olin (1991), for example, studied the power structure of Orange County, a suburban region outside of Los Angeles, over several decades. He discovered that the elite there changed according to the dominant business interests. Initially, the region was composed of ranches and farms, and the corporate agricultural interest dominated. When it was being developed for suburban housing, a land-based elite of construction and real estate interests took over. Lately, however, the region has matured into a multifaceted economy, and the elite has changed again to reflect globally linked corporate and financial interests, although land development continues to take place.

There is considerable evidence that cities are dominated by banks or finance capital because this faction of the business community still invests in downtown. Suburbs and some of the newer cities of the Sunbelt, on the other hand, possess dominating elites with interests in the corporate and construction industries, and some may indeed be controlled by real estate developers alone. Hence, when studying any local area, the sources of elite control are important to identify.

In sum, we have enough information about local government to suggest that as a state structure, it possesses the ability to generate and channel resources in society. This power is recognized by the business community and by all individuals who seek public office as a means of acquiring wealth. Despite an ideology of "free enterprise" that preaches minimal government involvement, local governments often have been used to promote parochial business interests. But because the state can channel resources, the public organizes itself and makes community demands on elected officials. They, in turn, must respond in some way in order to remain in office, thereby providing communities with benefits such as adequate parks or summer programs. The outcomes of politics depend not only on walking this tightrope between public and private needs but also on the particular way the apparatuses of representation and administration are set up. In the end, though, as a great deal of research shows, when really significant issues are involved, such as those that concern economic growth and fiscal stress, the business community wields the most power over local government regardless of structural shape or form.

The Drama of Local Politics

Empowerment: Ethnic and Racial Changes

The succession of economic elites is just one way to look at changes in local government, although it is perhaps the most important way. Politics is also a dramatic enterprise. It involves struggle, conciliation, coalition building, and conflict. For many years, our cities have been ruled by broadly based coalitions representing local neighborhoods as well as economic interests. The backgrounds of local politicians reflected immigrant origins in the early waves that arrived in this country. The late 1700s and 1800s witnessed the domination of WASPs such as Boss Tweed in New York. Later on, the Irish became adept at political control, as we have seen in the case of Boss Pendergast. For much of the twentieth century, cities have been run by coalitions of Irish, Eastern Europeans, Italians, and Jews. For example, Mayor Ed Koch, a Jew, led New York City from 1977 to 1990.

Most recently, the population of central cities has changed. Minority groups have become majorities. Over 300 U.S. cities, including our biggest urban areas, have minority mayors. Many are African Americans, but others are Hispanics, and recently a Chinese American candidate was nearly elected mayor of Los Angeles. The changeover from the ruling coalitions of Irish, Italians, Jews, and Eastern Europeans to minority leadership reflects today's realities, but has not necessarily gone smoothly. Change involved a struggle for political control or empowerment, where influence was captured because of voting power. The drama of minority empowerment is illustrated in Box 11.3.

Asians, for example, are often considered a "model minority" because many of the third-wave immigrants have done well economically (see Chapter 8). Yet many Asian Americans are simply scraping along in the United States and have needs that are being neglected by the existing power structure in local areas. In one such case, the Cambodians of Long Beach, California, decided to organize for empowerment rather than continue to be represented by other ethnic groups. Cambodians represent 10 percent of the Long Beach population. Previous ethnic groups relied on churches, ward machines, and even saloons as the places where voting blocs could be organized. The Cambodians had no such power bases. Under continual pressure to become active in politics because of the status quo's neglect of their needs, they began to organize themselves through the only institutional channel at their disposal, the Cambodian refugee agencies. According to Riposa (1992:16), these organizations blended social services for immigrants and cultural support in the transition to U.S. society. As a result of the struggle for empowerment, they were assigned a third task of political advocacy as the voice of the Cambodian community. Today these refugee organizations are one of many organized interests in Long Beach competing within the political arena.

Urban Social Movements

The previous section depicts one aspect of the drama of local politics, namely, the quest for power and control by organized ruling coalitions. There is another aspect, however, based on the concerns of citizens regarding their everyday life. Individuals and neighborhood associations often organize to influence local government. Despite the old saying "You can't fight city hall," many people do just that. When there are large enough numbers and defined demands, mobilized constituencies may even aggregate to the level of an *urban social movement,* that is, an organized mass of citizens making demands on local government for *structural* change (Castells, 1983). In the past, such movements have mobilized around the issues of welfare rights, tenants' rights, community control of schools, tax reduction, and control of growth.

In many cases, local protests are ad hoc and related to a specific issue. There may be some persisting irritant that afflicts a community, such as inadequate police protection or garbage removal. Residents will mobilize the community to appeal for more resources and the mayor's attention to their needs. Often these protests are resolved when the mayor's office negotiates with local citizens. These incidents constitute the very backbone of democratic freedom, even if the system itself cannot respond adequately to every demand. As might be expected, neighborhoods that are wealthier or better organized may receive more immediate attention. There is, therefore, an incentive for communities to keep a standing association that represents an organized voice for their needs. Many localities in both cities and suburbs have such neighborhood associations, and there is even a national network of block associations representing the voice of local communities (Boyte, 1980; Logan and Rabrenovic, 1990).

More organized efforts may become social movements that address fundamental issues such as rent control. For example, there is a class of protests that has been

BOX 11.3 NEW FACES, NEW REALITIES: ETHNIC POLITICS IN CHICAGO

For much of the last half-century, the story of Chicago and its neighborhoods has been the story of race. It's been a tale of black and white, of sharp contrasts and sharp collisions; of African American migration out of longtime ghettos and of white flight to the suburbs; of small triumphs of integration and, much more often, of another bleak cycle of resegregation. In a city dominated by a single party, race has become an organizing principle of politics. The black vote and the white vote are key elements in the political equation. Ward boundaries have been drawn around racial lines, and aldermen frequently rely on all-white or all-black constituent bases. Yet, at the threshold of the 21st century, a different Chicago is taking form—a much more complex Chicago, a much more diverse city, belonging to Latinos and Asians as well as blacks and whites.

Away from the tonier districts of the lakefront, Chicago has always been a city of immigrants, making local politics, then and now, ethnic politics. In places like the 35th Ward, voters don't worry too much about international trade or environmentalism. In the bungalows and two-flats of Chicago's interior, politics means a chance for a job, a curb or sidewalk repair, or simply a helping hand to navigate the bureaucracy of a new country with an unfamiliar language. Like the 35th Ward, many Chicago neighborhoods always have been works in progress. A group of immigrants come for a while until they are able to move up to the middle class and out to suburbia. Politicians don't skip a beat in courting the newcomers; they just adapt their patter to the new names on the voting lists. And if the past is any guide to the future, as each immigrant group becomes politically active, it will add still one more voice to the way Chicago will be run.

The once Jewish neighborhood of Albany Park became one of Korean shopkeepers; then they too moved out. That made room for a polyglot of peoples—Indians, Nigerians, Arabs, Filipinos. Once the Michigan Avenue of the city's Czech and Slovak communities, West 26th Street continues as a vibrant shopping street for the Mexican community, which is about 20 percent of the city's population. Those foreign-born residents of the 35th Ward and similar neighborhoods across the city, for all that they are divided by language, religion, and custom, share a common problem: how to tap into the American mainstream.

termed "poor people's movements" (Piven and Cloward, 1977) because such actions are organized efforts on the part of the working class to influence local government. In such cases, some issue has an impact on a large percentage of the population, cutting across neighborhood boundaries. Leaders will mobilize concerned citizens who demand structural reform. It is this demand for fundamental change directed at local government rather than at the business community that is most characteristic of an urban social movement. In these movements, issues concerning the quality of community life transcend class, race, or other divisions.

Under Mayor Richard M. Daley, the famous Democratic political machine is not what it once was. Federal court decisions have greatly weakened the party's ability to make working as a precinct captain or voting Democratic the prerequisite of a city job. Some would argue that the time of ethnic coalition politics has passed. They note that immigrants once lived in immense concentrations of their countrymen, making it easy for politicians and the community to trade services for votes. Today's newcomers reside in neighborhoods of myriad ethnicities where two dozen nationalities may share a single block.

Nick Gutu, a Romanian immigrant active in the 48th Ward Democratic organization, adds another reason why some of our most recent immigrants have been slow to organize. He canvasses buildings whose residents are Russian and Polish immigrants who came to Chicago from countries under totalitarian regimes. "They think of politics as a system where people have no choice. I try to explain that it's important to get involved in politics even if you don't know English and aren't yet a citizen and can't vote." Gutu uses the same techniques as 60 years ago. He helps those non-English speakers when they fill out government forms or deal with a city agency. He is confident that, little by little, his newcomer constituents will be tempted to take part in the political process.

Alderman Vilma Colom recalled that her father was reluctant to get involved in politics. Then his army buddy and business partner, a Polish immigrant, explained that that's not how to go about things in Chicago. "To survive here," he said, "you need to get involved in politics." After that lesson, Colom's father made her and her sisters do volunteer work. This led to a political career.

A generation earlier, Bernard Neistein's father, a tailor from Russia, had the same insight and got his 10-year-old son out onto the streets of the West Side passing out political fliers. Sooner or later, a Cambodian or Palestinian father is bound to give his children similar advice. As each community registers to vote, the politicians will be at their door with an age-old spiel. "If I was working one of those North Side neighborhoods now where everybody lives jumbled up together," Neistein said, "I'd knock on a Vietnamese family's door and talk to them about the political situation in their homeland and how I like their food."

"If it was a gay couple," he said, throwing his arms wide, "I'd say, ` Hey, I've joined you!' " (Reardon, 1999)

Suburban Social Movements

Cities are not the only places where social movements occur. Suburbs also have their share. As with the city, organized efforts at influencing city hall in suburbia can range from specific and temporary incidents to full-fledged movements that unite several communities. One common example of the former is neighborhood organization for greater traffic controls on streets; others involve movements to control development and tax revolts of homeowners.

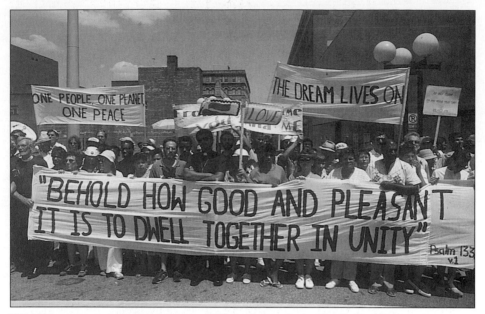

Racial harmony demonstration in 1991 in Greensboro, North Carolina.

The Struggle for Traffic Controls. Many suburban communities have a corner that has become particularly treacherous for pedestrians because of the emergent pattern of traffic flow to and from the houses of the development. Such a problem often occurs only *after* most of a subdivision's residents have moved in and the rush hour stream of cars makes itself felt on local streets. In such cases, the residents who are most affected will organize and demand from city hall aids to control the traffic, such as stop signs or a traffic light. In one suburban case study (Gottdiener, 1977), the affected residents could not acquire the support of their subdivision neighbors living on unaffected streets because the latter preferred the others' street as a traffic corridor. The result was political conflict between two neighborhoods *within* a subdivision, and this touchy affair became a power struggle that for a time polarized the community.

Growth Control Movements. To a great extent, suburban politics is homeowner politics because most of the issues that mobilize citizens concern their interest as owners of single-family homes. One issue that has successfully mobilized suburban residents across subdivisions is that of "growth control." In such cases, we can say that organized efforts to control growth qualify as a suburban social movement. Simply put, when suburban areas grow, the increase in residents brings problems that have an impact on the quality of life for those people who settled there first. Increased traffic, pollution, taxes, crowding in schools, and overburdening of public facilities such as recreational areas are but some of the problems that result when a region experiences sustained development. Often original inhabitants of a suburb will try to prevent future growth by passing a growth control measure or amendment to the town's zoning code.

BOX 11.4 THE WOODLAWN ORGANIZATION AND COMMUNITY REDEVELOPMENT

Between 1960 and 1970, the Woodlawn community on Chicago's South Side lost half of its population to white flight to the suburbs. Economic institutions were the next to leave; in 1971, the last bank in the community closed its doors. By the end of the 1970s, the once-thriving business district along 63rd Street had been replaced by boarded-up storefronts and residential areas had become vacant lots. The City of Chicago shut down the elevated train that ran above 63rd Street for repairs, and later announced plans to dismantle the line.

A coalition of over 100 neighborhood organizations, led by religious and block club leaders and with the assistance of Saul Alinsky, the famous community organizer, formed the Temporary Woodlawn Organization (TWO), later to be known as The Woodlawn Organization. TWO organized community residents to picket and threaten boycotts against merchants, landlords, and city bureaucrats responsible for the decline of the community, including demonstrations in front of the suburban homes of absentee landlords. When the University of Chicago sought to use urban renewal funds to clear the land between 60th and 63rd Streets and construct a park and upper-income housing to establish a buffer zone against the low-income neighborhood, TWO used the community participation requirement of the Urban Renewal program to prevent the displacement of low-income families.

In the 1970s, TWO began a wide range of social service programs, including prenatal and infant health care, Head Start programs for early child development, and programs for substance abuse, teenage pregnancy, and mental health care. By 1997, the organization was operating a social service network with a total budget of $4.2 million servicing more than 7,000 people each day. Recognizing that middle- and upper-class black families were following whites out into the suburbs, the Woodlawn Community Development Commission was created to attract middle-class black families back to the neighborhood and create a viable mixed-income community. Since 1968, TWO has rehabilitated or constructed more than 1,500 apartments and homes for low- and moderate-income families, senior citizens, and others.

TWO was the first organization in the country to sponsor a mixed-income homeownership project in which moderate- and low-income families would live next to one another. A small-business support program for local businesses gave way to large-scale commercial real estate development, including a shopping plaza to focus economic growth and create jobs within the community. Along 63rd Street and Stony Island Boulevard, vacant lots and abandoned hotels have been transformed into garden apartments for middle- and working-class families. In cities around the country, neighborhood organizations such as TWO have demonstrated that development strategies planned at the community level often produce results far superior to those of federal officials and city planners.

For example, in the medium-size city of Riverside, a rapidly growing suburban area in southern California, a movement arose to limit the development of hillsides and wild arroyos in the town. A growth control initiative was placed on the ballot for the 1980 election. Opposition to the measure was expressed by real estate interests and retailers who wanted to keep up the pace of growth. The initiative to block growth was passed by a majority of voters coming from a variety of backgrounds. In a statistical study of the election, class differences among voters were *not* found to be a significant factor (Gottdiener and Neiman 1982). Rather, all social groups in the community expressed a concern for maintaining the quality of life, and this interest dominated local suburban politics. A principal function of local government is preserving or enhancing the quality of life, and support for this effort comes from all segments of the community. The non-class-based nature of suburban social movements has commonalities with those of the central city in the United States and other countries that are also concerned with government's role in maintaining the quality of life; see Chapter 7's discussion of Manuel Castells (1983) and Chapter 14.

Growth control measures often result in "up-zoning," that is, the restructuring of land use by local planning departments to allow only large plots for homes. Such measures prevent the construction of high-density development, thereby reducing growth pressures. But they also push the value of new homes sky-high. For this reason, many communities that are in the path of development often opt for local growth controls. This places them at odds with state legislatures concerned about equal access to housing and developers who seek to build as many houses as they can, and often with landowners who want to sell their land to developers. The result is a potent brew for local political conflict.

Tax Revolts and the Crisis of Suburban Social Services. In several states, the demand of homeowners for tax relief not only cut across local suburban jurisdictions but struck a responsive chord in the majority of residents regardless of class. Such cases are social movements that result in a "tax revolt." California voters, for example, passed the Jarvis-Gann initiative—Proposition 13—in 1979. This measure restricted the property tax that could be charged to existing owners while allowing increases when property was bought by new owners. In effect, Proposition 13 made new buyers of property the bearers of increased taxes, and in June 1992 the United States Supreme Court upheld its constitutionality. The initiative was so successful that it sparked tax revolts in other states. Proposition 13 affects all the residents of the State of California because it places limits on the ability of local government to raise and spend tax revenue. At the same time, it has benefited immeasurably all long-time residents because their property taxes are so low, although it has greatly exacerbated social problems in the larger cities, as we saw in Chapter 9.

Local politics in both cities and suburbs is directed at concerns regarding the quality of life and limiting taxes. City government is expected to provide services, maintain law and order, and promote economic development while not adding to the tax burdens of local residents. This highlights the great contradiction of local politics in the United States: On the one hand, people want government to improve their quality of life; on the other, they are not willing to pay for it in taxes even though taxes in the United States are by far the lowest of any developed nation.

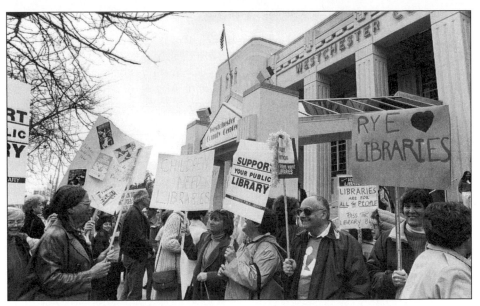

Suburbanites in Westchester County, New York, protest for more library funds.

Social movements that spring up from time to time that seek reforms and change are motivated by the same concerns that form the basis of local politics, namely, the role of city government in promoting the quality of life and in limiting taxation. One important outcome of research on urban and suburban social movements is that they are usually not class based; that is, their constituencies often cut across class lines. Hence, they constitute a *second* source of politics in society alongside worker-led industrial conflict.

The cross-class basis of local social movements is clearest in the suburban case of homeowner politics. As we have seen, concern over controlling the property tax or the rate of town development is shared by a variety of social groups. Threats to the quality of life cut across class lines. This is clearest in the city when diverse communities unite to block proposed projects that would overdevelop local areas or when traffic, crime, and other urban ills threaten neighborhood tranquility. It is for these reasons that urban and suburban social movements rank as a unique form of politics that differs from industrial conflict. Whereas the latter involves workers clashing with capitalists over wages and benefits, the former unites people of diverse backgrounds and confronts the state regarding concerns about taxation or the quality of life. This outcome occurs because Americans perceive that the function of local government is to sustain the quality of life. In many cases, people understand this and they work through their local governments to pressure business interests such as real estate developers to channel their investments for the public good. Whenever this occurs and the negative effects of uneven development can be brought under local control, democratic politics performs the function for which it was intended.

The Declining Power of Local Politics

Control of city and suburban government brings certain benefits from control over public decisions. The quality of life can be either enhanced or frustrated by the acts of those holding public office. This offers an incentive for citizens to become involved in local politics, even when the apparatus of government discourages direct participation. Involvement in politics may also be a means of acquiring wealth. Lawyers and politicians, along with their friends in real estate, construction, public services such as medicine, and banking and commercial interests, may benefit greatly from influence or control of city government. There is an incentive to fight for the right to manage city hall.

Despite the basis for participatory democracy, the power of local government declined after World War II. Both city and suburban governments have been hemmed in by constraints, making local politics weak. And over the last two decades, the drama of politics has been replaced by fighting over dwindling public resources, some of which heightens racial and ethnic divisions. There are three major reasons for this decline of city politics. First, participation in local elections is limited. Voter turnout is consistently less than half of all those eligible to participate. Community life once was characterized by high levels of citizen involvement, but if we consider voting, participation in the community has declined drastically. While some analysts do not consider this phenomenon as cause for alarm, it does suggest that a significant number of people have become alienated from the institution of politics and have limited faith in political leaders.

A second limitation of local politics is that if we consider metropolitan regions as a whole, we discover they are excessively fragmented by multiple municipal jurisdictions and overlapped with special service districts. The Chicago region possesses a chaotic array of over 1,000 separate public service districts. This makes metropolitan coordination of service delivery very difficult and regional planning almost impossible. In addition, central city governments are being overshadowed by their outlying suburban counties, which have matured and developed a strong array of services that rival those of the large city. In 1966, the city of Atlanta outspent its suburban counties by two to one in services. By 1987, however, Atlanta accounted for only 10 percent of spending on services among all places located within the metropolitan area (MSA). A single suburban county, Fulton, spent almost as much ($409.5 million) as the city of Atlanta itself ($586.7 million) (Fleischmann, 1991).

The third limitation of local politics is the ideology of privatism. According to Gregory Squires (1991:197), "the central tenet of privatism is the belief in the supremacy of the private sector and market forces in nurturing development, with the public sector as a junior partner whose principal obligation is to facilitate private capital accumulation."

Little connection is made between the need to promote the general quality of life and the desire of businesses to locate in areas that are attractive places to live as well as work. The ideology of privatism, therefore, is a very limited way of conceptualizing the guiding vision of local politics (see Chapter 15 for a more detailed discussion of public policy). It implies not simply the domination of business interests

BOX 11.5 UNEQUAL PARTNERSHIPS

The celebration of public-private partnerships has occurred in cities around the nation, at all levels of government, and among prestigious business organizations. Mayors and prominent business leaders from such cities as Cleveland, Milwaukee, Pittsburgh, New York, Oakland, and Salt Lake City have testified to the success achieved in their communities. In describing such partnerships, the Committee for Economic Development stated; "The linchpins of public-private partnerships are negotiation and cooperation. . . . Partnerships, almost by definition, require equitable commitment of capacity and investment."

The modus operandi of most partnerships—concentrating redevelopment decision making in quasi-public development entities—has also had negative consequences. Purposely insulated from public influence and dominated by downtown-oriented interests, these institutions have emphasized deal making and profit opportunities rather than systematic planning of how best to deploy public resources to create good jobs and address pressing neighborhood needs. Quasi-public corporations are insulated from public control to keep those groups deriving few benefits from partnership activity from interfering with the deal-making process. The depoliticalization of redevelopment decision making effectively stymies groups supporting alternative strategies; it insulates a crucial area of public policy from democratic impulses.

What has frequently been overlooked, however, is the inherently unequal nature of most partnerships. Frequently they exclude altogether the neighborhood residents most affected by development decisions. Public goals often go unmet, and democratic processes are undermined. Public support for public goals can dissipate if it is perceived (incorrectly) that the private sector is picking up the slack. The principal beneficiaries are often large corporations, developers, and institutions because the tax burden and other costs are shifted to consumers. And perhaps the most important public benefits—jobs—either are temporary and low paying or, in the case of good jobs, go to suburbanites or other out-of-towners recruited by local businesses. As Norman Krumholz has argued, "A nagging doubt arises. Does the publicly subsidized splendor of downtown and the institutional parts of our cities really have much to do with a city's recovery? The answer must be no. The recovery of cities is far more than brick and mortar projects. The city is people, and unless most of them are employed, self-respecting, and respected, the new towers of downtown are a mockery and a delusion." (Squires, 1989)

but political leadership, which has only a limited vision in addressing the social issues of growth.

For example, according to Gregory Squires, "no area of public life has suffered more from the current approach to economic development than the public schools." Local government has been spending its limited resources on subsidies to business, such as tax reductions or freezes in the tax rate. This results in a fiscal crisis as overall tax revenues in the local area fall. "As public officials grapple with growing financial problems, they often look to teachers' salaries as a source of savings. Strikes follow, morale on the part of teachers and confidence in the schools on the part of parents suffer, and the quality of public education deteriorates" (Squires, 1992:28).

But public subsidies to business have had only limited success in revitalizing cities (see Chapter 15). Redevelopment usually is centered on the downtown area and the construction of hotels, luxury housing, sports stadiums, and tourist attractions such as convention centers. These areas seem to function effectively by day but are devoid of life during other times. They provide only limited employment, usually in service industries and at minimum wage. They are places besieged by crime, the homeless, and deteriorating public facilities. Elsewhere in the city, neighborhoods and infrastructure deteriorate and education declines for lack of funds. In short, downtown business may have been improved by the policy of privatism, but the rest of the city has deteriorated.

Even more important with respect to our democratic institutions, privatism removes the goals and operations of government from both the political process and public accountability. Government decisions become merely a technical matter of choosing which economic policy to pursue. Public-private partnerships ensure that an increasing number of decisions previously open for public discussion are decided instead in political backrooms or, more likely, corporate corridors.

Redevelopment has created nonelective superagencies such as the Boston Redevelopment Authority and the Port Authority of New York and New Jersey, which carry out massive projects, such as the construction of the World Trade Center in Manhattan, with only minimal public input. Consequently, the quality of local politics has declined and communities no longer enjoy a democratic involvement in urban policies. In short, at present there is a crisis of political process and leadership at the local level and an alarming deterioration in the community quality of life for most residents of cities and suburbs.

Summary

Since the 1950s, the power of city government has progressively declined. At the same time, the demands made on it to ensure the quality of life have increased. As suburbanization drained the tax-paying middle class away from the city, first the federal government and then state governments cut aid to the cities. Now urban governments are being asked to do more and more with less and less to help the neediest groups in our society: the poor, minorities, and the aged.

Suburban governments have not fared much better. Although residents tend to be more affluent than those in the city, political jurisdictions are relatively small and their economic base is weak. Competition among suburban areas for new investment is always keen and usually results in a zero-sum game. As a consequence, suburban government also possesses a limited scope. Only the wealthiest communities are able to provide the kind of extensive services that rival those of the central city.

Some people assert that limited government is a good thing and that only liberals seek an extended political sphere, which usually does no more than tax excessively and fritter away public money. However, the kind of decline highlighted in this chapter is not about the limitations of government intervention but about the diminished quality of local democracy. At the local level, the declining power of government has meant constraints on the political process and on the democratic participation of all citizens in making effective decisions about the future of their own communities.

The history of municipal politics in the United States involves a struggle over the form that the representative and administrative apparatuses of local government within urban and suburban settlement spaces will take. Each of these is important for an understanding of the daily operation of government. But local politics also encapsulates dramatic struggles and themes. Because of the power of political decision making, both the business and the local residential communities strive to make their respective needs known. Municipal government can be the forum within which the desires of ordinary citizens are expressed and the injustices of uneven economic development are remedied. That is a democratic ideal. However, local politics is often controlled by business interests and poor political leadership. Too often municipal policy merely helps subsidize capital accumulation for the wealthiest groups in our society. This crisis of democracy may be measured not only by the extent to which business dominates local decisions but also by the failure of citizen participation and political leadership.

Local politics within urban and suburban settlement spaces has some important commonalities but also differences. In both, local governments must provide for education and other public services such as libraries and police and fire protection. In many large cities, government has reflected the popular interests of immigrant groups: In some communities, leadership and power have shifted into the hands of minorities that have become empowered after a long political struggle. But corporate, banking, and real estate interests are likely to set the agenda for urban and suburban governments. And the greater participation of minorities in city government has not resulted in a stronger commitment to alleviate social problems affecting these groups.

In the suburbs, concerns over the community quality of life dominate. Metropolitan growth itself has been perceived as a threat to the quality of life, and suburban politics has shifted to ways of managing growth. Political concerns in the suburbs also hold in common with the large city the need to overcome the injustices of uneven development. In both cases, these concerns are based not on class alone but on a cross-section of community interests.

In the 1800s, municipal boundaries enclosed the significant economic resources of manufacturing and banking activities, so that they had the capacity to enrich themselves as the economy prospered. This is not so today. At present, capital investing and manufacturing are dispersed not only across the metropolitan region but across world space. Attachment of capital to place is quite limited, although some businesses, such as public utilities, newspapers, and banks, have a permanent stake in neighborhood prosperity and growth. Consequently, local government lacks the same ability to raise revenue from the private sector that it once had.

Other factors add to the limitations of local politics. These include the continuing fiscal crisis at the state and local levels, the growing power of quasi-public agencies that push for economic development without community involvement; and the ideology of privatism, which restricts the redistributive role of local government and identifies its interest as the need to subsidize business.

The limitations on local government discussed in this chapter require reforms that address the nature of the local political process. Effective programs to address the social problems discussed in Chapter 10, for example, can come only if we understand how government might work better in the future, rather than by endorsing wholesale spending programs such as the urban renewal of the 1960s. Our discussion of problems and politics over the last several chapters creates the need to examine the nature of metropolitan policy. But first, let us examine the patterns of metropolitan growth in other countries of the world to obtain a comparative perspective on the issues raised in the preceding chapters.

12

URBANIZATION IN THE INDUSTRIALIZED WORLD:
Western and Eastern Europe and Japan

For many years, the study of urbanization in Europe was a relatively predictable affair. This is the oldest part of the globe having fully urbanized societies. In recent years, however, profound transformation has been taking place in both Western and Eastern Europe that is similar to the experience of the United States. Shifts in industry to high technology, declines in manufacturing employment, and growth in the service sector are common to both the United States and Europe. Social changes also share commonalities, such as the growing uneven development in metropolitan regions that results from the division between highly paid professionals and low-paid service workers; the increasing presence of immigrants, both legal and illegal, in city populations; and the intractable problems of the poor resulting from the combination of job loss in manufacturing and cutbacks in welfare services and segregation and social exclusion.

This chapter examines the case of Western Europe, which is closest to the U.S. experience. In subsequent sections we will discuss Eastern Europe, or the former Soviet bloc countries, and describe urban conditions there. The final section deals with the case of Japan, which exhibits certain similarities to, but also differences from, the restructuring of settlement space that has characterized metropolitan development in the United States in the post–World War II era.

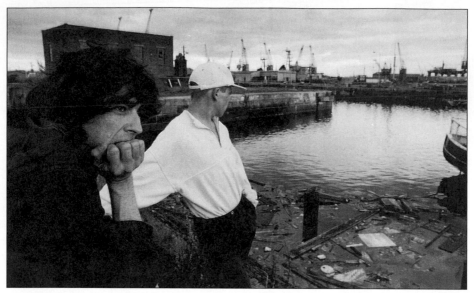

These two men recently lost their jobs at the Newcastle docks, which were closed due to deindustrialization in England.

Western Europe

The countries of Western Europe have been urbanized for centuries. They have a well-developed urban hierarchy with city populations ranging from over 5,000 to 100,000 to over 1 million. Recently, however, this region has experienced a restructuring of population and economic activities similar to those occurring in the United States. Many central cities are declining, and there is a marked increase in the development of suburban settlement space. At the same time, many new towns are experiencing rapid growth (Komniuos, 1989), resulting in metropolitan regions similar to those found in the United States.

According to Hall (1988), this pattern of change has varied. Some countries, such as the United Kingdom, Germany, and, to a lesser extent, Italy, have experienced decentralization of the population away from the large urban centers. Others, such as Belgium, Luxembourg, and, to some extent, France, continue to experience robust central city growth. Between 1970 and 1980, for example, Liverpool, Manchester, Birmingham, Belfast, and other cities in the United Kingdom all lost population. In Germany, Berlin, Essen, Dortmund, and other central cities also declined (Hall, 1988:121). Of course, since the unification, things have changed considerably in Germany, and urban decline may be stemmed in the western sectors of Germany while being shifted to the formerly eastern sectors.

As with the U.S. case, most of this change can be attributed to the restructuring of settlement space as a consequence of global economic shifts. Manufacturing has declined in many European countries, and more drastically in the United Kingdom.

TABLE 12.1
Cities and Their Transnational Corporate Headquarters: United States, Europe, and Japan in 1984

City	Metropolitan Population	Number of Headquarters
New York City	17,082,000	59
London (England)	11,100,000	37
Tokyo (Japan)	26,200,000	34
Paris (France)	9,650,000	26
Chicago, IL	7,865,000	18
Essen (Germany)	5,050,000	18
Osaka (Japan)	15,900,000	15
Los Angeles, CA	10,519,000	14
Hamburg (Germany)	2,250,000	10
Dallas, TX	3,232,000	9
Frankfurt (Germany)	1,880,000	7
Rome (Italy)	3,115,000	6
Stockholm (Sweden)	1,402,000	6
Turin (Italy)	1,191,000	5
Hartford, CT	1,020,000	5

Source: Adapted from Smith and Feagin (1988), pp. 6–7.

Cities have reduced their labor forces and converted to service economies, but with smaller employment bases than in the past. High-technology corridors, the European equivalent of Silicon Valley, and other "new spaces" of production have recently emerged. These have become new sources of employment and growth based on a professional, skilled labor force along with low-wage services. Industrial restructuring has resulted in declining urban cores with considerable unemployment of the working class, while the periphery has grown and developed into an affluent, middle-class population base. Welfare state programs have been cut back, leading to increasing problems with poverty and crime, just as in the United States.

Much of this change is attributed to the shifting patterns of investment in the global economy or the internationalization of capital. Many large corporations have become transnational and direct activities across a broad range of countries, including the location of manufacturing in low-wage, Third World nations. One indicator of the global integration of development is illustrated by Table 12.1, which shows the number of transnational corporations headquartered in cities of Europe, the United States, and Japan (compare this with Table 1.3, which lists the largest cities of the world). While U.S. cities figure prominently in this list, Table 12.1 also shows the important role played by companies in England, France, Germany, and Japan.

A look at individual countries shows the impact of the restructuring of settlement space in greater detail.

United Kingdom

Deindustrialization has been drastic in the United Kingdom. All the older industrial centers have experienced sharp employment declines due to factory shutdowns and wholesale job loss. Between 1978 and 1985 alone, manufacturing in Great Britain declined by 24 percent (Sassen, 1991:131). This followed a decade of comparable job loss. During this same period, employment in business services increased by 44 percent. Like the United States, Britain has undergone a shift from manufacturing to service industries.

Statistics for London are most revealing. Between 1960 and 1990, London lost over 800,000 jobs in manufacturing (Sassen, 1991:205). After 1980 it reaped a harvest of new jobs in the expanding service sector. It was not until 1985, and for the first time in 25 years, that net gains in employment finally outstripped net losses. The shift from a manufacturing economy to a service economy is graphically represented by the following figures: "In 1971 27% of all London jobs were in manufacturing and 68.6% were in services. By 1986 the shares were 15% and 80% respectively" (Sassen, 1991:205). Almost all of the new employment in services for London is a result of the continued historical functioning of the district known as "the City" as a global center of financial activities. London, New York City, and Tokyo today form three global centers for finance capital whose companies command and coordinate the increasingly dispersed world economy of manufacturing and marketing (Sassen, 1991).

New manufacturing centers tied to high-tech development have also emerged as part of this global restructuring. The M-4 highway corridor between London and Reading represents a center for electronics development that is similar to the I-128 peripheral outside of Boston, Massachusetts. In Cambridge, the government linked up with private venture capital and with the university to build a "science park." It contains 30 new enterprises on 55 hectares, and is similar to the "research triangle" located near Duke University and the college town of Chapel Hill in North Carolina.

New employment bases have been unable to compensate for job loss due to deindustrialization. England is currently undergoing a change that requires retraining of the labor force along with a smaller industrial sector. The need for drastic changes provided support for the Conservative Party in the 1980s. The Conservatives dismantled the British welfare state by increasing privatism and reducing publicly supported benefits (King, 1990). While a complete transfer from public financing to market-based services has not occurred in Great Britain, many welfare state programs have been partially converted to a pay-for-service basis or simply eliminated (Forrest, 1991). This record is comparable to the downsizing of domestic programs during the Reagan, Bush, and Clinton administrations in the United States. The selling off of formerly nationalized companies enabled the conservative regime in the United Kingdom to avoid massive debt financing of the economy in the 1980s, unlike the case of the United States. Presently the Liberal Party is in control of government, with Tony Blair as prime minister. Yet economic policies are little changed. Welfare, for example, remains under attack.

Privatization has brought increasing misery to the majority of the British working class. The appearance of uneven development on a national scale has also brought social changes to the entire country. According to one observer, shifts in national attitudes involve the replacement of a moral ethos that supported the welfare state and its reliance on redistributive policies to overcome uneven development with a new ethos based on social Darwinism, limited public programs, and a full reliance on the market economy (Mellor, 1989).

The outcome of restructuring over the last decade in the United Kingdom is that the police have had to expand their role as controllers of the population while crime and civil unrest have increased. As Mellor (1989:591) notes, "U.K. towns were, in international terms, safe places. Now burglary, often minimal in material effect, violates personal space and enforces discipline in the use of house and effects; assaults and/or harassment limit the freedom of movement of the elderly, children, black people, women and, increasingly, white men."

In the 1980s, Edinburgh, Scotland, had the highest rates of heroin use and, as a result, AIDS infection, of any European city. The consequences of the global restructuring of economic opportunity are graphically shown in the film *Train Spotting.*

There is also evidence that after years of successful redistributive policies under the welfare state, *social exclusion,* a term similar to our conception of the underclass, has greatly increased. A survey of households revealed that families whose major breadwinner has lost a job have had only limited success in placing any member in gainful employment. At present, England is facing the "spectre of an increasing number of households where *no*-one works, while there are also households with multiple wage earners" (Dale and Banford, 1989:482). In short, when a family can consistently count on the resources of a single wage earner, it has the resources to support the employment of others, even if their positions are not in high-earning capacities. However, those families suffering from job loss and periodic unemployment are falling behind and floundering in a sea of chronic poverty. One consequence of economic restructuring has been the rise of anti-immigrant and racist groups, particularly among urban youth. Opposition to these neo-fascist groups is brilliantly portrayed in *Rude Boy* (1980), the documentary film by The Clash.

As of the 1990s, few social repercussions have occurred from these changes in the United Kingdom despite the defeat of the Conservatives. Urban riots did occur, however, in 1989, when the Thatcher government attempted to levy an excessive poll tax on local voters. Urban violence has occasionally flared up in racially mixed neighborhoods such as Brixton. There have also been protracted and painful strikes, such as the nationwide strike of coal miners in the 1980s. The full social and political consequences of economic restructuring in the United Kingdom, as in the United States, will not be known for several decades.

Italy

For decades Italy remained one of the underdeveloped areas of Western Europe. The north was highly industrialized with an urbanized labor force centering on Milan and Turin. The south, in contrast, remained rural and dependent on agriculture (Martinelli, 1985). Population in the south was unstable as native sons often left home to migrate to cities in the north, or immigrated to other countries in search of employment.

Since the 1960s, the same force of economic restructuring that has operated in the rest of the industrialized West has changed the sociospatial pattern of development in Italy as well. The middle and southern regions, known as the *mezzogiorno,* have developed a vibrant industrial employment base concentrated in the small-craft tradition of the region. This includes apparel, textiles, footwear, wood products such as furniture, metal working, and clay and glass products. Firms in this region have been very successful by adopting custom design and flexible industrial methods. They engage in small-batch production, which can be changed and customized for new orders relatively easily. Some observers believe that these firms are a model for the new type of "flexible" manufacturing that will prosper in the global economy (Scott, 1988; Piore and Sabel, 1984), called post-Fordism.

Due to foreign competition, especially in the automobile industry, the northern region has been threatened with decline. The cities of Turin and Milan no longer are the employment meccas they were in the past. Changes were made in the industrial base to regain the competitive edge of such companies as Fiat Automobiles and Pirelli Tires. In Turin (see Table 12.1), existing plants were modernized according to the Japanese style that has also been copied by American automakers. Automation was introduced and aspects of the assembly line were turned over to robotics. Wholesale use of electronic or computer-assisted manufacturing was also incorporated into production. Finally, the "just-in-time" system (discussed in Chapter 7) was adopted by assembly plants to reduce operating costs by eliminating inventory problems. Under this system, assembly plants do away with holding large inventories of items they require in production. Instead, they work with suppliers outside the plant but within the region to provide what they need at the time they require it in the assembly process. Coordination of supplies is accomplished with the use of computers that monitor all aspects of the distribution and production schedules.

The successful adaptation of Italian industries to changes in the global marketplace has stabilized the migration patterns within the country. Transformations as a consequence of restructuring have been celebrated by some observers as a new model of growth that other advanced nations undergoing change should copy (Piore and Sabel, 1984). The fate of cities depends progressively more on their ability to attract and retain mobile capital investment. Capital, in turn, must restructure and acquire greater flexibility in responding to the increasing demands for small-batch, customized production. Caught by the decline in manufacturing employment and the threat of plant closings or layoffs, workers must settle for less job security and a growing need to work closely with business for the sake of their mutual survival.

Much of Italian industry is oriented toward exports. In the 1990s, the slowdown in the global economy hit Italy hard, especially in the mezzogiorno region. Once again the specter of layoffs and recession has destabilized politics as the standard of living for both working-class and middle-class households is threatened by economic restructuring. Fascist skinheads emerged in the 1980s, and anti-Semitism is on the rise despite the very small Jewish population. Not all of this activity is directly related to the current recession, and other, as yet undocumented factors may be playing a role as Italy enters a new period of social transformation.

France

As in England, the restructuring of settlement space in France is the result of industrial decline. Coal mining, steel production, and textiles, located in the north and west, have been particularly hard hit by plant closings and layoffs. In one year alone

(1982–1983), over 185,000 industrial jobs were lost (Body-Gendrot, 1987:244). Cities such as Metz, Dunkirk, Nancy, Lille, and Roubaix have taken on the feel of declining Rust Belt cities elsewhere. The French government sought to intervene and prop up failing industries to retain jobs and the community quality of life. When these policies were not successful (Zukin, 1985), supports were abandoned in favor of a competitive gleaning of unproductive businesses.

Industrial decline has resulted in a social crisis for many working-class families. According to one observer, "austerity brought about a deterioration of the social fabric: . . . racism, demonstrations of workers against arbitrary decisions benefitting other workers, and petty delinquency. At the workplace, competition rose between the working classes: . . . young vs. old, white vs. non-white, men vs. women, all fighting as the size of the pie was shrinking" (Body-Gendrot, 1987:244). The rise of right-wing racists can be attributed in part to this upheaval. Today racism is a major problem in France, and hate crimes target immigrants from North Africa, Jews and Arabs.

Some French industries have responded with modernization schemes, especially the French automakers, Renault and Citroën. Post-Fordist changes, such as flexible production, just-in-time supplying, and computer-assisted manufacturing in the manner of the Japanese industries, have also been adopted (see Leborgne and Lipietz, 1988). The French government has been very aggressive in supporting electronics-related industries, software companies, and biotechnology. In conjunction with universities and business venture capital, new technopoles have sprung up in the Grenoble, Montpellier, and Toulouse regions, among others. These resemble the Oxbridge complex in Great Britain (i.e., around Oxford and Cambridge), the larger university/high-tech industry regions of Silicon Valley, and the Research Triangle.

The push to high-technology industries has affected higher education in the country. As elsewhere, more emphasis is now placed on technologically sophisticated degrees in engineering and science. To date, the changeover to a modernized, flexible, and high-tech economy has met with some success; for example, the French military industries are world leaders. But the older industrialized cities and their problems of decline, unemployment, and renewed racism remain.

Germany

In western Germany, economic restructuring has had a pronounced effect on settlement space. Called the *süd-nord-gefälle* or the south/north cleavage, this pattern is very similar to the way economic changes have affected the United States, where, the Rust Belt cities once heavily based on manufacturing have all declined, and the Sunbelt cities have prospered. In Germany, the older, northern industrial cities such as Bremen and Hamburg have been hardest hit by restructuring, while southern towns such as Munich and Frankfurt have become affluent.

According to Hausserman and Siebel (1990), the north/south split is a consequence of Germany's shift to an export-oriented economy, similar to the Italian case. In Germany, the southern region contains the automobile industry and also high-technology-based manufacturing—two economic sectors that have done well in

BOX 12.1   PARIS AND CULTURE

When we think of France, we think of Paris, and when we imagine Paris, we associate that city with the riches of Western culture. Paris, France, is the very epitome of urban life. Consider the artist Manet:

> All those who knew him agreed that Manet was more than a resident of Paris; he "personified the sentiments and customs of Parisians, raised to their highest power." . . . The boulevards from the Porte Saint-Denis to the Madeleine, and especially the few hundred yards between the rue de Richelieu and the Chaussée d'Antin comprising the boulevard des Italiens, had been the center of Manet's social life since the late 1850s, as indeed they had been for several generations of worldly and talented Parisians for twenty years before that. Here were concentrated the most fashionable theaters, restaurants, and cafés— above all the Café Tortoni on the corner of the rue Taitbout, the very heart of boulevard society and of Manet's as well.
>
> It was also on the boulevard des Italiens, in the enterprising Galerie Martinet, a forerunner of those which later supported impressionism, that Manet had his first one-man exhibition in March 1863. Among the pictures he showed was the one in which, for the first time, he portrayed himself amid this boulevard society and made its elegant, allusive style his own—the *Concert in the Tuileries*. Some of those who have been identified in it were indeed among the leaders of that society: Gautier, the bohemian turned court writer and entertainer; Offenbach, the composer of lighthearted operettas; Aurelian Scholl, the journalist admired for his wit; Baudelaire, the poet and self-styled dandy; and Manet himself, the unofficial painter of this elite circle. (Sharpe and Wallock, 1987:136–138)

Concert in the Tuileries, by Edouard Manet, shows the lifestyle of the urban bourgeoisie in Paris in the nineteenth century.

Daimler-Benz truck assembly plant in Worth, Germany, demonstrates the scale of industrial restructuring in Europe as in the United States.

the global economy. Steel production and the shipping industry, which are concentrated in the north, have been unable to compete effectively in the world system; consequently, cities based on these sectors have declined. From 1980 to 1988, the northern region containing the cities of Bremen, Hamburg, and Bonn experienced a 6.4 percent decline in employment, while the southern region containing the cities of Munich, Baden, Frankfurt, and Stuttgart enjoyed an *increase* in employment (Haussermann and Siebel, 1990:377).

It is not clear how unification with East Germany will affect urban areas. It is expected that population will shift to centers of increasing employment wherever they are located in the nation. There is continuing difficulty in absorbing the formerly East German labor force. Unemployment is on the rise, as is racism as hate groups target immigrants and even the few Jews who reside there, despite the history of the Holocaust. Fascist skinheads perpetrating violence and hate crimes against immigrants and Jews threatened to destabilize the government in 1992. As in Italy and France, the renewal of racism in Germany has complex causes, although the recession is a contributing factor. Most Germans believe their economy can absorb the former population of East Germany; nevertheless, the effects of the global recession remain unpredictable.

Spain

Unlike the northern European countries, Spain is not highly industrialized and retains a large proportion of the population engaged in agriculture. Most of the manufacturing has been centered over the years in the Madrid region, and the urbanization pattern in this country is not as balanced as in the other European nations we have so far considered. In recent years, however, Spain has also been affected by the worldwide restructuring of the global economy.

Older industrial districts, such as Villaverde, have declined and are plagued by job loss and poverty. Small manufacturers, much like the businesses of Italy's mezzogiorno, have remained successful, especially those involved in metal working, crafts, and printing. In addition, a new, high-tech corridor running from Madrid past the airport and toward Barcelona has appeared recently that is expanding in employment. And the city of Madrid itself has been changing from a manufacturing economy to a service economy. A building boom of office towers along La Castellana boulevard caused by the growing importance of finance-related business services has produced an increase in service-related employment.

Spain is an interesting case because of the success of its industries during the 1980s under the direction of a socialist government. The 1992 summer Olympics served to showcase Spain's other large metropolis, Barcelona, as well as stimulate the nation's economy. The global recession, however, has hit this country hard, as it has all other export-oriented economies. Consequently, there is a current slowdown in the sociospatial restructuring of metropolitan areas.

Summary

Western European countries have undergone significant economic restructuring to service-based economies, with a reduced scale of government aid similar to that in the United States. New techniques of post-Fordist manufacturing have been introduced in the successful industries, including automation and Japanese-style flexible methods of production. High-technology corridors, such as the United States' Silicon Valley, have also appeared, such as the M-4 corridor in England. Finally, there is an increasing integration of large corporations or transnational firms that, like their American counterparts, conduct business around the globe.

Restructuring has also brought an increasing array of urban problems. Crime, poverty, and the declining quality of life, almost unheard of as European concerns, are now becoming serious. Hate crimes, anti-immigrant sentiments, and racism are on the rise. Poverty and unemployment are growing because of related economic changes that have hit the working class especially hard. In Ireland, for example, 33 percent of households receive some form of public assistance; in Denmark the figure is 25 percent; and about the same percentage is characteristic of Germany and England (Abrahamson, 1988:21).

Cutbacks in the traditional European welfare state have made the problem of poverty more severe. Since the level of funding for public assistance now varies greatly among the countries of Western Europe, fears have been expressed about the possibility of "social dumping." This phenomenon arises when one geographical area has appreciably better social programs than another during a time of economic hardship. Poor populations migrate to the area with better benefits. As the European community moves to common market integration, it is feared that large movements of relatively poor people will occur and inundate places such as Scandinavia that have attractive welfare programs still in place (Abrahamson, 1988:7). Such movements strain the political and social fabrics of host countries and lead to government instability. They might also lead to anti-immigrant hate crimes and social unrest that are unfortunate reminders of World War II.

A different form of social dumping has already been experienced by European countries and, to an extent, the United States. Since the 1970s, large numbers of workers from the Third World have entered developed societies in the hope of obtaining work, as we discuss in Chapter 13. Several million Turks, Kurds, and Greeks, for example, live in Germany. Millions of North Africans have migrated to France, and even the Danes, who have always lived in a homogeneous society, are now concerned about the high Muslim birth rate in their country. It is now quite common to have African, Middle Eastern, or Asian cab drivers in cities such as Paris, London, and Berlin (not just in Los Angeles and New York). Domestic servants, undocumented workers, and low-skilled, labor-intensive factories or sweat shops composed of Third World workers are increasingly common in all these cities. Even Japan, which restricts immigration, has a growing number of illegal aliens from Asia who come there in search of work.

Global economic restructuring therefore brings an increasingly mobile flow not only of capital investment and goods but also of people. Immigration from Third World countries to Europe has affected the social order of these once relatively homogeneous societies in notable ways. The growing presence of foreigners is reflected in the increasing mix of ethnic restaurants that have sprung up in city centers. This drawing together of the First and Third Worlds in a common urban experience is increasingly characteristic of contemporary Western cities.

Eastern Europe

Eastern Europe was under communist domination for the last 70 years, but has now joined the capitalist West. Most countries exhibit a pattern of primate city development. Only Russia seems to have been able to develop a balanced urban hierarchy. However, its capital, Moscow, remains quite large, with a population estimated in 1990 to be over 8 million. Table 12.2 illustrates the growth in population for the four largest cities from 1960 to 1980.

Discussion about Eastern European cities among urbanists most often centers on whether there is a specific difference in patterns of growth that can be attributed to communism. According to Friedrichs, however, "except for a short period in the early 1920s, there are no specific socialist types of land use, distribution of new housing, internal organization of residential blocks, or location of companies" (1988:128). Consequently, communist societies have built environments similar to those in capitalist countries. Yet there are fundamental differences between communism and capitalism,

TABLE 12.2
Population of Major Eastern European Cities, 1960–1994

	Budapest	Moscow	Prague	Warsaw
1960	1,805,000	6,242,000	1,133,000	1,139,000
1980	2,064,000	8,302,000	1,186,000	1,629,000
1994	2,061,000	8,436,000	1,216,000	1,643,000

Source: Adapted from Friedrichs (1988). 1994: United Nations Statistics Division, Demographic Yearbook.

especially with regard to the absence in the former of separate factions of capital and separate markets. Consequently, there are some peculiarities of land use and population distribution among such cities that differ from patterns in the West. These involve the nature of the central city due to an absence of the finance capital sector, the pattern of population distribution and the housing shortage, and, most important, an absence of a capitalist real estate market.

Central City Decline

All Eastern European countries have large capital cities. Some, such as Hungary and Poland, approach the condition of primate status due to the dominance of their main centers—Budapest and Warsaw, respectively. Others, such as the Czech Republic and Russia, have a more balanced system of cities. In every case, the central sections of the major cities are quite old, dating back several hundred years to their founding. Under the communist governments, original buildings in the city center were not torn down. They remain standing and are, in most cases, in terrible shape. The lack of ambitious office building schemes, characteristic of the communist city, stands in contrast to the capitalist city, where finance capital and its associated business services, such as accounting and legal consulting, have taken over the downtown. In most communist countries, the state directed investment; thus, their downtowns do not contain an active real estate market of office buildings that services the needs of corporate and finance capital. As a result, the shift to the service-oriented economy is occurring more slowly in these countries than elsewhere in Europe.

The Demographic Pattern of Land Use

Family income differences in Eastern European cities are not as segregated as in the rest of Europe or the United States (Ladanyi, 1989). In the United States, both the wealthy and the poorest classes are highly segregated. In Eastern European cities, such as Budapest, the upper classes are highly segregated but the poorest people are only somewhat segregated, and the rest of the population is evenly spread out in the city despite some differences in family income.

The reason for this contrast seems to be the operation of government subsidies for housing, which has prevented the poorest people from being concentrated within urban spaces. Thus, a major difference between formerly communist societies and

TABLE 12.3
Housing Shortages in Warsaw, Budapest, and Moscow, 1960 and 1980

	Year	Households	Number of Dwellers	Deficit of Dwelling Units
Warsaw	1960	396,100	307,500	88,600
	1980	594,200	514,000	80,700
Budapest	1960	659,000	535,000	154,000
	1980	807,000	727,000	96,000
Moscow	1960	2,214,000	880,000	1,333,900
	1980	3,323,000	2,479,000	844,000

Source: Adapted from Friedrichs (1988).

capitalist ones such as the United States is the active role of government in providing affordable housing for the poor (although, as we will see below, the total volume of housing provided is inadequate). Paradoxically, however, under the communist governments, the more affluent people have also enjoyed considerable state housing subsidies (Ladanyi, 1989). Consequently, it is not the market that has created uneven development in formerly communist countries, as it does under capitalism, but state intervention itself. This kind of uneven development and privilege produced by state favors for the elite has been a common complaint about communist practice for decades; however, it is comparable to the economic advantages of the capitalist class in the United States.

With the fall of communism, housing subsidies are declining, and as the market takes over, segregation is also increasing. More privately produced housing represents efforts to alleviate the chronic shortage of housing in these societies. However, a shift to an active capitalist real estate market is also producing the first significant signs of capitalist-style uneven development within urban settlement spaces, such as a growing number of homeless people and a sharp rise in the cost of rental housing, which hits elderly pensioners particularly hard.

Housing Shortage

Unlike those in Western Europe, the cities of the communist societies have suffered a housing shortage for many years. State-planned construction has never been able to keep pace with demand, unlike the market experience of the capitalist West. In addition, countries such as Russia have restricted the growth of cities. Yet population has increased as migrants from agricultural areas move to the city looking for work. Table 12.3 details the deficit in housing stock for Warsaw (Poland), Budapest (Hungary), and Moscow (Russia) from 1960 to 1980. As can be seen, while significant strides have been made since 1960, the deficit ranged from over 80,000 for Warsaw to 96,000 for Budapest and 844,000 for Moscow in the 1980s. This peculiar communist-produced shortage has, over the decades, resulted in an unexpected style of life: Households often double up and share one apartment, and married children often live with their parents for years.

According to Friedrichs, migration to the city and natural increase have produced this housing shortage, much as they have in the Third World. But the failure of state-directed housing programs has also compounded the shortage. Under communism, because land use was strictly controlled by the state, no shantytowns or street people were tolerated. This is currently changing with the switch to a free market in real estate, as we have discussed. In addition, as the urban economy grew under communism, new industry had to locate on the outskirts because of the lack of space within the central city and the absence of the kind of urban renewal that is characteristic of Western capitalism. As a consequence, population has been slowly deconcentrating and following employment opportunities to the outer rim. This is the reverse of the occupational/residence pattern of the old industrial city during the early stages of communist rule, which maintained its working-class districts and employment opportunities within the city center (Friedrichs, 1988:150).

The Emergence of Free Markets

Eastern Europe is now the scene of immense social changes as the changeover is made from communism to a market economy. Potentially the most significant change is the growth of the real estate market and a new, second circuit of capital for formerly communist countries. It remains to be seen how this restructuring will affect settlement space areas; however, we can use the U.S. case as a guide for future projections. Some indications already suggest that within the large cities, segregation will increase, deconcentration of population will accelerate as suburbanization occurs, and the service economy will replace manufacturing as the principal sector. It remains to be seen how slowly or quickly land use in the centers of cities such as Budapest, Warsaw, Prague, and Moscow will also change. Old buildings remain, and to date there is little new office construction, but this situation most likely cannot last as the capitalist urban land market takes over and the pressures to switch to a service-based economy prevail there as they have in the capitalist West. We can even expect drastic renovation or renewal programs, led by private investment, for the construction of high-rise office towers in the Eastern European cities of the future.

Japan

One of the world's greatest economic powers, Japan has contained large cities for hundreds of years (Bestor, 1985). Tokyo, for example, had over 1 million people as early as the 1700s when it served as the capital (called Edo at the time) of the shogun empire. Since World War II, Japanese cities have developed as large regional agglomerations or multicentered metropolitan regions. The Tokyo/Yokohama metropolitan area, for example, contains more than 17 million people, 25 percent of the entire population of Japan, while the city of Tokyo alone contained 11,828,000 in 1985. The Osaka metropolitan area to the south contained 15,900,000 people in 1984. The urbanization of the Japanese population, 77 percent of the total, is roughly comparable to that of Western countries such as the United States and Britain (Population Reference Bureau, 1990).

Tens of thousands of shoppers swarm Tokyo's busiest shopping street, Ame-yoko, on the year's last Sunday as they prepare foodstuffs for the coming New Year holiday.

Japanese cities developed trading and commercial centers during the sixteenth and seventeenth centuries. When industrialization was occurring in the nineteenth century, it was embraced by Japanese business along with the aid of the monarchy. By the beginning of the twentieth century, Japan was already a major industrial power. After the massive loss of labor and industrial production as a consequence of World War II, Japan initiated ambitious, export industry–led industrialization schemes that were remarkably successful in establishing Japan as a global economic power (Lee, 1982; Berry, 1989). Box 12.2 describes the city of Tokyo during this period.

Japanese cities are not deconcentrated in the pattern of U.S. cities, nor have they undergone a shift to services on the same scale as have cities in the United States and older industrialized countries. Today manufacturing remains important to the Japanese economy. Work is highly centralized within city boundaries even though the suburban population is growing. For example, Tokyo employed almost 6 million people in 1985 (Sassen, 1991:161), many of whom had manufacturing jobs. Each day several million commuters ride into the central city by public transportation, often traveling as much as two hours each way. Japan is unlike the United States in other respects. Due to a free market in real estate, a general shortage of land in the country, and the centralization of employment within large cities, housing and rental prices are astronomical. It has become increasingly difficult to own one's own home there, and most housing space, in terms of square feet, is extremely small by U.S. standards.

The success of Japan's export-oriented industries in the global economy has resulted in important changes in settlement space patterns for the entire Pacific Rim. Japanese industries innovated a number of techniques, such as "just-in-time" methods, that helped their competitiveness. They also embarked on regional schemes of manufacturing in search of cheap labor (much like U.S. companies), which had an impact on other Asian countries, in particular South Korea and Taiwan. But the real impact occurred because of Japan's success in foreign trade earnings. Within a few decades, it became a major repository of the world's finance capital. Tokyo alone contains almost half of the top 50 banks of the world, and since 1985 it has ranked first in total banking assets (Sassen, 1991:176), surpassing London and New York. The flow of money into Japan has meant a major source of development funds for surrounding areas in the Pacific Rim. While the U.S. economy inched along at an annual increase of only 2 percent of its gross domestic product, Japan's economy grew by 6 percent (Berry, 1989:176). Most gains were in those export-oriented industries that have proved successful for Japan, namely, textiles, clothing, automobile manufacturing, and consumer electronics.

Several notable trends characterize Japanese industrial and urban development. The global recession has affected Japan's economy, but not to the extent that it has Italy's or Spain's. Export industries are still doing well. More significant is the profits squeeze from the increasing costs of Japanese labor. This has resulted in the kind of response enacted by U.S. firms, namely, the shift of some production to other countries with cheaper and more compliant sources of labor. While marketing and control remain located in Japan, the past two decades have witnessed an increase in the amount of component part production farmed out to Taiwan, South Korea, and Singapore (Douglas, 1988; Berry, 1989:203).

Japan is experiencing another trend common to the United States and Europe. Japan has always restricted its immigration, which is why its labor force and urban populations have remained more stable than in countries such as the United States. Lately, however, illegal immigration is becoming noticeable as the global flow of investment and people integrates the Pacific Rim countries. Typically, such immigration occurs because the low-wage, menial jobs that are necessary in a developed economy are no longer being filled by the domestic population because of increases in the quality of life and training levels. This has been the experience of the United States and, increasingly, of Japan. Sassen (1991:308) notes that since the late 1980s, there has been a rapid increase in the number of illegal aliens working in Japan:

> Typically, they have entered the country with tourist visas and overstayed their officially permitted time. The estimate is that by mid-1988 there were 200,000 illegal male workers in Japan in manual work, from construction to restaurant kitchens. Almost all of these were from Asia. The estimate is that the largest single groups were from Taiwan, South Korea, Bangladesh, the Philippines, and Pakistan.

BOX 12.2 TOKYO: CITY OF PARADOXES

Of all the world cities, Tokyo is richest in paradoxes. In terms of population it is the largest city authority, and the second largest metropolitan area in the world; but its public services are structured for a city between one-fifth and one-half the present size. Its factories produce some of the most technologically sophisticated products in the world; yet its wage levels and living standards are noticeably below those of the other world cities . . . and they contrast sharply in turn with relative poverty in Japan's provincial agrarian regions, only a few hundred miles away. Its rate of population growth is by far the highest of any of the very big cities of the world; it has the biggest problems in accommodating the extra millions. It is a metropolis where, in 1964, an elaborate network of expressways is in an advanced stage of construction, but where only 23 percent of the city's ten million people enjoy main drainage. Of all world cities it is the one whose citizens have devised the most varied and original solutions to their problems; but also the one where almost all schemes have a habit of failing for lack of funds. (Hall, 1966)

Over one-quarter of the entire population of Japan is crowded into the greater Tokyo metropolitan area, which includes the districts of Tokyo prefecture, Kanagawa, Saitama, and Chiba City. Unlike Western developed cities, manufacturing still takes place there, principally in the eastern and southern zones. Lately, however, factory employment has been declining to the benefit of service and commercial activities (Dogan and Kasarda, 1988:136). Tokyo prefecture alone contains over one-fourth of the corporate headquarters in Japan. It is also the nation's capital.

Tokyo has virtually no racial or ethnic problems, although Koreans and lower-class Japanese are discriminated against. Poverty is a growing concern, but the rates are extremely low. The city has several slums "inhabited by ragpickers, day laborers and the like" (Dogan and Kasarda, 1988:138).

In another respect, Japanese urban culture differs markedly from that of the United States. Unlike here, Japan relies on the strength of local neighborhood associations. "Almost every neighborhood in Tokyo has an association (*chokai* or *jichikai*) which assists the government in the co-production of muncipal services, promotes neighborhood solidarity, and acts to articulate neighborhood demands to the government . . . Their prevention of social atomization and active observation of local goings-on contributes to the astonishingly low crime rate in Tokyo" (Dogan and Kasarda, 1988:140).

Japanese cities are not characterized by the kind of social segregation found in the West, although the wealthy are isolated from the rest of the masses. However, they exhibit uneven development with regard to the lack of services and facilities. Almost half of Tokyo's population lacks flush toilets (Kasarda, 1988), and extreme housing and space shortages affect the city's inhabitants. There are few parks, medical facilities, and community centers in Tokyo. The city does contain an extensive mass transit network, as do other Japanese cities, but all Japanese cities suffer from pollution, smog, noise, and overcrowding (Nakamura and White, 1988). Other areas of the country are plagued by extensive pollution resulting from industrial development that the government has not controlled.

Much recent development in Japan involves the construction of new spaces that bypass traditional urban agglomerations. This is especially the case for the new technopoles that have been energetically constructed with massive government help, a feature that differs from the United States, which has yet to undertake such federally sponsored development. Most projects are joint ventures by the state, universities, and private capital, such as the giant Tsukuba "science city" centered on "Skuba" university outside of Tokyo. More recently, technopoles have been developed in the peripheral regions of Japan—those areas previously bypassed by development—such as Hokkaido, Tohoku, Kyushu, and the area along the Sea of Japan. One of the most ambitious of these projects is the "silicon island" developed on Kyushu, centered in Kumamoto City. This region has become a leading producer of microchips and contains a population of over 700,000 (Fujita, 1988).

Japan exhibits some of the characteristics of Western industrialized countries. Its traditional urban centers continue to grow. At the same time, new spaces have been created to house the "knowledge industries." These are similar to technopoles found elsewhere, but Japan's government is energetic in its support of such new development. Japan's urban system shows symptoms of overurbanization and is dominated by Tokyo and other large agglomerations, such as Osaka and Nagoya. Due to the high cost of land and the very high price of housing, there is little suburbanization and residential construction. As a result, Japanese people must contend with long commutes to work in crowded facilities and cramped living quarters at home.

Summary

Western Europe, which has been urbanized for centuries, has recently undergone the same restructuring of settlement space found in the United States. Manufacturing has declined, and service employment is on the rise. New industrial spaces centered on high-technology industries have appeared and are growing. The movement of people and activities to suburban settlement space is increasing. New forces of centralization associated with command and control functions for the finance capital sector keep inner-city development alive. Finally, the integration of economies due to the globalization of capital and the growing demand for low-wage labor has resulted in the flow of migrants across national borders.

All of these elements have combined to produce changes in the social order of once homogeneous European societies. Uneven development in wage levels creates a growing disparity between well-off professionals and low-wage service workers. Migration and ethnic cultural influences have met with increasing numbers of hate crimes, racism, and, most ironically, anti-Semitism in a post-Holocaust Europe.

Asian urban development is led by the modern economy of Japan. It too suffers from uneven development. Japanese housing and real estate issues are worrisome, and the shortage of affordable units will provoke a crisis of business location as fewer and fewer workers find places to live within commuting distances of jobs. But many negative effects are outweighed by the success of Japanese economic growth. Industrial expansion brings the growth of multicentered metropolitan regions outside of Japan's traditional manufacturing centers—Tokyo, Osaka, and Nagoya. Financial investment flowing from Japan fuels the economies of the new Asian tigers, and thereby restructures the entire Pacific Rim (as well as the United States, Canada, and Australia, in addition to the less developed countries of Asia and Latin America) for a new round of growth.

Common problems abound in Europe, Japan, and the United States, including the growing lack of affordable housing, challenges from the flow of immigrants who are often illegal aliens, declines in manufacturing employment, and the uneven development of economic opportunities for city populations due to the restructuring of the economy and the emphasis on high-tech skills. With few exceptions, however, no industrialized country has experienced the kind of decay in the social conditions of everyday life comparable to the U.S. experience. In this respect the United States presents a unique case to the world, although parallels may be found in Third World cities such as Calcutta and Nairobi.

CHAPTER
13
THIRD WORLD URBANIZATION

Urban development in the United States illustrates the spatial pattern of deconcentrated development characteristic of an advanced capitalist society. While large cities remain important centers of commerce and culture, many of them have reached slow or stable population growth. Despite continual renovation and gentrification in the centers, most development occurs outside the large city in the suburban settlement space. Land use is mixed and shared among densely populated cities, minicenters of various kinds, and expanding suburban regions of residential housing. As we have seen, our society faces problems that are accentuated by locational inequities. Both income and racial segregation are common and lead to serious inequalities in employment, housing, education, medical care, and recreation. Despite the problems, most Americans are well housed and well fed. While unemployment has been high in recent years, the majority can find work and even pursue careers.

In many parts of the world, cities have a different relationship to society, and people's individual fortunes are plagued by dangers and disparities unheard of in more affluent societies. Box 13.1 depicts life in Lagos, Nigeria, a place of great opportunity but also serious problems. In this chapter, we will examine the urban condition in Asia, Africa, and Latin America. These regions contain three-fourths of the world's population and most of its land mass. The societies range from democracies to totalitarian dictatorships. What they have in common is an inability to sustain economic development and, with some notable exceptions, a declining quality of life for most of their urban residents.

Changing Perspectives on Third World Urbanization

In approaching the issue of urbanization in developing countries, a number of misconceptions must be dispelled. First, such societies are commonly thought to be primitively

BOX 13.1   LAGOS, NIGERIA

> Lagos was unlike anything I had seen before in Africa; it was more like an over-crowded city in India. It is an island with a lagoon between it and the mainland. Perhaps 400,000 people are jammed into this area, almost all of them selling something to someone. . . . Whole sections of the town are devoted to headscarves, and women walk nonchalantly down the street with two- or even three-foot piles of these scarves on their heads. . . . All night the city is alluring: candle flames flickering in small shops or on stalls by the roadside, green or pink electric light bulbs casting eerie shadows in beerparlors. . . . Always the city is intensely vital. All night long, people move up and down, never still. (Baker, 1974:16)

Lagos is the capital of Nigeria, one of the most populous countries in Africa. Due to extensive supplies of crude oil, it is also one of the richest countries on that continent. The British took control of Nigeria from the Portuguese and established a colony at Lagos in 1866. In 1960, Nigeria achieved independence. By 1972, the greater Lagos region contained 1.8 million people. By 1985, the population was 4 million and still growing. At present it is an example, all too frequently repeated in other areas of the Third World, of urbanization out of control. As one observer notes:

> Lagos today continues to function as the nerve center of the most populous and prosperous country in sub-Saharan Africa. But it presents a disturbing picture of a community overwhelmed by urban problems encountered in both the developed and developing worlds. Like many western cities, it is suffering from serious housing shortages, chronic traffic jams, an increase in the crime rate, inner city decay, pollution, weak financial resources, and a largely unstable urban population. These difficulties are compounded by uncontrolled expansion and growth, painfully poor social services, an inadequate administrative staff, unsanitary environmental conditions, corruption in official circles, and widespread unemployment, particularly among young school leavers who form the bulk of newly arrived immigrants. (Baker, 1974:viii)

developed compared to the United States. In fact, however, countries such as Brazil, Mexico, and Korea are highly industrialized, with factory workers numbering in the hundreds of thousands. Some of the largest cities in the world, such as São Paulo and New Delhi, not only are located in developing countries but are also vibrant, dynamic urban centers (see the next section). However, these societies seem to share a pattern of uneven development that is even more extreme than that found in the older, developed nations. We will discuss this issue shortly.

Second, the ecological theory discussed in Chapter 6 argues that developing countries are very much like the developed societies, only they are at an earlier stage and will "modernize" in time (Kasarda and Crenshaw, 1991). The sociospatial perspective disagrees with this view because it considers factors such as the roles of the state, classes, global capital investment, and economic changes in the First World—all of which are neglected by the ecological approach—as critical for an understanding of urbanization in developing countries. Thus, it suggests that countries having a differ-

Lagos, Nigeria, including the port district and downtown.

ent economic structure will develop in different ways. Close observers of growth patterns in areas such as Latin America (Roberts, 1978) and Asia (Berry, 1989) seem to agree that the explanatory variables stressed by the sociospatial approach are most important, while not necessarily subscribing to the perspective itself. In opposition to the ecological view of similar modernization trajectories, the process of urbanization is *different* from the First World pattern and involves factors such as elite power, differences in state policies, integration into the global economy, and the effects of class structure (Smith and Timberlake, 1993).

A third change in perspective concerns the increasing relevance of the global economy. Prior to the 1970s, there seemed to be a sharp distinction between First and Third World economies. Countries such as the United States were still operating under "Fordist" arrangements of production during this time, meaning that most manufacturing was carried out domestically and foreign countries were viewed principally as markets for U.S. goods. Less developed countries were sources for agricultural goods such as coffee or winter fruits, but were otherwise disconnected from our own society, except perhaps as places for tourists to visit. Developmental theories of the time proposed the "peripheral urbanization" concept, which emphasized the marginal nature of the Third World (Harvey, 1973; Castells, 1977; Walton, 1982).

Since the 1970s, however, vast changes have occurred in the United States as Fordist arrangements of production were dropped and the country underwent deindustrialization (see previous chapters). During the 1970s and 1980s, much U.S. manufacturing employment was shipped overseas, and countries such as Mexico, Malaysia, Singapore, Brazil, and the Dominican Republic were used as effective sites for labor. By the 1990s, it had become commonplace for consumers in the United States to find that the products they purchased, whether articles of clothing, sports equipment, or cars, were assembled in foreign places. Thus, a pattern of manufacturing for world markets was established in many areas of the Third World, and people's lives in the United States were connected by multinational corporations to formerly peripheral societies (Peet, 1987).

Recent studies of Third World urbanization now reject previous approaches that emphasized world system marginality or dependency (Datta, 1990). Instead, it is argued that these countries are increasingly linked to the global economy (Smith and Timberlake, 1993). The cycle of investment, manufacturing, consumption, and profit making that leads to more investment integrates U.S. consumers and producers with manufacturing, banking, and consumption activities in other countries, including the Third World. This effect is often called the "internationalization of capital" (see Chapter 1). As Smith and Timberlake remark, "Thus, to the extent global linkages are considered, the once sharp distinction between the 'comparative' study of urbanization and urbanization in the U.S. is beginning to break down" (1993:15). In this chapter, a continuation of Chapter 12, we will further highlight these commonalities as well as the differences from the U.S. experience.

The sociospatial perspective acknowledges the influence of the global system of capital, and especially the internationalization of capital, on locality. But urbanization processes in both developed and developing countries involve combinations of global, national, and local factors that are relatively independent of the global economy. The kinds of governments that Third World countries have at the national level play a key role in the success of their development schemes. Korea (Barone, 1983) and Singapore have aggressive national policies in pursuit of growth and governments that actively aid capital investment. Other countries, such as many Latin American societies, are plagued by "crony capitalism" and government corruption and dictatorships that squander national wealth.

At the most local level, there are also independent effects that are related to but not determined by the global level. For example, it was recently observed (Roberts, 1991) that Third World cities are moving rapidly from the stage of developing economies to postindustrial relations, that is, skipping many of the features of industrialization that inform the experience of Western, developed nations. Large cities in the Third World, like their First World counterparts, are experiencing shifts to a service-oriented employment base due to their increasing role as command and control centers of capital investment. As a result of new employment opportunities created for professional workers, there is a growing wage differential between well-paid and working-poor residents. How this increasingly diverse class structure manifests itself politically varies from country to country and involves new patterns of local political activity that are independent of, and in some cases oppositional to, global system needs (see the section on social movements).

In sum, the sociospatial perspective on Third World urbanization emphasizes global linkage, differences in the class structure, the effect of national state arrangements, and differences in local politics as key factors for an understanding of current trends. Third World urbanization processes also have many features in common that contrast with First World experiences. These can be identified by considering the nature of population growth and change, or demography, which we will do next.

Demography and Third World Urbanization

When dealing with rapid population changes such as those that affected the United States in the 1800s and affect developing countries today, the science of demography becomes most important. Demographers track the dynamics of population growth. They concentrate on rates of change, such as the frequency of births, deaths, and average number of children per mother. Demographers are also interested in rates of migration, especially changes in the rural and urban populations. For any given population, the rate of increase that depends on the number of births minus deaths is known as the *natural increase.* Population changes within any given settlement space can arise from natural increase or from migration.

For most of human history, the high birth rate was offset by an equally high death rate and populations grew very slowly. Following World War II, the introduction of modern medical techniques and preventive measures to the Third World resulted in a population explosion that is called the *demographic transition.* When new techniques of medical intervention lowered the death rates in these countries, the societies experienced a *permanent* rise in the rate of natural increase because they maintained a high birth rate. In the developed world, the demographic transition was eventually adjusted by means of a declining birth rate or the social norm of smaller families as industrialization prospered over several centuries. Many European countries now have low or even negative growth rates. That stage has yet to occur in the Third World, although some countries, such as Brazil, have drastically lowered their growth rates in recent years. But for most of the Third World, birth rates still outstrip death rates, and overpopulation is a serious social and environmental problem.

The demographic problems of the Third World are compounded by the limited success of economic development. Faced with a population explosion, rural areas have been hard pressed to grow enough food for everyone. Despite the best efforts of developmental economists, the standard of living in rural areas has declined drastically since the 1950s in most Third World countries. People simply have too many mouths to feed. The dilemma facing families was poignantly depicted in a Mexican film by Luis Buñuel, *Los Olvidados.* A farmer comes to the city with his young son. They move toward a crowd in the center of the city. When the father is satisfied that his son is distracted, he seizes his chance and runs away. Many Third World cities are teeming with such abandoned children, many of whom are exploited by a growing sex industry catering to foreign tourists. As might be expected, they have a short life span.

The failure of rural agricultural efforts to mass produce enough to sustain the quality of life has led excess population to migrate to the cities. Despite the hardships of life found there, the move holds out the promise of improvement, and this encourages others to come. As a result, Third World cities suffer from a *double* population explosion: a high rate of natural increase *and* a high rate of in-migration. In the city, there is little room for poor people's housing. In many cities, urban migrants find space on the outskirts and put up makeshift shelters that lack the basic necessities of homes, such as running water, sanitation facilities, and even adequate ventilation for heating. These shantytowns, or squatter settlements, have many names all over the world—*favellas* (Brazil), *bustees* (India), *barriadas* (Mexico), *poblaciones* (Chile), *villas miseria* (Argentina), *bidonvilles* (Africa), and *Kampongs* (Southeast Asia). But they have many features in common, including frequent public health crises, crime, crushing poverty, and no future for the next generation since few countries provide them with schools. We will discuss shantytowns in more detail later.

A third effect of demographic changes in Third World countries involves their common experience of social, economic, and political exploitation under European and American colonialism. Western powers took control of underdeveloped countries in Africa, Asia, and South America beginning in the sixteenth century, and in 1898 the United States gained control of the former Spanish colonies: the Philippines, Hawaii,

Pedestrians and rickshaws in the busy shopping center of Chandni-Chowk in Old Delhi, India.

Cuba, and Puerto Rico. Their principal goal was to acquire natural resources such as gold, spices, and, later, cheaply produced manufactured goods. Because colonialism or imperialism depended on trade with the conquering country, effective links to the global world system were established early. A result of colonialism was the construction of large cities that were usually located near the coast, such as Hong Kong, Manila, Lagos, Singapore, Bombay, and Bangkok. Over the years these cities grew immensely, but few other cities were founded because the colonial powers did not deem them necessary.

Over the years, many Third World countries have been able to launch development programs that have overcome the legacy of colonial control. However, the success of these programs has been limited due to changes in geopolitics and in the world economy, as well as to national issues such as crony capitalism and civil conflict. These factors may hinder the balanced growth of cities in these countries. As a result, many Third World countries today possess a single, gigantic *primate city* that is *overurbanized,* or excessively populated, and remains the center for most investment and economic growth, while retaining a relatively *underurbanized* interior with no large cities. Primate cities are characteristic of an unbalanced pattern of urbanization that remains quite different from that found in the developed countries of the world. Let us examine this unique feature in more detail, as well as other characteristics of Third World urbanization, including shantytown development, household coping strategies and the informal economy, and new urban social movements.

Primate City Development Patterns

In developed countries such as the United States, there is an even distribution in the number of cities according to size (see Chapter 4). Some, such as New York with over 7 million people, are quite large; others fill in the ranks lower down with populations of between 500,000 and 1 million, such as San Diego; between 100,000 and 500,000, such as Minneapolis; and so on down the hierarchy. Such a profile constitutes "balanced" urbanization, and it provides both businesses and people with a *variety* of locational choices and urban environments.

Primate cities dominate and distort development within their countries. *Overurbanization,* or the presence of primate cities, is measured by comparing the size of the largest city with other large cities within a given country. In the developing world, the disparities among urban centers may be very great. In Thailand, for example, the population of the capital city of Bangkok was 5,876,000 in 1990, 30 times larger than that of the next largest city. Countries with primate cities lack locational flexibility. As a result, primate cities are locked in a migratory cycle. Like a magnet, they pull mobile populations from the countryside at the expense of other locations.

Primate city development questions the legitimacy of ecological theory, as discussed earlier. According to this perspective, developed nations should be the model for poorer countries. They should industrialize and urbanize as rapidly as possible.

When they do, ecological theory suggests that the populations in industrialized cities will increase their incomes and acquire a better quality of life. By encouraging urban growth, the entire society benefits.

The sociospatial perspective disagrees with this view. Third World countries can grow economically, but only in conjunction with world system priorities and investment flows. Consequently, rapid urbanization may have negative effects because its principal cause is the needs of global capital and not the quality of life for local populations (Smith, 1985). As a result, Third World countries can suffer from extreme examples of uneven development despite impressive modernization efforts, and primate cities are often the sociospatial consequence. While the *average* income of primate city residents may be greater than that of rural counterparts, the inequality of income and of quality of life is so severe in primate cities that the standard of living is lower than in rural areas (Bradshaw and Fraser, 1989). Thus, the growth of primate city economies does not help the majority of citizens who are victims of uneven and inequitable development.

Shantytown Development

Each month more than 20,000 people come to Mexico City from impoverished rural states looking for employment. The sheer number of urban migrants is too great for either the private or public sector to provide adequate housing or shelter, and thus many families end up in squatter settlements. The common conception is that life in these places is totally peripheral to the vibrancy of the urban economy of the capital city. But many shantytowns support robust economies in themselves—including areas of real estate investment—and are also large residential districts where the working class often lives. Marginality of shantytown inhabitants is largely a myth (Perlman, 1976).

The status of shantytowns varies from city to city and country to country. In many places, they are simply illegal settlements built on the outskirts of cities, and they exist under the threat of annihilation by state authorities. In other places, however, shantytowns have acquired legitimate status through political activism, and they constitute working-class suburbs that have many services, including electrical power, running water, and schools. Box 13.2 illustrates the variety of shantytown environments and squatter residents.

Many shantytowns possess a robust social order (Aina, 1990; Cooper, 1987). They often are the location for small-business enterprises started by urban migrants. Shantytowns may also be the site for small and medium-size factories. In addition, recent penetration of multinational corporations as part of the restructuring of the global economy has brought the support of subcontracting in Third World countries (Safa, 1987). This phenomenon of vertical disintegration (see Chapter 7) creates new manufacturing jobs and helps local entrepreneurs while integrating shantytowns into the world economy.

Shantytowns are often the only places where the working class can find affordable housing. Consequently, many of the individuals who build these settlements are

BOX 13.2 TYPES OF SHANTYTOWN RESIDENTS

There is great variation in the types of shantytowns, or squatter settlements, found in developing nations. They differ not only in location, building materials, and physical appearance, but also in the types of groups that live in them. Some settlements suffer from social disorganization and crime, while others have been characterized as "slums of hope." In older shantytowns, many families may rent their building from other squatters. Charles Abrams (1977) discovered five different types of squatters during his research in South American cities:

1. **Owner squatters.** This group conforms to our common idea of the urban squatter: the individual or household owns its own building, but not the land on which it was built.
2. **Squatter tenants.** This group is composed of new in-migrants to urban centers who do not live in their own buildings but rent this space from other squatters. Because the "landlord" does not pay taxes or upkeep of the structure, substantial profit may be realized from this business enterprise.
3. **Speculator squatters.** Like regular landowners, this group understands that occupying land and gaining property rights is a way to make a profit. Squatting is viewed as a business venture in the hope of obtaining title to the land.
4. **Store or business squatters:** This group consists of individuals who operate businesses and often live within the squatter settlement. Because they pay no rent or taxes, they may be able to make substantial profits.
5. **Semisquatters:** Individuals or households in this group construct a building on private land but later come to terms with the owner as to rental or even purchase price for the space. The boundary between the legal tenant and the semisquatter may be blurred, particularly within Third World economies.

real estate entrepreneurs. According to one estimate (Datta, 1990), the majority of shantytown dwellers live in rental housing. Real estate investment brings in much needed income. However, as in the First World, there are also problems with a privatized housing market. According to Schteingart (1990), for example, due to the increasing cost of construction materials, shantytown housing around Mexico City has become excessively expensive, and new pressures have been placed on the government to address the issue of affordable housing in that country.

In general, shantytowns continue to grow because they are where the growing working-class populations and rural migrants to the city can obtain shelter (Nash, 1992). They must be viewed, therefore, less as slums than as workers' suburbs that require greater attention and services from local government.

A shantytown at the edge of the city in Caracas, Venezuela.

The Informal Economy and Coping Strategies

In previous chapters we noted that many urban sociologists follow the ecological approach. They focus on individual behavior and the aggregation of separate interests in the public and private sectors. The sociospatial perspective, in contrast, recognizes that while society is composed of individuals, a focus on groups, such as classes and networks, is a preferred way of understanding metropolitan dynamics. In Chapter 11 we saw that urban politics has a class component but cannot always be explained by class conflict alone. Homeowner politics and the struggle to control territory and its quality of life are also important political considerations. When studying the Third World, the nature of class structure and especially the control by select elites through the government and military are important factors. Urban researchers also assert that Third World urban dynamics is not exclusively a class phenomenon. They suggest that the appropriate unit of analysis for the study of urban populations in developing nations is the household (Datta, 1990).

Roberts (1991) argues that the household and its coping strategies are basic to an understanding of urban life everywhere, that is, in the First as well as the Third World. Households are collective units that share housing and food, trade clothing and other consumer durables, and are composed of individuals who pool monetary resources. According to Mingione (1988), not all the members of a given household are immediate family. Households may contain distant relatives and even friends. The collective pooling of resources does not preclude differences among household members, such as conflicts between men and women. What counts most with this emphasis is that it conforms better to the reality of urban life in many countries than does the focus of mainstream sociology on individual decision making or of Marxists on class alone.

The study of household survival strategies shows that the poor do not accept their adversity in a passive manner. They innovate and find ways to support themselves and others. This dynamism makes shantytown life quite complex and leads to both positive and negative outcomes such as the reproduction of generations despite poverty and the existence of criminal activity. Households cope with adversity by making collective decisions rather than allowing the burden of poverty to fall on each individual's shoulders alone. To reduce expenses they may engage in *self-provisioning,* which "includes domestic processing or production of food, making clothes, undertaking repairs, self-construction of housing" (Roberts, 1991:142). Other household coping strategies include reducing the number of members (often children, as in the earlier example of the Buñuel film) and connecting with the *informal economy.*

The issue of the informal economy is an important focus of Third World urbanization research, and is increasingly an equally relevant topic for the First World (Safa, 1987). In this sector, whose activities are considered "off the books" or illegal, people sell everything from drugs, cigarettes, and convenience store items (such as sodas) to produce (such as fruits and vegetables)—and even their own bodies for sex. As global restructuring expands in Third World cities, bringing with it highly paid professional services, poor people find informal or casual employment as shoeshiners, messengers, deliverypersons, and domestic helpers, in addition to the burgeoning demand for restaurant and other commercial laborers. Many laborers, especially domestic servants and babysitters, are hired off the record.

The informal sector is dominated by a market economy, although this is not the same as capitalism because barter or trade as well as monetary exchange prevails and no formal structures dominate pricing (Korff, 1990). Work is precarious and does not bring the kinds of benefits that people in the First World identify with full-time employment, such as health insurance or social security. Researchers of this phenomenon note that the numbers of people and activities in the informal sector are growing in all countries (Datta, 1990), a fact we have noted in connection with the illegal drug industry's role in poor ghetto areas of the United States.

The study of household coping strategies and the informal economy paints a multidimensional picture of shantytown life and illustrates how individuals may take advantage of opportunities in cities that are not usually noted when attention is given only to formal economies and our own limited, culture-bound conceptions of everyday life.

Urban Social Movements and Politics

Another important topic that is often neglected in discussing urbanization in the Third World is the significance of political struggles within the city (see Castells, 1983; Walton, 1987; Cooper, 1987). According to one observer, Third World urban movements are characterized by a

> gradual transition during the last decade from essentially comprising local movements with limited socio-political goals to being more conscious movements making much greater demands on the state and with social and political effects no longer limited to the local arena. (Datta, 1990:44)

An example of this change concerns the broadening movement for affordable housing (Castells, 1983; Ramirez, 1990) and the drive to make squatter and shantytown settlements legal. Organized efforts of poor people have pitted them against the government with demands for better health, education, and neighborhood services—a phenomenon that is also characteristic of First World communities and that transcends class distinctions. Another recent development is the growing number of class-based union activities that take place in cities. Deindustrialization has meant the decline of manufacturing jobs in the First World and with it the drastic decline in the power of unions. But as manufacturing jobs have been shunted to the Third World, an associated rise in union activity and class struggles has resulted. Countries such as Brazil and India, for example, have formidable industrial labor forces, and with them have come active trade union movements and class-based political action.

Special attention must be given to the role of women in Third World politics. When women migrate to the city in traditional Third World countries, they acquire new opportunities for marriage and male–female relations, "even if social conservatism may also be exacerbated by the novelty and difficulties of urban life" (Coquery-Vidrovitch, 1990:77). African and Latin American studies show that women take advantage both of the informal economy and of shantytown dwellings to earn a living, although some fall victim to male domination and criminal exploitation such as prostitution (Schlyter, 1990). One important measure of the freer status of city women is their important role in urban social movements. Coquery-Vidrovitch (1990:77) suggests that this important representation may be the result of the active involvement of women in voluntary associations connected with urban shantytown life.

Uneven development and the proliferation of shantytowns may lead to political instability. The national government is not viewed as an avenue for the solving of ordinary people's problems. This makes struggles at the most local level increasingly important as a vehicle for change. According to one African study (Mabogunje, 1990:361), the government of Nigeria

> is seen as no more than the instrument of the dominant class, committed to perpetuating an unbalanced distribution of income and wealth and preserving the dominance of capitalist ideology and political power. Reports of the performance in government of different groups, whether military or civilian, reveal a cynical use of state apparatus to enrich individuals at the expense of the commonwealth.

From time to time, leaders arise claiming to address the immense disparities of wealth. Often this occurs at the local level, and urban social movements help organize residents to fight for political influence. Beneditas Das Silvas, a black from the major favella in Rio de Janeiro, Brazil, ran for the office of mayor in December 1992 on the Socialist Party (PT) ticket. Beneditas, as her supporters call her, symbolizes the forces of change that challenge the inequities of uneven development. Her presence in a local election shows how relevant this issue is for growing urban areas.

Urban social movements are connected to the global economy. Workers in Third World countries comprise a complex social order with many different class statuses (Portes and Walton, 1981). Changes in the activities linked to global investment have differential effects on the Third World working class. These differences are reflected in different political positions and complex ideological issues among trade union parties, some of whom are active socialist or communist organizations, although there are conservative and reactionary political elements as well. In other words, Third World national and urban politics involves a variety of organized political positions despite the greater presence in many countries of worker-oriented or left-wing movements than in the developed nations.

The global economy also affects urban social movements directly through its agents of international control. In the 1970s, for example, the International Monetary Fund (IMF), which controls most of the Third World debt and national financing, called for austerity measures and reductions in state expenditures among all its client countries in the Third World. In turn, national governments responded by eliminating subsidies on food and other consumer goods. This placed a severe burden on households. In response to the threat of hunger or increased misery, residents of cities began rioting in protest of food subsidy cutbacks. The "IMF" riots (Walton, 1987; Cleaver, 1989), as they came to be called, were powerful political events that affected the stability of state regimes in diverse places around the globe, including Africa, Latin America, and Asia. As summarized by Datta (1990: 45):

> food riots caused the fall of the Tolbert regime in Liberia in 1979 and threatened the imminent collapse of the regimes in Tunisia and Morocco in 1981, in the Dominican Republic in 1984 and 1985, in Brazil in 1983, in Chile in 1983 and 1985.

As a result of organized opposition to global restructuring agents such as the IMF or to multinational corporations and industrial development, urban social movements have broadened their perspectives to deal with issues that affect all levels of society, including the local, the national, and the global.

Urban social movements are important in the Third World and take many forms. In Chile, for example, between 1968 and 1972, 400,000 people converged on the city of Santiago and established free squatter settlements, or *campamentos* (Schneier, 1990:349). Similar self-governing squatter communities can be found in Mexico, where they are a powerful political force in urban areas (Castells, 1983). In Nigeria, shantytowns have been organized into neighborhoods that have demanded greater political representation. According to one African study, "The mobilization of people at such a level within a city should at least encourage improved information flows and increase the prospect of greater participation by all in the governance (as distinct from the government) of the city" (Mabogunje, 1990:364). Thus, as we saw in Chapter 11, urban social movements are common among city dwellers in both the developed and undeveloped countries of the world.

We have been discussing phenomena that Third World countries have in common. These include the presence of primate cities, the complex social order of shantytowns, household coping strategies and the informal economy, and the changing complexion of urban social movements and politics. Much of the research on these topics has been published only since the 1970s, when they were brought into sharper focus for the audience in developed, westernized countries.

Above all, studies show that the "comparative" perspective on global urbanization that conceptualized a break between the First and Third Worlds must give way to the sociospatial perspective, which acknowledges the growing commonalities and links between metropolitan restructuring patterns in both the First and Third Worlds. Along with increasing acknowledgment of global links is the recognition of certain differences that exist among countries. Not everything is determined by global processes alone. National and local differences also add to the complexity of Third World urbanization. In the final section of this chapter, we will look briefly at these local sources of variation in a region-by-region analysis.

Patterns of Third World Urbanization

Latin America

Latin America contains the world's largest city, Mexico City, with a population of 26 million in 1990, and several of the world's most rapidly growing metropolises: Rio de Janeiro and São Paulo in Brazil, Buenos Aires in Argentina, Caracas in Venezuela, and Bogotá in Colombia. The continent of South America, along with Central America and Mexico, was urbanized hundreds of years ago as a result of the Aztec, Mayan, and Inca civilizations, which founded great cities during the European Middle Ages. In the seventeenth and eighteenth centuries, the Spanish and Portuguese conquests founded new towns and administration centers. The uneven spatial development engendered by colonialism created primate cities in most countries. Many of the cities were located on the coast because of the dominance of trade with the colonial power, although Mexico City, the capital of the ancient Aztec empire, remains an inland magnet for migration.

In recent years, countries such as Brazil, Argentina, and Mexico have benefited from the global search for cheap labor. Mexico, for example, is host to the successful *maquilladoras* program, which locates primary manufacturing in a band of space along the U.S. border for shipment back to the United States as finished products to be sold in that country. Maquilladoras systems, such as enterprise zones, are becoming increasingly popular with Third World countries as First World deindustrialization continues. They allow First World multinationals to retain control of production and marketing while still benefiting from the exploitation of cheap labor in foreign countries with the active support of their governments. The maquilladoras program relies heavily on the use of female labor, which has been made compliant by the culture of paternalism (Fernandez-Kelly, 1991) and enjoys active subsidies from both the Mexican and U.S. governments.

Some Latin American countries, such as Argentina and Brazil, have industrialized. However, in order to be successful and compete with foreign competition, they must use the most sophisticated techniques to make products that will sell on the global market. Most often this means using capital-intensive methods, such as automation, that require little labor. Consequently, even in countries that have achieved some industrialization, factories are run without significant labor forces. New employment opportunities are not created at a pace that could absorb the excess rural population. The result is the perpetuation of shantytown growth despite industrial development.

Brazil is a graphic example of the dilemma presented by world system competition. Brazil has a rather successful indigenous steel industry. It can compete on the world market principally because it is capital intensive and uses the latest techniques of production. But this also means that it employs comparatively few people. Hence, it is not a major source of employment, something Brazil also desperately needs. As Cochrane (1982:16) illustrates, in the 1870s England was the world's leader in steel production, reaching the million-ton mark. At that time, England's steel industry employed 400,000 workers. Brazil today routinely produces four times that amount of steel, but does so using only around 28,000 workers. Modern technology and production techniques make a difference that is surely a mixed blessing to developing countries, and the need to compete in the world system constrains the types of development policies those countries can pursue.

Latin America is the scene of the most explosive growth on this planet. São Paulo, Brazil, had a population of less than 3 million in 1950, for example; today its population is approaching 24 million. Estimates assert that the total Brazilian population, which was 136 million in 1985, will almost double to 246 million by the year 2025 (United Nations, 1985). Of this population, it is estimated that over 90 percent will reside in urban areas. In the next 30 years, Brazil will become a country of giant cities. To feed these people, Brazil can exploit its arable land mass—but many of these new lands are the rain forest. A potential ecological disaster of global magnitude is in the making.

Mexico expects to double its 1985 population by the year 2025 (from 79 million to 154 million). Unlike Brazil, the country is semiarid and lacks appreciable agricultural resources. It has already cultivated virtually all of the available land. Population pressures will force people into the cities or to "El Norte," the United States. As observers note:

> The urban population is expected to increase from 55 million in 1985 to 131 in 2025, the equivalent of 13 cities of ten million each. Is there a limit to Mexico City's growth, this bowl constrained by a circle of pollutant-trapping mountains? Guadalajara and Veracruz might become enormous metropolises. How many new cities of over a million will spring up in the Mexican "desert"? How many Mexicans will head for California, either legally or clandestinely? (Dogan and Kasarda, 1988:24–25)

In addition to immense population pressures, Latin American countries share a history of political instability. They have been controlled for over a century by the dictates of U.S. foreign policy and by the demands of its corporations. Over the years, developmental strategies have been hemmed in by such global constraints.

There is a great need to nurture domestic industrial development. Yet political problems and periodic military coups seem to hamstring such efforts. Instability is also fostered by inequalities in the class system, which is one of the most skewed in the world. The factors of class structure, government control, and global power figure prominently in understanding development in Latin America.

After World War II, Argentina possessed the ingredients to become a world power. It had an industrialized labor force, a large proportion of European trained professionals, and abundant natural resources. The country quickly fell victim to totalitarian government under Juan and Eva Peron and a succession of military dictatorships. The corruption and inefficiency of such regimes failed to realize the Argentinian promise.

At present, democratic governments in countries such as Peru (with recent martial law proclaimed by its president), Brazil, Colombia, and Chile remain unstable. This affects long-term chances for economic development, because capital is reluctant to flow into such countries. As observers have noted (Geisse and Sabatini, 1988), the primate cities of Latin America generate economic growth, but when industrialization strategies are sandbagged by corruption and totalitarian politics, and when the quality of life declines for most of the population due to uneven development, the prospects for realizing the economic potential of urban areas remain bleak.

Asia

The global region of Asia represents great diversity and contains at least half of the world's population. The two largest countries, China and India, share a similar pattern of settlement. They are "underurbanized" as nations, with a large segment of the population remaining in rural areas and, in the case of India more so than China, "overurbanized" because of the presence of primate cities. In China, close to 80 percent of the population resides in rural areas. The remaining 20 percent is heavily concentrated in the few cities with populations of over 500,000, such as Shanghai and Beijing. In India, slightly less than 80 percent of the population lives in rural areas, while the majority of urbanites reside in cities of over 1 million in population.

India and China display differences in their patterns of urbanization because of different national policies; as in Latin America, the factors of state control and local class structure explain a great deal about development. China's communist government, for example, has restricted the size of China's largest cities. In the 1980s, China's largest city, Shanghai, had a population of under 7 million, Beijing was 5,550,000, and Tianjin was 5,130,000 in 1982 (Chen, 1988:233), although their surrounding areas also had large populations. In contrast, India's largest city, Calcutta, contained over 9 million people in the 1980s, while Bombay had 8.2 million and Delhi had 5.1 million (Nagpaul, 1988:254). It is estimated that by the year 2000, these three cities will have populations of 19.6, 19.0, and 13.2 million, respectively (Nagpaul, 1988:256).

Of all the rapidly growing population areas of the globe, only China seems to have controlled the rate of urbanization to match its development potential in the past. China's government pursues a balanced growth process of rural and urban development. Under the *hukou* system, the rural population is prevented by law from moving to cities (Kim, 1988). This outlaws the kind of in-migration to the cities from rural areas that is common in the rest of the developing world.

Such balanced growth has had positive effects, and living in one of China's large cities may actually improve the quality of life (Bradshaw and Fraser, 1989). More recently, however, China has launched an extensive drive to integrate into the world economy, particularly by manufacturing consumer items. Recently the government has adopted rapid modernization policies that have canceled China's measured urban growth. It is now estimated that by the year 2000, China's two main cities will have populations slightly larger than India's: 23.7 million projected for Shanghai and 20.9 million projected for Beijing (Chen, 1988:247). It remains to be seen whether or not they will also develop the characteristic pattern of uneven development that plagues other societies.

China and India can also be contrasted with regard to the quality of life in their cities. Just the mention of India's cities (Calcutta, Bombay, Delhi) conjures up images of extreme poverty. To an extent, these images are accurate. The first two cities have large homeless populations, and all possess a declining quality of life. India's cities are surrounded by shantytowns, called *bustees,* that grow each day. Their presence has not prevented the city center from experiencing terrible overcrowding. The population density of Calcutta, for example, has been estimated at 45,000 residents per square kilometer, with the overwhelming majority living below the poverty line. Misery, disease, squalor, and malnutrition afflict the hordes of urban street people. The urban implosion of India is the consequence of rural push factors as well as urban pull. The "green revolution" that modernized India's agriculture has been relatively successful, which has led to a decline in the number of people needed to grow food in rural areas. As a result, in recent years more Indians are looking toward the cities for livelihood. Estimates are that by the year 2001, the urban population will have increased to 33.1 percent from 23.3 percent in 1981, or a *doubling* of the population living in cities (Nath, 1989:258).

The uncontrolled influx of people to India's cities is making a bad situation worse. As one observer notes:

> The most serious problems are related directly or indirectly to the extreme shortage of housing, and to inadequacy of physical and social infrastructures to meet the needs of the urban low- and middle-income groups. . . . The shortages are the principal cause of the progressive deterioration of the urban environment during the past 20–25 years.
> Proliferation of slums is the most visible symptom of the environmental deterioration. The other major symptom is the rapid increase in the levels of air and water pollution in or near the cities, far above the internationally accepted levels for maintaining human health and safety. (Nath, 1989:264)

Some of India's cities, such as Delhi, have large areas that are middle class and quite prosperous. Bombay was planned by the British as a colonial center and still retains its planned streets and residential districts that allow services to be delivered with some efficiency. It is a major center of industrial and service employment. In short, despite the declining quality of life, India's cities are not all mired in extreme poverty and deprivation (Misra, 1978).

Under the communists, the Chinese cities have fared comparatively better. One of the first acts of the Maoist regime in the 1950s was to eradicate the poverty and prostitution endemic to the streets of Shanghai, the focal point of global colonial interests. City services throughout China are regulated by the state and function to maintain the quality of life. There is little crime and few signs of poverty. The Chinese government has also pushed strict measures of birth control. In fact, most families are not permitted to have more than one child. This state policy of restricting population growth in a country of over 1 billion people has had some success in the cities, but is less successful in the countryside.

There is a visible contrast between India and China, as noted by Whyte and Parish (1984:2–3) with regard to Chinese cities:

> Slums and squatter settlements seemed absent, conspicuous consumption and foreign oriented life styles were not visible, a high degree of economic equality and security seemed to prevail, unemployment seemed absent, close-knit neighborhoods and families seemed to persist, and crime, drug addiction, prostitution, and other forms of deviance seemed minor or nonexistent.

In one area, however, Chinese cities seem to be worse than their counterparts elsewhere: pollution. Under the communists, no environmental regulations or controls were imposed on industrial development. The outcome has produced levels of pollution so high that they threaten the well-being of the population (see Chapter 14 for an extended discussion of the environment).

Shanghai, for example, may well be the world's most polluted city. Less than 5 percent of the city's sewage is treated, and 4 million cubic meters of raw sewage enter the city's river, the Huangpu, daily (Murphy, 1988:175). The Huangpu is Shanghai's principal source of drinking water. Industrial plants upstream also discharge untreated chemical wastes directly into the river. The long-term effects of this pollution on the population have yet to be documented. In addition to the problem of unclean drinking water, Shanghai shares with other Chinese cities an increasingly threatening air pollution problem. The major source of heating fuel is soft coal. This is an especially dirty energy source, spewing ash and poisonous gases such as sulfur dioxide into the air. One estimate is that 1,600 tons of fly ash and 1,500 tons of sulfur dioxide for each square kilometer of the city fall each year—a level unprecedented across the globe. Beijing has similar air pollution problems, especially during the cold winter, when the sun itself is obscured by coal smoke. At present, the Chinese government continues to ignore pollution problems and has done little in the way of environmental regulation.

Asia contains other rapidly growing regions (see Table 13.1). By the year 2000, the British Crown Colony of Hong Kong is expected to have 6.5 million people; Japan's urban population will be 111 million; North Korea's, 19.9 million; South Korea's, 36.2 million; Indonesia's, 64.1 million; Malaysia's, 8.8 million; the Philippines', 37.8 million; the city-state of Singapore's, 2.3 million; and Thailand's, 15.9 million. In

TABLE 13.1
Cities in Asia with Population over 10 Million by Location *(population in millions)*

City	1994	2015 (projection)	Density (square miles)
Tokyo-Yokohama, Japan	26,518	28,700	24,463
Shanghai, China	14,709	23,400	87,659
Bombay (Mumbai), India	14,496	27,400	120,299
Beijing, China	12,030	19,400	37,816
Calcutta, India	11,485	17,600	54,607
Seoul, South Korea	11,451	13,100	45,953
Jakarta, Indonesia	11,017	21,200	122,033
Osaka-Kobe, Japan	10,585	10,600	27,833
Tianjin, China	10,376	17,000	97,291

Sources: United Nations, Department for Economic and Social Information and Policy Analysis; *Statistical Abstract of the United States 1991,* U.S. Department of Commerce, Economics and Statistics Administration, Bureau of the Census, Table 1437, pp. 835–836.

all these countries, the primate cities—Tokyo-Yokohama, Pyongyang, Seoul, Taipei, Jakarta, Kuala Lumpur, Manila, and Bangkok—represent the centers of economic growth and development (Yeung, 1988:162). For example, Tokyo accounts for 60 percent of Japan's elite business leaders and 60 percent of the total capital invested, along with a third of all department store sales. Seoul contains 78 percent of South Korean business headquarters and 90 percent of all large enterprises, while accounting for 27.9 percent of South Korea's GNP. Finally, Bangkok houses one-third of Thailand's manufacturing and almost 80 percent of its banking, and contributes 26.8 percent toward the country's GNP (Yeung, 1988:162).

In all of these countries, urban development programs are often given a high profile. Among the issues that must be confronted is the lack of an adequate infrastructure to meet the demands of the growing urban population. The case of urban redevelopment in Manila is instructive. The Philippines suffered from the crony capitalism of the Marcos dictatorship for two decades before electing Cory Aquino (wife of the political opposition leader assassinated by Marcos' security forces) president of the country in 1986. Millions of dollars from the World Bank and other international agencies lined the pockets of the military leaders, while underdevelopment continued to plague the country; more than 80 percent of its export crops are owned by the Dole Pineapple conglomerate, and many Filipinos in rural areas work in a plantation system characterized by Ligaya McGovern (1996) as a "militarized zone." With perhaps the highest birth rate in all of Asia, overpopulation has led many Filipinos to leave rural communities for the capital city of Manila. The result has been uneven development within the Metro Manila region, where neighborhoods not much different from those in any modern city exist alongside squatter settlements. Box 13.3 describes efforts of the Philippine government to resettle nearly 6,000 squatter families from just one of these areas in the capital city.

BOX 13.3 RELOCATION OF SQUATTER SETTLEMENTS IN MANILA

The Pasig River Rehabilitation Program is about giving renewed life to one of the most important natural legacies of the Philippines. In the early 1950s, the Pasig River could still give water for homes, fish for the table, and irrigation for farms. But even then, the river was already slowly but steadily dying as people and industry used and abused it without much thought for the future. By the 1970s, all fish and water plants had disappeared. People could no longer swim in it or even use it to wash their clothes. There used to be an entire cottage industry of *lavanderas* along the banks of the river. That industry, which employed hundreds of women as well as men, collapsed as the river waters became dirtier and smellier.

Metro Manila has always been a socioeconomic magnet for the country's poor. A substantial number of them end up in the squatter colonies that continue to line stretches of the Pasig River. About 12,800 squatter families immediately fall within the scope of the river rehabilitation plan and need to be relocated. The squatter resettlement operations are guided by a master plan approved in 1994. Census and tagging of affected families living on easements of the Pasig River system is another component of resettlement. Started in 1996, this component has so far tagged 3,894 physical structures and interviewed 5,872 squatter families.

As of 1997, some 1,267 families had been relocated to a resettlement site in Dasmarinas Bagong Bayan, Cavite. The remaining families are within the jurisdiction of Pasig City. They have not been moved because of the city government's reluctance to issue a demolition order. Other factors that slowed the resettlement operation included the 1998 local elections (local politicians tend to rely heavily on votes from squatter colonies) and the refusal of local government officials to issue demolition notices (again, probably due to the elections).

Case studies show that most families started as migrants from the provinces. They came to Manila usually at a young age (one woman was 13 years old when she arrived, alone, in Manila to look for the parents who abandoned her while still a baby). Their idea of good fortune was going to the city where, according to them, life would be better. With very few exceptions, many ended up marrying young and usually had to stop going to school. In spite of the poverty they experienced as squatter dwellers, none of them thought seriously about going back to their provinces. Each case study depicts how a relocated family is coping with the stress of reestablishing their life in a resettlement site.

A typical story is that of Lorna, who was 16 years old when she and her sister left their home village in rural Visayas to try their luck in Manila. In the city, they stayed in the home of a rich aunt. It was here that Lorna met and eloped with her husband, who was then her aunt's personal driver. Lorna ended up living with her husband at a squatters' colony in Santa Mesa, Manila. In 1995, Lorna's family, by then numbering four children, was among 57 families relocated to Dasmarinas, Cavite.

Also among the studies is the story of Jennifer, a young mother of one, who has adjusted relatively quickly to resettlement. Holder of a college degree in education, she quickly found work as a full-time elementary school teacher at the resettlement site. A single parent (her husband left her in 1997), she lives with her parents and a teenage brother. Ambitious and hard working, Jennifer is doing her master's studies at Philippine Christina College.

In contrast, Purificacion's story is one of bitterness. Three years after being relocated, she and her husband can barely make ends meet to support four children and two grandchildren. As a squatter dweller in Manila, Purificacion had a thriving food vending business. That business disappeared when her family was resettled. She earns some money by doing odd jobs, such as sewing. Given a chance to reestablish her old *carinderia* in Manila, Purificacion says she will immediately leave the resettlement site.

In between these two extremes are case studies of individuals who find that life in the resettlement site is healthier, safer, and more secure. Difficulties remain, to be sure, especially because income opportunities are more limited than in Manila. Each study shows an individual family's unique response to the experience of socioeconomic dislocation. Most have made the commitment to stay, however, and many have used the helping opportunities to reestablish or even improve the income levels that they had while living as squatters in Manila. If there is a common characteristic that emerges from the people depicted in the case studies, it is their resilience, pragmatism, and determination to build a better life for themselves and their children.

Children from squatter settlements scavenge from garbage dumps outside Makati, the business and financial center of Manila.

BOX 13.4 SINGAPORE

Singapore is an island nation that is also a metropolitan area. For that reason, it is unique in the world. In 1965 the city/island of Singapore, with an area of 240 square miles, became independent of Malaysia. In 1984 its population was 2,616,000, composed mainly of Chinese, Malay, Tamil, and English people, and since its founding it has been ruled by Prime Minister Lee Kwan Yew, the head of a socialist party. From its beginnings, it already possessed the best harbor in Southeast Asia and a flourishing international trade. Over the last 20 years, it has become a banking and manufacturing center that attracts considerable foreign capital. As a result, Singapore has achieved the second highest per capita income (after Japan) in Asia.

Part of the reason for its success lies with the strict government control that is exercised over people's lives. In Singapore the national government operates a compulsory savings scheme, with all workers contributing 16.5 percent of their wages and employers contributing an additional 20.5 percent. The hundreds of millions of dollars collected each year from this scheme by the government are then used for economic development. These compulsory savings cannot be drawn out by workers until their retirement. However, workers are allowed to borrow from the fund to pay for government-constructed housing. As a result, about half the population lives in such government housing (Palen, 1990).

Singapore is a contradiction. It is a society that works extremely well as a dynamic economy with adequate housing, education, and medical care. The price that has been paid for such development is the complete government regulation of everyday life in the city, where the length of men's hair is fixed by law and even chewing gum is illegal. As one observer notes:

> To the visitor Singapore is clean, green (for years the government planted trees and bushes and grass in preference to making pavements), orderly, efficient and apparently perfectly safe . . . this general impression of safety, tolerance and efficiency is accurate enough. But behind this screen hides another Singapore, a city of violence, with a prison population proportionately half as big again as that of Britain. . . . Keeping Singapore clean and green needs more than propaganda broadcast over radio and television, though this goes on the whole time. For tossing his cigarette butt into a drain, Ng Ah Chai was fined $40. He was lucky; he could have been fined $500. (Josey, 1980:8)

In recent years several Asian nations, such as Korea, Taiwan, and Singapore, have exploded the myth of Third World dependency and the notion of "peripheral" development by growing rapidly as industrialized countries. They have been helped along by the influx of capital investment from Japan and the search for cheap labor by multinational corporations from across the globe. Many of the enterprises are joint domestic and foreign operations. Analysts today refer to the four "Asian tigers"—Hong Kong, Taiwan, South Korea, and Singapore—as especially successful areas of industrial development. In the 1980s, the Asian tigers led the world in percentage growth of gross domestic product at 7 percent a year (Berry, 1989:176), helped by the continuing demand for consumer goods—especially electronics, textiles, and clothing. This pattern of "export-led" development has also been tried successfully in Spain and Italy (see Chapter 12) among other countries.

An important characteristic of the Asian tiger development is the large role played by the national government in promoting growth. This intervention is not restricted to subsidization of capital investment and development but also includes strong control of unions and, often, harsh methods of regulating the working-class population; unions are not allowed, and child labor, low wages, and sweatshop conditions are common (see Box 13.4 on Singapore; Lee, 1982; Palen, 1990).

The presence of the Asian tigers changes the dynamics of global capital investment. In the future, countries such as South Korea may prove to be as competitive in manufacturing as established First World societies, or more so. This Asian *Pacific Rim,* which is linked to Japan (see Chapter 12) as well as the United States, contains economic forces that are emerging as a major sphere of power and development for the next century (Berry, 1989). Box 13.4 illustrates the dynamic aspect of Asian growth with the case of Singapore.

Africa and the Arab Countries

Of all the continents, Africa presents the clearest case of the overurbanization/ underurbanization dilemma. For the most part, this represents a legacy of years of colonial rule (Simon, 1989). South of the Sahara, the primate cities were all founded as trading centers and located near the coasts or with easy access by water to the coast. Some countries, such as Nigeria, have a moderately developed urban hierarchy containing several cities: Lagos, Ibadan, Kano, and Oshogbo. However, most, such as Kenya, are classic cases of primate city development. Kenya's capital, Nairobi, contains over half (57 percent) of the country's population. Here, as in most of Africa, the intermediate level of the urban hierarchy (i.e., cities with populations greater than 100,000 but less than 1,000,000) is notably absent.

Africa contains 54 separate countries, and it is sometimes difficult to generalize about the scale of development or urbanization. The north, which contains Arab countries, is highly urbanized. In 1980, 54 percent of the Libyan population and 53 percent of Tunisia's population were living in cities. Egypt contains one of the world's most populated cities, Cairo, with over 8 million people. At the other extreme, only 2 percent of the population in Burundi and 4 percent of the Rwandan population in eastern and central Africa were urbanized.

It is estimated that by the year 2000, almost one-half of the African countries will contain an urban population of at least 50 percent of the total (Rondinelli, 1988:295). In addition, urbanization is now proceeding rapidly. In 1950, only nine cities had a population of over 1 million. Estimates are that "by the end of the 1990s, 29 cities will have a population of between one and two million, another 17 cities will have between two and four million residents, and 11 more will exceed four million (Rondinelli, 1988:300).

Most African countries have a primate city land-use pattern similar to that of other Third World countries. The center consists of wide boulevards loaded with traffic and passing in between high skyscrapers built in the common "international style" of the developed West. Affluent natives and the foreign community make their home there. Beyond the glitter domes of development, the core is surrounded by mile upon mile of shantytowns—the most depressing agglomeration of ersatz housing imaginable—where entire families follow a precarious existence and play the "life lottery," hoping to acquire some meager portion of the wealth circulating through the center.

According to O'Connor (1978:86), around the central city

> is an extensive peripheral zone of crudely built shacks sometimes disparagingly termed a "septic fringe." In several cities such areas . . . now house over half the urban population and informal sector housebuilding constitutes a major economic activity.

Years of dominance by colonial powers, coupled with political conflict and poor local leadership, have left Africa in an undeveloped state. Countries continue to rely on natural resources and tourism for economic growth. With the discovery and exploitation of oil, Nigeria has acquired considerable capital, just as is the case with Libya. However, most countries remain locked in the grip of poverty, with limited industrial schemes and weak rural economies. Without extensive agricultural development, migration to the cities is an inevitable result. Extensive squatter settlements, or "bidonvilles," are characteristic of urban development (Aina, 1990; Schlyter, 1990).

The Arab cities are also scenes of uneven development. Cairo is known for its cosmopolitan population but also for its squatter settlements, such as the inhabitants of the immense cemetery, the City of the Dead, or the people known as the *zebaleen,* who live off of other people's garbage at the massive city dump (Abu-Lughod, 1969). Most Arab countries have medium-size cities and have not experienced a large rural exodus because their hinterlands have always been sparsely settled. The oil kingdoms of the Middle East have utilized their great wealth to create cities with modern architecture, such as Riyadh in Saudi Arabia and Baghdad in Iraq. These cities have remained showcases that are dependent on the oil industry monoculture.

Because islamic civilization advanced through the founding of cities, most Arab places have a long history of urban life. These were either trading or administrative centers (see Chapter 2). Cities were divided into quarters and provided people with stable neighborhoods. The *casbah,* or fortified area, is probably the most familiar name for such city quarters. Semiotic signs and symbols enable the pedestrian to negotiate what is often a maze of twisting streets (Boudon, 1986). Because of their age, many city thoroughfares were designed for donkey traffic and are quite narrow and confining. Finally, Arab cities contain the original shopping malls, or *bazaars.* They can be quite expansive, as in Istanbul, Turkey, occupying many city blocks where just about everything is bought and sold. In sum, quarters; narrow, winding streets; zigzags, courtyards, and alleyways; and bazaars are the distinguishing features of traditional Arab cities. To this urban fabric has been added, in some of the countries, the modern highways and megastructures financed by the oil monoculture.

Summary

Many Third World countries are mired in the vicious cycle of overurbanization/under-urbanization. The failure of agriculture means future populations face starvation or migration. The limited success of urban economic growth means that Third World cities will continue to play a marginal role in the global economy. Without balanced policies of development, these countries will face a bleak future. The issue is not simply growth and industrial development financed by the wealthy First World. Rather, there is a need for linked policies that improve agricultural production on the one hand and urban economies on the other. Especially in places such as Asia and Africa, it is essential that rural populations be stabilized so that the migration pressures on cities can be relieved. Yet development that is simply led by global capital investment will not head countries in that much-needed direction.

For example, over two decades ago the World Bank and the International Monetary Fund encouraged developing countries to build enterprise zones of manufacturing that would capture global investment. It is estimated that over 1 million people are now employed in industrial free-trade zones across the Third World (Peet, 1987:203). However, this development has come with a price. Much of the labor force consists of young women between 16 and 25 years old. The movement of young women from their home villages to employment in the city disrupts traditional family structures, and often this cheap supply of labor simply expands the patriarchal dominance over females in Third World countries. These women once constituted the backbone of traditional agriculture. With the young female population working in factories, rural agriculture in many countries is on the verge of collapse (Fuentes and Ehrenreich, 1987:203). Decline of rural economies pushes more and more people into the cities to seek a livelihood. As we have seen, this cycle of growth has disastrous results.

Shantytowns are growing rapidly in response to continued population expansion. São Paulo, Brazil, and Calcutta, India, respectively, have over 1 million and 2 million residents in their *favellas* and *bustees,* while Mexico City's *barriadas* contain over 4 million. The pattern of shantytown/central core *uneven* development is the exact opposite of that in the United States. As we have seen, the latter possesses maturing and relatively affluent suburbs surrounding a declining urban core. Third World cities reverse this pattern. But more graphically, the gap between the wealthy and the majority of the population is quite enormous.

For the most part, Third World governments have failed to achieve a better quality of life for their citizens. Ruling class domination of the economy and government leads to harsh measures of social control, hyperaggressive police, death squads, and repressive political dictatorship rather than enlightened policies of social reform. The passion of the Third World peoples manifests itself as a political clash between the fortunate few backed up by the government and the afflicted and disadvantaged many who face a declining quality of urban life.

The last two chapters presented a comparative perspective on urbanization. Once such an approach would have stressed the unique differences between advanced countries like the United States and developing nations such as Ghana in Africa. To be sure, such differences still exist. The formerly communist countries of Eastern Europe, for example, contain cities that have a primate role and centers that are neglected—in stark contrast to other nations of the world. Yet we have also seen in these two chapters that differences can be increasingly explained by a common connection to global processes of economic restructuring. As manufacturing decentralizes in search of cheap and compliant labor, investment circulates from country to country. Command and control centers coordinate the new flows of capital and commodities, with some (such as the finance capital concentrations in New York City, London, and Tokyo) becoming global cities. Thus, marked discontinuities no longer characterize the comparative perspective on urbanization; increasingly, we live in one world, not three.

CHAPTER

14

ENVIRONMENTAL ISSUES AND METROPOLITAN PLANNING

On October 1, 1980, the Love Canal section of the small town of Niagara, New York, located near the Canadian border, was declared an environmental disaster by President Carter. He ordered the permanent evacuation of all families from their homes. This action followed after two previous evacuations beginning in 1978 (Gibbs, 1981:5). Between 1920 and 1953 the area, an uncompleted canal, was used as a dump site for toxic chemicals from both the private sector and the federal government, particularly the U.S. Army. Homes had been built on top of landfill after the site was no longer used for dumping. Residents who lived along the canal had been exposed for many years to carcinogens from the toxic wastes that leaked into groundwater and oozed to the surface. In the 1970s, some of the 1,000 families that lived near the canal site began to complain about the high incidence of cancer, birth defects, miscarriages, and central nervous system diseases (Gibbs, 1981:3). Once the full extent of the poisoning became known, evacuations proceeded, but this action came too late to save many people from contracting cancer and other environmentally caused health problems from the area.

On April 26, 1986, a nuclear power plant located in Chernobyl, near the Ukrainian capital city of Kiev, exploded (Marples, 1988). The blast ignited the graphite moderating core of the reactor and resulted in the unleashing of intense radiation across a wide area of the former U.S.S.R. and Western Europe. Fallout from the disaster was measured as far away as the United States, and showed up in the dairy production of countries such as Norway, but the most severe effects were to hundreds of thousands

A damaged reactor at the Chernobyl nuclear power station is below the chimney at the center of this photo taken on May 9, 1986. The accident caused damage to the building, destroyed the reactor, killed at least 31 people, and raised levels of radiation throughout Europe.

of people living in the small towns of the area. Had the winds been blowing northward at the time, the Ukrainian people's historic city of Kiev (population: 2.4 million) would have been destroyed along with countless lives.

Official figures from the U.S.S.R. listed 31 people killed by the accident, but other estimates are as high as 500 (Marples, 1988:42). It was also estimated that as many as 50,000 people may have been directly exposed to excessive radiation, with nearly 500,000 long-term deaths predicted over the next few decades. The disaster forced permanent evacuation of persons and homes from a 30-kilometer zone, but over 100,000 children outside this area were also taken from their families to avoid exposure. Thousands of people were treated for radiation sickness. To this day, the region contains "hot spots" that are a threat to life.

Unfortunately, the above examples are not isolated cases. The United States, for instance, had its own potential nuclear catastrophe when the Three Mile Island reactor near Middletown, Pennsylvania, began emitting radioactive steam on March 28, 1979. That emergency was controlled without immediate loss of life or property. Many countries around the world—too many, in fact—have toxic pollution sites and unsafe radioactive facilities within their borders that affect the health of citizens every day. According to the Environmental Protection Agency, the United States alone contains between 30,000 and 50,000 toxic waste dumps (Gibbs, 1981:1).

In this chapter, we will use the sociospatial perspective to study environmental issues that result from, and create problems within, the expansion of urban and suburban settlement space. Because the effects of living and working arrangements in modern societies have impacts on the health and well-being of all residents, questions raised about environmental quality have as much to do with spatial issues as does the nature of economic development.

The environmental question and its relation to sociospatial development raise a variety of issues. One set inquires about the nature of constructed space, or "second nature," as Henri Lefebvre (1991) calls it. These issues involve the activity of *planning,* which seeks to obtain the best living and working arrangements in developing cities. The built environment—any built environment, such as a city or a mall—possesses attributes that may enhance or hinder the functioning of its use. Elements of the environmental fabric such as streets, pedestrian pathways, automobile corridors, and housing complexes can be placed in harmony with one another to facilitate the movement of people and vehicular traffic throughout the constructed space. Planning and architectural design address these kinds of issues, and we will consider them in the second section of this chapter.

A separate set of questions involves the inherent *quality of the environment.* How nurturing are the outcomes and by-products of social activities? What effects do the different types of activities, such as manufacturing, have on population groups within their vicinity? Who pays the environmental costs for development? What is the environmental impact of growth on the health and well-being of citizens? These and other questions frame the discussion of urban and suburban settlement spaces as a built environment. Let us explore this topic first and relate it to metropolitan considerations.

Environmental Quality

All societies seek to improve their quality of life through industrial development. Some countries, such as the United States, already possess a heritage of over 100 years of industrialization. While all human activities produce waste products that may adversely affect others, such as the effluent problem in an ancient city like Beijing, the scale and intensity of the environmental costs of industrialization are unprecedented. Manufacturing results in by-products that are toxic to animal and plant life; energy generation affects the temperature and quality of water and air with consequent effects on living things; and the extraction of "natural" resources, such as gold, results in environmental damage, such as the releasing of mercury into forest streams.

Societies around the globe have always put developmental desires above environmental concerns. In places such as China, Brazil, and sections of Europe, the health-related impacts of industrialization weren't even publicly recognized until quite recently, as we saw in the Chapter 13 discussion of Shanghai. For many centuries, all societies have held an unwavering belief in the idea of progress. Technology, science, and industrial growth, it is commonly understood, hold the promise of making our lives better and better. At present this assumption, which is at the core of modernist ideology (discussed shortly), has been called into question by some environmentally conscious individuals. According to Murray Bookchin (1990:20), "the certainty that technology and science would improve the human condition is mocked by the proliferation of nuclear weapons, by massive hunger in the Third World, and by poverty in the First World."

Most Americans appreciate the quality of life made available to them by the accomplishments of industrialization, but environmental activists suggest that this comfort for the relative few, globally speaking, has been acquired at a phenomenal cost to the many around the world. Furthermore, the unprecedented scale of human development today has resulted in global effects such as the widening hole in the ozone layer, global warming, acid rain, the eradication of entire plant and animal species, and the increasing threats to fresh drinking water. In response, environmentalists have called for a new ordering of global priorities that would seek out environmentally enhancing methods of industrial production and safe technologies (Naess, 1989; Gore, 1992). This means redefining the relationship between humans and settlement space on this planet.

As the level of awareness about these environmental issues increases across the globe, perhaps the issues of growth and development will be reexamined. New, environmentally sound methods of production and safe technologies such as rechargeable electric cars may usher in a transformed relation between people and the earth that preserves the well-being of both. Environmental concerns translate into new jobs and industries so that persisting development can be compatible with saving the planet (Kazis and Grossman, 1982).

The above concerns have been part of the environmental movement in the United States for some time. In the classical phase of activism, which began in the 1800s, Americans sought to protect large areas of the country from development and endangered species from destruction. Naturalists such as John Muir (1838–1914), who won protection for places like Yosemite and led the fight to establish the National Parks System, and organizations such as the Audubon Society, which has been at the forefront of the fight to save native birds and other wildlife, are examples of the classical phase of environmentalism (Bullard, 1990).

In the twentieth century, the mature phase of activism attacked the unbridled nature of industrialization in the United States. Concerned citizens fought for regulatory agencies, the passage of environmental statutes, and the establishment of industrial standards for control of pollutants. Over the years, regulations and legally binding statutes have been passed by both the federal and state levels of government. In 1970 the mature phase efforts culminated in the establishment of a separate federal agency under the executive branch, the Environmental Protection Agency (EPA), which serves as the public's advocate and coordinates research on environmental issues. In the 1970s the EPA was granted powers to regulate mileage standards for automobiles, thereby leading to the production of fuel-efficient engines. While there is still much work to be done and an imminent need for residents of the United States to rethink their relationship with the settlement space of advanced industrial society, the classical and mature phases of environmental activism have accomplished a great deal. This is especially the case when we consider the sensitivity many Americans have acquired in the last several decades to the need for fuel economy, recycling of waste products, and the search for safe technologies.

A third type of activism is *grassroots* or community efforts. Advocates of grassroots mobilization point out that while social concern about environmental quality is quite high in the United States, there is little appreciation for the social equity and social justice aspects of environmental impacts (Gale, 1983). These impacts are distributed inequitably across settlement space, creating a particular sociospatial dimension to the differential impact of costs. As one observer puts it:

> An abundance of documentation shows blacks, lower-income groups and working-class persons are subjected to a disproportionately large amount of pollution and other environmental stressors in their neighborhoods as well as in their workplaces. (Bullard, 1990:1)

The classical and mature phases of environmental activism have drawn in thousands of people, but the overwhelming majority of them and the concerns they express are middle class. The environmental costs paid by poor and minority people have been ignored. This sociospatial pattern of environmental costs is most revealing. Love Canal in New York State was situated within a white, working-class community, and it was these people who paid the price of toxic pollution. In Alabama, the town of Triana is judged the "unhealthiest town in America" (Reynolds, 1980:38). The residents of Triana are black, and they have been poisoned by the pesticide DDT and the chemical PCB from a creek whose quality is the responsibility of the federal government. Time and again research shows that society continues to produce toxic pollution and that poor and minority communities are its victims (Bullard, 1990; Berry, 1977; Blum, 1978).

Many of the hazards that differentially affect minorities and the poor are the consequence of industrial location patterns. Factories, chemical plants, mills, and the like are located in areas isolated from middle-class residential space. Because housing costs are lower in settlement spaces constructed around manufacturing areas, this is where poor people are more likely to live. Chemical emissions, spillovers of toxic by-products, unpleasant smells, and loud noises are just some of the hazards that affect these relatively powerless communities. These areas are often selected for unwanted land uses (or LULUs) such as landfills, toxic waste dumps, and effluent treatment plants. Hence, even though regulations have increased for safeguarding environmental quality, they have also led to injustices in the disposal of environmental threats, especially because of the inequitable siting of toxic dumps and landfills. For example:

> Four landfills in minority zip code areas represented 63 percent of the South's total hazardous-waste disposal capacity. Moreover, the landfills located in the mostly black zip code areas of Emelle (Alabama), Alsen (Louisiana), and Pinewood (South Carolina) in 1987 accounted for 58.6 percent of the region's hazardous-waste landfill capacity. (Bullard, 1990:40)

The differential locational impacts of environmental costs and the issues of social equity that they raise have yet to be addressed. Most communities seek to avoid becoming hosts to activities that represent social problems, such as outpatient mental clinics, halfway houses for criminals, and drug treatment centers. They advocate "not in my backyard" or NIMBY politics, which makes location a struggle that the least powerful community loses. The same is true for LULUs such as hazardous waste dumps or landfills. But allowing the stronger to make the weaker pay for all of society's costs violates principles of social justice.

In recent years, grassroots activists have organized poor and minority communities to fight for their rights. They are forcing the larger society to rethink environmental issues. If toxic dumps are unfair to any community, why not design production operations to minimize environmental damage? If landfills are becoming a problem, can't recycling and other, even more imaginative schemes be considered for the ever-increasing volume of garbage we all produce? How can we reorder our priorities to avoid having people pay unfairly for pollution? These and other questions will frame the agenda for grass-roots organizing and environmental activism in the years to come. This agenda will be aided by the way we have tried to relate the effects of our activities to the sociospatial organization of society.

Environmental concerns also raise issues related to the way we have designed settlement space and how best we can improve our arrangements for living and working together. The remainder of this chapter looks at people's attempts to change their circumstances through the specific manipulation of space, design, and public policy. We consider the case of planning, the use of rational schemes of land use, home construction, and environmental design to make metropolitan life better in general and to improve the quality of life of specific groups of individuals. We will consider public policy, the active intervention of the government at various levels to bring about social changes through public means, in Chapter 15.

Metropolitan Planning

Pruitt-Igoe was a massive public housing project constructed in the early 1950s in St. Louis, Missouri. It was inspired by the work of the leading architect of the post-war generation, Le Corbusier of France, and executed in design by several famous architects, including Minoru Yamasaki. The project consisted of 33 eleven-story buildings with a total of 2,700 apartment units on a site that stretched out to almost 60 acres (about one-tenth of a square mile). The project represented the zenith of government-sponsored high-rise/low-income housing construction. Yet residents experienced problems almost immediately after Pruitt-Igoe opened in 1954 (Montgomery, 1988). Elevators broke down and were not repaired. Children were injured playing in corridors or stairwells that could not be monitored adequately by adults. Crime began to terrorize residents due to the large scale of design that allowed muggers to remain hidden. People complained of isolation from friends and neighbors.

Within five short years after opening, occupancy rates were already on the decline despite the subsidized rent. By 1970, vacancy rates in the buildings had reached more than 50 percent. The St. Louis housing authority made the fateful decision that the problems with the project were insurmountable and ordered its complete demolition. By 1976, the entire project was torn down. Pruitt-Igoe was a combination of architecture design following modernist principles that pursued progress in human/spatial relations and, simultaneously, a type of government intervention that made apartments at subsidized rents available to poor people. Architectural critic Charles Jencks sets this date as the time when modernist ideas about the promise of architecture as promoting social progress gave way to the postmodern period with its abandonment of such lofty aspirations (Holston, 1989). With the failure of Pruitt-Igoe, and other public housing projects, came the realization that modernist architecture and government intervention in public housing required reexamination. In Chicago, the in-

The demolition of Pruitt-Igoe on April 21, 1972. Compare this case with the vision of Le Corbusier on page 322.

famous Cabrini-Green projects are now being dismantled and replaced by single-family town houses (see Box 14.1).

Within the metropolitan region, we would find separate agencies devoted to planning that employ significant workforces at each level of government—including each city, suburb, and township within the metropolitan area, plus a countywide and regional planning department! Yet our metropolitan environments seem to be characteristically unplanned. This "planning paradox" (see Gottdiener, 1977) exists because in the United States planners have very little direct power to enact their schemes and for the most part are confined instead to advisory roles. The civic culture of the United States has always resisted direct intervention in the market by government. In the early stages of urbanization during the nineteenth century, most cities were constructed with little planning. Yet the market, as economists know, does not provide adequate amounts of the infrastructure—roads, streets, utilities, and transportation facilities—needed by society.

In addition, early industrial cities possessed a chaotic mix of land uses. Working-class homes were sited next to factories belching pollution. Narrow streets wandered in and out of districts without plan, restricting movement. Construction was not attuned to the aesthetic principles of architectural design. This ugliness and haphazard growth finally stimulated a response. Around the turn of the century, the "City Beautiful" movement sought to inspire localities to adopt aesthetically pleasing architecture and land-use planning principles. These ideas were showcased in the 1898 World's Fair in Chicago (see Chapter 3). Proper design was touted as the means of improving the urban quality of life, and the leaders of many cities were inspired by this exposition to give comprehensive urban planning a try.

BOX 14.1 REDEVELOPMENT OF CABRINI-GREEN

In 1929 Harvey Zorbaugh published his study *The Gold Coast and the Slum*, a description of Chicago's wealthy lakefront neighborhoods along Lake Michigan (the Gold Coast) and of the slum area of tenement housing just half a mile inland. In the 1950s, the slum area was cleared and replaced with some two dozen high-rise public housing units called Cabrini-Green. In the early years most of the occupants were white, but by the 1960s the area was almost entirely composed of poor black families. The film *Cooley High* (1966) was shot at the local high school of the same name. By the 1980s the projects, sometimes called the worst in America, had become symptomatic of all that was wrong with public housing in the United States: All of the residents had incomes below the poverty line; most units were single-parent households; and drugs, gangs, and crime were rampant. In 1996 Dantrell Davis, a seven-year-old boy, was shot and killed while walking to the elementary school across the street from the project, still holding his mother's hand.

For years the site remained not simply a black spot in the city's history but also a controversial area with respect to plans for urban redevelopment. Many floors of the buildings were boarded up and some of the buildings were vacant, while the remainder sported large graffiti showing which gangs controlled the buildings. The *Chicago Tribune* sponsored a design competition for the best redevelopment plan for the area. Neighborhood organizers charged that the city wanted to turn the land over to real estate developers for middle- and upper-class housing close to the downtown area, and city planners looked for ways to relocate low-income households that would be displaced by the removal of the buildings. Finally, in 1998 and 1999, eight of the high-rise buildings were demolished in a scene reminiscent of the earlier destruction of the Pruitt-Igoe projects in St. Louis (see the photo on page 313).

In the area adjacent to the project, new townhomes selling for $180,000 were built by a developer, seeming to confirm the fears of neighborhood activists. But along with the 65 new units in the Mohawk North condominium

In short, because the U.S. culture has a commitment to free-market solutions, only when the problems of growth were acknowledged did adequate community support for planning appear. Since the turn of the century, most cities and counties have retained a planning staff to help with the problems of development. But rather than discuss the history of planning per se, let us consider some sociological aspects of the profession.

The Sociology of Land-Use Planning

The most basic kind of planning involves *zoning* for land use. Based on the principles that like activities should be located near one another and that industrial activities and residential areas should be separated, zoning partitions metropolitan space into distinct areas for development are 16 units of public housing. From the outside, the public housing units are indistinguishable from the private development, and the floorplans of each unit are similar "railroad flats" common to both older and newer housing in this area of the city (see the accompanying photo). By dispersing low-income households and creating, in effect, a mixed-income housing development the city hopes to eliminate the problems of concentration and isolation of poor families described by Massey and Denton in *Urban Apartheid*. In the coming decade, the high-rise public housing developments will disappear, to be replaced by new rowhouses—perhaps the end of the slum described some 75 years earlier in *The Gold Coast and the Slum*.

New housing in Mohawk North that replaces high-rise public housing at Cabrini-Green.

each activity. Space is partitioned into zones reserved for residential use, commercial activities, and industrial work, among other functions. Planners use detailed maps to draw up land-use guides that constitute the zoning master plan. In most cases, such a plan needs to be adopted by local residents or their elected representatives. Changes and modifications are always a possibility with land-use schemes, but once zoning has been adopted by the local city council, it carries the weight of law. Through the political power to control the use of land, planning agencies can shape the pattern of metropolitan development. Their powers, however, are dependent on the local political authority.

Planners also work with elected officials and representatives from the business community to develop new uses of land. They may set aside land or help design an industrial park for factories and businesses, an office tower or city skyscraper complex, a mall, or a large residential development. New developments require infrastructure planning as well as the construction of the buildings themselves. Roads have to be put in along with sewer and utility lines and the like. The impact on the surrounding area also requires careful thought and planning. New developments, just like zoning schemes, must be approved by local political authorities. Sometimes citizens object to new growth, and developments can be blocked or changed according to local residents' desires. Most of the time, however, local elected representatives approve growth, since that is the priority of city government. Local communities often feel they must compete against one another to develop new industrial parks, shopping malls, and office centers, adding to the pressures for growth across the metropolitan region. Box 14.2 describes the efforts of planners and politicians in Minnesota to control these problems.

Physical Determinism

Planners believe that the optimal living and working arrangements for people can be achieved through the use of construction, design, and landscaping technology. This approach assumes that people's behavior can be controlled or channeled into desirable forms through the manipulation of physical design. As Herbert Gans (1968:28–33) has argued, this commits the fallacy of assuming that physical design will determine personal behavior. As social scientists are aware, behavior is determined by a complex relation of various social processes interacting in and with spatial forms rather than the influence of the physical environment alone. In practice, planners and architects seem to ignore the social basis of behavior and falsely believe that construction design by itself can bring about desired change, such as increasing the frequency of neighborly interaction. Physical determinism, which privileges the abstract space of the planning professional over social space, has been responsible for some spectacular failures of planning, including the Pruitt-Igoe and Cabrini-Green housing projects, where it was thought that new architectural designs would somehow alleviate the social problems brought about by social exclusion. We shall discuss some of these failures below when we consider how the "utopian" impulse has influenced the design of human environments.

Elitist/Populist Dilemma

Professional planners work within a political milieu because local citizens are endowed with the authority to approve many development schemes. Because of their training in graduate programs of architecture and planning, many urban planners acquire the elitist assumption that they know best what a good plan should be like since they are the technical experts. They, along with the politicians or elected representatives, also assume there is some easily defined public interest that planning can fulfill. But many dimensions of the democratic process of planning are often ignored, such as public participation in the selection of development goals—that is, the open discussion of what kind of community people really want and the open search for alternatives to any proposed growth scheme. A true democratic relationship among planners, politicians, and the public would involve such an open search for desirable goals and alternative growth schemes.

BOX 14.2 THE TWIN CITIES FISCAL DISPARITIES PROGRAM

The Minnesota Fiscal Disparities Act of 1971 created the only metropolitan-wide tax base sharing system in the United States. Under the program, each taxing jurisdiction in the seven-county area contributes 40 percent of the growth in the value of its commercial-industrial tax capacity base since 1971 into a regional pool. Taxing jurisdictions in the program include municipalities, counties, school districts, and special districts, and number roughly 300. However, contributions to, and distributions from, the pool are computed at the municipality level (195 in 1995). Municipalities receive a distribution of tax base from the pool based on population and total market value of property per capita relative to the rest of the region. A muncipality with average market value per capita receives a portion of the pool equal to its share of regional population. If its market value per capita is lower than average, it receives more than its population share.

Overall, Fiscal Disparities cleverly balances regional goals with local autonomy. It is designed so that it both narrows property tax rate disparities by taxing part of the local tax base at a uniform rate and maintains local control over local property tax rates. By 1992, the pool represented nearly $300 million, or $125 per capita, in tax capacity. By 1995 the absolute size of the pool had declined by roughly 17 percent ($50 million) from its peak in 1992 and by slightly more (18 percent) in per capita terms. However, increases in the tax rate on the pool offset much of the decline. As a result, revenues from the pool increased from about $114 in 1990 to a high of $157 per capita in 1994. Despite some recent erosion in the size of the pooled tax base, the Fiscal Disparities pool still generates significant revenues.

More than twenty years later, the Minnesota Fiscal Disparities is still the only system of its kind. However, tight local conditions at both the federal and state level in the 1990s have focused attention again on tax base sharing. At the state level, tight budgets in the early 1990s led to lower than average growth or real declines in state aids to local governments and school districts in many states. Because of budget concerns, federal aid to states is also likely to decline by significant amounts during the next decade, placing further stress on state-local finance systems. Current trends clearly imply that the federal declines will be concentrated in redistributive programs, increasing the need for state and local approaches to general equity concerns. At the same time, American metropolitan areas continue to decentralize in ways that may be both inequitable and inefficient. In such an environment, tax base sharing at either the regional or state level is a likely candidate for discussion. (Luce 1998)

The elitist/populist dilemma concerns the contradictory role of planners who function as technical experts who know what is best for the community, but must nevertheless acquire community support for their plans. This *politics of planning* does not always achieve the optimal results. Planners must court citizen support for a plan to be approved, but planners and citizens rarely work together in an open process of preparing for the community's future. This process presents a limited version of what democratic planning would be like; it represents a dilemma. Only in some instances have citizens and planners achieved an appropriate balance of democratic process, citizen participation, and planners' goals, such as in the active planning for rent control in the city of Santa Monica, California, and the efforts toward balanced growth achieved by Burlington, Vermont (Clavel, 1985). Box 14.3 illustrates the case of Bellevue, Washington, where citizens worked together with planners and local politicians to preserve the city's quality of life.

The planning process is a complex one, and sociologists studying the three-way relation among politicians, planners, and the public have observed interesting aspects of social decision making (Gans, 1968). Because development goals are often the expression of special interests, and because projects are often renegotiated in response to the public's concerns, the outcome of metropolitan planning appears to lack the coherence that technical ideas profess. An example of the *unintended* consequences of planning due to community politics is a case study of a suburban area on Long Island, New York (Gottdiener, 1977). In this town, planners worked with local politicians and businesses to build a shopping center adjacent to a large residential development. The residents were in favor of the center, but after it opened, they discovered that it increased traffic on their local streets. This outcome was not considered in the original plans.

Residents rallied to place political pressure on the local government to supply traffic lights to slow traffic down. Their concerns were not addressed until the residents had organized themselves to maintain constant pressure on local politicians. The planners and government refused to install the stop lights, however, because the volume of traffic was not great enough. In a compromise, stop signs were installed within the development. No one wanted stop signs, and from a planning point of view they are not the best controls of traffic, but that is what the residents received as a consequence of the negotiation process. A result that no one desired became the outcome of compromise because negotiations and political struggle are also part of the planning process.

Utopian Schemes: Howard, Le Corbusier, and Wright

Idealistic thinkers in centuries past lamented the evils of civilization and created a genre of literature known as *utopian* writing. Plato's *Republic* might be the earliest example, but the consummate vision belongs to Thomas More's *Utopia.* These accounts of some fictional paradise provide us with a means of measuring the prospects of human endeavor by showing how we can perfect ourselves and our society even while exploring our all too frail shortcomings as a species. Over the centuries, utopian literature has provided important inspiration to socially concerned individuals, as has the equally fascinating genre of dystopian writing, especially science fiction's dystopian accounts of life in future cities (such as the film *Blade Runner*).

Utopia, from the Greek word meaning "no place," and *dystopia,* a more recently coined expression that means an imaginary place of dread, are examples of places that exist elsewhere in time and space. While the former usually signals the modernist theme of progress, the latter represents our fears about the myth of progress. This yearning for the perfection of settlement space and the realization that it may never be

BOX 14.3 COMMUNITY PLANNING IN BELLEVUE, WASHINGTON

In much of the United States, recent patterns of development have fostered suburbanization that has torn the city apart. Few cities have been able to resist this process, which eventually leads to the deterioration of the downtown. When faced with this dilemma, the citizens of Bellevue, Washington, decided that they wanted to preserve the city and its urban way of life in the face of suburbanization pressures. They enacted a series of land-use regulations and initiated projects that channeled development into preserving the urban form. The city was small enough and people were able to cooperate sufficiently with politicians, planners, and one another to make this happen. According to the account of William H. Whyte (1988:307–308),

> The central business district that Bellevue is building does not sprawl; it has a tight pattern of development with well-defined edges. Within the core of the CBD, developers can put up buildings with a floor-area ratio as high as 8 by providing bonusable amenities—up to 10 by providing specified public spaces. Beyond the CBD, however, developers must build low, with the maximum floor-area ratio a meager .5. This represents a clear public decision to concentrate and direct development rather than simply let it happen.
>
> Downtown, as a consequence, remains quite compact—an easy walk from one side of it to the other. . . . Bellevue people insist that there is indeed more walking and that within the past two years the increase in walking in the core area has been quite noticeable. Because of the concentration, there are more people there and more amenities to prompt them to walk. . . . They believe the very structure of downtown is likely to induce more walking. Bisecting downtown is a central pedestrian corridor. At one end there is an attractive shopping mall; at the other, a unique transit center, with lots of seating and overhead cover. Developers along the corridor contribute segments to it, and via incentive zoning, bonuses are given to provide a rich townscape of trees, handsome paving, lighting, and canopies to temper the Northwest's drizzle. . . .
>
> The car is being tamed. Instead of more parking, the city is mandating less. New buildings used to have to provide a standard five spaces per thousand square feet of office space. This has been cut to three spaces. To pinch matters further, commercial parking lots and garages are forbidden in the CBD. About half of all new employees working in downtown will have to join car pools or take a bus to get there.

The case of Bellevue represents some important ways urban life is being preserved, such as livable streets, the discouragement of deconcentration, and the development of attractive amenities downtown. The success of this makeover, however, depends on the support of the people, because planning is political as well as technical. So far, according to Whyte, Bellevue has been successful.

---

attained due to the limitations of our civilization constitute an important strain in Western literature and cinema. The philosopher Henri Lefebvre (1991) calls all such spaces that exist in our minds as imaginary places *heterotopias*. As mental conceptions, heterotopias have the ability to influence our behavior and to define prospective schemes for architects and planners.

In nineteenth-century Europe, when the evils of industrialization and urbanization became a major social concern, individuals exercised the utopian spirit by conceiving of alternative urban environments. Some of these modernist visions were highly influential on the planning and architectural professions, and indeed by the twentieth century, architects no longer confined themselves to the design of individual buildings but composed manifestos and schemes that addressed the living and working arrangements of the entire city space itself. Among the important conceptualizers of new urban environments are Ebenezer Howard, Le Corbusier, and Frank Lloyd Wright. The modernist vision of each was expressed, respectively, as the Garden City, the Radiant City, and Broadacre City.

The Garden City

Ebenezer Howard, who lived during the turn of the last century, was a social reformer in England. Like others of his time, including Friedrich Engels, he was appalled at the social costs of British industrialization. Some thinkers, such as Robert Owen, responded by founding a utopian movement that advocated the construction of communities (such as New Harmony, Indiana) that would counteract the evils of the industrial city but required a fundamental break with acceptable ways of family or social life. Howard's response was to propose an alternative way of living that everyone could follow, even those uninterested in the utopian movement's social change.

To Howard, the city represented the future of economic growth, but it was, to express it directly, a lousy place to live. In contrast, the rural areas remained in organic harmony with their surroundings, but they were afflicted with limited economic opportunity. Howard's vision combined the two. He proposed that all new industrial growth be channeled to new locations in outlying areas that would combine industrial employment with country living on a moderate, human scale. These "garden cities" would represent the very best of city and country living.

The concept of the garden city proved to be very powerful. Capitalist industrialization in the nineteenth century knew no bounds. The older cities were crowded and polluted, and large cities gobbled up their adjacent countrysides in a relentless process of accretion. Because planners understood that growth was inevitable anyway, they were attracted to Howard's idea of breaking urban expansion off and aspiring to locate new industry and housing in moderate-size communities.

Howard's ideas influenced the "new town" movement in England, which has been responsible for building hundreds of such places, as well as the measured establishment of medium-size cities in Russia, although the latter case does not embody the ideal of the "garden," or suburbanized urban environment. In the United States a group of architects, notably Clarence Stein, popularized Howard's approach. Working with local authorities and developers, they constructed several places across the country, including Garden City, New York, outside of Manhattan, and Baldwin Hills, California, located in Los Angeles. Ebenezer Howard lived to see the opening of the New York community in 1928.

In practice, most of the American garden cities lack their own industry and hence are little more than middle-class suburban housing developments with some interest-

The Garden City plan of Ebenezer Howard. Housing was integrated with parks and gardens, while railway lines and manufacturing were zoned out to the periphery.

ing features, such as shared public spaces. These ideas, all derivative of Ebenezer Howard's vision, are still put in practice by developers of large suburban residential projects such as planned unit developments, or PUDs, which we shall discuss shortly.

The Radiant City

Le Corbusier was the professional name of the Swiss-born French architect Charles-Edouard Jeanneret (1887–1965). Along with several German architects, such as Walter Gropius and Ludwig Mies van der Rohe, Le Corbusier is considered the founder of the *international style* of design and one of the leaders of the modernist movement in architecture. The type of building associated with this movement is familiar to anyone who has seen the skyline of a large city, because the design concepts took over the world of architecture following World War II. International style buildings are clean, straightforward, rectangular shapes with flat roofs. They are framed in steel and feature large glass windows that are sealed shut. Not until the postmodern architectural revolt of the 1980s were downtown office buildings liberated from the dictates of this concept.

Le Corbusier was influential because he propagated certain ideas about city living instead of confining his practice to building design. He believed in the triumph of technology over social conditions of industrialization. Buildings themselves were to be "machines for living," that is, the most efficient designs for the sustenance of everyday activities. The urban environment would itself have to be changed to conform to the dictates of more enlightened architectural design. Because Le Corbusier lamented the terrible social costs of industrialization, he proclaimed the modernist rallying cry, "Architecture or Revolution," sincerely believing that capitalist countries had little choice but to follow his ideas or confront the revolt of the urban masses.

Le Corbusier's ideas and those of his contemporaries constituted the ideology of *modernism,* which legitimated the notion of progress and the improvement of human conditions year after year through the intervention of technology. Modernist ideology asserted that the lot of individuals could be improved by the acquisition and application of knowledge—scientific, technological, architectural, social, and psychological. Part of modernist culture was the celebration of architecture and "modern" ideas about city planning.

Le Corbusier's plan for an entire metropolis, the "radiant city," reordered social space across a large, industrial aggregation. Instead of the relatively low density of housing and chaotic land use that was characteristic of the cities at that time, Le Corbusier proposed that buildings should be high-rises. By condensing the living space using building height, open spaces would be liberated, and Le Corbusier envisioned these spaces as parks that would surround residential clusters, thereby transforming the congested, sprawling industrial city into an open, airy, and efficient place of mobility and light.

A second important feature of the new design followed from Le Corbusier's and the modernist belief in the virtues of technology. Le Corbusier believed that the widespread use of public transportation and auto modes of transport would vastly improve

The Radiant City. Le Corbusier's plan for Antwerp (1933), never built. From *La ville radieuse* (1935). See the photo on page 313 for comparison of how Le Corbusier's ideas went wrong.

the efficiency of urban scale. He proclaimed the "death of the street," that is, the pedestrian thoroughfare characteristic of all cities in the past. He envisioned instead rapid movement facilitated by autos, trains, highways, and feeder roads of people and commodities between the various nodes of urban space—residences, factories, shops, and government buildings.

The lesson of Pruitt-Igoe (discussed earlier) illustrates the deeply ingrained physicalist fallacy of Le Corbusier. Construction design, which disregards social process, cannot alone change everyday life. Unfortunately, the modernist ideas of the international style, and especially the concepts of Le Corbusier, were highly influential in urban planning through the 1960s. Along with Pruitt-Igoe, another major tragedy of planning in this vein is exemplified by the case of Brasília, the capital city of Brazil, which was constructed following Le Corbusier's idea of the radiant city.

Designed by the architects Lucio Costa and Oscar Niemeyer in 1960 and located in the interior 600 miles from the Rio de Janeiro coast, Brasília looks like a giant bird from an aerial view. But on the ground, its limitations have become legendary. The "death of the street" produced an austere, alienating environment in which urban life is shrouded in anonymity. Neighboring and community interaction have all but disappeared because of the inability to overcome the automobile-based lifestyle and the imposing superhuman social scale, which has led to feelings of isolation and anonymity among residents (Holston, 1989).

Crime plagues the vacant parks, ramps, and open spaces. With all buildings looking the same, a horrible ennui afflicts local residents who live and work in interchangeable modules. The city was built to be the country's new capital, and so government administrators and their support staffs find employment there. However, Brasília has failed to attract the diverse kinds of industry and everyday life that would convert it to a major city. Brasília, among other austere creations of modernist city planning, reminds us graphically of the perils of physical determinism and the need for architects to work in conjunction with social science to bring about an improvement of urban conditions.

Broadacre City

Frank Lloyd Wright (1869–1959) was the premiere U.S. architect for most of the past century. His ideas, unlike Le Corbusier's, remain appreciated today, even if some of his designs have become outdated. Wright was no modernist. In fact, he was much influenced by the crafts movement in the United States and by Oriental architecture, particularly the Japanese use of interior space. Wright believed that structures should be organic extensions of natural environments. Houses, for example, should emerge from the crown of the hill rather than being built at the top, since the latter should be reserved for nature. They should embody a fluid connection with the world outside, and their construction should celebrate natural materials and settings, as exemplified by the Kaufmann home, Falling Water House (built in 1936), outside Pittsburgh, Pennsylvania. This summer home is made of concrete that is stacked like pancakes on three levels (called *cantilevering*) so that it sits on a rock above a forest stream. The water flows under the lower level and out over a falls. Sitting in the living room, one can watch the water flow and hear the stream as it runs over the rock below.

Frank Lloyd Wright was not enamored with the American city that he saw developing after World War II, and wrote that with each new skyscraper he saw only the death of the city. Wright's vision of the new city possesses some similarities with that of Ebenezer Howard, especially the desire to merge the city and the country, except Wright thought in modular terms. Instead of a single, human-scale community, Wright envisioned an immense metropolis whose internal structure reduces space to a human scale through modular design. Each family would be assigned a single-family home on an acre of land! The space would enable families to grow their own food and to modify their surroundings according to their own personal tastes. Houses would be arrayed on an expansive grid. Wright also liked the possibilities of the auto, and his Broadacre City assumed that the car would be the basic means of transportation. Each place would be accessible by interconnected roads and highways feeding into and out of grids. Commercial shopping would take place in regularly spaced shopping centers, and industry would be isolated in specifically designed factory areas that were zoned exclusively for business.

Wright's scheme seems almost like the massive suburban environments of today—and indeed Wright saw little need for the city. He was one of the earliest architects to think up the concept of the shopping center, and his factory-zoned area is recognizable as the industrial park of the present, a common feature of metropolitan environments. The key element of Wright's vision, however, seems elusive—namely, the one-acre allotment of land that resolved the city/country dilemma at the smallest scale of each individual family. While suburban residences often have ample backyards, these are reserved for leisure activities, including, perhaps, a swimming pool. But Wright's vision of every family providing for its sustenance through backyard farming seems far removed from the realities of metropolitan life.

Our review of architectural visionaries provides us with some alternative ways to think about massive metropolitan environments and points out that urbanized landscapes do not necessarily have to assume the form they now possess. The present-day givens of metropolitan development patterns seem to find no other way of building except unending sprawl. But alternatives are possible; only the continuing belief in physical determinism, which wrongly suggests that architecture and urban planning can alter social processes, needs to be abandoned. Developers combining proper design with environmentally aware social science that uses the legacy of utopian ideas have had some successes, such as the new towns of Columbia, Maryland, and Garden City, New York.

Planning Critics: Jacobs, Krier, and the Goodmans

Ideas about planning have benefited from the work of critics who have taken both architects and the planning profession to task for neglecting the human values embodied within social space (Mayo, 1988). Four of the most influential critics are Jane Jacobs, Leon Krier, and the team of Paul and Percival Goodman.

Jane Jacobs

Jane Jacobs (1961) is concerned that we preserve the city as a viable place to live. She believes that the best cities have a vital and active street life. Her critique of urban planning claims that too many projects have ignored the role of human interaction as providing the life blood of city culture when most city inhabitants live in apartments with restricted space. For Jacobs, active urban life can never be planned because people invent uses for space. They accommodate the pursuit of their needs to the streets, parks, and playgrounds that they find around them. City planning that discourages this social interaction through the limiting of public or social space winds up also destroying the city itself.

For example, adolescents in the city spend a good deal of time out on the streets where they live. Over the years, an incredible variety of street games has arisen using this space, and many of these have been handed down through the generations, such as "Ring-a-Levio," "Johnny on the Pony," "Hop-Scotch," rope-jumping games, and stick ball. Skateboarders and others make use of urban spaces in ways never envisioned by architects and planners (Bordain, 1999). Projects planned only in terms of efficient automobile traffic (such as Le Corbusier's radiant city or Brasília, the capital of Brazil) arrange for wide thoroughfares that are heavily traveled. But such efficiency in the name of transportation destroys the ability of children to use the streets for play. Can you imagine active street games in the immense auto corridors of Los Angeles or on the well-traveled two-way streets in your own community? In contrast, Jacobs celebrates the streets and advocates blocking them off on a periodic and temporary basis to allow for neighborhood interaction. This is just what many cities now do when they sponsor neighborhood festivals during the summer months.

According to Jacobs, human-scale public spaces in the city, such as sidewalks, parks, and playgrounds, provide people with a number of resources: (1) They constitute learning environments for children, (2) they allow for parents' surveillance of the neighborhood and their children's activities, and (3) they facilitate intimate, primary relations among neighbors, thereby providing a strong sense of community (see the case studies of street corner societies in Chapter 8).

Jane Jacobs's ideas have had a strong impact on the way urbanists and planners think about city life. Local governments encourage park use, street festivals, temporary blocking of community roads, and toleration of sidewalk vendors. But not all of Jacobs's ideas have been accepted. Some of her followers advocated the elimination of elevators in apartment buildings to facilitate neighborly interaction—but with disastrous results for the residents of these buildings. Planners who emphasize revitalizing streets and city parks must take the high crime rate into account; in many cities, downtown revitalization efforts using Jacobs's ideas have failed due to the fear of urban crime on the part of suburban residents.

Jacobs's ideas about community may also be passé. Many city residents socialize with networks of friends and relatives who do not live nearby, as we saw in Chapter 9. Teenagers may prefer to travel to their own friendship networks rather than socialize on the street. On the whole, however, Jane Jacobs's ideas have influenced urbanists because she has captured the heart and soul of urban culture. Her importance lies in convincing us that urban culture depends on the relationship between personal interaction and public space. The fact that this culture is in danger of dying today is certainly not the fault of her conception. As we direct our attention to metropolitan regions, it is important to ask whether her ideas are equally relevant for suburban settlement spaces.

Leon Krier

As a contemporary architect practicing in Germany, Krier's ideas have been highly influential in the United States in recent years. Like Jacobs, his main concern is in revitalizing urban culture. He views this as principally a problem of scale: The contemporary city has grown too large to shelter a livable environment, and it is necessary to return urban building to a human scale. Krier's model of the city is the preindustrial town, and he advocates a return to the type of building characteristic of societies hundreds of years ago. In this sense, Krier is a critic of modernist ideology and one of the inspirations for *postmodern* architecture.

According to Krier, settlement space should be divided into districts with no more than 15,000 people in each subdivision. Ample use is made of squares, monuments, and public spaces, which should have the proportions of the classical preindustrial towns. All of these changes, inspired by "retro" thinking, would return urban space to a human scale.

Krier also has his critics (see Dutton, 1989). More so than Jacobs, he commits the fallacy of physical determinism. He ignores social process and the larger societal forces that make up the modern city and would make the kind of transition in scale that he envisions difficult for all but the most affluent residents. Krier's proposal, like those of most architects, also commits the elitist/populist fallacy. He never asks what people want; he only dictates design prescriptions through abstract space.

Despite these drawbacks, Leon Krier's work has had an enormous influence on architects designing new communities in the United States who seek to overcome modernist ideology. Among the most significant is the team of Andres Duany and Elizabeth Plater-Zyberk, who are identified with the new traditionalist movement, or the new urbanism (Langdon, 1988). The new traditionalists are especially concerned with the design and social failures of suburbia. They consider suburbs to be sterile environments that prevent an active community life and, by their very nature, promote excessive use of the automobile.

Duany and Plater-Zyberk have designed several planned communities, such as Seaside, located 100 miles west of Tallahassee, Florida. Seaside is a community of 300 homes and 200 apartments that lies on 80 acres. Its human scale is accentuated by residential housing that is consciously based on the forms of 100 years past. All houses have front porches, and most are located on pedestrian paths rather than roads. Lots are small and narrow to facilitate social interaction among neighbors. There are ample walking paths and places where residents can meet and enjoy interaction within the public space of the community. Communities such as Seaside also incorporate many construction features dictated by architects that play an uncertain role in promoting a new sense of community, such as the mandated use of tin roofs or tall, narrow house windows. The elitism of architectural choice may not appeal to everyone.

The new urbanism has been influential because there is a growing sense that typical suburban communities have isolated people unnecessarily (see Box 14.4). At the same time, these ideas, like those of Leon Krier, seem destined to be enjoyed by the most affluent but unavailable to the average family interested in a suburban home. Nevertheless, the work of the new urbanists is notable because at long last they have provided alternatives to the ways cities and suburbs have been built, and they remind us of the need for human scale and community feeling.

Paul and Percival Goodman

Most of the planners and critics we have discussed so far focused on construction design and the living arrangements of cities. Recall in the utopian vision of Ebenezer Howard that plans for garden cities included a balanced relationship between residences and industry. Paul and Percival Goodman (1974) asserted that planning could never be effective if it did not integrate working and living arrangements. The focus on residential construction alone ignores the most basic characteristic of social life: that people must work for a living and take care of their families.

The Goodmans also avoided the fallacy of physical determinism. They argued that good plans try to address political and social relations, not just architectural design needs. Community life should be political in the positive sense; that is, it should involve all individuals and groups. They proposed the construction of communities that would employ participatory democracy both at the place of work and within the local community. Their ambitious scheme involves the creation of a societal decision-making apparatus entirely different from the one we now possess. In the new, democractic-anarchist social order, all decisions related to work and community needs would be based on strict participatory democracy. Needless to say, their ideas have not been applied in the United States, because they would involve a change in the structure of government. However, the Goodmans' work, along with the continuing legacy of Ebenezer Howard, has been influential in the balanced construction of new developments in some formerly socialist countries such as Sweden and Israel—in particular, the Israeli kibbutz (Strong, 1971).

Trends in Planning Today

In recent years, development projects in both urban and suburban settlement spaces have involved an increase in scale. Projects such as the building of a garden city—Columbia, Maryland—or the construction of Battery Park City at the tip of Manhattan are large in scope and involve many acres. Land has been freed up from agricultural use in the suburbs or as the result of slum clearance and renovation in the cities.

BOX 14.4   NEW URBANISM OR NEW SUBURBANISM?

Many New Urbanists have written eloquently about the problems engendered by suburbanization. In "The Second Coming of the American Small Town," for example, Alex Duany and Elizabeth Plater-Zyberk charged that America's current city building is responsible (at least partly) for impoverishing central cities and for cutting off "a whole generation of Americans . . . from direct contact with people from other social classes." The resulting "mutual incomprehension and fear accounts for no small share of the tensions in our national political life." In a similar vein, Peter Calthorpe, in *The Next American Metropolis*, criticized American urban policy for impoverishing those who live in central cities while undermining environmental standards and eliminating open space elsewhere. New Urbanists recognize the increasing gap between poor cities/inner suburbs and prosperous outer suburbs.

Like other New Urbanists, Andres Duany has argued that pedestrian scale, density, and public space can improve how diverse people relate to each other. If the New Urbanists' communities ended up offering places as homogeneous and privatized as most suburbs, one suspects they would consider their work a failure. They are reluctant to insist on building communities with a genuinely diverse population because they fear that to do so would threaten their market. Yet they are reluctant not to insist on diversity because failure to do so would undermine the value of what they are doing. Although Duany realizes that the communities he envisions could foster New Urbanism or new suburbanism, depending on where—and at what price—they are built, he seems overwhelmed by the difficulties involved in fostering diversity.

This is understandable because fostering diversity requires confronting and overcoming the increasing fear Americans have of unfamiliar people—a fear that is palpable when one observes white Americans tensing up, even crossing the street, when they encounter a young black male. For many, such a moment is so frightening that they organize their lives to avoid neighborhoods where it may occur. Yet racial tension, while the most serious symptom of the currently pervasive fear of unfamiliar people, is by no means its only manifestation. Many people prefer suburban malls to downtown streets because they are comfortable only in an atmosphere of homogeneity, free of homeless people, street peddlers, weirdos. More and more people live in gated communities and work in office parks that enable them to isolate themselves not just from crime, but also from "them." This instinct for withdrawal is shared by African Americans and Latinos, who themselves avoid shopping malls where they are made to feel uncomfortable. They, too, often settle in homogeneous neighborhoods. These divisions collectively threaten to undermine the central characteristic of urban life and "public space": the daily experience of encountering—on the street, in the parks, on the subway—people different from oneself.

New Urbanist designs could create communities with such public spaces. Pedestrian scale, density, and well-located public buildings can enhance the variety of people that one contacts or at least tolerates. But architecture cannot by itself create new attitudes. Changes in police practices, in financing mechanisms for public schools, and in housing policies that now favor suburban homeowners over the urban poor, for instance, are equally necessary. The task, then, is to link New Urbanists with people from other disciplines equally interested in making the political, legal, and institutional changes necessary to promote diversity. They need jointly to address questions such as: How can political alliances be built that would help solve problems like crime, bad schools, and joblessness? To what extent does the legal system—through annexation laws, zoning laws, the organization of school financing, the allocation of voting rights, etc.—now promote fragmentation and division? What changes in the organization of local governments might lead to diverse communities? New Urbanists should not have to resign themselves to building in the outer suburbs.

But they can avoid doing so only if they are part of a larger strategy to reformulate the American dream from one of escape to one of revitalized urban living (Frug, 1997).

Architectural model of Seaside, Florida.

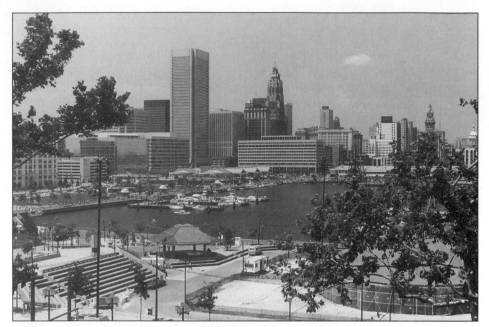

The redevelopment of Baltimore Harbor includes shops, restaurants, and entertainment areas.

These megaprojects usually incorporate mixed-use developments of housing and commercial shops. Due to the influence of planning critics, however, many of these designs incorporate human scaling despite their large size.

Among the most successful developers of large but human-scale projects is James Rouse, whose corporation built the Baltimore Inner Harbor, Faneuil Hall in Boston, the New York South Street Seaport in Manhattan, and the Santa Monica Mall. The Baltimore, Boston, and New York projects in particular were constructed on deteriorating, unused land that was revitalized. Rouse's success involved a blending of open spaces, reasonably priced eating places of great variety, and upscale shops. Such redevelopment transformed spaces of bleak prospect into vital urban centers with an active public life. The Baltimore Harbor project, for example, consists of a large horseshoe of open space that comprises the shore of the harbor inlet. Concrete steps lead to benches and play areas. One section is devoted to an array of alternative and moderately priced eateries. Two attractions, the Baltimore Aquarium and the Revolutionary War battleship *Constellation,* also draw in visitors.

Rouse also successfully developed Columbia, Maryland, a new town that mixes apartment and single-family home construction with accessible and usable open space and shopping areas. The entire project has been planned to conform to human scale and includes pathways totally dedicated to pedestrian use that link the various sections of the town. As one observer notes:

> In Columbia the size of residential areas was determined primarily by the number of households needed to support an elementary school. The Rouse Co., as developer, insisted that within a block of the school there be a swimming pool, a community building, and a convenience store, and that people be able to walk or bike to these facilities without crossing any major streets. Three to five neighborhoods made up a village, which offered more facilities, including a supermarket, a bank branch, and other businesses—also accessible by the community's forty-seven miles of walking and biking paths, as well as by car. (Langdon, 1988:52)

The success of the Rouse Corporation has influenced the way other megaprojects have been designed. In New York City, for example, a 92-acre section of the dilapidated downtown with few residential units was demolished to build Battery Park City. The project consists of high-rise apartments, offices, and shopping facilities. Located at the tip of Manhattan, the new development makes ample use of its view of the Hudson River. Residential blocks are integrated with an esplanade that includes spaces to sit and socialize with neighbors. Many other projects across the country, such as Riverplace in Portland along the Willamette River, also use the successful approach of human-scale residential blocks, mixed commercial and housing land use, and pedestrian amenities to provide a more attractive environment for residents.

While the above cases provide examples of developers' attempts to encourage the formation of community, other trends are symptomatic of the many problems cities and suburbs face. For example, it is also popular to construct "gated" developments where security and surveillance are given prime importance. These barricaded communities (called *condominium fechado* in Rio de Janeiro) do not seek an integration with urban surroundings and an active street life, but instead isolate themselves from the urban fabric (see Box 14.5). Fences protect the perimeter. Guards supervise the coming and going of both residents and their guests. The uninvited are simply not allowed in. One such project, Studio Colony, is located in the Studio City section of Los Angeles and consists of 450 upper-middle-income apartments. The residences are sealed off in high-rise buildings with parking garages located underneath the guarded structures. Studio Colony provides security from the high crime rate of Los Angeles, but, as one observer notes,

> What Studio Colony does not do is shape the outdoor areas into coherent, genuinely inviting spaces; it is hard to imagine that anyone would want to walk from one end of Studio Colony to the other even once. (Langdon, 1988:59)

In sum, principally due to the increase in the social problems of metropolitan living, architectural schemes for communities have changed in recent years. The shift is from the utopian influenced plans of the nineteenth century to the current mix of postmodern design that seeks a return to human scale and the barricaded, guarded environments that seek isolation from the dystopia of the city.

BOX 14.5 ENCLAVES OF FEAR

The phenomenon of walled cities and gated communities is a dramatic manifestation of a new fortress mentality growing in America. Gates, fences, and private security guards, like exclusionary land-use policies, development regulations, and an assortment of other planning tools, are means of control, used to restrict or limit access to residential, commercial, and public spaces.

Gated communities are residential areas with restricted access in which normally public spaces are privatized. They are security developments with designated perimeters, usually walls or fences, and controlled entrances that are intended to prevent penetration by non-residents. They include new developments and older areas retrofitted with gates and fences, and they are found from the inner cities to the exurbs and from the richest neighborhoods to the poorest. Some communities with round-the-clock security require all cars to pass the guard, issuing identification stickers for residents' cars. Others use video cameras to record the license plate numbers and sometimes the faces of all who pass through. Entrances without guards may have intercom systems, some with video monitors, that residents may use to screen visitors.

These developments in part reflect the notion of community as an island, a social bulwark against the general degradation of the urban social order; they also reflect the increasing attempt to substitute private controls for public organization, for the joint responsibilities of democratic citizenship all of us share. Gates and walls are not necessary or natural consequences of these social trends, or causes of them; they are, rather, a dramatic manifestation of them.

Gates and fences around our neighborhoods represent more than simple physical barriers. Gated communities manifest a number of tensions: between exclusionary aspirations rooted in fear and protection of privilege and the values of civic responsibility; between the trend toward privatization of social public services and the ideals of the public good and general welfare; and between the need for personal and community control of the environment and the dangers of making outsiders of fellow citizens.

The gated communities phenomenon has enormous policy consequences. It allows some citizens to secede from public contact, excluding others from sharing in their economic and social privilege. This result raises an ideological question that prompts polarized viewpoints. Are gated communities a metaphor of the exclusionary fortress, creating walls between citizens, or are they refuges from the forces that threaten family, economic security, and quality of life?

The real issue is not about the actual gates and walls, but why so many feel that they need them. What is the measure of nationhood when the divisions between neighborhoods require guards and fences to keep out other citizens? When public services and even local governments are privatized, when the community of responsibility stops at the subdivision gates, what happens to the function and the very idea of a social and political democracy? (Blakely and Snyder, 1997)

Summary

People in the United States regard planning with suspicion. They prefer to defend individual property rights and the home rule prerogative of local government control over land use. While every jurisdiction, no matter how small, seems to have its own planning department, professional experts are relegated to an advisory position. Planners must maneuver within this politically constrained milieu by exercising their influence on developers, speculators, homeowners, renters, local community activists, and public officials (Weiss, 1987). It is not an easy task. In the main, the professional planners employed by business and government devote their time to working out the ordinary details of mandated land use and construction requirements. They pursue the unglamorous job of drafting site usage plans for developers, reviewing and updating zoning maps for local governments, and assessing traffic studies. They also collect and review demographic information on the present and future growth patterns of individual towns. But this bureaucratic domain of activity remains removed from the active task of fashioning environments in which other people will live.

As we have seen, the limitations placed on professional planners have not prevented individuals from dreaming their dreams of the perfect city. Visionaries and utopian thinkers have tried their best to lead citizens of modern society toward some Eden that actualizes the promise of industrial progress. Some ideas, such as Howard's garden city, have been influential enough to affect future generations. Colossal failures, such as the superhuman building blocks of Le Corbusier's radiant city (actualized in every high-rise public housing project, not to mention the ashes of Pruitt-Igoe), have also been helpful because they have shown what we cannot or should not do. Happily, visionary plans are tried sometimes, and, even more happily, most of the time on a small scale so that the human cost of failure is not dear. We learn from mistakes and successes as our knowledge of planning human environments accumulates.

One important lesson that has recently been learned concerns the yearning for human-scale places in the face of unending metropolitan sprawl and the experience of immense, impersonal city space. Developments today feature an informed use of space. Macro environments, such as the Santa Monica enclosed mall, are composed of many mini environments that nurture sociability. The monstrous Battery Park City project opens itself out to the surrounding urban fabric and natural setting, providing for social interaction via micro public spaces and the extended esplanade on the Hudson River. Finally, as we have seen, new towns developed in their entirety (such as Columbia, Maryland) succeed by devoting space to pedestrians and thereby providing alternatives to automobile transportation to perform everyday tasks such as shopping, leisure activities, and commuting to work or school.

But a return to human scale alone, even through the best efforts of planners, will not save the declining quality of life in either our central cities or our massive, sprawling suburbs. As revealed in Chapter 10, the high level of crime has taken an immense toll on the free use of urban space, not to mention its cost in lives. We can rightly wonder what will happen to the Hudson River Esplanade and its pedestrian traffic if it becomes a haven for muggers. How enjoyable would the miles of pedestrian paths of Columbia, Maryland, be if the community were not isolated from the realities of homelessness and destitution characteristic of inner-city residents? The growing problems of land use, congestion, traffic jams, housing blight, environmental pollution, and sprawl spur the public to search for planned solutions to urban growth. These and other problems may yet encourage local citizens to give up their traditional and narrow concern with protecting their own property rights in favor of a more coordinated approach to development. Yet the problems of the metropolitan region have societal roots that are not easily addressed by technical recommendations without massive social change.

These contradictions are clearest when we study the impact of environmental pollutants on communities. As we have discussed, the burden of costs for society's progress seems to fall on poor and minority neighborhoods. Government at all levels participates in producing this pattern of discrimination. In many communities, air pollution affects and endangers the lives of everyone, rich or poor. Environmental problems are found in all metropolitan regions and require economic, political, and social responses in addition to better-quality spatial design.

As sociologists have noted, professional planners, government officials, and architects would probably remain limited by their own outlook even if they were provided with more power. They preach the fallacy of physical determinism, which holds a blind faith in the power of construction technology and design to alter social relationships. Rarely do they profess what the Goodman brothers or Frank Lloyd Wright saw as the organic, holistic needs of families and households. They are more comfortable with limited prescriptions that conform to the dictates of their professions— building design and construction for architects, landscaping or land-use schemes for planners, or political expediency for politicians. Much more is needed to control the forces of development in the United States, but little public debate seems to be devoted to the issue of planning or the search for alternatives to our deteriorating environment. Increased public involvement in the planning question can focus concern on those issues that affect our daily lives rather than on profits to be created from real estate and commercial development, or increased tax revenues that may accompany urban growth. It is up to the leaders of our society, therefore, to involve citizens in a protracted dialogue regarding the kind of environments they would prefer to have, much like the model of Bellevue, Washington (see Box 14.2).

One last source of reform remains unexamined so far: the activities surrounding the drafting and execution of public policy and state intervention. We will consider this topic next.

CHAPTER

15

METROPOLITAN SOCIAL POLICY AND THE FUTURE OF URBAN SOCIOLOGY

In the previous chapter, we considered one form of intervention: planning. We have examined both its prospects and its limitations. Attempts by society to fashion a living environment that is beneficial to all citizens do not end by exhausting planning options. A separate approach, one that is often initiated in conjunction with planning, involves government intervention guided by policy. The state has the authority to allocate money from tax revenues for social programs and to authorize deficit spending to address social needs. Government actions not only can direct behavior by prohibition—that is, by passing laws that prohibit certain acts—but can also provide incentives and opportunities to channel resources in specific ways. This push-versus-pull feature of policy is an important one to keep in mind when examining the issue of political intervention. While this chapter will be devoted to the role of government in improving metropolitan life, it is worthwhile noting that intervention, such as the publicly directed dumping of toxic waste in poor communities, can also create problems. Just "how much" intervention is needed and in "what forms" remain critical issues for any discussion of government policy.

The Tragedy of the Commons and Uneven Development

U.S. society possesses a civic culture that is adverse to government intervention in the market. We have identified this perspective as *privatism,* the belief that government should restrict its role to helping the business community and seeking market solutions to social problems. But this reliance on the market leads to certain problems. In the previous chapter, we saw that the desire to plan the development of metropolitan regions arose because the private market is not capable of providing the infrastructure required in our modern metropolis. There are other problems with the market as a mechanism for allocating resources. These include the difficulty of maintaining the quality of life when public resources are involved and the problem of uneven development in a capitalist society.

The Tragedy of the Commons

There is an old fable in academic circles that economists use to show why individual choice can lead to socially undesirable effects. The fable has many variations. Here is ours: Consider a village of farmers, each with a herd of cows and an open field adjacent to the village that is held in common. Each farmer seeks to use the public resource of the field to private advantage. Therefore, they all attempt to graze their cows as often and as long as possible on the common green. Pretty soon the grass is all eaten and the common field is reduced to a muddy, barren plot of land.

If the farmers are interested in improving their situation, they have few alternatives. They could each buy a farm that would be owned privately with sufficient grazing land—an expensive move. Or they could band together and create a community scheduling agreement that would recognize the need of each farmer *and* the need of the field to regenerate itself. Because the users of this public resource might have disputes, the individuals involved would also have to arrange for arbitration in the event of disagreements or abuse. In short, this tragedy of the commons points to the need for the social institution of public authority or local government, which safeguards the benefits to the many from the abuses of the few.

Settlement spaces in modern society contain many public resources such as air, water, and recreational areas. Safeguarding these common environmental resources becomes increasingly difficult as the population and frequency of use rise (see Chapter 14). As a consequence, government must develop active public policies to deal with the many problems arising from large populations living in the same settlement space. Often these policies involve laws that are passed that restrict individual rights but are considered necessary to preserve public resources.

To take one brief example: In New York City, partly as a consequence of a rising crime rate, apartment dwellers purchased dogs in great numbers. By the 1970s, piles of dog excrement made walking the city streets a hazardous affair. The city was compelled to pass a "pooper scooper" law mandating that owners clean up after their dogs in public. This law made it a crime not to comply. To this day, any tourist can observe dog owners from all social backgrounds scooping up after their animals to keep the streets clean. The law is an infringement on individual rights, but it is sanctioned by our society because it leads to a greater good: public enjoyment of a common resource, public space. Most environmental policy is of this type, and support for such measures requires a public culture that is committed to protecting environmental resources.

In the United States, many such laws limit the free market for the public good. Some of the most restrictive are the southern California anti-air-pollution statutes, which are regulated by an independent state agency and affect everything from automobile exhaust systems, to by-products of industrial activity, to homeowner burning of trash and outdoor barbecue use. The air-quality control board has authority to limit daily activities when pollution is hazardous in the Los Angeles metropolitan region. Over the years, southern California has lost many businesses because they preferred to move rather than pay the extra cost of compliance. But that has not diminished public support for government policy. Rather, in such an environment, where pollution is a clear and present danger, intervention is the only solution until the causes of air pollution are eliminated by other means. Hence, while we dislike government intervention, we find it useful. Sustaining the quality of life in metropolitan regions is an especially difficult task without the aid of government policy and regulation because the free market is incapable of doing so on its own.

Uneven Development and Policy: Redistributive Programs

In capitalist society, resources tend to flow to those who are most powerful. There are many reasons for this, and not all of them imply wrongdoing on anyone's part. Under pure market conditions, when individuals compete in business with one another, one's prosperity is supposed to spur the others to copy success. Thus, the market serves to discipline businesspeople to adopt the best and most efficient means of pursuing a profit. What holds for business, however, does not necessarily apply to individual people. Issues of inequality plague our society (as we saw in Chapter 10) and those of other countries (see Chapters 12 and 13). They also undermine the social order and lead to conflict.

While we have a public philosophy of privatism in this country, we also have a public commitment, guaranteed by the Constitution, to equality of opportunity. This last feature leads to dilemmas for Americans because inequality and powerful special interests produce patterns of uneven development. For example, all children within the same public school district are supposed to have a right to receive the same quality of education. What do we do when we find that schools in richer neighborhoods have more resources than schools in poorer ones? And shouldn't *all* children in the United States receive the same quality schooling? Can we all afford to move to the best districts? Should we do so as the only solution, even if we could? Should only the more affluent receive an adequate education, including college, especially when public higher education is supported by everyone's taxes?

As another example, doctors in the United States are capitalists; they charge what the market will bear. Those people who have the most money can get the best medical care. But what happens to people who are too poor to pay? Why do some people have adequate insurance while others do not? Shouldn't all Americans, as a right of citizenship, have equal access to adequate health care? Or should quality of care depend on ability to pay?

Finally, the housing industry in our society is also a capitalist enterprise. Those individuals who can afford a private home can get one. The more you can afford to spend, the better your home will be. But what about those individuals who cannot afford the price? What happens to the truly poor who cannot even afford rent? Should we sanction poverty, homelessness, premature death, or the ruination of elderly persons who must pay for health and housing expenses they cannot afford?

Over the years, all capitalist societies have had to face the social costs of uneven development. In the United States, government has enacted legislation at all levels supporting social programs that address social ills. Social welfare programs are designed to pool resources so that all persons may have access to them (as is the case with

Medicare programs for the elderly) or to redistribute them (in the case of rent vouchers for low-income households). Using certain criteria of inclusion, government officials decide what is needed and who should be eligible to receive assistance. These programs are supported by taxing the more affluent or by special government borrowing; hence, they *redistribute* the wealth from the relatively well-off to the poor, although, as we will discuss shortly, such schemes are not without their abuses or critics (Jencks, 1992).

In its most basic form, then, the issue of uneven development and public policy involves a question of money, because sustaining the quality of life has private and social costs. Government programs may address the issue of inequitable wealth, but, as Christopher Jencks (1992) has argued, only income redistribution can directly address the problem of poverty. Hence, many social programs are destined to fail because they do not consider the fundamental cause of the problems they seek to address.

Public policy is created by government representatives in conjunction with research staffs and various academic aides. Some policies find the government directly intervening in the production of new resources such as the building of dams, highways, housing, and nuclear energy facilities. These directly aid private-sector business interests as well as the general welfare. In other cases, incentives are created to channel individual behavior in certain directions, such as the tax subsidy provided to people who purchase single-family homes. The enactment of programs often requires new staff and administrators. Government at all levels is a major employer in the United States, accounting for more than 25 percent of the entire workforce. Social programs run by government also support immense bureaucracies, such as the welfare departments in each state. Hence, not only the less affluent but also state workers benefit from public intervention.

There are many ways that government policy redistributes wealth and channels resources toward the public good. The welfare program and Medicaid are meant to protect the quality of life among those individuals who are less affluent or whose incomes are restricted because they are single parents or are retired and elderly. State boards of education try to equalize school resources among different public districts, regardless of neighborhood family incomes. Public health crises such as the AIDS epidemic are also addressed by government policy. Finally, housing programs exist in a variety of forms; there are even public programs to deal with homelessness.

In addition, government policies aid the business community directly and subsidize its activities, as the discussion of privatism suggests (see below). Public programs aimed at aiding individuals in need may be co-opted by private-sector involvement toward the pursuit of profit by business. This co-optation of government intervention is a serious limitation of public policy in the United States, and it alone causes programs to fail, as the experience with low-income housing programs run by HUD shows (see Box 15.1, pp. 340–341). Other limitations include the failure of individual programs themselves because they cannot attain desired goals—as in the case of welfare aid—or because intervention actually makes problems worse (Jencks, 1992).

Most of the examples discussed so far concern the general problems of inequity in our society rather than issues specifically relevant to metropolitan areas, although issues of inequity certainly have major impacts on the quality of life of urban spaces. Let us look more closely at some of the programs aimed particularly at the needs of both cities and suburbs, and the various political, economic, and social ramifications of government policy in metropolitan areas. In the previous chapter, we discussed how the desire for planning is associated with the "modernist" belief that increased rationality of land use and architectural design can improve our lives and lead to progress for all. Some countries, such as the welfare capitalist societies of Scandinavia, hold a modernist belief in government policy as also aiding progress through rational state intervention. The United States is characterized by a different public ideology called *privatism,* which requires government to aid business interests through the market. While our approach has had some success, it also leaves public programs vulnerable to co-optation by powerful interests. As we will see next, due to the characteristics of public policy, the pursuit of social justice often fails even when government intervenes with the best intentions.

Urban and Metropolitan Policy

There is no escaping the fact that public policy is shaped by fundamental philosophical positions and ideologically held beliefs regarding government intervention. As we have seen, the dominant belief in the United States is that government should always play a limited role in the economy and that market solutions are usually best—but also that it is appropriate for the government to subsidize private business. This attitude contrasts with those of industrialized countries in Western Europe, for example, which have more active public policy and more publicly supported benefits such as national health care schemes (although, as we discussed in Chapter 12, some of these countries, such as the United Kingdom, have lately limited their public welfare programs).

The United States, therefore, is *ambivalent* regarding government intervention. Different political positions support different types of criticisms directed against state programs. On the one hand, many liberals lament the takeover of public programs by powerful business interests. On the other, many conservatives point to the inefficient and deleterious effects of government intervention. In addition to the philosophy of privatism, a second drawback to intervention is that under the federalist arrangements between the national government and the states, the condition of cities is the responsibility of the states, yet many urban problems, such as crime and inadequate health care, are national in scope. Over the years, the respective roles of the federal versus state level have become an issue of political debate (see the concluding section).

The urban renewal program of the 50s, 60s, and 70s provides an illustrative case of the relationship between business and government as well as the limitations of policy. Urban renewal grew out of the 1930s Roosevelt administration's commitment to rescue the housing and banking industry from the Depression, a serious economic crisis indeed. The Housing Act of 1934, for example, established the Federal Housing Authority, which guaranteed home loans. The 1937 Housing Act mandated the government to provide funds for the support of low-income house construction and slum clearance. These powers were amplified in the Housing Act of 1949 under Title I assistance and in subsequent acts passed in 1954, 1961, 1968, and 1970. The Department of Housing and Urban Development (HUD) grew into a massive bureaucracy that oversaw the many programs associated with renewal.

It is important to note that housing intervention was aimed primarily at aiding the real estate industry, one of the three largest in the U.S. economy, rather than being a showcase of modernist ideas mixing planning with policy, as in the Scandinavian countries. Providing homes for people and caring for their community needs was only

BOX 15.1   THE CASE OF PUBLIC HOUSING

As part of the recovery from the Great Depression, the federal government passed a number of acts that aimed to fight social problems such as unemployment as well as spur industrial growth. During World War II, much American industry benefited from the allied effort; however, the housing industry was still in the doldrums. Congress passed the 1949 Housing Act to stimulate that industry. As drafted, the act embodied the contradiction of U.S. public policy because it was aimed principally at subsidizing the housing industry, but it also proposed to alleviate the problem of slums. The act authorized the construction of 135,000 public housing units each year.

The architects of the bill were two famous senators, Robert Taft and Paul Douglas. Both believed that living in a "decent home" was the right of every American. According to Charles Abrams's commentary:

> Senator Robert Taft, who had been the measure's most forceful advocate, would not allow himself to be distracted by those who had pressed for an enlargement of purpose beyond housing, for the good senator was a Christian at heart to whom "no room at the inn" was a gnawing deficiency in a great and progressive society.

> "I do not believe that public housing is socialism," Senator Taft told me in an interview, "if it is confined to the furnishing of decent housing only to that group unable to provide housing by its own means." (1965:81)

Soon after, however, the commitment to public housing was watered down by Congress. After 1954 the authorization was cut to between 35,000 to 45,000 units per year, hardly enough to accommodate those slum dwellers displaced by renewal.

In subsequent years, the commitment to the construction of public housing became a low priority compared to the use of urban renewal legislation to make the housing industry profitable. According to Abrams:

> It was only one of many examples of how legislation passed with the best of intentions is ultimately perverted during the administrative process. In the long run, the profit motive somehow operates as the designated but effective legislator while the public obligation is pushed under the rug. (1965:84)

Another drawback to the housing legislation was that the programs were not monitored carefully regarding their impact both on the industry and on the public housing tenants. We have already seen how life in the few large public projects led to a high crime rate and disaffection of the tenants, many of whom moved out, as in the case of Pruitt-Igoe. In Chapter 10, we also learned of Ruby and her family, who lapsed into welfare dependency,

a secondary goal of the U.S. program. As a result of this contradiction, metropolitan housing policy has had only mixed results. It proved to be a great boon to business but was less effective in attaining its social goals. Box 15.1 discusses the case study of federal support for public housing in more detail.

During the period from 1950 to 1990, government intervention aimed at aiding cities went through three separate phases, each of which reflected the dominant role of drug use, and poverty for several generations after moving into the massive Cabrini-Green housing project in Chicago. While public housing did *not* cause these problems, it concentrated them and made their solution difficult, especially because of the ghettoization of the poor, as we have seen.

But the abuses of profit entrepreneurs are also cause for alarm when public programs are not adequately monitored. In the case of the 1949 and 1954 housing acts, scandal eventually tarnished the intentions of Taft and Douglas. The acts amplified a wartime provision that provided federal funds for military housing, notoriously known as Section 608. This provision was meant to stimulate the rapid construction of rental housing, and it provided for as much as 90 percent of the costs to be covered by the government. The postwar housing acts sought to use Section 608 to stimulate the construction of affordable rental housing after urban renewal had torn slums down.

The program was renewed in 1946, but not monitored for 12 years. Frequent abuse by the private sector occurred, such as the use of dummy leases, purposely enacted defaults to acquire FHA insurance, and the selling of units to wholly owned subsidiaries to hide profits. To illustrate the massive ripoff of public funds, Abrams notes:

> Three speculators [in one illustration of the ripoff] put up only $6,000 for a $12,500,000 project [in 1954 dollars] in Virginia. They each went on the payroll for $20,000 a year; each got his $6,000 back in a few weeks, and when the building was completed, there was $2,250,000 left over from the mortgage, which they promptly pocketed. (1965:88–89)

The above illustrates an important point about the abuses of government programs. They are not committed solely by those blamed in public discourse as "welfare cheats" but also by white-collar criminals who plunder millions of dollars from the public. The abuses of Section 608 seem reminiscent of the present-day savings and loan scandal, which will require billions of public dollars to remedy. These scandals remind us of the power of the business establishment to co-opt government programs to increase personal wealth through both legal and illegal means.

Public housing in the United States has been a failure, but not because of the particular evils of either white-collar criminals or welfare dependency. It has failed because our society does not support a social welfare program of such magnitude. Government policy is most often directed at subsidizing industries, such as housing. Instead of doing both of these well, government funds wind up lining the pockets of ripoff artists, often to the detriment of honest people. Without adequate monitoring of programs, the abuses often amount to billions of dollars.

business in defining the interventionist agenda. Initially, funds targeted slum removal and construction of affordable housing. Then social goals were dropped and the focus turned to the support of economic development for local business. Finally, government funds were used to subsidize economic development for global competition. In all three phases, local government operated less as a vehicle for social justice than as an aid to businesses experiencing declining profits.

Support for Slum Removal

Beginning with the late 1950s, the amount of federal money allocated for central city slum clearance and renewal increased greatly each year. Combined expenditures were $706 million in 1960, $1.8 billion in 1966, and $3.8 billion by 1970, or an increase of over 500 percent in 10 years (Mollenkopf, 1975).

There were many reasons for HUD's spending spree. By the 1950s, central cities were being devastated by the immense outflow of people to the suburbs. This shift, as we already discussed, was made possible by government highway and housing programs. As a result, downtown retailers and their department stores were in danger of being shut down because of the success of suburban shopping malls, while entire residential sections of the city gave way to blight and decline as middle-class people moved out. City politicians appealed to the federal government for help in rescuing downtown areas. A second cause involved the national response to the ghetto riots of the 1960s, which also highlighted the deterioration of inner-city areas. Funding for HUD projects more than doubled after 1966, the year of the worst rioting.

During the 1950s, urban renewal was aimed at revitalizing the downtown areas of cities and clearing away slums or blighted dwellings. Programs were supposed to replace cleared land with affordable housing and income-earning civic projects. According to some estimates, over 5 million low- to moderate-income housing units in U.S. cities were candidates for destruction and replacement (Flanagan, 1990:292). By the end of 1961, renewal programs had eliminated over 126,000 substandard housing units, but only 28,000 new dwellings were built (Robertson and Judd, 1989:307). The net result was a decline in the number of dwelling units for low-income households and an increase in housing costs in poor neighborhoods.

At that time, observers noted that the policy seemed to be more effective in the removal of black and/or poor residents than at replacing slums with affordable housing. In fact, during the 1960s, urban renewal was dubbed "Negro removal." Over 75 percent of all people displaced by renewal projects were black (Robertson and Judd, 1989:307).

While some low-income residents were helped by the ambitious redevelopment schemes subsidized by the federal government, much of urban renewal involved the clearing away of slums to allow private real estate interests to use downtown land for profit making, including the building of middle- and upper-middle-income housing projects and the regeneration of central city commerce through the construction of plazas, civic centers, and pedestrian malls.

Paradoxically, at the same time HUD programs were intervening in renewal, other federal housing policy in the form of tax subsidies to homeowners was destroying city neighborhoods by promoting suburbanization. These subsidies, which amounted to billions of dollars each year, were responsible for the massive shift to the suburbs, or white flight. By the 1970s, it was already clear that the United States had become segregated by race and class, with middle-class whites dominating the suburbs while the inner cities were increasingly populated by minorities and those whites who either could not afford to move to suburbia or preferred to live in the city in newly built or renovated upper-middle-income housing. Thus, government intervention not only was less interested in social justice than in subsidizing business but was also not rational, and it worked against itself in the fight to save the city.

Many central cities contain hundreds of vacant housing units and many acres of empty land—a consequence of failed public policies in the post-World War II period.

Support for Economic Development

By the late 1960s, the goals of urban policy had changed as a result of political pressures. Commitment to the revitalization of slums was abandoned in favor of using government programs to bolster private business interests in the city. It was now apparent that urban economies, which had been dependent on manufacturing, were in decline. Deindustrialization had taken over the country, and cities needed to retool themselves to compete with other communities within their metropolitan region for new employment. Downtown business interests, along with local politicians, regrouped and worked together to use federal funds for revitalization projects. The focus of renewal shifted from slum clearance to support for economic development, such as the construction of sports stadiums, hotel and tourist complexes, and high-rise service centers. For example, in the 1960s the city of Los Angeles used urban renewal funds to bulldoze the blighted section of Bunker Hill near the downtown. But instead of replacing the structures with affordable housing and preserving the community, the city and its partners in the business sector constructed a music center, high-rise banking offices, and expensive high-rise apartment complexes. Slightly east of this redevelopment, the city eradicated another blighted residential neighborhood and replaced it with a sports facility—Dodger Stadium—instead of low-income housing (Davis, 1990).

Such projects, backed by powerful political and business interests, were responsible for the eradication of inner-city neighborhoods and small businesses, while the signs of "progress" greeted all residents with visible advertising for the joint government/business

BOX 15.2   THE WORLD TRADE TOWERS

The World Trade Center was proposed as a complex of twin towers, each with 110 stories. They were constructed on the lower west side corner of Manhattan Island in 1972, adding 4.5 million square feet of office space to the downtown area. The site on which they were built was not vacant. It consisted of blighted buildings along with several vibrant neighborhoods, including the Cortlandt Street complex of independent and highly competitive small businesses dealing in electronics.

One might think that this trade-off of small commercial interests and ethnic neighborhoods for a world-class center of international banking was exactly the kind of project urban renewal programs had in mind. According to a report by Ralph Nader and associates (Leinsdorf et al., 1973), however, local residents opposed the project: New York City did not require such a massive increase in office space at the time, and there were limited transportation facilities servicing the site area. To this day the towers are plagued by excessive vacancy rates, and they have failed to spark development in the surrounding area.

The project was the brainchild of a group of private-sector banks, including First National City, Chase Manhattan, Morgan Guaranty Trust, Chemical Bank, and Marine Midland Grace (Leinsdorf et al., 1973:143). But this group, known as the Downtown Lower Manhattan Association (DLMA), did not build the towers. Instead, the Port Authority of New York, a quasi-public agency, constructed the complex on land cleared by urban renewal. This quasi-public agency has the government's powers of *eminent domain*

---

ventures. In many cases, city neighborhoods that did not represent high-yield profit making for business were bulldozed despite the objections of local residents. Box 15.2 illustrates this trend with the example of World Trade tower construction in Manhattan, but examples from every city abound (Robertson and Judd, 1989; Stone, 1989; Davis, 1990).

In the 1960s and 1970s, economic development as an urban policy meant that privatism had taken over, not just through co-optation as it had in previous periods, but overtly as part of city revival schemes. As the argument went, business concerns come first in a period of recession because when business prospers, the tax coffers of the city are also enriched. Housing programs and community redevelopment had to take a back seat, as did the fight for social justice and against the problems of uneven development. As in other periods, while some federal programs aided business directly, others also helped the middle class. City government could not stem the tide of middle-class white flight during this period because the pull of subsidized suburbanization was too powerful (see Chapter 5). Government could try to make the city a better place to do business, but it could not make it a better place to live.

Support for Global Competition

The shift to a financial and service economy for the downtown had now turned into global competition. Each place was in competition for limited investment that was at-

(i.e., the right to take over private property for public use despite owner objections) and the authority to extend tax exemptions; it is not directly responsible to the public, but has the authority to collect user fees for the area's infrastructure of bridges, tunnels, and roads and use the money for development projects.

To finance the project, the Authority borrowed millions of dollars from a consortium of 13 banks, most of which were members of the DLMA. As the Nader report observes,

> On December, 31, 1968, the Port Authority had 276 million dollars, or 93 percent of its time deposits in the same banks that were receiving tax-exempt interest on the 210 million dollar loan. . . . The Authority deposited the proceeds from its bonds in the same banks that were receiving its tax-exempt interest payments. If the banks took tax deductions for the interest they paid on the Port Authority's time deposits, then they were violating the law. (Leinsdorf & Etra, 1973:148)

Even if the Nader group's conclusion was wrong and no laws were violated, this example illustrates how special and powerful interests were able to use urban renewal to further their own desires. The construction of the twin towers is only one example of a pattern that was repeated in many cities, namely, the influence of finance capital in channeling public resources toward the preservation of central city land values. According to a newspaper report about downtown development in Los Angeles, "Federal law prohibits banks from speculating on real estate, but they may own property they use for bank business. Such bank holdings account for perhaps one-fifth of total property values downtown" (*Los Angeles Times*, April 25, 1982, Section A-3).

tuned to worldwide opportunities within the marketplace of global capitalism. National programs that supported private enterprise would bypass local bureaucracies and downsize the role of government planning. Issues of social justice were ignored. This restructuring of the federal–city government relationship reached its zenith during the eight years of the Reagan administration and resulted in the cutback of urban policy until there was little left of renewal funding.

Several reasons have been advanced for the federal abandonment of HUD city renewal programs, most of which are political. The Republican administration in the 1980s ran on a platform that deemphasized the needs of cities. The plurality of active voters lived in the suburbs, and they were attracted by President Reagan's call to get government "off the backs" of people. This meant that under the Reagan and Bush administrations, there were severe cuts in public welfare programs but not in military spending. The new regime followed a conservative philosophy that favored market solutions to social ills. It also reaffirmed the political principle of federalism (mentioned at the beginning of this chapter), which made the condition of cities a responsibility of the states. This principle suggests that local and state governments were better able to deal with local problems and that urban revitalization should be market driven rather than pulled along by federally financed and planned projects. Such sentiments were supported by a majority of voters, who backed President Reagan's conservative agenda and later elected George Bush.

The cuts to federal programs were unprecedented. As Robertson and Judd (1989:314) observe about national aid to cities:

> Overall spending dropped from $6.1 billion in fiscal year 1981 to $5.2 billion in fiscal year 1984. The $5.2 billion spent for the fiscal year 1984–1985 amounted to a decline of almost 20 percent when corrected for inflation. By the 1989 budget year, money for urban programs was cut $4.4 billion—a further reduction of about 40 percent when the effects of inflation are considered.

> Nearly all subsidies for the construction of public housing were ended. . . . Urban mass transit grants were reduced 28 percent from 1981–1983 and were cut another 20 percent by 1986. CETA [Comprehensive Employment and Training Act] funds were eliminated after 1983.

The Clinton administration has brought little in the way of new ideas or new aid to urban areas. Cities and states have had to fend for themselves in supporting metropolitan programs. As discussed in Chapter 10, the fiscal crisis that set in during the 1970s severely restricted the ability of local areas to finance policy aimed at social goals, even when good ideas circulated freely. As the fiscal crisis spread to the states in the 1980s and 1990s, they could no longer support social justice–oriented policies at the local level. With little public money available both cities and states had to scrap many social projects and have since concentrated on economic development.

Local governments in particular faced a crisis when the federal level slashed urban funds and proclaimed a "market led transition to a postindustrial economy" (Barnekov and Rich, 1989). City politicians now work directly with business to revive ailing urban economies. This represents an extreme example of privatism, because the reduction or elimination of policy aimed at improving social well-being has occurred at *every* government level since the 1980s. This trend continued through the 1990s as the Clinton administration issued waivers to states that sought to eliminate welfare programs and replace them with a variety of "work incentive" programs. The result has been a substantial reduction in the number of welfare recipients—but this does not mean that former welfare recipients now participate in the paid labor force. Fewer than half of the persons removed from welfare rolls over the last decade have found permanent employment, and the number of families seeking assistance from food pantries and other private-sector charities has increased substantially. It is one thing for the federal government to claim that the local quality of life is a matter for local jurisdictions, but it is quite another matter when no level of government addresses this need due to fiscal crisis cutbacks and the subsidization by taxpayers of economic recovery.

According to Desmond King (1990), local policy now comprises either supply- or demand-side incentives to business. The former consists of packaging incentives such as tax breaks, rent free land, and local bond financing that will attract capital to the area. The latter consists of city development activities that attempt to create new industries with the aid of the private sector by underwriting development costs, such as in the creation of high-tech industrial parks. In both cases, the policies of the 1990s are in stark contrast to those of 30 years ago, because the emphasis is on economic recovery without the rhetoric that once obscured the emphasis on privatism by, at least, acknowledging issues of social equity and injustice.

Privatism and Issues of Social Justice

Has the support of private enterprise and abandonment of active intervention in cities been successful? Our analysis of metropolitan problems (Chapter 10) shows just the opposite. What are the limitations of the ideology of privatism and the present constraints on pursuing social justice? The limitations of privatism and government subsidy for economic development include the failure to realize benefits from development, especially by low-income residents; the proliferation of beggar-thy-neighbor competition among different cities, which does not benefit local areas; the subsidization of capital investment that is not reinvested locally; and the destruction of public resources without benefit from the public subsidization of private-sector growth (Barnekov and Rich, 1989).

Lack of Community Benefits from Public Investment

Oakland, California, obtained a package of loans and tax subsidies to support the private development of airport improvements and an industrial park. The rationale for the public subsidy of the project was that it would help provide steady work for the city's hard-core unemployed. But only an estimated 65 jobs out of many hundreds that were created went to hard-core unemployed workers (Pressman and Wildausky, 1973). Other studies indicate that publicly supported growth does not bring the kind of benefits purported by boosters of public–private partnerships (see Box 15.3). In Houston, which claims to be a city based on private enterprise, business has used government funds in many ways to develop infrastructure, subsidize industry, and grease the wheels of profit making. During the city's growth, the costs of development were passed along to residents. By maintaining a low tax rate on business, the city failed to plan adequately for highways, sewage systems, garbage collection, water quality, and road maintenance. Houston's traffic jams are legendary. And future residents will be saddled with the immense public bill to finance the missing infrastructure and the costs of growth (Feagin, 1988). The experience of Houston has been duplicated in other U.S. cities, which now face immense infrastructure problems of their own while continuing to spend millions in taxpayer money on "development" projects such as sports stadiums, convention centers, and luxury housing. The alleged "crisis" of the infrastructure and of public support for the quality of life is not, as some political leaders maintain, a crisis of funding alone, but represents some skewed priorities when all available money is spent on civic development projects of dubious value.

Other case studies reveal that privatism twists the intent of public–private partnerships to the full benefit of business. As Barnekov and Rich (1989:216) observe:

> Local economic development programs designed to use public funds to leverage private investment frequently result in reverse leverage—that is, private enterprise often leverages public funds to accomplish its own development objectives and, in the process, may hold local governments hostage if they do not come forth with generous subsidies.

Case studies have shown how the competition for investment dollars simply forces local jurisdictions to make excessive sacrifices. This is especially the case as capital has become increasingly mobile in the global economy. In the last decade, we

BOX 15.3 THE DESTRUCTION OF POLETOWN

An extreme case of the failure of public–private partnerships involves the city of Detroit's subsidy of a new General Motors assembly plant. In 1980 Chrysler Corporation closed its Dodge Main plant in Detroit, eliminating the jobs of thousands of employees. The same year, General Motors—the third largest corporation in the world, with annual profits in the $100 millions —indicated that it would build its new assembly plant outside of Detroit unless the city would locate and pay for the development of a new site large enough for the plant. The city responded with the Central Industrial Park Project, which located a 400-acre site on the western edge of the city. The area had long been known as Poletown because of the prominence of the ethnic Polish population in the neighborhood. Some community activists opposed the project, claiming that a smaller area would be sufficient for the plant. But other community leaders supported it, believing the project would save much-needed jobs within the city. Finally, the Michigan supreme court ruled that the city of Detroit had the right to condemn properties within the community and to sell this land to General Motors. Over 1,200 homes and apartments, 155 businesses, 16 churches, 2 schools, and a hospital were destroyed, and more than 3,500 people were displaced. Community residents observed that even in the former Soviet Union no government official dared to destroy churches, but the Poletown project did so with impunity.

More than $200 million in local, state, and federal funds was used to condemn and purchase the land, relocate displaced families, and then demolish the churches, businesses, and homes that stood in the way of "economic development." The land was then turned over to General Motors for $8 million. This meant that the city would have paid more than $60,000 for every new job created by the factory. But the company also demanded—and received—a 50 percent tax abatement from the city for not leaving Detroit. Although General Motors had promised 6,500 new jobs, the plant has operated with just one shift of some 3,000 workers. And with a new assembly plant built by public money up and running, the company announced the closure of two older plants in 1987—at a loss of some 6,000 jobs. Regardless of how the final cost is figured—and some have suggested that the benefits to the city will never outweigh the costs of the Central Industrial Park Project—this example suggests some of the problems that can occur with the use of public funds for economic development projects in American cities.

have seen cities and states offering incredible tax breaks and other incentives to attract new or relocating industrial plants—another use of public funds to support private business. Some observers have called this ruthless competition among places for investment the "new arms race." In the chase after global dollars, social equity programs are cut or abandoned. As a result, cities have a diminished capacity to support socially beneficial programs and to sustain the community quality of life (Kanter, 1987:510–511). The problems of uneven development within and between metropolitan regions are of deep concern (see Chapter 10).

The Decline of Democracy in Local Politics

The new public–private partnerships in pursuit of economic development usually work outside the democratic process of government decision making. Nonelective superagencies such as the Port Authority of New York and New Jersey (see Box 15.2) and similar ad hoc development agencies are not monitored by the voters. This means that public investment and oversight through the democratic process is itself diminished in the pursuit of growth (see Chapter 11).

Government policy involves an often unproductive struggle between the dominant priority to support business and the lesser goal, often passionately pursued by social movements, of social justice. Spatial competition among places for limited public and private investment also affects the success of policy, because the United States has no overarching national program for metropolitan revitalization. In the 1950s, competition was between central cities and their suburbs; in the 1960s, it was between regions of the country—especially between areas that were not experiencing a decline in manufacturing (such as the Sunbelt) and those that were (e.g., the Frostbelt). By the 1980s and 1990s, however, all places were involved in a universal global competition for scarce resources. These policies pitted place against place to the advantage of capital and at the expense of local taxpayers. Only recently have government policy experts been willing to reexamine this one-sided relation between people and increasingly mobile capital, because in many areas the benefits of business decisions to locate have been stripped away by the costs of incentive packages.

As crime, homelessness, housing deterioration, and other urban problems (see Chapter 10) intensify, renewed pressure is being placed on the federal government to intervene once more to stem the decline in the quality of community life. If such a turnaround does occur, it will come only with a renewed debate on the philosophy of intervention. This has *not* occurred under the Clinton administration in the 1990s.

Urban Policy: The Political Debate

Over the past two decades, debate has raged regarding whether traditional liberal or conservative solutions to the urban crisis should be applied. Most analysts of urban problems discuss solutions in terms of precisely this clash of ideologies. In this section, we will discuss policy recommendations along ideological lines. In a later section, we will point to a course of action that offers the possibility of rising above this clash of perspectives by addressing the limitations of present public policy arrangements.

Liberal Positions on Urban Problems

Liberals tend to focus on the limitations of existing social institutions and to seek remedies that equalize the ability of all citizens to overcome those limitations. They support government intervention and spending as a means of combating social ills. Most urban problems are caused, in this view, by the inequities of the resource distribution system in our society. Poverty and associated problems of uneven development are the inevitable consequence of the fact that economic rewards and social opportunities are not equally available to all citizens.

The liberal agenda uses government intervention as a tool to overcome uneven development. It supports active involvement of policy to identify, address, and help resolve serious urban problems of the less affluent. Economic deprivation and persistent racial segregation are contributing factors in the rise of crime and drug use rates. Programs could be designed, as they were in the 1960s, for job training, long-term unemployment assistance, and even government-subsidized corporate internships that might provide hope and job possibilities for the most disadvantaged city residents. In addition, government subsidized medical care, family assistance, and aid for the homeless, such as the present program of Aid to Dependent Children, could provide a social safety net below which U.S. citizens would not fall. This would improve the life chances of the less affluent and remove from the city streets some of the worst cases of need that threaten the quality of life for everyone.

Conservative Approaches to Urban Problems

Conservatives, in contrast, believe in limited government intervention and severely restricted government spending. They accuse liberals of squandering society's wealth through excessive public spending. Consequently, they are opposed to the kinds of programs sponsored by liberals precisely because they cost money and must be supported by taxes on private income or corporate profits. Conservatives also address the issue of uneven development. In their view, less advantaged people and places must make themselves more competitive so that they will be in the contest for capital investment. It's up to people and places themselves to become more attractive.

Conservatives believe that many of the problems of the poor reside in their *own* personalities and family traits. Analysts such as Edward Banfield (1974), for example, suggest that poor people are not motivated to find legitimate jobs and that they prefer welfare programs because they have been encouraged to do so by eager liberals seeking to exercise their agenda and support the growth of government bureaucracy (see Jencks, 1992). James Murray's influential book *Losing Ground* argued that welfare and other government programs actually increased poverty and caused the increase in the number of unwed mothers. This book was referred to (by conservatives) as the Bible of the Reagan administration.

Recently a variant of the conservative position has been taken up by black critics of liberalism such as Shelby Steele (1990). They argue that urban liberals and their programs, such as affirmative action, have ruined the moral character of blacks while the latter have languished in the ghettos of northern cities. Blacks have been made dependent and are losing the ability to cultivate their own inner resources as a consequence of city bureaucracies and their liberal programs of aid. Consequently, the immense problems of the ghettoized poor (formerly called the "underclass") are really the outcome of decades of liberal policies that forced blacks to become wards of the state.

It must be pointed out that even if people favor government intervention for the pursuit of social justice, our study of the record of government metropolitan policy over the last 50 years shows that expensive public programs have continually been co-opted by the business community. Hence, there is considerable evidence against returning to the blind faith of liberals and active public spending to combat social ills, even if we could do so.

Overcoming the Liberal–Conservative Impasse

What hope exists for the urban future? The lessons of history teach us that either/or choices are unfair. We must look beyond the clash of liberal and conservative ideology and beyond all ideological means of understanding urban problems. What possible solutions might overcome the liberal–conservative ideological impasse?

An important but neglected dimension to the debate on urban problems involves recognizing the fact that local governments have only limited ability to plan adequately for social change. The ideological debate between liberals and conservatives misses an important dimension, namely, the limitations of local government as administrative structures. It also fails to address the particular relationships among the federal, state, and local levels that have always worked against adequate planning and public policy in the United States.

Within metropolitan areas, there are so many levels of government, each with its own limited administration, that power is both highly fragmented and weakly applied. Social programs initiated by cities are ineffective because they must tackle problems that are regional in scope. So cities simply control too small a piece of the regional pie to fight the immense problems of uneven development, such as the need for affordable housing. In fact, it can be argued that the city is not the place to initiate programs aimed at social problems of broad scope or at alleviating the inequities of uneven development. Suburbs and cities share similar problems, and the growth patterns of one are linked to those of the other. Hence, a *metropolitan* perspective on improving the quality of life becomes imperative for adequate public policy. Problems that are national in scope, such as crime or the crisis of health care, must be returned to the responsibility of the national and state levels of government, where they belong. By understanding the relationship between spatial and social levels in the study of policy, we can sort out what should and should not be the responsibility of local government. And by adopting a metropolitan, regional perspective, we can design better ways of attacking the problems of social justice and uneven development.

There is strong evidence that the political fragmentation of metropolitan regions in the United States is responsible for uneven sociospatial development. For example, Detroit and Toronto are industrial cities located just some 230 miles apart. Detroit has long been in the throes of economic crisis. While the metropolitan region contains more than 4 million people (and many wealthy suburbs), the city of Detroit lost half of its population from 1950 to 1990. Its murder rate increased 10 times during this same period, from 6 per 100,000 persons in 1950 to 60 per 100,000 in 1989. Entire city blocks are now vacant, the housing long since abandoned due to white flight to the suburbs and destroyed by arson. Some of these neighborhoods have actually been reclaimed by "urban forests," and deer have returned to the city. Today the city is overwhelmingly black and poor, with apparently few opportunities for economic revival due to the restructuring of the auto industry that brought the city to greatness in the 1950s.

In contrast, Toronto has doubled its population since 1950, going from slightly more than 1 million to 2.3 million in 1990. Compared to Detroit, Toronto is relatively crime free, with a murder rate of less than 5 per 100,000 people, lower than any U.S.

city of 1 million or more population. Yet Toronto has a diversity of people with a mix of racial, ethnic, and class groups living within its borders. According to one report:

> One thing does much to explain Toronto's success: the enactment in 1953 of a federal form of government for the 13 previously independent municipalities in the area. The original 13 have consolidated into six. They are responsible for local affairs, while the Metro council handles area affairs, including Metro-wide planning. (*The Economist,* May 1990:17)

The Metro-wide government consolidates resources in the entire region and coordinates the growth of both the central city and its suburbs. As a result, many of the problems brought about by uneven sociospatial development that have plagued Detroit have been avoided by the Toronto region. For example:

> Metro-wide co-ordination of the education system has given Toronto civilized schools. Detroit has some civilized and well financed schools too, but they are in the suburbs; the city schools are mainly deprived, like their pupils. (*The Economist,* May 1990:18)

Regional government has worked in Toronto. In contrast, Detroit cannot possibly find the resources to address its ills because it is cut off from the affluent suburbs. Should this society tolerate the extreme forms of deprivation and affluence that can be readily seen in this region, even if all metro Detroit people suffer from the current recession and the severe problems of the auto industry?

Due to the autonomous home rule of local communities that discourages regional forms of government, suburban settlement spaces have effectively insulated themselves from the need to address the problems of uneven sociospatial development. But the contrast is not only one of spatial organization. Canada has a system of national health care that is run by the national government; the United States does not. The two federal governments differ regarding what they have chosen to bear as national responsibilities, and this also affects the quality of life for metropolitan residents. The issue of national concern for social justice cannot be separated from that of local policy.

In sum, we may not know all the answers to the present case of urban decline, but one very good try at finding a solution that avoids ideological debates focuses on the *structural* limitations of city government and the excessive fragmentation of local jurisdictions. Along with these sociospatial concerns are jurisdictional dilemmas among local, state, and national levels that must be faced to determine who shares the burden of responsibility for the quality of life in the United States—the individual alone (as conservative policy dictates), the city, the state, or the federal government.

Without metropolitan coordination, and lacking support from higher levels of government, cities simply do not possess the resources they need to address commanding problems of everyday life. At some point in the future, national leaders must provide the vision necessary to share the responsibility for social concerns at the federal and state levels, where it belongs. Until then, the quality of life not only in central cities but across metropolitan regions as a whole will be dependent on the well-being of local business concerns within an increasingly competitive global economy.

Future Prospects for the Metropolitan Region

In the nineteenth century, industrial manufacturing was centered in the large city. This form of settlement space also concentrated capital and the essential resource of labor. The social world of urban life revolved around home, work, and neighborhood, all located within the space of a short walk or a ride on public transport.

After World War II, the scale of urban life changed forever. The mass movement to the suburbs and the decline of central city manufacturing transformed the way home, work, and neighborhood were knit together. Automobile commutation or complex mass transportation lines of railroads, subways, and buses became the threads that helped weave a new, regional urban fabric. People's homes were located miles from their jobs, while the places where they lived took on new importance as a commodity with the mass introduction of homeownership. Jobs changed from an almost exclusive reliance on manufacturing to the more educationally demanding careers of service industries and their deskilled counterparts in office work and clerking. Finally, it was not so much that the neighborhood changed as that the activity of neighboring changed. People no longer relied on those most adjacent to them to fulfill the needs of intimacy and sociality. They ranged across the metropolitan region participating in friendship networks that were deployed across space.

The new scale of settlement space life was propelled by the process of deconcentration, which we have defined as combining both decentralization of people and resources and recentralization in new spaces of agglomeration. Deconcentration disassembled the old, compact industrial city and replaced it with a regional, multicentered form of social organization. Factories, department stores, religious institutions, hospitals, universities, banks, and specialty stores no longer needed the proximity of central city location. They decentralized and dispersed throughout the metropolitan region. Deconcentration was helped along by government programs that encouraged the flight of people, who were overwhelmingly white and middle class, to the suburbs, thereby providing both a market and a labor force for relocated business activity. Department stores, malls, and fast-food outlets peppered the metropolitan region with branch outlets that originally were designed to capture dispersed consumer markets but now lead and distort the expansion of settlement space into the far reaches of the metropolitan region.

At the same time, the process of deconcentration transformed the large, central city. Its population has become a study in contrasts—between the affluent and the poor especially, but also between the housed or pampered and the homeless, the high-status professional and the new working class of service employees, and the established and the new immigrant. A shift to service industries within the central city has meant demanding, professional employment opportunities for those with skills, and a burgeoning but relatively low-paid array of jobs in services that cater to the needs of the professional class. As central cities fell under the domination of finance capital and its links to global patterns of investment, the population stabilized or declined. In contrast, metropolitan regions that included these large cities grew steadily, if not rapidly, over the last two decades.

The growth of multicentered metropolitan regions pushes us forward into the twenty-first century. Global economic changes have caused the transformation of

Two contrasting views of the future: Frank Lloyd Wright's vision (top) and the dystopia depicted in *Blade Runner* (bottom).

cities both in the United States and elsewhere. Large, central cities have become the command and control centers of the world economy. New centralized spaces have sprung up based on new ways of making money in increasingly automated or high-technology industries. Located principally within suburban settlement space, the new high-tech spaces such as Silicon Valley or Route 128 in the United States, the Oxbridge complex in England, and the Scuba complex outside of Tokyo became the growth poles of the new advanced economies. The minicenters of employment in the United States helped to define suburban space as a series of residential developments serviced by commercial centers and malls, fast-food outlets, branch banking, and drive-in services.

Tying all this together are the seemingly limitless miles of invisible microwave and fiber optic links that reach across the metropolitan landscape and around the globe. Business is conducted at the office, in the car, and at home using telephone modems, fax machines, cellular phones, desktop PCs, laptops, and revolving pools of clerical helpers and subcontractors. For many people, these new arrangements seem the natural outcome of available choices. The concentrated city of the nineteenth century has exploded. But each individual must make his or her own choice about where to live, where to work, where to go to school, where to shop, and where to worship within the expanding matrix of separate places that make up the metropolitan region—places that have been planned to produce profit within the real estate sector, not to enhance equal opportunity or the quality of life.

The puzzle comes together through personal decisions constrained by available budgets, and invariably involves a good deal of commuting if gainful employment can be obtained. Only the purchase of a home seems to anchor families within a chosen sphere of travel. While an incredible variety of jobs, leisure activities, shopping outlets, and recreational amenities are available to metropolitan residents, they are rarely all found in the same place. Thus, at present everyday life depends on the daily round of commuting and chaffeuring between activities, some of which are located in far-flung places of the metropolis.

The future prospects of this new, multicentered mode of settlement space involve issues of equity, planning, and policy. In recent years, for example, not only have extreme forms of inequality, such as homelessness, surfaced in the United States and elsewhere, but other, more subtle forms, such as the inability of first-time buyers to find affordable housing, have also appeared. The quality of community life has been on the decline in central cities for over a decade, but now also plagues suburban settlement space within the metropolis. Educational, transportation, environmental, recreational, crime, and employment issues increasingly define the dilemmas of daily life. The problem of uneven development not only haunts the central city, where the disparities of life chances are on view in the extreme, but also characterizes the suburbs and increasingly defines the nature of all societies, rich and poor alike. The more affluent generally have been relatively sheltered from social problems such as violent crime, whether they lived in barricaded urban enclaves such as the security-guarded high rises of U.S. cities, the *condominium fechado* of Rio in Brazil, or the supreme isolation of affluent suburbs. Today this shielding is increasingly less possible.

One possible future prospect is for everyday life to become progressively more inconvenient for all members of the metropolitan region. Another prospect is that public policy may continue to make problems manageable in the future. However, several limitations now are placed on policy interventions. Perhaps the most formidable is the fiscal crisis of the state, which prevents adequate funding of programs. Another drawback is the inadequacies of government intervention, perceived by both progressives and conservatives. The very idea of intervention must be rethought, with special attention to the sociospatial or structural arrangements of policy. Modernist ideas of unbridled progress arising from government intervention and rational planning seem unable to work, even when they have some promise of success.

The massive, complex weave of the multicentered, regional fabric must be retailored to provide a more human scale of daily life and a more equitable manner of living and working arrangements. In the United States, people have always been satisfied with the most minimal planning, especially when they have been willing to sacrifice community goals entirely in return for the ability to purchase an affordable home. In the future, we should not settle for so little. Instead, we should return to the fundamental lessons of the sociospatial approach, which prefers that decisions about the built environment be made by the majority rather than by the current, select few who pursue profit at the expense of social equity.

It is possible that we may decide to jettison the utopian impulse altogether and allow the metropolis to find its own level of prospect and decline; this would amount to a policy of limited intervention. This is not only the program of Republican administrations under Ronald Reagan and George Bush but also the result of policies put into place by the Clinton administration. Or we might return to some well-thought-out ideas about shaping present growth for future prospects and the renewed use of a government role in advancing the quality of life. As with other philosophical and political decisions, the choice will be ours to make if we don't surrender to the wishes of special interests.

The Future of the Urban Inquiry

For many urbanists, analyzing metropolitan phenomena involves a choice between the competing paradigms of human ecology and political economy. While human ecology has been useful because it appreciates the role location plays in social interaction, it undertheorizes this role and adopts one-dimensional, technologically deterministic explanations for sociospatial processes. In contrast, the political economy approach deals with a host of important concepts and issues that ecology neglects, such as the role of capital and class in the urban drama. It too is limited, however, because it neglects aspects of culture and politics that cannot be reduced to class phenomena. Sadly, it also ignores the important features of spatial relations by considering location merely as a container for economic processes.

By adopting the social spatial perspective, we pass beyond the limitations of political economy to explain how the built environment changes and develops. Political economy's focus on the restructuring of global capitalism cannot alone explain the changes experienced by metropolitan development. The missing element is supplied by a focus on real estate interests as the leading edge of change that channels growth in specific directions. Once spatial patterns are altered in one region of the metropolis, this alteration affects all other parts. Hence, social space operates as both a product and a producer of changes in the metropolitan environment.

Both ecological and political economy perspectives assume that the state has only a weak role as an agent of change. Ecology simply ignores government intervention. Political economy often treats the state as simply the direct agent of capitalist interests. But the involvement of the state in sociospatial development is both critical and complex. First, government policies help provide the "pull" factors of growth. Second, they are the focus of urban and suburban social movements that aim for a redistribution of both wealth and social costs. Third, government officials are relatively autonomous agents who do not simply follow the needs of capital alone but pursue interests of their own to bring about social change. Finally, national policies of taxation and spending can transfer wealth from one region of the country to another; hence, programs such as military spending are critical causes of regional growth or decline, in addition to private-sector investment patterns. As we have seen demonstrated in a variety of contexts, private- and public-sector efforts often work hand in hand.

The sociospatial perspective utilizes a semiotic approach to understand how culture and ideology define sociospatial processes, such as the appeals to progress and modernism in urban renewal or the use of religious belief to structure the ancient cities of the past. The sociospatial approach considers all built environments as meaningful social spaces. Behavior occurs within these social spaces, but our own behaviors may change the actual meaning and use of that space. The sociospatial approach further captures the special articulation between territory and culture that produces lifestyle networks and variation in daily community life within the metropolis. Ethnic, gender-oriented, or racially defined lifestyles enact themselves within the built environment. The street corner, the mall, the game arcade, the local bar, the school cafeteria, and the commuter train, car, or bus are all special venues where social networks interact.

Finally, the sociospatial perspective takes an integrated view of the multicentered metropolitan region. We have considered both urban and suburban settlement space. The traditional field of urban sociology possessed too narrow a focus on the central city. Urban texts invariably treat suburbs only in a special chapter devoted to that purpose, while the remainder of the text specializes in the study of the large, central city, even though a majority of population, employment, and business activity is located within expanding metropolitan environments. Urban or suburban concerns are largely metropolitan concerns, and any governmental efforts should begin from a regional rather than a local perspective.

The future of the metropolitan inquiry will mean important conceptual changes. In place of traditional urban sociology, we should have a field called the "sociology of settlement space" that would deal with all forms of human settlement—tribal spaces, cities, suburbs, metropolises, megalopolises, and so on—so that we no longer privilege the city. In place of a contentious and often confusing clash of different paradigms (ecology for aggregate data analysis, political economy for economic issues, and the culturist approach for ethnography), we can look forward to integrated discussions of all levels (micro, macro, and meso) following the synthesis of the sociospatial approach. Finally, by critically evaluating planning efforts because they neglect the importance of space, we have a means by which we can construct and live in more humane and enjoyable environments that confront, rather than hide from, the seemingly intractable issues of social justice.

BIBLIOGRAPHY

Abrahamson, P. 1988. *Welfare States in Crisis: The Crumbling of the Scandinavian Model.* Copenhagen: Forlaget Sociologi.

Abrams, C. 1965. *The City Is the Frontier.* New York: Harper & Row.

———. 1977. "Squatting and Squatters." In J. Abu-Lughod and R. Hay, Jr., eds., *Third World Urbanization.* Chicago: Maaroufa Press.

Abu-Lughod, J. 1969. "Testing the Theory of Social Area Analysis: The Ecology of Cairo, Egypt." *American Sociological Review* 34 (April):313–343.

Adams, C. 1986. "Homelessness in the Postindustrial City." *Urban Affairs Quarterly* 21:527–549.

Aina, T. 1990. "Shanty Town Economy: The Case of Metropolitan Lagos, Nigeria." Pp. 113–148 in S. Datta, ed., *Third World Urbanization: Reappraisals and New Perspectives.* Stockholm: HSFR.

Alford, R. 1975. *Health Care Politics.* Chicago: University of Chicago Press.

Alicea, M. 1990. "Dual Home Bases: A Reconceptualization of Puerto Rican Migration." *Latino Studies Journal* 1, 3:78–98.

Alihan, M. 1938. *Social Ecology: A Critical Analysis: Ideological and Interest Group Barriers to Reform.* New York: Columbia University Press.

Allen, O. 1990. *New York, New York: A History of the World's Most Exhilarating and Challenging City.* New York: Atheneum.

Althusser, L. 1971. *Lenin and Philosophy.* New York: Monthly Review Press.

Anderson, E. 1978. *A Place on the Corner.* Chicago: University of Chicago Press.

———. 1990. *Streetwise: Race, Class and Change in an Urban Community.* Chicago: University of Chicago Press.

———. 1999. *Code of the Street: Decency, Violence, and the Moral Life of the Inner City.* New York: W.W. Norton.

Anderson, M. 1964. *The Federal Bulldozer.* Cambridge, MA: MIT Press.

Applebome, P. 1991, January 28. "Although Urban Blight Worsens, Most People Don't Feel Its Impact." *New York Times,* p. A20.

Arax, M. 1987, April 6. "Monterey Park: Nation's First Suburban Chinatown." *Los Angeles Times.*

Armstrong, R. 1972. *The Office Industry: Patterns of Growth and Location.* Cambridge, MA: MIT Press.

———. 1979. "National Trends in Office Construction, Employment and Headquarters Location in the United States Metropolitan Areas." In P. Daniels, ed., *Spatial Patterns of Office Growth and Location.* New York: John Wiley.

Auletta, K. 1983. *The Underclass.* New York: Random House.

Bachrach, P., and M. Baratz. 1962. "Two Faces of Power." *American Political Science Review* 56:947–952.

Bacon, E. N. 1967. *Design of Cities.* New York: Viking Press.

Baker, P. 1974. *Urbanization and Political Change: A Study of the Politics of Lagos.* Los Angeles and Berkeley, CA: University of California Press.

Baltzell, E. D. 1958. *Philadelphia Gentlemen: The Making of a National Upper Class.* Glencoe, IL: Free Press.

Banfield, E. 1974. *The Unheavenly City Revisited.* Boston: Little, Brown.

Baran, P., and P. Sweezy. 1966. *Monopoly Capital.* New York: Monthly Review Press.

Barbanel, J. 1992, February 18. "Robberies on the Rise on Long Island." *New York Times,* p. A15.

Barnekov, T., and D. Rich. 1989. "Privatism and the Limits of Local Economic Development Policy." *Urban Affairs Quarterly* 25:212–238.

Barnes, J. A. 1954. "Class and Committees in a Norwegian Island Parish." *Human Relations* 7:39–58.

———. 1972. *Social Networks.* Addison Wesley Modular Publications, Number 26.

Barone, C. 1983. "Dependency, Marxist Theory, and Salvaging the Idea of Capitalism in South Korea." *Review of Radical Political Economy* 16:1.

Barthes, R. 1973, *L'Empire des Signes.* Geneva: Albert Skira.

———. 1986. "Semiology and the Urban." Pp. 87–98 in M. Gottdiener and A. Lagopoulos, *The City and the Sign.* New York: Columbia University Press.

Baumgartner, M. 1988. *The Moral Order of a Suburb.* Oxford: Oxford University Press.

Bean, F., and M. Tienda. 1987. *The Hispanic Population of the US.* New York: Russell Sage.

Benard, D., and E. Schlaffer. 1993. " 'The Man in the Street': Why He Harasses." Pp. 338–391 in L. Richardson and V. Taylor, *Feminist Frontiers III.* New York: McGraw-Hill.

Berak, B. 1991, May 5. "A Shelter for Rage, Fear, Crack." *New York Times,* pp. A1, A24.

Berger, B. M. 1960. *Working Class Suburb.* Berkeley: University of California Press.

Berman, M. 1981. *All That Is Solid Melts into Air: The Experience of Modernity.* New York: Simon & Schuster.

Bernard, R., and B. Rice. 1983. *Sunbelt Cities: Politics and Growth since World War II.* Austin: University of Texas Press.

Berry, B. (ed.). 1977. *The Social Burden of Environmental Pollution.* Cambridge, MA: Ballinger.

Berry, B., and J. Kasanda. 1977. *Contemporary Urban Ecology.* New York: Macmillan.

Berry, B. J. L., and P. Rees. 1969. "The Factorial Ecology of Calcutta." *American Journal of Sociology* 74:445–491.

Berry, M. 1989. "Industrialization, De-industrialization and Uneven Development: The Case of the Pacific Rim." Pp. 171–216 in M. Gottdiener and N. Komninos, eds., *Capitalist Development and Crisis Theory.* New York and London: Macmillan.

Berry, W. 1972. *The Unsettling of America*. New York: Avon.

Bestor, T. 1985. *Japanese Urban Life*. Palo Alto: Stanford University Press.

Blake, W. 1977. "London." P. 150 in *Songs of Innocence and of Experience*. New York: Oxford.

Blakely, E. J., and M. G. Snyder. 1997. *Fortress America: Gated Communities in the United States*. Washington, DC: Brookings Institution.

Blau, J. 1992. *The Visible Poor: Homelessness in the United States*. New York: Oxford University Press.

Bluestone, B., and B. Harrison. 1982. *The Deindustrialization of America: Plant Closings, Community Abandonment and the Dismantling of Basic Industry*. New York: Basic Books.

Blum, B. 1978. *Cities: An Environmental Wilderness*. Washington, DC: Environmental Protection Agency.

Blumer, M. 1984. *The Chicago School of Sociology: Institutionalization, Diversity, and the Rise of Sociological Research*. Chicago: University of Chicago Press.

Body-Gendrot, S. 1987. "Plant Closures in Socialist France." Pp. 237–251 in M. Smith and J. Feagin, eds., *The Capitalist City*. Oxford: Blackwell.

Boer, L. 1990. "(In)formalization: The Forces Beyond." *International Journal of Urban and Regional Research* 14:404–422.

Bollens, J., and H. Schmandt. 1965. *The Metropolis: Its People, Politics, and Economic Life*. New York: Harper & Row.

Bookchin, M. 1974. *The Limits of the City*. New York: Harper & Row.

———. 1990. *The Philosophy of Social Ecology: Essays on Dialectical Naturalism*. Montreal: Black Rose Books.

Borchert, J. 1967. "American Metropolitan Evolution." *Geographical Review* 57:301–332.

Bordan, I. 1999. "Skateboarders, Urban Space, and Urban Planning." In R. Hutchison, ed., *Research in Urban Sociology,* Vol. 5. Greenwich, CT: JAI Press.

Bott, E. 1971 [1957]. *Family and Social Network*. New York: Free Press [London: Tavistock].

Boudon, P. 1986. "Rewriting of a City: The Medina of Tunis." Pp. 303–322 in M. Gottdiener and A. Lagopoulos, eds., *The City and the Sign*. New York: Columbia University Press.

Bourne, L., and J. Simmons (eds.). 1978. *Systems of Cities: Readings on Structure, Growth, and Policy*. New York: Oxford University Press.

Boyte, H. 1980. *The Backyard Revolution: Understanding the New Citizens Movement*. Philadelphia: Temple University Press.

Bradshaw, Y., and E. Fraser. 1989. "City Size, Economic Development, and Quality of Life in China: New Empirical Evidence." *American Sociological Review* 54:986–1003.

Braudel, F. 1973. *Capitalism and Material Life: 1400–1800*. New York: Harper & Row.

Bullard, R. 1990. *Dumping in Dixie: Race, Class and Environmental Quality*. Boulder, CO: Westview Press.

Bullard, R., and J. Feagin. 1991. "Racism and the City." Pp. 55–76 in M. Gottdiener and C. G. Pickvance, eds., *Urban Life in Transition*. Newbury Park, CA: Sage.

Burgess, E. 1925. "The Growth of the City: An Introduction to a Research Project." In R. Park, E. Burgess, and R. McKenzie, eds., *The City*. Chicago: University of Chicago Press.

Buss, T., and F. S. Redburn. 1983. *Shutdown at Youngstown: Public Policy for Mass Unemployment*. Albany: SUNY Press.

Castells, M. 1977. *The Urban Question*. Cambridge, MA: MIT Press.

———. 1983. *The City and the Grass Roots*. Berkeley and Los Angeles: University of California Press.

Cavan, R. S. 1928. *Suicide.* Chicago: University of Chicago Press.

Chambers, I. 1986. *Popular Culture: The Metropolitan Experience.* London: Methuen.

Chase-Dunn, C. 1985. "The System of World Cities, A.D. 800–1975." Pp. 269–292 in M. Timberlake, ed., *Urbanization in the World Economy.* Orlando: Academic Press.

Chen, X. 1988. "Giant Cities and the Urban Hierarchy in China." Pp. 225–251 in M. Dogan and J. Kasarda, eds., *The Metropolis Era,* Vol. 1. Newbury Park, CA: Sage.

Childe, V. G. 1950. "The Urban Revolution." *Town Planning Review* 21:4–17.

———. 1954. *What Happened in History.* New York: Penguin Books.

Clavel, P. 1985. *The Progressive City: Planning and Participation, 1969–1984.* New Brunswick, NJ: Rutgers University Press.

Cleaver, H. 1989. "Close the IMF, Abolish Debt, and End Development: A Class Analysis of the International Debt Crisis." *Capital and Class,* No. 39, pp. 17–50.

Cochrane, A. 1982. *Patterns of Urban Development.* Unit 29, Block 7. Milton Keynes: Open University Press.

Cooper, F. 1987. *On the African Waterfront: Urban Disorders and the Transformation of Work in Colonial Mombasa.* New Haven, CT: Yale.

Coquery-Vidrovitch, C. 1990. "A History of African Urbanization: Labor, Women and the Informal Sector—A Survey of Recent Studies." Pp. 75–89 in S. Datta, ed., *Third World Urbanization: Reappraisals and New Perspectives.* Stockholm: HSFR.

Coughlin, R. 1979. "Agricultural Land Conversion in the Urban Fringe." In M. Schept, ed., *Farmlands, Food and the Future.* Ankers, IA: Soil Conservation Society of America.

Cressey, P. 1932. *The Taxi-Dance Hall: A Sociological Study in Commercialized Recreation and City Life.* Chicago: University of Chicago Press.

———. 1956. "The Ecological Organization of Rangoon, Burma." *Sociology and Social Research* 40:166–69.

Crump, S. 1962. *Ride the Big Red Cars: How Trolleys Helped Build Southern California.* Los Angeles: Crest Publications.

Dahl, R. 1961. *Who Governs? Democracy and Power in an American City.* New Haven, CT: Yale University Press.

Dale, A., and C. Banford. 1989. "Social Polarization in Britain: 1973–82, Evidence from the General Household Survey." *International Journal of Urban and Regional Research* 13:482–494.

Darley, J., and B. Latane. 1970. *The Unresponsive Bystander: Why Doesn't He Help?* New York: Appleton-Century-Crofts.

Datta, S. 1990. *Third World Urbanization: Reappraisals and New Perspectives.* Stockholm: HSFR.

Davis, M. 1986. *Prisoners of the American Dream: Politics and Economy in the History of the U.S. Working Class.* London: Verso.

———. 1987. "Chinatown, Part Two? The Internationalization of Downtown Los Angeles." *New Left Review* 164:65–84.

———. 1990. *City of Quartz: Excavating the Future in Los Angeles.* New York: Verso.

Dear, M. J., H. E. Schockman, and G. Hise. 1996. *Rethinking Los Angeles.* Newbury Park, CA: Sage.

Defoe, D. 1966 [1722]. *A Journal of the Plague Year.* New York: Penguin.

Dinnerstein, L., R. Nichols, and D. Reimers. 1990. *Natives and Strangers: Blacks, Indians and Immigrants in America.* New York: Oxford University Press.

Dogan, M., and J. Kasarda. 1988. *The Metropolis Era,* Vols. 1 and 2. Newbury Park, CA: Sage.

Dooley, D., and R. Catalano. 1980. "Economic Change as a Cause of Behavioral Disorder." *Psychological Bulletin* 87:450–468.

Dorsett, L. 1968. *The Pendergast Machine.* New York: Oxford University Press.

Douglas, M. 1988. "Transnational Capital and Urbanization on the Pacific Rim: An Introduction." *International Journal of Urban and Regional Research* 12:343–355.

Drake, St. Clair, and H. Cayton. 1945. *Black Metropolis: A Study of Negro Life in a Northern City.* New York: Harcourt Brace.

Dreiser, T. 1900. *Sister Carrie.* Boston: Houghton Mifflin.

DuBois, W. E. B. 1899. *The Philadelphia Negro.* Philadelphia: University of Pennsylvania Press.

Durkheim, E. 1933 [1893]. *The Division of Labor in Society.* Translated by George Simpson. Glencoe, IL: Free Press.

Dutton, T. 1989. "Cities, Cultures and Resistance: Beyond Leon Krier and the Postmodern Condition." *JAE* 42:3–9.

The Economist. 1990, May 19. "Toronto and Detroit: Canadians Do It Better," pp. 17–20.

Ehrenreich, B. 1990. *Fear of Falling: The Inner Life of the Middle Class.* New York: HarperCollins.

Eisenstadt, S., and A. Shachar. 1987. *Society, Culture and Urbanization.* Beverly Hills, CA: Sage.

Engels, F. 1973. *The Condition of the Working Class in England: From Personal Observations and Authentic Sources.* Moscow: Progress Publishers.

Ernst, R. 1970. "Immigrants and Tenements in New York City: 1825–1863." Pp. 113–126 in R. Mohl and N. Betten, eds., *Urban America in Historical Perspective.* New York: W. and T. Publishers.

Espiritu, Y., and I. Light. 1991. "The Changing Ethnic Shape of Contemporary Urban America." Pp. 35–54 in M. Gottdiener and C. G. Pickvance, *Urban Life in Transition.* Newbury Park, CA: Sage.

Farley, R., and W. Allen. 1987. *The Color Line and the Quality of Life in America.* New York: Russell Sage.

Fava, S. 1980. "Women's Place in the New Suburbia." Pp. 125–149 in G. Wekerle, R. Peterson, and D. Morley, eds., *New Space for Women.* Boulder, CO: Westview Press.

Feagin, J. 1983. *The Urban Real Estate Game: Playing Monopoly with Real Money.* Englewood Cliffs, NJ: Prentice-Hall.

———. 1988. *Houston: The Free Enterprise City.* New Brunswick, NJ: Rutgers University Press.

———. 1992. "Why Not Study the American 'Overclass'?" *Contemporary Sociology* 21, 4:449–451.

Feagin, J., and M. Smith. 1987. "Cities and the New International Division of Labor: An Overview." Pp. 3–36 in M. Smith and J. Feagin, *The Capitalist City.* Oxford: Blackwell.

Fernandez-Kelly, M. 1991, December 6. "Labor Force Recomposition and Industrial Restructuring in Electronics." Paper presented at symposium: "Crossing National Borders: Invasions or Involvement." Columbia University.

Fiery, W. 1945. "Sentiment and Symbolism as Ecological Variables." *American Sociological Review* 10:140–148.

Fischer, C. 1975. "Toward a Subcultural Theory of Urbanism." *American Journal of Sociology* 80:1319–1341.

———. 1976. *The Urban Experience.* New York: Harcourt Brace.

————. 1982. *To Dwell among Friends: Personal Networks in Town and City.* Chicago: University of Chicago Press.

Fishman, R. 1987. *Bourgeois Utopias: The Rise and Fall of Suburbia.* New York: Basic Books.

Flanagan, W. 1990. *Urban Sociology: Images and Structures.* Boston: Allyn and Bacon.

Fleischmann, A. 1991. "Atlanta: Urban Coalitions in a Suburban Sea." Pp. 97–114 in H. Savitch and J. Thomas, eds., *Big City Politics in Transition.* Newbury Park, CA: Sage.

Fong, T. P. 1991. *The First Suburban Chinatown: The Remaking of Monterey Park, California.* Philadelphia: Temple University Press.

Form, W. 1954. "The Place of Social Structure in the Determination of Land Use." *Social Forces* 32:317–323.

Forrest, R. 1991. "The Privatization of Collective Consumption." Pp. 169–195 in M. Gottdiener and C. Pickvance, *Urban Life in Transition.* Newbury Park, CA: Sage.

Frazier, E. F. 1932. *The Negro Family in Chicago.* Chicago: University of Chicago Press.

French, R., and F. Hamilton (eds.). 1979. *The Socialist City: Spatial Structure and Urban Policy.* New York: J. Wiley and Sons.

Frey, W. 1979. "Population Movement and City-Suburban Redistribution: An Analytic Framework." *Demography* 15:571–588.

Frey, W., and A. Speare. 1988. *Regional and Metropolitan Growth and Decline in the United States.* New York: Russell Sage.

Friedrichs, J. 1988. "Large Cities in Eastern Europe." Pp. 128–154 in M. Dogan and J. Kasarda, eds., *The Metropolis Era,* Vol. 1. Newbury Park, CA: Sage.

Frobel, F., J. Heinrichs, and O. Krege. 1980. *The New International Division of Labor.* New York: Cambridge University Press.

Frug, G. E. 1997. "New Urbanism or New Suburbanism." *Harvard Design Magazine* (Winter/Spring):54.

Fuentes, A., and B. Ehrenreich. 1987. "Women in the Global Factory." Pp. 201–215 in R. Peet, ed., *International Capitalism and Industrial Restructuring.* Boston: Allen and Unwin.

Fujita, K. 1988. "The Technopolis: High Technology and Regional Development in Japan." *International Journal of Urban and Regional Research* 12:573–581.

Fussell, P. 1983. *Class: A Guide through the American Status System.* New York: Summit Books.

Gale, R. 1983. "The Environmental Movement and the Left: Antagonists or Allies?" *Sociological Inquiry* 53:179–199.

Gallup, G. 1982. *The Gallup Poll: Public Opinion 1981.* Wilmington, DE: Scholarly Resources.

Gans, H. 1962. *The Urban Villagers: Group and Class in the Life of Italian-Americans.* New York: Free Press.

————. 1968. *People and Plans: Essays on Urban Problems and Solutions.* New York: Basic Books.

————. 1968. "Urbanism and Suburbanism as a Way of Life: A Reevaluation of Definitions." Pp. 34–52 in H. Gans, *People and Plans.* New York: Basic Books.

————. 1990. "Deconstructing the Underclass: The Term's Dangers as a Planning Concept." *American Planning Association Journal* 56 (Summer):271–277.

Geisse, G., and F. Sabatini. 1988. "Latin American Cities and Their Poor." Pp. 322–336 in M. Dogan and J. Kasarda, eds., *The Metropolis Era,* Vol. 1. Newbury Park, CA: Sage.

Geruson, R., and D. McGrath. 1977. *Cities and Urbanization.* New York: Praeger.

Gibbs, L. 1981. *Love Canal: My Story.* Albany, NY: SUNY Press.

Girouard, M. 1985. *Cities and People: A Social and Architectural History.* New Haven, CT: Yale University Press.

Glaab, C., and A. T. Brown. 1967. *A History of Urban America.* New York: Macmillan.

Glaberson, W. 1992, April 21. "Swaddling Shoppers: A Mall's Cocoon Effect." *New York Times,* p. A10.

Glazer, N., and P. Moynihan. 1963. *Beyond the Melting Pot: The Negros, Puerto Ricans, Jews, Italians and Irish of New York City.* Cambridge, MA: MIT Press.

Goffman, E. 1963. *Behavior in Public Places: Notes on the Social Organization of Places.* New York: Free Press.

———. 1971. *Relations in Public: Microstudies of the Public Order.* New York: Basic Books.

Golledge, R., and G. Rushton (eds.). 1976. *Spatial Choice and Spatial Behavior.* Columbus: Ohio State University Press.

Goodman, P., and P. Goodman. 1974. *Communitas: Means of Livelihood and Ways of Life.* New York: Vintage.

Gordon, D. 1977. "Class Struggle and the Stages of Urban Development." In A. Watkins and R. Perry, eds., *The Rise of the Sunbelt Cities.* Beverly Hills, CA: Sage.

———. 1984. "Capitalist Development and the History of American Cities." Pp. 21–53 in W. Tabb and L. Sawers, eds., *Marxism and the Metropolis,* 2nd ed. New York: Oxford University Press.

Gordon, M. 1964. *Assimilation in American Life: The Role of Race, Religion and National Origins.* New York: Oxford University Press.

Gore, A. 1992. *Earth in the Balance: Ecology and the Human Spirit.* Boston: Houghton Mifflin.

Gorrie, P. 1991. "Farewell to Chinatown: An Era of Isolation Ends with the Transition to Toronto's Suburbs." *Canadian Geographic* (August/September):17–28.

Gottdiener, M. 1977. *Planned Sprawl: Public and Private Interests in Suburbia.* Beverly Hills, CA: Sage.

———. 1982. "Suburban Crime: Testing the Police Hypothesis." *Journal of Police Science and Administration* 10, 4:425–434.

———. 1985. *The Social Production of Urban Space.* Austin: University of Texas Press.

———. 1986. *The Decline of Urban Politics: Political Theory and the Crisis of the Local State.* Beverly Hills, CA: Sage.

———. 1990. "Crisis Theory and State Financed Capital." *International Journal of Urban and Regional Research* 14:383–403.

Gottdiener, M., and J. Feagin. 1988. "The Paradigm Shift in Urban Sociology." *Urban Affairs Quarterly* 24:163–187.

Gottdiener, M., and G. Kephart. 1991. "The Multinucleated Metropolitan Region: A Comparative Analysis." Pp. 31–54 in R. Kling, S. S. Olin, and M. Poster, eds., *Postsuburban California.* Berkeley and Los Angeles: University of California Press.

Gottdiener, M., and N. Komninos. 1989. *Capitalist Development and Crisis Theory.* New York: Macmillan.

Gottdiener, M., and A. Lagopoulos. 1986. *The City and the Sign: Introduction to Urban Semiotics.* New York: Columbia University Press.

Gottdiener, M., and N. Neiman. 1981. "Characteristics of Support for Local Growth Control." *Urban Affairs Quarterly* 17:55–73.

Gottdiener, M., and C. G. Pickvance (eds.). 1991. *Urban Life in Transition.* Newbury Park, CA: Sage.

Green, C., and B. Wilson. 1992. *The Struggle for Black Empowerment in New York City: Beyond the Politics of Pigmentation.* New York: McGraw-Hill.

Greenberg, J. 1990, September 3. "All about Crime." *New York,* pp. 20–32.

Grief, G. 1985. *Single Fathers.* Lexington, MA: Lexington Books.

Habermas, J. 1989. *The Structural Transformation of the Public Sphere: An Inquiry into a Category of Bourgeois Society.* Cambridge, MA: MIT Press.

Hacker, A. 1992. *Two Nations: Black and White, Separate, Hostile, Unequal.* New York: Scribner's.

Hagedorn, J. 1988. *People and Folks: Gangs, Crime and the Underclass in a Rustbelt City.* Chicago: Lakeview Press.

Hall, P. 1966. *The World Cities.* London: Weidenfeld and Nicolson.

———. 1988. "Urban Growth and Decline in Western Europe." Pp. 111–127 in M. Dogan and J. Kasarda, eds., *The Metropolis Era,* Vol. 1. Newbury Park, CA: Sage.

Handlin, O. 1951. *The Uprooted.* Boston: Little, Brown.

Hannerz, U. 1969. *Soulside: Inquiries into Ghetto Culture and Community.* New York: Columbia University Press.

———. 1980. *Exploring the City: Inquiries toward Urban Anthropology.* New York: Columbia University Press.

Hareven, T. 1982. *Family Time and Industrial Time: The Relationship between the Family and Work in a New England Industrial Economy.* New York: Cambridge University Press.

Harrington, M. 1962. *The Other America: Poverty in the United States.* New York: Macmillan.

Harris, C., and E. Ullman. 1945. "The Nature of Cities." *Annals of the Academy of Political and Social Science* 242:7–17.

Harrison, R., and D. Weinberg. 1992. "Changes in Racial and Ethnic Residential Segregation, 1980–1990." Paper prepared for the American Statistical Association Meetings in Boston, MA, August.

Harvey, D. 1973. *Social Justice and the City.* Baltimore: Johns Hopkins University Press.

———. 1975. "Class-Monopoly Rent, Finance Capital and the Urban Revolution." In S. Gale and E. Moore, eds., *The Manipulated City.* Chicago: Maaroufa Press.

———. 1976. "Labor, Capital and Class Struggle around the Built Environment." *Politics and Society* 6:265–295.

———. 1982. "The Urban Process under Capitalism: A Framework for Analysis." Pp. 91–122 in M. Dear and A. Scott, eds., *Urbanization and Urban Planning in Capitalist Society.* New York: Methuen.

———. 1985. *The Urbanization of Capital: Studies in the History and Theory of Capitalist Urbanization.* Baltimore: Johns Hopkins University Press.

Haussermann, H., and W. Siebel. 1990. "The Polarization of Urban Development in the Federal Republic of Germany and the Question of a New Municipal Policy." *International Journal of Urban and Regional Research* 14:369–382.

Hawley, A. 1950. *Human Ecology: A Theory of Community Structure.* New York: Ronald Press.

———. 1956. *The Changing Shape of Metropolitan America: Deconcentration since 1920.* Glencoe, IL: Free Press.

———. 1981. *Urban Society: An Ecological Approach,* 2nd ed. New York: J. Wiley and Sons.

Hayden, D. 1981. *The Grand Domestic Revolution: A History of Feminist Designs for American Homes, Neighborhoods, and Cities.* Cambridge, MA: MIT Press.

Hayner, N. 1936. *Hotel Life.* Chapel Hill, NC: University of North Carolina Press.

Henslin, J. 1972. "What Makes for Trust?" In J. Henslin, ed., *Down to Earth Sociology.* New York: Free Press.

Herbert, D., and R. Johnston. 1976. *Social Areas in Cities,* Vol. II. New York: John Wiley and Sons.

Hero, R., and R. Durand. 1985. "Explaining Citizen Evaluations of Urban Services." *Urban Affairs Quarterly: A Comparison of Some Alternative Models* 20:344–354.

Higham, J. 1977. *Strangers in the Land.* New York: Atheneum.

Hightower, J. 1975. *Eat Your Heart Out: Food Profiteering in America.* New York: Crown Publishers.

Hilkevitch, J., and P. Kendall. 1999, February 8. "Infrastructure Rust Never Sleeps: Aging Roads, Utilities, Sewers Are Reaching the Breaking Point." *Chicago Tribune.*

Hill, R. C. 1986. "Economic Crisis and Political Response in the Motor City." Pp. 313–338 in W. Tabb and L. Sawers, eds., *Sunbelt/Snowbelt.* New York: Oxford University Press.

Hochschild, A., and A. Machung. 1989. *The Second Shift.* New York: Viking.

Holston, J. 1989. *The Modernist City: An Anthropological Critique of Brasília.* Chicago: University of Chicago Press.

Hoover, D. 1971. *A Teacher's Guide to American Urban History.* Chicago: Quadrangle.

Hoyt, H. 1933. *One Hundred Years of Land Values in Chicago.* Chicago: University of Chicago Press.

Hughes, E. 1928. "A Study of a Secular Institution: The Chicago Real Estate Board." Ph.D. dissertation, University of Chicago.

Hummon, D. 1986. "Urban Views: Popular Perspectives on City Life." *Urban Life* 15:3–36.

Hunter, A. 1979. "The Urban Neighborhood: Its Analytical and Social Contexts." *Urban Affairs Quarterly* 14:267–288.

Hunter, F. 1953. *Community Power Structure: A Study of Decision Makers.* Chapel Hill, NC: University of North Carolina Press.

———. 1980. *Community Power Succession: Atlanta's Policy Makers Revisited.* Chapel Hill, NC: University of North Carolina Press.

Hutchison, R. 1988. "The Hispanic Population in Chicago: A Study in Population Growth and Acculturation." Pp. 193–229 in C. Marrett and C. Leggon, eds., *Research in Race and Ethnic Relations.* Greenwich, CT: JAI Press.

———. 1993. "Blazon Nouveau: Gang Graffiti in the Barrios of Los Angeles and Chicago." Pp. 137–172 in S. Cummings and D. J. Monti, eds., *Gangs: The Origins and Impact of Contemporary Youth Gangs in the United States.* Albany: State University of New York Press.

Hutchison, R., and C. Kyle. 1993. "Hispanic Street Gangs in Chicago Public Schools." P. 136 in S. Cummings and D. J. Monti, eds., *Gangs: The Origins and Impact of Contemporary Youth Gangs in the United States.* Albany: State University of New York Press.

Jackson, K. 1985. *Crabgrass Frontier: The Suburbanization of the United States.* New York: Oxford University Press.

Jacobs, J. 1984. *The Mall.* Prospect Heights, IL: Waveland Press.

Jacobs, J. 1961. *The Death and Life of Great American Cities.* New York: Random House.

———. 1970. *The Economy of Cities.* New York: Vintage Books.

Janowitz, M. 1956. *The Community Press in an Urban Setting.* Chicago: University of Chicago Press.

Jefferson, T. 1977. *Notes on the State of Virginia.* B. Wishey and W. G. Leuchtenberg, eds. New York: Harper & Row.

Jencks, C. 1992. *Rethinking Social Policy: Race, Poverty and the Underclass.* Cambridge, MA: Harvard University Press.

Jencks, C., and P. Peterson (eds.). 1991. *The Urban Underclass.* Washington, DC: Brookings Institution.

Jezierski, L. 1988. "Political Limits to Development in Two Declining Cities: Cleveland and Pittsburgh." Pp. 173–189 in M. Wallace and J. Rothschild, eds., *Deindustrialization and the Restructuring of American Industry.* Greenwich, CT: JAI Press.

Josey, A. 1980. *Singapore.* London: Andre Deutsch Ltd.

Judd, D. 1995. "The Rise of the New Walled City." Pp. 146–166 in H. Ligget and D. C. Perry, eds., *Spatial Practices*. Newbury Park, CA: Sage.

Kain, J. 1970. "The Distribution and Movement of Jobs and Industry." Pp. 1–44 in J. Q. Wilson, ed., *The Metropolitan Enigma*. Garden City, NY: Anchor.

Kanter, P. 1987. *The Dependent City: The Changing Political Economy of Urban America*. Glenview, IL: Scott, Foresman.

Karp, D., G. Stone, and W. Yoels. 1977. *Being Urban: A Social Psychological View of City Life*. Lexington, MA: D.C. Heath.

Karp, D., and W. Yoels. 1986. *Sociology and Everyday Life*. Itasca, IL: Peacock Publishers.

Kasarda, J. 1988. "Economic Restructuring of America's Urban Dilemma." Pp. 56–84 in M. Dogan and J. Kasarda, eds., *The Metropolis Era*, Vol. 1. Newbury Park, CA: Sage.

Kasarda, J., and E. Crenshaw. 1991. "Third World Urbanization: Dimensions, Theories, and Determinants." *Annual Review of Sociology* 17:467–501.

Kazis, R., and R. Grossman. 1982. *Fear at Work: Job Blackmail, Labor, and the Environment*. New York: Pilgrim Press.

Keller, S. 1968. *The Urban Neighborhood: A Sociological Perspective*. New York: Random House.

Kephart, G. 1991. "Economic Restructuring, Population Redistribution, and Migration in the United States." Pp. 12–34 in M. Gottdiener and C. G. Pickvance, eds., *Urban Life in Transition*. Newbury Park, CA: Sage.

Kim, J. 1988. "China's Modernizations, Reforms and Mobile Population." *International Journal of Urban and Regional Research* 12:595–608.

King, D. 1990. "Economic Activity and the Challenge to Local Government." Pp. 265–287 in D. King and J. Pierre, eds., *Challenges to Local Government*. London: Sage.

Kling, R., S. S. Olin, and M. Poster. 1991. *Postsuburban California*. Berkeley and Los Angeles: University of California Press.

Komninos, N. 1989. "From National to Local: The Janus Face of Crisis." Pp. 348–365 in M. Gottdiener and N. Komninos, eds., *Capitalist Development and Crisis Theory*. New York and London: Macmillan.

Korff, R. 1990. "Social Creativity, Power and Trading Relations in Bangkok." Pp. 168–185 in S. Datta, ed., *Third World Urbanization: Reappraisals and New Perspectives*. Stockholm: HSFR.

Ladanyi, J. 1989. "Changing Patterns of Residential Segregation in Budapest." *International Journal of Urban and Regional Research* 13:556–566.

Ladd, F. 1967. "A Note on the World across the Street." *Harvard Graduate School of Education Association Bulletin* 12:47–48.

Lagopoulos, A. 1986. "Semiotic Urban Models and Modes of Production: A Semiotic Approach." Pp. 176–201 in M. Gottdiener and A. Lagopoulos, eds., *The City and the Sign*. New York: Columbia University Press.

LaGory, M., and J. Pipkin. 1981. *Urban Social Space*. Belmont, CA: Wadsworth.

Lamarche, F. 1976. "Property Development and the Economic Foundations of the Urban Question." Pp. 85–119 in C. Pickvance, ed., *Urban Sociology: Critical Essays*. New York: St. Martin's Press.

Lamb, M. (ed.). 1986. *The Father's Role: Applied Perspectives*. New York: Wiley.

Landry, B. 1987. *The New Black Middle Class*. Berkeley: University of California Press.

Langdon, P. 1988. "A Good Place to Live." *The Atlantic* 261, 3:39–60.

Larkin, R. 1979. *Suburban Youth in Cultural Crisis.* New York: Oxford University Press.

Lawson, C. 1991, September 12. "A Writer Reveals the 'Dark Underside of Suburbia': Car Pools," *New York Times,* p. C-1.

Leborgne, D., and A. Lipietz. 1988. "Two Social Strategies in the Production of New Economic Spaces." *CEPREMAP Working Papers #8911.* Paris: CEPREMAP.

Lee, E. 1982. *Export-Led Industrialization and Development.* Geneva: ILO.

Lefebvre, H. 1991. *The Production of Space.* Oxford: Blackwell.

Leinsdorf, D., and D. Etra. 1973. *Citibank: Ralph Nader's Study Group Report on First National City Bank.* New York: Grossman.

Lemann, N. 1991a, January 13. "Four Generations in the Projects." *New York Times Magazine,* pp. 16–21, 36–38, 49.

———. 1991b. *The Promised Land: The Great Black Migration and How It Changed America.* New York: Alfred A. Knopf.

Leshner, A. 1992. *Outcasts on Main Street: Report of the Federal Task Force on Homelessness and Severe Mental Illness.* Washington DC: National Institute of Mental Health.

Lévi-Strauss, C. 1963. "Do Dual Organizations Exist?" Pp. 132–163 in *Structural Anthropology,* Vol. 1. New York: Basic Books.

Levine, M. N. 1989. "The Politics of Partnership: Urban Redevelopment since 1945." Pp. 12–34 in G. D. Squires, ed., *Unequal Partnerships: The Political Economy of Urban Redevelopment in Postwar America.* New Brunswick, NJ: Rutgers University Press.

Levy, F. 1987. *Dollars and Dreams: The Changing American Distribution.* New York: Russell Sage.

Lieberson, S. 1962. "Suburbs and Ethnic Residential Patterns." *American Journal of Sociology* 67:673–681.

———. 1980. *A Piece of the Pie: Black and White Immigrants since 1880.* Berkeley and Los Angeles: University of California Press.

Lieberson, S., and M. C. Walters. 1988. *From Many Strands: Ethnic and Racial Groups in Contemporary America.* New York: Russell Sage.

Lin, J. 1998. *Reconstructing Chinatown: Ethnic Enclave, Global Change.* Minneapolis: University of Minnesota Press.

Lindio-McGovern, L. 1997. *Filipino Peasant Women: Exploitation and Resistance.* Philadelphia: Pennsylvania State University.

Lineberry, R., 1977. *Equality and Urban Policy: The Distribution of Municipal Public Services.* Beverly Hills, CA: Sage.

Lineberry, R., and I. Sharkansky. 1978. *Urban Politics and Public Policy,* 3d ed. New York: Harper & Row.

Lipsky, M. 1976. "Toward a Theory of Street-Level Bureaucracy." In W. Hawley et al., eds., *Theoretical Perspectives on Urban Politics.* Englewood Cliffs, NJ: Prentice-Hall.

Logan, J., and H. Molotch. 1987. *Urban Fortunes: The Political Economy of Place.* Berkeley and Los Angeles: University of California Press.

Logan, J., and G. Rabrenovic. 1990. "Neighborhood Associations: Their Issues, Their Allies, and Their Opponents." *Urban Affairs Quarterly* 26, 1:68–94.

Long, J. 1981. *Population Deconcentration in the United States.* Washington, DC: Bureau of the Census.

Longstreet, S. 1973. *Chicago: 1860–1919.* New York: David McKay.

Los Angeles Times. 1982, April 25, p. A3.

Luce, T. "Regional Tax Base Sharing: The Twin Cities Experience." Pp. 234–254 in Helen F. Ladd, ed., *Local Government Tax and Land Use Policies in the United States: Understanding the Links.* Northampton, MA: Edward Elgar.

Lynch, K. 1964. *The Image of the City.* Cambridge: MIT Press.

Lynd, R. S., and H. M. Lynd. 1937. *Middletown in Transition: A Study in Cultural Conflicts.* New York: Harcourt Brace.

Mabogunje, A. 1990. "Organization of Urban Communities in Nigeria." *International Social Science Journal* 42:355–366.

MacDonald, M. 1984. *America's Cities: A Report on the Myth of Urban Renaissance.* New York: Simon and Schuster.

Mandel, E. 1975. *Late Capitalism.* London: Verso.

Marples, D. 1988. *The Social Impact of the Chernobyl Disaster.* New York: St. Martin's Press.

Marshall, D. 1990. "Continuing Significance of Race: The Transformation of American Politics." *American Political Science Review* 84:611–616.

Martinelli, F. 1985. "Public Policy and Industrial Development in Southern Italy." *International Journal of Urban and Regional Research* 9:48–56.

Marx, K. 1967. *Capital.* New York: International Publishers.

———. (n.d.). *The 18th Brumaire.* Moscow: Progress Publishers.

Massey, D. S., and N. A. Denton. 1993. *Urban Apartheid: Segregation and the Making of the Underclass.* Cambridge, MA: Harvard University Press.

Mathews, F. H. 1977. *Quest for an American Sociology: Robert E. Park and the Chicago School.* Montreal: McGill-Queen's University Press.

Matrix Collective. 1984. *Making Space: Women and the Man-Made Environment.* London: Pluto.

Matzer, J., Jr. 1986. "Local Control of Fiscal Stress." Pp. 63–80 in M. Gottdiener, ed., *Cities in Stress.* Newbury Park, CA: Sage.

Mayo, J. 1988. "Urban Design as Uneven Development." *Environment and Behavior* 20:633–663.

McDowell, B. 1984. "Mexico City: An Alarming Giant." *National Geographic* 166:138–178.

McDowell, L. 1991. "Restructuring Production and Reproduction: Some Theoretical and Empirical Issues Relating to Gender, or Women in Britain." Pp. 77–105 in M. Gottdiener and C. G. Pickvance, eds., *Urban Life in Transition.* Newbury Park, CA: Sage.

McInerney, J. 1984. *Bright Lights, Big City.* New York: Vintage.

McKenzie, R. 1933. *The Metropolitan Community.* New York: McGraw-Hill.

———. 1944. *The Metropolitan Community.*

McKeown, T. 1976. *The Modern Rise of Population.* London: Edward Arnold.

Mehta, S. K. 1969a. "Patterns of Residence in Poona (India) by Income, Education, and Occupation (1937–1965)." *American Journal of Sociology* 73:496–508.

———. 1969b. "Patterns of Residence in Poona (India) by Caste and Religion: 1822–1965." *Demography* 6:473–491.

Mellor, R. 1989. "Transitions in Urbanization: Twentieth Century Britain." *International Journal of Urban and Regional Research* 13:579–592.

Melman, S. 1983. *Profits without Production.* New York: Knopf.

Mingione, E. 1988. "Urban Survival Strategies, Family Structure and Informal Practices." Pp. 297–322 in *The Capitalist City.* Oxford: Blackwell.

Minsky, H. 1989. "Financial Crises and the Evolution of Capitalism: The Crash of '87." Pp. 391–403 in M. Gottdiener and N. Komninos, eds., *Capitalist Development and Crisis Theory.* New York: Macmillan.

Misra, R. (ed.). 1978. *Million Cities of India.* New Delhi: Vikas Publishing House.

Mollenkopf, J. 1975. "The Postwar Politics of Urban Development." *Politics and Society* 5:247–296.

Mollenkopf, J., and M. Castells. 1991. *The Dual City: Restructuring New York.* New York: Russell Sage.

Monkkonen, E. 1986. "The Sense of Crisis: A Historian's Point of View." Pp. 20–38 in M. Gottdiener, ed., *Cities in Stress.* Newbury Park, CA: Sage.

———. 1988. *America Becomes Urban.* Berkeley and Los Angeles: University of California Press.

Montgomery, R., and K. Bristol. 1987. *Pruitt-Igoe: An Annotated Bibliography.* Chicago, IL: Council of Planning Librarians.

Moore, J. W. 1976. *Mexican Americans,* 2nd ed. Englewood Cliffs, NJ: Prentice-Hall.

———. 1978. *Homeboys: Gangs, Drugs and Prison in the Barrios of L.A.* Philadelphia: Temple University Press.

———. 1991. *Going Down to the Barrio: Homeboys and Homegirls in Change.*

———. 1991. *Homeboys: Gangs, Drugs, and Prisons in the Barrios of Los Angeles.*

Morawska, E. 1990. "The Sociology and Historiography of Immigration." Pp. 187–238 in V. Yans-McLaughlin, ed., *Immigration Reconsidered: History, Sociology and Politics.* New York: Oxford University Press.

Muller, P. 1981. *Contemporary Suburban America.* Englewood Cliffs, NJ: Prentice-Hall.

Mumford, L. 1961. *The City in History.* New York: Harcourt Brace Jovanovich.

Murphy, R. 1988. "Shanghai." Pp. 157–183 in M. Dogan and J. Kasarda, eds., *The Metropolis Era,* Vol. 2. Newbury Park, CA: Sage.

Murray, J. 1984. *Losing Ground: American Social Policy 1950–1980.* New York: Free Press.

Naess, A. 1989. *Ecology, Community, and Lifestyle: Outline of an Ecosophy.* New York: Cambridge University Press.

Nagpaul, H. 1988. "India's Giant Cities." Pp. 252–290 in M. Dogan and J. Kasarda, eds., *The Metropolis Era,* Vol. 1. Newbury Park, CA: Sage.

Nakamura, H., and J. White. 1988. "Tokyo." Pp. 123–156 in M. Dogan and J. Kasarda, eds., *The Metropolis Era,* Vol. 2. Newbury Park, CA: Sage.

Nardulli, P., and J. Stonecash. 1981. *Politics, Professionalism and Urban Services: The Police.* Cambridge, MA: Oelgeschlager, Gunn, and Hain.

Nash, G. 1974. *Red, White and Black: The People of Early America.* Englewood Cliffs, NJ: Prentice-Hall.

Nash, N. 1992, November 15. "Latin America's Shantytowns Grow as People Flock to Cities." *Press Enterprise,* p. A18.

Nath, V. 1989. "Urbanization and Urban Development in India." *International Journal of Urban and Regional Research* 13:258–269.

National Institute of Justice. 1990. *Drug Use Forecasting, Annual Report, 1988.* Washington, DC: U.S. Department of Justice.

New York Times. 1990, September 30. International Section:17.

———. 1991, December 7. "Wider Mosaic: Suburbs' Jobs Lure Immigrants to Greater Opportunity." Metro Section:L–28.

Noyelle, T., and T. M. Stanback, Jr. 1984. *The Economic Transformation of American Cities.* Totowa, NJ: Rowman and Allanheld.

Oakes, J. 1985. *Keeping Track: How Schools Structure Inequality.* New Haven, CT: Yale University Press.

O'Connor, A. 1978. *The Geography of Tropical African Development,* 2nd ed. Oxford: Pergamon.

Olin, S. 1991. "Intraclass Conflict and the Politics of a Fragmented Region." Pp. 223–253 in R. Kling, S. S. Olin, and M. Poster, eds., *Postsuburban California.* Berkeley and Los Angeles: University of California Press.

Omi, P., and H. Winant. 1992. *Racial Formation in the United States: From the 1960s to the 1990s.*

Orfield, M. 1997. *Metropolitics: A Regional Agenda for Community and Stability,* rev. ed. Washington, DC: Brookings Institution.

Palen, J. 1990. "Singapore." Pp. 626–640 in W. Van Vliet, ed., *International Handbook of Housing Policies and Practices.* New York: Greenwood Press.

———. 1991. *The Urban World.* New York: McGraw-Hill.

Pallas, A., G. Natriello, and E. McDill. 1989. "The Changing Nature of the Disadvantaged Population: Current Dimensions and Future Trends." *Educational Researcher* 18:16–22.

Park, R. E. 1915. "The City: Suggestions for the Investigation of Human Behavior in an Urban Environment." *American Journal of Sociology* 20:577–612.

Peet, R. (ed.). 1987. *International Capitalism and Industrial Restructuring: A Critical Analysis.* Boston: Allen and Unwin.

Perlman, J. 1976. *The Myth of Marginality: Urban Poverty and Politics in Rio de Janeiro.* Berkeley: University of California Press.

Peroff, K. 1987. "Who Are the Homeless and How Many Are There?" Pp. 33–45 in R. Bingham, R. Green, and S. White, eds., *The Homeless in Contemporary Society.* Beverly Hills, CA: Sage.

Philips, K. 1990. *The Politics of Rich and Poor: Wealth and the American Electorate in the Reagan Aftermath.* New York: Random House.

Pickvance, C. (ed.). 1976. *Urban Sociology: Critical Essays.* New York: St. Martin's Press.

Piore, M., and C. Sabel. 1984. *The Second Industrial Divide: Possibilities for Prosperity.* New York: Basic Books.

Piven, F., and R. Cloward. 1977. *Poor People's Movements.* New York: Pantheon.

Polsby, N. 1980. *Community Power and Political Theory.* New Haven, CT: Yale University Press.

Popenoe, D. 1977. *The Suburban Environment: Sweden and the United States.* Chicago: University of Chicago Press.

———. 1980. "Women in the Suburban Environment: A U.S.–Sweden Comparison." In G. Wekerle, R. Peterson, and D. Morley, eds., *New Space for Women.* Boulder, CO: Westview Press.

Population Reference Bureau. 1990. *1990 World Population Sheet.* Washington, DC.

Portes, A., and R. Rumbaut. 1990. *Immigrant America: A Portrait.* Berkeley: University of California Press.

Portes, A., and J. Walton. 1981. *Labor, Class, and the International System.* New York: Academic Press.

Pred, A. 1973. *Urban Growth and the Circulation of Information: The United States System of Cities, 1790–1840.* Cambridge, MA: Harvard University Press.

Press Enterprise. 1992, January 19. "School Integration into Revenge," pp. A1, A7.

———. 1992, May 17. "Our Altered Planet," p. AA-1.

Pressman, J., and A. Wildavsky. 1973. *Implementation.* Berkeley: University of California Press.

Pye, R. 1977. "Office Location and the Cost of Maintaining Contact." *Environment and Planning* 9:149–168.

Quante, W. 1976. *The Exodus of Corporate Headquarters from New York.* New York: Praeger.

Raban, J. 1974. *The Soft City.* New York: Dutton.

Ramirez, R. 1990. "Urbanization, Housing and the (Withdrawing) State: The Production-Reproduction Nexus." Pp. 204–234 in S. Datta, *Third World Urbanization: Reappraisals and New Perspective.* Stockholm: HSFR.

Reardon, P. T. 1999, February 10. "New Faces, New Realities: In a City Where Race Still Dominates the Political Order, Increasing Neighborhood Diversity May Change the Rules." *Chicago Tribune,* pp. 1, 8.

Reckless, W. 1933. *Vice in Chicago.* Chicago: University of Chicago Press.

Reff, T. 1982. *Manet and Modern Paris: One Hundred Paintings, Drawings, Prints, and Photographs by Manet and His Contemporaries.* Washington, DC: National Gallery of Art.

Repplier, A. 1898. *Philadelphia: The Place and the People.* New York: Macmillan.

Reynolds. 1980, August 18. "Triana, Alabama: The Unhealthiest Town in America." *National Wildlife.*

Rhodes, R. F. 1995. *Architecture and Meaning on the Athenian Acropolis.* Cambridge, UK: Cambridge University Press.

Riposa, G. 1992. "Urban Empowerment: The Cambodian Struggle for Political Incorporation in California." Working Paper. Department of Political Science, Long Beach State College.

Roberts, B. 1978. *Cities of Peasants: The Political Economy of Urbanization in the Third World.* Beverly Hills, CA: Sage.

———. 1991. "Household Coping Strategies and Urban Poverty in a Comparative Perspective." Pp. 135–168 in M. Gottdiener and C. Pickvance, *Urban Life in Transition.* Newbury Park, CA: Sage.

Robertson, D., and D. Judd. 1989. *The Development of American Public Policy: The Structure of Policy Restraint.* Glenview, IL: Scott, Foresman.

Robertson, I. 1987. *Sociology,* 3rd ed. New York: Worth.

Rondinelli, D. 1988. "Giant and Secondary City Growth in Africa." Pp. 291–321 in M. Dogan and J. Kasarda, eds., *The Metropolis Era,* Vol. 1. Newbury Park, CA: Sage.

Rubin, J. 1970. "Canals, Railroads and Urban Rivalries." Pp. 127–139 in Mohl and Betten, eds., *Urban America in Historical Perspective.* New York: W. and T. Publishers.

Safa, H. 1987. "Urbanization, the Informal Economy and State Policy in Latin America." Pp. 252–274 in M. Smith and J. Feagin, eds., *The Capitalist City.* Oxford: Blackwell.

Sale, K. 1975. *Power Shift: The Rise of the Southern Rim and Its Challenge to the Eastern Establishment.* New York: Random House.

Sandburg, C. 1944. "Chicago." *Chicago Poems.* New York: Harcourt Brace Jovanovich.

Sassen, S. 1989. "New Trends in the Socio-Spatial Organization of the New York Economy." In R. Beauregard, ed., *Economic Restructuring and Political Response.* Newbury Park, CA: Sage.

———. 1991. *The Global City: New York, London, Tokyo.* Princeton, NJ: Princeton University Press.

Sassen-Koob, S. 1984. "The New International Division of Labor in Global Cities." In M. Smith, ed., *Cities in Transformation.* Beverly Hills, CA: Sage.

Schlyter, A. 1990. "Housing and Gender: Important Aspects of Urbanization." Pp. 235–246 in S. Datta, ed., *Third World Urbanization: Reappraisals and New Perspectives.* Stockholm: HSFR.

Schneier, G. 1990. "Latin America: A Tale of Cities." *International Social Science Journal* 125:337–354.

Schnore, L. 1957. "Metropolitan Growth and Decentralization." *American Journal of Sociology* 63:171–180.

———. 1963. "The Socio-Economic Status of Cities and Suburbs." *American Sociological Review* 28:76–85.

———. 1965. *The Urban Scene.* New York: Free Press.

Schteingart, M. 1990. "Production and Reproduction Practices in the Informal Sector: The Case of Mexico." Pp. 105–117 in S. Datta, ed., *Third World Urbanization: Reappraisals and New Perspective.* Stockholm: HSFR.

Schwartz, D., P. Ferlauto, and D. Hoffman. 1988. *A New Housing Policy for America: Recapturing the American Dream.* Philadelphia: Temple University Press.

Schwirian, K. (ed.). 1974. *Comparative Urban Structure: Studies in the Ecology of Cities.* Lexington, MA: D.C. Heath and Company.

Scott, A. 1980. *The Urban Land Nexus and the State.* London: Pion.

———. 1988. *Metropolis: From the Division of Labor to Urban Form.* Berkeley and Los Angeles: University of California Press.

Scott, J. 1972. *Comparative Political Corruption.* Englewood Cliffs, NJ: Prentice-Hall.

Seeley, J., R. Sim, and E. Loosley. 1956. *Crestwood Heights.* New York: Basic Books.

Serrin, W. 1992. *Homestead: The Glory and Tragedy of an American Steel Town.* New York: Times Books.

Sexton, P. 1961. *Education and Income: Inequalities of Opportunity in Our Public Schools.* New York: Viking Press.

———. 1965. *Spanish Harlem.* New York: Harper & Row.

Shannon, T., N. Kleiniewski, and W. Cross. 1991. *Urban Problems in Sociological Perspective,* 2nd ed. Prospect Heights, IL: Waveland Press.

Sharpe, W., and L. Wallock. 1987. *Visions of the Modern City: Essays in History, Art and Literature.* Baltimore: Johns Hopkins University Press.

Shaw, C. S. 1930. *The Jackroller: A Delinquent Boy's Own Story.* Chicago: University of Chicago Press.

Shevky, E., and W. E. Bell. 1955. *Social Area Analysis: Theory, Illustrative Application and Computational Procedures.* Westport, CT: Greenwood.

Shevky, E., and M. Williams. 1949. *The Social Area of Los Angeles: Analysis and Typology.* Berkeley: University of California Press.

Shover, J. 1976. *First Majority-Last Minority: The Transformation of Rural Life in America.* DeKalb: Northern Illinois University Press.

Simmel, G. 1950. "The Metropolis and Mental Life." Pp. 409–424 in K. Wolff, ed., *The Sociology of Georg Simmel.* Glencoe, IL: Free Press.

Simon, D. 1989. "Postcolonial Africa and the World Economy." *International Journal of Urban and Regional Research* 13:68–92.

Sjoberg. 1960. *The Pre-Industrial City.* New York: Free Press.

Sleeper, J. 1990. *The Closest of Strangers: Liberalism and the Politics of Race in New York.* New York: W.W. Norton.

Smith, C. 1985. "Theories and Methods of Urban Primacy: A Critique." Pp. 87–117 in M. Timberlake, ed., *Urbanization in the World-Economy.* Orlando, FL: Academic Press.

Smith, D. 1992, October 15. "Valley of Gloom." *Press Enterprise,* pp. A1, A7.

Smith, D., and M. Timberlake. 1993. "World Cities: A Political Economy/Global Network Approach." In R. Hutchison, ed., *Urban Theory in Transition.* Greenwich, CT: JAI.

Smith, M., and J. Feagin. 1987. *The Capitalist City: Global Restructuring and Global Politics.* Oxford: Blackwell.

Snell, B. 1979. "American Ground Transport." Pp. 239–266 in J. Feagin, ed., *The Urban Scene.* New York: Random House.

Snipp, C. 1989. *American Indians: The First of This Land.* New York: Russell Sage.

South, S., and D. Poston. 1982. "The United States Metropolitan System." *Urban Affairs Quarterly* 18:187–206.

Sowell, T. 1981. *Ethnic America.* New York: Basic Books.

Spain, D. 1992. *Gendered Spaces.* Chapel Hill, NC: University of North Carolina Press.

Spear, A. 1967. *Black Chicago: The Making of a Negro Ghetto: 1890–1920.* Chicago: University of Chicago Press.

Squires, G. D. 1989. "Public-Private Partnerships: Who Gets What and Why." Pp. 1–11 in G. D. Squires, ed., *Unequal Partnerships: The Political Economy of Urban Redevelopment in Postwar America.* New Brunswick, NJ: Rutgers University Press.

———. 1991. "Partnership and the Pursuit of the Private City." Pp. 196–221 in M. Gottdiener and C. G. Pickvance, *Urban Life in Transition.* Newbury Park, CA: Sage.

———. 1992, December 28. "Economic Development Is Killing Education." *In These Times,* pp. 28–29.

Stack, C. 1974. *All Our Kin: Strategies for Survival in a Black Community.* New York: Harper & Row.

Stahura, J., K. Huff, and B. Smith. 1980, March 15. "Crime in the Suburbs." *Urban Affairs Quarterly,* pp. 291–316.

Steele, S. 1990. *The Content of Our Character: A New Vision of Race in America.* New York: St. Martin's Press.

Stone, C. 1989. *Regime Politics: Governing Atlanta, 1946–1988.* Lawrence, KS: University of Kansas Press.

Storper, M. 1984. "The Spatial Division of Labor: Labor and the Location of Industries." In L. Sawers and W. Tabb, eds., *Sunbelt/Snowbelt.* New York: Oxford University Press.

Storper, M., and R. Walker. 1983. "The Theory of Labor and the Theory of Location." *International Journal of Urban and Regional Research* 7:1–41.

Strong, A. 1971. *Planned Urban Environments.* Baltimore: Johns Hopkins University Press.

Strong, J. 1891. *Our Country.* New York: Baker and Taylor.

Stubbing, R., and R. Mendel. 1986. *The Defense Game.* New York: Harper & Row.

Susser, L. 1982. *Norman Street: Poverty and Politics in an Urban Neighborhood.* New York: Oxford University Press.

Suttles, G. 1972. *The Social Construction of Communities.* Chicago: University of Chicago Press.

———. 1990. *The Man Made City.* Chicago: University of Chicago Press.

Sweetser, F. L. 1965. "Factorial Ecology: Helsinki, 1960." *Demography* 2:372–385.

Taeuber, K., and A. Taeuber. 1965. *Negroes in Cities: Residential Segregation and Neighborhood Change.* Chicago: Aldine.

Taylor, G. 1915. *Satellite Cities: A Study of Industrial Suburbs.* New York: Appleton.

Taylor, R. 1991. "Urban Communities and Crime." Pp. 106–134 in M. Gottdiener and C. G. Pickvance, *Urban Life in Transition.* Newbury Park, CA: Sage.

Thorne, B. 1993. "Girls and Boys Together . . . But Mostly Apart: Gender Arrangements in Elementary Schools." Pp. 115–126 in C. Richardson and V. Taylor, eds., *Feminist Frontiers III.* New York: McGraw-Hill.

Thrasher, F. 1927. *The Gang: A Study of 1,313 Gangs in Chicago.* Chicago: University of Chicago Press.

Tobio, C. 1989. "Economic and Social Restructuring in the Metropolitan Area of Madrid: 1970–85." *International Journal of Urban and Regional Research* 13:324–335.

Toennies, F. 1957 [1887]. *Community and Society [Gemeinschaft und Gesellschaft]*. Ed. by Charles P. Loomis. East Lansing, MI: Michigan State University.

———. 1971. *Ferdinand Toennies on Sociology: Pure, Applied, and Empirical*. Ed. by W. J. Cahnman and R. Heberle. Chicago: University of Chicago Press.

United Nations, Department of International and Social Affairs. 1985. *Estimates and Projections of Urban, Rural, and City Populations, 1950–2025: The 1982 Assessment*. (ST/ESA/SER.R./58). New York.

U.S. Bureau of the Census. 1990. *Census of Population*. Washington, DC: U.S. Government Printing Office.

USA Today. 1991, November 11. "Segregation: Walls between Us," pp. A1–3.

Vance, J. 1977. *This Scene of Man: The Role and Structure of the City in the Geography of Western Civilization*. New York: Harpers College Press.

———. 1990. *The Continuing City: Urban Morphology in Western Civilization*. Baltimore: Johns Hopkins University Press.

Veblen, T. 1899. *The Theory of the Leisure Class*. New York: Viking Press.

Vidich, A. J., and J. Bensman. 1968 [1958]. *Small Town in Mass Society: Class, Power, and Religion in a Rural Community*. Princeton, N.J.: Princeton University Press.

Vigil, J. 1988. *Barrio Gangs: Street Life and Identity in Southern California*. Austin: University of Texas Press.

Wagenknecht, E. 1964. *Chicago*. Norman, OK: University of Oklahoma Press.

Wakefield, D. 1959. *Island in the City: Puerto Ricans in New York*. New York: Citadel Press.

Walloch, L. (ed.). 1988. *New York: Culture Capital of the World*. New York: Rizzoli.

Walton, J. 1982. "The International Economy and Peripheral Urbanization." Pp. 119–135 in N. and S. Fainstein, eds., *Urban Policy under Capitalism*. Beverly Hills, CA: Sage.

———. 1987. "Urban Protest and the Global Political Economy: The IMF Riots." Pp. 364–386 in M. Smith and J. Feagin, *The Capitalist City*. Oxford: Blackwell.

Warner, S. B., Jr. 1962. *Streetcar Suburbs: The Process of Growth in Boston*. Cambridge, MA: Harvard University Press.

———. 1968. *The Private City: Philadelphia in Three Periods of Its Growth*. Philadelphia: University of Pennsylvania Press.

Warren, D. I. 1975. *Black Neighborhoods: An Assessment of Community Power*. Ann Arbor: University of Michigan Press.

Warren, R., and D. I. Warren. 1977. *The Neighborhood Organizer's Handbook*. Notre Dame, IN: Notre Dame University Press.

Weber, A. F. 1899. *The Growth of Cities in the Nineteenth Century*. New York: Macmillan.

Weber, M. 1958. *The Protestant Ethic and The Spirit of Capitalism*. New York: Scribner's.

———. 1966. *The City*. New York: Free Press.

———. 1968. *Economy and Society*. New York: Bedminster Press.

Weiner, M. 1985. "On International Migration and International Relations." *Population and Development Review* 11:441–455.

Weiss, M. 1987. *The Rise of Community Builders: The American Real Estate Industry and Urban Land Planning*. New York: Columbia University Press.

————. 1988. *The Clustering of America.* New York: Harper & Row.

Wellman, B. 1979. "The Community Question." *American Journal of Sociology* 84:1201–1231.

————. 1988. "The Community Question Re-evaluated." Pp. 81–107 in M. Smith, ed., *Power, Community and the City.* New Brunswick, NJ: Transaction.

Wellman, B., and B. Leighton. 1979. "Networks, Neighborhoods and Communities." *Urban Affairs Quarterly* 14:363–390.

Whitt, J. A. 1982. *Urban Elites and Mass Transportation: The Dialectics of Power.* Princeton, NJ: Princeton University Press.

Whyte, M., and W. Parish. 1984. *Urban Life in Contemporary China.* Chicago: University of Chicago Press.

Whyte, W. F. 1955. *Street Corner Society: The Social Structure of an Italian Slum.* Chicago: University of Chicago Press.

Whyte, W. H. 1956. *The Organization Man.* Garden City, NY: Simon & Schuster.

————. 1988. *City: Rediscovering the Center.* New York: Doubleday.

Wilkerson, I. 1991, March 19. "How Milwaukee Boomed but Left Blacks Behind." *New York Times,* pp. A1, D22.

————. 1992, April 15. "The Loop Is Still Dark." *Press Enterprise,* pp. A1, A8.

Williams, T., and W. Kornblum. 1985. *Growing Up Poor.* Lexington, MA: D.C. Heath.

Wilson, J. 1992, May 1. "Anarchy Spreads on Day 2." *Press Enterprise,* p. A1.

Wilson, W. J. 1987. *The Truly Disadvantaged: The Inner City, the Underclass, and Public Policy.* Chicago: University of Chicago Press.

————. 1996. *When Work Disappears: The World of the New Urban Poor.* New York: Random House.

Wirth, L. 1928. *The Ghetto.* Chicago: University of Chicago Press.

————. 1938. "Urbanism as a Way of Life." *American Journal of Sociology* 44:3–24.

Wohl, R., and A. Strauss. 1958. "Symbolic Representation and the Urban Milieu." *American Journal of Sociology* 63:523–532.

Wright, T. 1998. *Out of Place: Homeless Mobilizations, Subcities, and Contested Landscapes.* Albany: State University of New York Press.

Yago, G. 1984. *The Decline of Transit: Urban Transportation in German and United States Cities: 1900–1970.* New York: Cambridge University Press.

Yago, G., H. Korman, and S-Y Wu. 1984. "Investments and Disinvestment in New York: 1960–1980." *Annals of the American Academy of Political and Social Science* 475 (September):28–38.

Yeung, Y. 1988. "Great Cities of Eastern Asia." Pp. 155–186 in M. Dogan and J. Kasarda, eds., *The Metropolis Era.* Newbury Park, CA: Sage.

Zhou, M. 1992. *Chinatown: The Socioeconomic Potential of an Urban Enclave.* Philadelphia: Temple University Press.

Zorbaugh, H. 1929. *The Gold Coast and the Slum: A Sociological Study of Chicago's Near North Side.* Chicago: University of Chicago Press.

Zukin, S. 1985. "The Regional Challenge to French Industrial Policy." *International Journal of Urban & Regional Research* 9, 3:352–367.

————. 1990. *Loft Living: Culture and Capital in Urban Change.* Baltimore: John Hopkins University Press.

ACKNOWLEDGMENTS

Photo Credits

5 Top, Courtesy Naval Research Laboratory; bottom, Roy Bishop/Stock, Boston **9** Top, David M. Grossman/Photo Researchers; bottom, Stock, Boston **16** Top, Peter Menzel/Stock, Boston; bottom, Marixsa Alicea, DePaul University **24** Corbis–Bettmann **28** American School of Classical Studies **29** Art Resource/ SCALA **31** Top, Corbis–Bettmann; bottom, Art Resource **43** North Wind Pictures **49** Photo Researchers **53** The Granger Collection, New York **54** Corbis–Bettmann **58** The Granger Collection, New York **60** Corbis–Bettmann **62** Corbis–Bettmann **67** Archive Photos **73** Superstock **79** Corbis–Bettmann **88** Van Bucher/Photo Researchers **89** Robert A. Isaacs/Photo Researchers **93** William Johnson/Stock, Boston **99** Alex S. MacLean/ Landslides **107** Photoreporters **112** Courtesy The University of Chicago Office of Press Relations **116** The University of Chicago Library–Special Collections **129** Corbis–Bettmann **133** Pierre Verdy/AFP Photo **143** Spencer Grant/Stock, Boston **144** Corbis–Bettmann **153** Ray Ellis/Photo Researchers **156** Rich LaSalle/Tony Stone Images **162** R. M. Collins III/Image Works **171** Barbara Rios/Photo Researchers **173** Spencer Grant/Photo Researchers **179** Ray Hutchison, University of Wisconsin–Green Bay **185** Collection of The Whitney Museum of American Art, NY **195** Roy Gumpel, Liaison International **198** Cary Wolinsky/Stock, Boston **219** Reuters-Bettmann/Corbis **225** Ray Hutchison, University of Wisconsin–Green Bay **232** Bridget Montgomery **235** Rapho/Photo Researchers **241** Corbis–Bettmann **252** M. Greenlar/The Image Works **255** Roberta Hershesnon/Photo Researchers **262** Steve Conlan/Select **268** Superstock **269** Courtesy The German Information Center **275** Reuters/Bettmann **283** George Gerster/Comstock **286** Arvind Garg/Photo Researchers **290** Peter Menzel/Stock, Boston **301** Melvyn Calderon/The Gamma Liaison Network **308** AP/Wide World Photos **313** Corbis–Bettmann **315** Ray Hutchison, University of Wisconsin–Green Bay **322** From La Ville Radieuse (1935) **329** Alex S. MacLean/Landslides **330** Tom Bross/Stock, Boston **343** Barros/ Liaison International **354** Top, Courtesy The Frank Lloyd Wright Foundation; bottom, Photofest

Illustration and Text Credits

23 Excerpt from D. Fitts, 1966; *Greek Plays in Modern Translation,* p. 156. Reprinted with permission of Holt, Rinehart, and Winston. **37** Excerpt from Lewis Mumford, *The City in History: Its Origins, Its Transformations, and Its Prospects,* Copyright © 1961 and renewed 1989 by Lewis Mumford, reprinted by permission of Harcourt, Inc. **38** Excerpt from "Chicago" from *Chicago Poems* by Carl Sandburg, Copyright 1916 by Holt, Rinehart and Winston and renewed 1944 by Carl Sandburg, reprinted by permission of the publisher. **38** Excerpt from G. Keynes, 1977, "London," in William Blake, *Songs of Innocence and*

Experience. NY: Oxford University Press.   **71** Map of electrified trolley routes of Los Angeles © Spencer Crump.   **80–81** Excerpt from "The Valley of Gloom . . ." reprinted with permission of *The Press Enterprise.*   **100** Excerpt from Michael J. Dear, *Rethinking Los Angeles* (Sage Publications, 1996). Reprinted by permission of Sage Publications.   **104** Excerpt from pp. 227–228 in Ferdinand Toennies, *Community and Society* (Gemeinschaft und Gesellschaft), Michigan State University Press, 1957. Reprinted by permission of Michigan State University.   **104** Selection from p. 69 in *Ferdinand Toennies on Sociology: Pure and Applied* (Werner J. Cahman and Rudolf Heberle, eds.; University of Chicago Press). Reprinted by permission of the publisher.   **109** Robert Park, "The City: Suggestions for the Source Investigation of Human Behavior in an Urban Environment." *American Journal of Sociology,* 1915, pp. 577–612. Copyright © 1915 by The University of Chicago Press. Reprinted by permission of the publisher.   **113** Map of Chicago from Ernest Burgess, "The Growth of the City: An Introduction to a Research Project," in Ernest Burgess, Robert E. Park, and Roderick McKenzie. *The City* (Chicago: University of Chicago Press). Copyright © 1925 by The University of Chicago Press. Reprinted by permission of the publisher.   **120–121** Map of Gangland Chicago from Frederick Thrasher, *The Gang: A Study of 1,313 Gangs in Chicago* (University of Chicago Press, 1927). Copyright © 1927 by The University of Chicago Press. Used with permission of the publisher.   **123** Diagram from E. Shevky and W. Bell, *Social Area Analysis* (Stanford University Press, 1955). © 1955 by the Board of Trustees of the Leland Stanford Junior University.   **138–139** Selection from D. Harvey, *The Urbanization of Capital and the Urban Experience,* pp. 133–134 (Baltimore: Johns Hopkins University Press, 1983). © 1983 by Johns Hopkins University Press.   **154** Excerpt from E. Digby Baltzell, *Philadelphia Gentlemen,* reprinted by permission of E. Digby Baltzell.   **157** Excerpt from M. Weiss, 1988, *The Clustering of America.* Reprinted with permission from HarperCollins Publishers.   **157** Excerpt from Jay McInerney, *Bright Lights, Big City.* Copyright © 1984 by Jay McInerney. Reprinted by permission of Vintage Books, a Division of Random House, Inc.   **159** Excerpt from Jerry Jacobs, *The Mall: An Attempted Escape from Everyday Life.* © 1984 by Waveland Press, Inc., Prospect Heights, Illinois.   **159** Excerpt from Peter O. Muller, *Contemporary Urban America,* © 1981, pp. 10, 72, 74–75. Adapted by permission of Prentice-Hall, Englewood Cliffs, New Jersey.   **161** Excerpt in Box 8.4 from Terry Williams and William Kornblum, *Growing Up Poor.* Copyright © 1985 by Lexington Books. Reprinted with permission of Lexington Books, an imprint of Macmillan, Inc.   **175** Excerpt from "Farewell to Chinatown" (*Canadian Geographic,* August/September 1991), reprinted with permission of Peter Gorrie.   **187** Excerpt from *The Urban Villagers: Group and Class in the Life of Italian-Americans.* Updated & Expanded Edition by Herbert J. Gans. Copyright © 1962 by The Free Press. Copyright © 1982 by Herbert J. Gans. Reprinted with permission of The Free Press, a Division of Simon and Schuster, Inc.   **192** Excerpt from p. 6 of "Urban Views: Popular Perspectives on City Life," from *Urban Life* by D. Hummon, reprinted by permission of Sage Publications.   **194** Diagrams from Frances Ladd, "A Note on the World Across the Street." *Harvard Graduate School of Education Association Bulletin,* Vol. 12, 1967. Reprinted with permission of Frances Ladd.   **196** From Dennis Judd, "The Rise of the Walled City," in Hellen Ligget (ed.), *Spatial Practices* (Sage Publications, 1996). Reprinted by permission of Sage Publications.   **212–213** Selection from *American Apartheid* by Douglas S. Massey and Nancy A. Denton. Copyright © 1993 by the President and Fellows of Harvard College. Reprinted by permission of Harvard University Press.   **213** Excerpt from the article "Segregation: Walls between Us, USA at Home: Streets Still Isolate Races." Copyright 1991, USA TODAY. Reprinted with permission.   **215** Excerpt from "As Urban Blight Worsens, Victims Find Their Isolation Is Deepening," copyright 1991/92 by The New York Times Company. Reprinted by permission.   **217** Excerpt from "How Milwaukee Boomed But Left Blacks Behind," copyright

1991/92 by The New York Times Company. Reprinted by permission. **218** From *When Work Disappears* by William Julius Wilson. Copyright © 1996 by William Julius Wilson. Reprinted by permission of Alfred A. Knopf Inc. **226** Map by Matt Moody, from Rich Connell and Robert J. Lopez, "A Decade of Death" (*Los Angeles Times,* November 17, 1999). Used by permission of *The Los Angeles Times.* **250–251** Selection from "New Faces, New Realities" by Patrick Reardon (*Chicago Tribune,* February 10, 1999). Copyrighted © 1999 by the Chicago Tribune. All rights reserved; used with permission. **257** Excerpt from Gregory Squires, "Public-Private Partnerships: Who Gets What and Why?" (pp. 2–3) and Marc Levine, "The Politics of Partnership: Urban Redevelopment (pp. 27–28) in Gregory D. Squires (ed.), *Unequal Partnerships: The Political Economy of Redevelopment in Postwar America,* Rutgers University Press, 1989. Reprinted by permission of Rutgers University Press. **268** Excerpt from *Manet and Modern Paris,* by T. Reff, © 1992, Board of Trustees, National Gallery of Art, Washington, D.C. Reprinted with permission. **277** Excerpt from P. Hall, 1966, *The World Cities.* Published by George Weidenfield and Nicolson, Ltd. Publishers. **282** Excerpt from pages viii and 16 from Pauline Baker, *Urbanization and Political Change: The Politics of Lagos, 1917–1967.* Copyright © The Regents of The University of California. **300–301** Excerpt from *Annual Report of the Pasig River Rehabilitation Program.* Reprinted with permission of the Pasig River Rehabilitation Program, Republic of the Philippines. **302** Excerpt from A. Josey, *Singapore.* Copyright © 1980 by Andre Deutsch, Ltd. Reprinted by permission of the publisher, Andre Deutsch, Ltd. **317** Thomas Luce, "Regional Tax Base Sharing: The Twin Cities Experience," from Helen Ladd (ed.), *Local Government Tax and Land Use Policies in the U.S.* (Edward Elgar, Inc., 1998). Reprinted by permission of the Lincoln Institute of Land Policy, Cambridge MA. **319** Excerpt from *City: Rediscovering Its Center,* by William Whyte. Copyright © 1989 by William H. Whyte. Used by permission of Doubleday, a division of Random House, Inc. **328–329** Selections from Gerald F. Frug, "New Urbanism or New Suburbanism." First published in *Harvard Design Magazine,* Winter/Spring 1997. **332** Selections from Edward J. Blakely and Mary Gail Snyder, *Fortress America: Gated Communities in the United States.* Copyright © 1997 The Brookings Institution. **340–341** Excerpts from pages 81, 84, 88, 89 from *The City Is the Frontier* by Charles Abrams. Copyright © 1965 by Charles Abrams. Reprinted by permission of HarperCollins Publishers, Inc.

INDEX